Critical Essays on
HENRY MILLER

CRITICAL ESSAYS
ON
AMERICAN LITERATURE

James Nagel, General Editor
University of Georgia, Athens

---◆---

Critical Essays on
HENRY MILLER

---◆---

edited by
Ronald Gottesman

G. K. Hall & Co. / New York
Maxwell Macmillan Canada / Toronto
Maxwell Macmillan International / New York Oxford Singapore Sydney

Twayne Publishers
Macmillan Publishing Company
866 Third Avenue
New York, New York 10022

Maxwell Macmillan Canada, Inc.
1200 Eglinton Avenue East
Suite 200
Don Mills, Ontario M3C 3N1

Macmillan Publishing Company is part of the Maxwell Communication
Group of Companies.

Library of Congress Cataloging-in-Publication Data

Critical essays on Henry Miller / edited by Ronald Gottesman.
    p.   cm.—(Critical essays on American literature)
  Includes bibliographical references and index.
  ISBN 0-8161-7319-2
  1. Miller, Henry, 1891–   —Criticism and interpretation.
I. Gottesman, Ronald.   II. Series.
PS3525.I5454Z6593   1992
818'.5209—dc20   92-16873
                                                      CIP

The paper used in this publication meets the minimum requirements of
American National Standard for Information Sciences—Permanence of
Paper for Printed Library Materials. ANSI Z3948-1984.∞™

10 9 8 7 6 5 4 3 2 1

Printed in the United States of America

To Beth Shube in love and friendship

Contents

◆

General Editor's Note

◆

This series seeks to anthologize the most important criticism on a wide variety of topics and writers in American literature. Our readers will find in various volumes not only a generous selection of reprinted articles and reviews but original essays, bibliographies, manuscript sections, and other materials brought to public attention for the first time. This volume, *Critical Essays on Henry Miller* is the most comprehensive collection of essays ever published on one of the most important modern writers in the United States. It contains both a sizable gathering of early reviews and a broad selection of more modern scholarship as well. Among the authors of reprinted articles and reviews are Jay Martin, Kate Millet, Lawrence Durrell, Ezra Pound, Edmund Wilson, Erica Jong, Warner Berthoff, and Alan Trachtenberg. In addition to a substantial introduction by Ronald Gottesman there are also four original essays commissioned specifically for publication in this volume, new studies by Mary Kellie Munsil, Jeffrey Bartlett, Welch D. Everman, and Richard Kostelanetz. There is also a section of new tributes to Miller with statements from Isaac Bashevis Singer, Jerzy Kosinski, Robert Creeley, Robert Snyder, and Diane Miller. We are confident that this book will make a permanent and significant contribution to the study of American literature.

James Nagel
University of Georgia

Publisher's Note

◆

Producing a volume that contains both newly commissioned and reprinted material presents the publisher with the challenge of balancing the desire to achieve stylistic consistency with the need to preserve the integrity of works first published elsewhere. In the Critical Essays series, essays commissioned especially for a particular volume are edited to be consistent with G. K. Hall's house style; reprinted essays appear in the style in which they were first published, with only typographical errors corrected. Consequently, shifts in style from one essay to another are the result of our efforts to be faithful to each text as it was originally published.

Acknowledgments

♦

My debt to Jay Martin is primary and double. His deeply imagined biography of Henry Miller stimulated my serious interest in the man and his literary achievement, and ever since Jay has been a steady and generous source of encouragement of that interest (and many others). Fine teacher that he is, Jay knows how to help without getting in the way. I am glad to acknowledge his friendship over the years.

Another biographer of Miller—Bob Snyder—has also inspired me by his creative example and comforted me with his friendship—often over breakfast, always with a wondrous mixture of utter seriousness and unrestrained laughter. His film *The Henry Miller Odyssey* made a gift to me many years ago of the living presence of Miller. More recently, Bob instigated what has become this large book. Our frequent companions in eating, talking, and laughing were Noel Riley Fitch and Michael Hargraves, who between them knew everyone who had written or were writing on Miller and Anaïs Nin (and scores of related topics). They were full of good advice, practical information, and sound judgment.

Many other people have also contributed to the completion of this collection. Annelore Stern in the Reference Department and Mary Hollerich, Assistant Head of Access Services, of the University of Southern California's Doheny Library were very helpful, as were their colleagues in the Inter-Library Loan Service. Jerry Kamstra, Director of the Henry Miller Memorial Library in Big Sur, supplied information promptly and in a cordial fashion. Patricia Middleton of the Beinecke Rare Book and Manuscript Library at Yale University expedited my inquiries, and Octavio Olvera in Special Collections made my use of Special Collections at UCLA efficient and pleasant.

I want to say a special word of thanks to two groups of people. Among those who have written on Miller, Bert Mathieu was especially generous both with his own scholarship and in supplying the letter written by Isaac B. Singer for a publication planned by Mathieu many years ago. He was, moreover, gracious about supplying translations to French passages in the selections from his fine book on Miller. Warner Berthoff, Louis Budd, Erica Jong, Norman Mailer, Jay Martin, Patricia Middleton, Barbara, Tony, and Valentine Miller, Ann Barret Perlès, Bern Porter, Alan Trachtenberg, and George Wickes were instrumental in making materials available either free of charge or for a very token fee. Many publishers were similarly cooperative and should have the gratitude of the scholarly community: Straight Arrow Press, New Directions, Farrar Straus and Giroux, Duke University Press, Da Capo Press, the Scott Meredith Literary Agency, the *Virginia Quarterly Review*, Omni Publications International. They certainly have mine.

Jeffrey Bartlett, Welch Everman, James Goodwin, and Mary Kellie Munsil, prepared original essays for this volume at the rate of something like ten cents an hour. And they paid their own postage. All who use this volume are, like me, in their debt.

Several students of mine in recent years have written papers on Miller for seminars in modernism, and all of them have stimulated my thinking about Miller and his works. It is a pleasure to acknowledge the contributions of Paul Hansom, Andrea Ivanov, and John Whalen-Bridge. Two research assistants did invaluable leg and finger work and I am grateful to (Karen) Hyon Hui Oh and Tracey M. Harris for efficient help cheerfully rendered.

Finally, I am pleased to thank two family members for their assistance. Allison McCabe took time from her school break to type footnotes and to prepare, meticulously, the index. Beth Shube, to whom this book is dedicated, did large parts of the intellectual and clerical work that went into the preparation of this book. But I am even more grateful for her emotional support, which made it possible for me to carry on with my part of the work.

I alone, of course, am responsible for any errors of fact and judgment that remain.

Introduction

RONALD GOTTESMAN

But the quality of the imagination is to flow, and not to freeze.
—Ralph Waldo Emerson, "The Poet"

By the time I was handed my birth certificate my criminal instincts were already fully developed. It was only natural that I should become a rebel, an outlaw, a desperado. I blame my parents, I blame society, I blame God. I accuse. I go through life with finger lifted accusingly. I have the prophetic itch. I curse and blaspheme. I tell the bitter truth.
—Henry Miller, "Uterine Hunger"

Henry Miller wrote too much and too much has been written about him and his work to make it possible to cover all his writings or the vast range of responses to them in this one volume. Selections had to be made and the choices and their arrangement will not please everybody. More space might have been given to Miller's post-Paris writings, to Miller's lifelong role as a literary commentator, to theoretically sophisticated gender-conscious criticism, to other current theoretical interests (for example, a Bakhtinian analysis of Miller's carnivalesque), to the vast body of criticism in languages other than English, and to Miller as one of the most extraordinary letter writers of the past century. Many of the dozens of Henry Millers (to say nothing of the hundreds of commentators) are inevitably absent from this volume.[1] Still, the reprinted material and the essays commissioned specifically for this volume do provide a richly varied set of perspectives on Miller the man and his writings, and surely this collection will not be the final or "definitive" one for a writer of such power and originality.[2]

If it is usually difficult to separate a writer from his work, in the case of Henry Miller it is virtually impossible to do so. As Miller himself observed: "I don't care who the artist is, if you study him deeply, sincerely, detachedly, you will find that he and his work are one."[3] Another guiding assumption

1

behind the selection of materials and the interpretations offered in this introduction is that there is not one Henry Miller but many. (Norman Mailer suggested twenty, fifteen of whom are very good.)[4] It is also true that although an immense amount of ink has been expended on both the life of the man and his work, we are still discovering a great deal about the person called Henry Miller, about his several literary personae, and about the two score of volumes of letters, fiction, autobiographies, essays, travel writings, plays, literary, art, and film commentary, and miscellaneous writings he left as his literary legacy.[5] *Crazy Cock*, a previously unpublished early novel by Miller, appeared in 1991, two new biographies were published in the centennial year of his birth by Mary Dearborn and Robert Ferguson, and Erica Jong is at work on a memoir focussing on Miller.[6] This volume is part of the upsurge of interest in the legacies of Henry Miller, and it has a double purpose—to acknowledge and characterize the earlier critical responses to Miller and his works, and to indicate some of the ways in which a new generation of readers is responding to the man and his writings.[7]

EARLY MILLER

The collection opens with a vivid and sensitive appreciation by Emil Schnellock, one of Miller's earliest and most intimate friends—the one who Miller credited with crystallizing his ambition to become a writer.[8] Schnellock's portrait calls attention to a number of character traits not usually associated in the public mind with Miller—his generosity, his capacity for sympathetic attentiveness, and the undercurrent of tenderness that runs beneath the nihilistic and despairing surface of *Tropic of Cancer*. We are hardly surprised to be told about Miller's animal energy, the "tremendous gusto" of a young man who "could caper like a goat," a man who had the disconcerting habit of laughing in your face when he sensed falseness of utterance, a man whose capacity for talk was marked by a manic intensity "in which he spoke all languages at once." After all, one of Miller's mottoes was "Always merry and bright," a motto adopted in the face of experience that was often painful and dark. We may be surprised, however, to hear of Miller's early sense of being a misfit (of being, as his friend Lawrence Durrell put it, "stillborn") and of his attempted suicide (with its comic and symbolically predictable outcome). Of even greater interest, I think, are three of Schnellock's observations: his intriguing reference to Miller's tendency to fall into trances "at the most unusual, unexpected moments," his description of Miller's "joyful frenzy" in the act of painting, and, in particular, Schnellock's astonishment at the "cascade" of letters Miller wrote to him (as he did to many others) over the years of their long friendship. Schnellock's account of Miller is surely one of the best brief impressions we have of Miller as a young man. Written with the eye of an artist and the heart of a devoted friend, it is a biographical gem.

Miller's first published and still best-known book is *Tropic of Cancer* (1934), and it has seemed worthwhile to devote a good deal of attention to this work's genesis, its compositional and publication histories, and the responses it has evoked over the past half century. Virtually everything written about Miller addresses *Tropic of Cancer*, but the next few items in this collection do so in a concentrated way.

Michael Fraenkel, a businessman turned poet and philosopher, was introduced to Miller in the spring of 1931 by the expatriate American poet Walter Lowenfels.[9] Fraenkel, obsessed with the notion of the spiritual death of the Western world, immediately took Miller in hand (and into his apartment, the Villa Borghese of *Tropic of Cancer*), where the two of them engaged in nonstop oral autopsies of Western civilization. Fraenkel's essay enjoys the benefit of a decade of hindsight, but its reconstruction of both the mood of the times in which *Cancer* was composed and the biographical circumstances of its composition has the ring of truth (and none of its facts or interpretations were gainsaid by any of the principals).

Fraenkel clearly had a fine instinct for Miller's imaginative power and for what Miller needed to do to realize that power as a writer. Responding to what he took to be Miller's "absolute simplicity," his natural, open artlessness (which he also recognized were connected with Miller's anarchic impulses), Fraenkel offered his new friend advice he was ready to heed, partly because Miller had already begun to act on it (as one can plainly see in the extraordinary letters Miller had been writing for some time to Emil Schnellock). Still, Fraenkel deserves credit for encouraging Miller to put his imitative literariness behind him and to begin to close the gap between the rhythms of his mind and emotions and the movement of his prose. Fraenkel's observations about the way the moment-to-moment nature of the lives depicted in *Cancer* are made manifest in the narrative's "desperate swing and beat" reveal that Fraenkel had a literary as well as a philosophic sensibility. Fraenkel, moreover, perceptively insists that the book *is* the author, "the living man going on," and that central to the power of both was *"talk"*— this "wild, mad, fantastic talk that swelled and grew and gathered momentum—a stream, a torrent, a flood." The power of Miller's speech, Fraenkel observes, is "something pathological," but as Miller brought it under control in the act of writing and revising, it became one of the salient features of his style, giving a distinctive immediacy to his writing that lives as much in the mind's ear as in the mind's eye.[10]

Throughout his life Miller had an extraordinary capacity to make and sustain friendships, and he made many lifelong friends during his Paris years. Of these none was deeper or more complex than his relationship with Anaïs Nin, which, as Gunther Stuhlmann has noted, was "firmly founded on [their] shared need to create themselves through writing."[11] Anyone familiar with the various documentations and interpretations of this relationship is already aware of its romantic, literary, and practical aspects, and especially of the emotional and material support Nin provided Miller, who was, when they first met, better known as a "desperado" or bohemian "gangster" than as a writer. What is of special importance is her unparalleled understanding of Miller as a man and a writer from the moment of their first meeting as recorded in Nin's astonishing diaries—that vast and artful repository of one of the most finely tuned sensibilities of her generation.

Nin immediately picked up on Miller's complexity of character, sensing the intensity of his curiosity, his capacity to install himself without reserve in the present moment, the tension between his acquiescent passivity and his rebellious anger, and, perhaps most presciently, Miller's deep need for revenge against life's insults, especially those by women; "his work," she noted, "is a struggle to triumph over woman, over the mother, over the woman in himself" (p. 165).[12] Once she had read some of his (then unpublished) work, she remarked, as many critics since have, on its "ugly, destructive, fearless, cathartic strength." "He uses," she went on, "the first person, real names; he repudiates order and form and fiction itself. He writes in the uncoordinated way we feel, on various levels at once" (pp. 10–11). The diaries are studded with such perceptive observations, and if Nin could venture the shrewd opinion that Miller's distinctive contribution to letters is his "dementalization" of fiction, it is because she, like Miller, had a "small, round, hard photographic lens" in her eyes (p. 258). And while this is not the proper place to explore the subject in detail, the importance to Miller's life and writing of his engagement with his dream life beginning in 1933 would be hard to exaggerate, and this too was in large part a gift from Nin. Her suggestion to Miller that he hold on to his dreams, that "they will make a new kind of work, of book" proved invaluable (p. 225).[13]

Many of the canny observations about Miller and his writings recorded as her diary entries find their way into what is still one of the best pieces of criticism devoted to *Cancer*—Nin's famous preface to the book (she pointedly refrained from calling it a novel). Indeed, much later critical commentary owes a debt to her aphoristic notation of the unresolved tensions embedded in the book, its "obedience to flow," its descent to a " 'pre-artistic level,' " the pioneering character of its form, the book's ability "to startle the lifeless ones from their profound slumber"—all deriving from its origins in, and paradoxically controlled allegiance to, the unconscious, the world of personal and cultural dream and nightmare.[14]

Jay Martin's chapter "The Last Book" (Miller's first title for *Tropic of Cancer*) is a model of biographical writing, combining as it does the spirit of the time, the facts of the place, the interplay between the inner life of the subject and the often exuberant dailiness of his life. But it is as *literary* biography that this chapter of *Always Merry and Bright* is most impressive.

Martin deftly traces the way Miller stitches significant episodes and small details of his life into the design of the book, identifies Miller's growing sense of his destiny as a writer, fills in the circumstances surrounding the titling and publication of the book, and convincingly argues that at "the end of the book the man who can write the book is born." Martin, of course, has other fresh and critically acute things to say about Miller and his diverse writings, but the chapter reprinted here has the form, finish, and heft that distinguishes the best literary biographies of our time.

The next contributions deal in various ways with *Tropic of Cancer* as a published book, and they are chosen from among many noteworthy candidates.[15] While *Cancer* was, in several senses, notorious from the moment of its birth on 1 September 1934, it was a critical success as well. Blaise Cendrars, the Swiss-French writer, published the first review in *Orbes* (Summer 1935), 9–10, characterizing Miller as a "good down-to-earth realist," who wrote of Paris with a European sensibility.[16] As Jay Martin tells us, in response to Miller's request for his opinion, T. S. Eliot had written at about the same time: "*Tropic of Cancer* seems to me a very remarkable book . . . a rather magnificent piece of work. . . . a great deal better both in depth of insight and of course in the actual writing than *Lady Chatterley's Lover.*"[17] Miller had sent copies of his first published book to other influential writers, critics, and editors, and many of them admired the book for one reason or another.[18]

Some of the most interesting early reactions to *Cancer* were not published for many years. Perhaps the best-known of these early responses, however, came from the least-known writer among them—young Lawrence Durrell. Durrell, then in his early twenties, wrote Miller a fan letter in August 1935 (included in this volume) in which he celebrated the book as "the only man-size piece of work which this century can really boast of." Durrell particularly gloried in the antiliterary qualities of the book, the way "it really gets down on paper the blood and the bowels of our time," the way it violates conventions that insist on the well-mannered, the sentimental, the superficially pretty. It already is, he concluded, "the copy-book for my generation."

Ezra Pound wrote privately on 28 March 1935 to T. S. Eliot, asking him to reserve four pages of each issue of the *Criterion* so that Pound could tell readers what was fit for them to read. He immediately went on to note that Henry Miller had recently published "presumably the only book a man cd. read for pleasure," a book which "if not out Ulysseeing Joyce" was at least "more part of permanent literature than such ½ master slime the weakminded, Woolf female" had written. Less than two years later (11 December 1937), Pound wrote to Montgomery Butchart: "Miller has considerable talent. Ultimately bores me, as did D. H. Lawrence." Pound qualifies this judgment by pointing out that he is not "the general reader; and Miller is too good for them."[19]

Pound's review of *Cancer* was apparently written for the *Criterion*, in

1935, but it has not been published until now. Perhaps T. S. Eliot, the journal's editor, objected to the almost free-associational quality of Pound's characteristically strong and strongly worded opinions of English writers, but he seems likely to have shared Pound's admiration of the book's truthfulness to experience, Miller's sense of values, and his "eminent fairness." Not the least interesting of Pound's perceptions is his insistence that the book is "incurably healthy," bawdy but not obscene, and his Poundian claim that in it the "sense of the sphericality of the planet presides."

Walter Lowenfels, to whom Miller had given the first draft of the first fifty pages of *Cancer* in 1931, wrote what apparently is the first notice of the book, though the notice was not published until more than thirty years later. This stylishly elliptical piece makes little effort to hide its contempt for Miller and his work in progress. Lowenfels begins by attacking the egotism of Miller and quickly characterizes what he had seen as "the most destructive book I have ever read." He moves on to make, for the first time, a now-familiar observation about Miller's depiction of women: "As for the poor girls! I never smelt anything more like garbage—huge female gobs of it. How he hates them all, the vinegar of human kindness." Waxing more (half-seriously) splenetic as he goes along, Lowenfels concludes: "Miller ought to write this one book and then be shot."[20]

Herbert Faulkner West published the first American notice of *Cancer* in 1937 (in *Dartmouth Alumni* 29 [January]:8–9, 72). His commentary is mostly devoted to Miller's *Aller Retour New York* (1935), and although West praises *Cancer* and *Black Spring* as "amazing pieces of sustained lyrical prose" and calls attention to Miller's "honesty," he also offers the opinion that his work "very often loses rather than gains by his vocabulary."

Something of this same tolerant patrician squeamishness informs Edmund Wilson's well-known early notice included in this collection. As Jeffrey Bartlett observes in his essay written for this volume, the problem with Wilson's response is not so much its lack of generosity—he praises Miller's "sure hand at color and rhythm"—as Wilson's fundamental misunderstanding of the nature of the book, which Bartlett sees as a "species of autobiography" rather than, as Wilson does, a novel. Rather than paying attention to *Cancer's* formal innovations Wilson concentrates on it as "the epitaph for the whole generation of American writers and artists that migrated to Paris after the War."

Miller was a very different kind of cultural critic from Wilson, and it is to his credit that George Orwell was the first major writer to respond at length to that difference (in the widely available essay "Inside the Whale" [1940]). What Orwell likes most about *Cancer*, however, are the ways in which it reinforces his own gloominess about the horror of modern life and the prospects for apocalypse. Orwell's lament over "the disintegration of our society and the increasing helplessness of all decent people" leads inevitably to the prediction that the "autonomous individual is going to be stamped out of existence," views that perhaps tell us more about Orwell and his deep concern for the independent self than they do about Miller, whose inexplicable happiness in the face of this cultural collapse Orwell does note.

Orwell is all the same responsive to the innovations in this "very remarkable book," calling attention to Miller's capacity to give the reader the feeling of "being understood," that the author's mind and the reader's mind are one—a quality Orwell believes is also to be found in Joyce. Perhaps even more remarkable is Orwell's extravagant praise of Miller's prose, which he finds "astonishing" and which he most perceptively associates with Miller's distinctive ability to treat English "as a spoken language." For all that he saw *Cancer* and *Black Spring* through the lens of his own angst, Orwell did understand Miller's accomplishment: "Here in my opinion," he concluded, "is the only imaginative prose-writer of the slightest value who has appeared among the English-speaking races for some years past." But to suggest, as he also did, that Miller was "essentially a man of one book" may have had as much to do with Orwell's sense of the imminence of world cataclysm as with his conviction regarding Miller's potential for survival as an imaginative writer.

By the end of the 1930s Miller had published a body of work sufficient to make early retrospective assessments possible (though the first of his books to be published in the United States did not appear until 1939). One of the very best of these early overviews is Herbert J. Muller's "The World of Henry Miller," *Kenyon Review* 2 (Summer 1940), 312–18.[21] Though he opens by paying tribute to Miller's "remarkable personality, remarkable talent," Muller chides the author for his anti-intellectual and antisocial proclivities, expressing an indulgently school-masterly impatience with Miller's "ultra-romantic passion for utter freedom" and his apparent rejection of "all formal disciplines." (Two decades later, Frank Kermode, in a rather more peevish tone, will complain that Miller is "in thrall to the conventions of modern Romantic primitivism" and that his work "frighten[s] away *mesure*".)[22] Muller does recognize Miller as a "highly self-conscious writer of literature whose sense of life is authentic—" earned, not learned. Comparing Miller favorably to Thomas Wolfe, Muller is apparently the first critic to insist that Miller is "American to the core." For Muller the nature of this Americanness, shared by Wolfe and Miller, consists of an "immense appetite for experience, the feeling of wonder and awe, the teeming memory and blazing imagination, the gift of headlong eloquence." Having indulged Miller, Muller reins him in again with the rather pious concluding hope that "his subsequent work may be more measured and restrained." By contrast, most subsequent critics favorably disposed to Miller have argued that this measured and restrained quality is at the root of the comparative falling off of Miller's success as a writer from the 1940s on.

A much less grudging appreciation of Miller was written by Herbert Read, the brilliant English poet, scholar, and critic.[23] Read, who had been writing to Miller since the mid-1930s, embraced Miller's oppositional stance, and claims that it is precisely Miller's violation of conventional aesthetic, moral, religious, and philosophical expectations that has made it possible for him to make "one of the most significant contributions to the literature of our time." Unlike Muller, who accepts Miller's obscenity but finds that it diverts attention from other aspects of his work, Read cheerfully acknowledges that Miller is probably "the most obscene writer in the history of literature," but sees this fact as a tribute to his "devastating honesty" and a key sign of his vitality. Also unlike Muller, who wished to keep the artist and the social philosopher in Miller separated, Read insists that what "makes Miller distinctive among modern writers is his ability to combine, without confusion, the aesthetic and the prophetic functions." Finally, rather than calling on Miller to exercise more decorum and self-control, Read endorsed Miller's anarchistic spirit and welcomed the prospect of a time when, as Miller observed, man's "aim will be not to possess power but to radiate it."

Philip Rahv is another of those critics who sought, above all else, to be judicious—at least where Miller was concerned.[24] Rahv reviews what has already taken shape in the accumulating critical reaction to Miller as some of his books (but not the *Tropics* or *Black Spring*) became available in the United States. Miller, he suggests, is unfairly ignored or dismissed by highbrow critics on formalistic or moral grounds, but he points out as well that Miller is also too easily overrated by those who fail to distinguish between "the art of exploiting one's personality and the art of exploiting material . . . for creative purposes." Allowing that Miller "at his best . . . writes on a level of true expressiveness, generating a kind of all out poetry, at once genial and savage," Rahv at the same time worried about Miller's amoral stance and the tendency of his writings to expose "more fully than any other contemporary novelist in English the nihilism of the self which has been cut off from all social ties and released not only from our allegiance to the past but also from all commitments to the future."[25] Echoing Orwell's observation that Miller was "Whitman among the corpses," Rahv went further in separating these two American writers, suggesting, indeed, that the "peculiarly American affirmation voiced by Whitman was . . . completely negated in Miller." What, in the end is to be said for Miller, this writer possessed of an "insatiable naturalistic curiosity?" The "final impression we have of his novels," Rahv suggested, "is that of a naturally genial and garrulous American who has been through hell."

Poet and critic Kenneth Rexroth wrote early and frequently (and not always favorably)[26] about Miller, and, in "The Reality of Henry Miller" (1959), selected for this volume, he first called attention to a number of matters unnoticed by other commentators. Rexroth pointed out, for example, that outside the United States Miller is read by "common people"—those who in his native land would be readers of comic books—and that Miller's works have become "part of the standard repertory of reading matter" everywhere except in England and America. It was not primarily salaciousness that attracts such working-class readers, Rexroth argued, but Miller's capacity to provide convincing representations of their familiar reality available nowhere else in print. He "tells about the Emperor, about the pimples on his behind, and the warts on his private parts, and the dirt between his toes." Miller is not like Sade or Céline, Rexroth insisted; both of them were in some sense thesis-driven, whereas Miller is concerned, in a masculine, comic way, only to tell the whole truth about the "utter tragedy of life." Indeed, Miller has preserved, Rexroth claimed, a pagan innocence about life and literature and his only social message is: This is what life is like. Rexroth made the interesting suggestion, against the view of Orwell, that Miller was a writer of the 1920s, that what Miller found in the Paris of the 1930s was the Brooklyn of the 1910s, the afterglow of his first experience of Paradise as a young boy in Brooklyn.

Rexroth also anticipated a number of critics who have written on Miller's representation of women. In connection with what he characterized as Miller's "rank, old-fashioned masculinity," Rexroth wrote: "He characteristically writes about his wives as bad boys talk of their schoolteachers. When he takes his sexual relationships seriously, the woman disappears in a sort of marshy cyclone. She becomes an erotic giantess, a perambulating orgy." To his credit, Miller doesn't pretend to have found a "sacramental marriage"— one that "transmutes and glorifies the world"—though disappointment in that fantasy, it has been argued, by Millett, for example, drives much of *The Rosy Crucifixion*.

George Wickes, who has been the most informative and even-handed of Miller's critics over the years, provides the most detailed yet briefest account of Miller's Paris years we have. He helps us to understand, in the chapter reprinted in this collection, why Miller went to Paris in the first place, where, how, and with whom Miller lived over the nine years he spent there, and what he read and wrote during those years. He enables us to sense the dominant moods of euphoria and exaltation in which Miller's first trilogy was composed as well as the shifting intention that informs each of these books. It is important to understand, for example, Miller's mood as he readied himself to write what would become *Tropic of Cancer*. "I will explode in the Paris book," he wrote: "The hell with form, style, expression and all those pseudo-paramount things which beguile the critics. I want to get myself across this time—and direct as a knife thrust." Having done what he could to finish his novel *Crazy Cock*, he wrote to Emil Schnellock on 24 August 1931: "I start tomorrow on the Paris book: first person, uncensored, formless—fuck everything."[27] He was clearly ready to make a jump—and without a net.

PHALLIC MILLER

Any number of explanations have been offered to account for and to mitigate Henry Miller's derogation of women, but it makes as little sense to deny Miller's sexism as it does to insist that Henry Miller was *only* (or mainly) a sexist. All the same, unlike Faulkner, Hemingway, or Fitzgerald, Miller is, in Mailer's words, "not a social writer but a sexual writer."[28] Miller was, as Mailer also reminds us in the "Narcissism" selection in this volume, a product of "a milieu where sex had something wrong with it if it [was] not sordid." In turn-of-the-century Brooklyn, Mailer continues, "[s]ex and filth were components of the same equation," and Miller's "first and fundamental relation to a woman is detestation." Noting the coldness of Miller's mother (a fact that haunted Miller into old age),[29] Mailer underscores Miller's early tendency to seek out idealized love objects. His first passion, altogether unrequited, was for a "blond blue-eyed near mythical girl."[30] There appeared to be for Henry Miller—as before and since for so many men—a clear choice to be made between madams and madonnas, and Miller chose to worship the virgins while punishing the whores with his phallus. "The first of the lovers in him," Mailer observes, "and it will never leave him altogether, is the stud with a rock for a cock and a rock for a heart—so he will present himself." These observations may tell us as much about Mailer as they do about Miller, who was from the start, and remained, a man capable of great emotional tenderness as well as wanton cruelty.

Miller's first serious sexual liaison was with a woman old enough to be his mother, and his first wife was puritanical, passionate, and guilt-stricken about sex. The great love of Miller's life, of course, was June Edith Smerth, who later became the Mara/Mona of several of his "auto-novels." June represented many things to Henry; she was beautiful, sexually exciting, radically unconventional, highly original and imaginative, and perhaps most important, she made Henry believe that he could become a great writer. She was the first woman to recognize his potential as an artist, and if she and he had been different kinds of people theirs might have been one of the great love stories of our time. As it was, Henry wrote about her for more than thirty years, yet she eluded him in imagination as she did in life. What Henry learned from June, Mailer suggests, was his lack of identity, his need to "re-create himself every morning," as June did. (Though Mailer doesn't say it, Henry's need was perhaps not so much to fill women as it was to use women to fill himself—a not uncommon confusion.)

Mailer's most provocative speculation has to do with the couple's narcissism. Henry and June, he suggests, were both narcissists, and narcissists "have a passionate affair to the degree each allows the other to resonate more fully than when alone." What typically occurs in such relationships, he notes, is not so much love as "fine tuning," and once Miller and Mansfield (as she later called herself) were separated by the Atlantic after she sent him to Paris in 1930 to write full-time, they both had to seek out new tuning forks. After the Sturm und Drang of seven years with Mansfield, who professed her belief in him but spent her time with others (as did Miller), it is not surprising that Miller for a time considered taking up a relatively straightforward and relatively uncomplicated relationship with a prostitute. If June was still his muse, his first significant publication was devoted to "Mademoiselle Claude."[31]

Kate Millett's analysis of Miller's sexism in *Sexual Politics* (1970) was the first extensive one, and it is still the most detailed. In the chapter reproduced in this collection, Millett does give Miller credit of a sort: "Miller's genuine originality," she writes, "consists in revealing and recording a group of related sexual attitudes which, despite their enormous prevalence and power, had never (or never so explicitly) been given literary expression before." In her first footnote she also praises his "considerable achievement as an essayist, autobiographer, and surrealist." Even so, the charges against Miller are many and extensively documented. Millett, moreover, attempts to cut off one obvious line of defense—that critics should not confuse texts with their authors. Indeed, what for some critics is one of Miller's strengths, she sees as "the major flaw in his oeuvre—too close an identification with the personal 'Henry Miller'—[which] always operates insidiously against the likelihood of persuading us that Miller the man is any wiser than Miller the character."

The charges against Miller and his persona are several: that Miller depersonalizes women, that he depicts them as pawns to be exploited in an essentially adolescent power game of machismo, that he uses them in childishly fantasized ways to demonstrate male dominance, and as so many toilets into which he can evacuate. So, in Millett's view, Miller must be seen as suffering from the neuroses he depicts and as therefore offering us a vision not of liberation but of confinement within a pernicious ideology. (Essentially the same charges are made against Norman Mailer.)[32]

Michael Woolf proposes, in "Beyond Ideology: Kate Millett and the Case for Henry Miller," that "Millett is torn between a political and ideological alienation from Miller's work, and a responsiveness to his creative method and artistic vision." This underground connection, Woolf argues, is revealed most clearly in Millett's novel *Sita* and, especially, in *Flying*. In these novels, he urges, one can see Millett as sharing with Miller a conviction not only that consciousness is mobile, fluid, and dramatic, but also that their common discovery is of an "essential self in a state of liberation from social restraint and convention." For both of them, "sex is the mechanism through which the private or essential self is realized," and, in the fiction of both, "sexual action is both an expression of liberation and freedom, and simultaneously the reverse: a prison of obsession." On the ideological surface, then, Millett and Miller are "strangers," but "in the innermost chambers of the contradictory heart" they both "draw upon a rich vein of creativity which transcends issues of sexual politics and pornography."

There is an immense amount of material available on the legal, political, sociological, and ideological issues associated with "obscenity" and (the newer word) "pornography" in Miller's work, and for much of the Anglo-American reading public these are still, in fact, the only issues associated with Miller's name. He is, for a large nonreading public, a pornographer plain and simple, and his salacious books constitute a danger to young people and others with too little impulse control. In the memorable words of Justice Michael Musmanno of the Supreme Court of Pennsylvania, *Tropic of Cancer* was the equivalent of "the sweepings of the Augean stables, the stagnant bilge of the slimiest mud scow, the putrescent corruption of the most noisome dump pile, the dredgiest filth in the deepest morass of putrefaction."[33] What makes such high dudgeon and strained rhetoric particularly amusing is the way the desperation of Musmanno's outrage unintentionally demonstrates the utility of certain short words of the kind to which, among other things, he is apparently objecting. Much of the testimony and many of the legal charges against *Cancer* are laughable in their hyperbole and their confusion of aesthetic and moral criteria.

But Musmanno and others found (and still find) more to object to than Miller's use of Anglo-Saxon words. They object to his "subject matter," that is, his explicit representation of certain parts of the human body in certain kinds of conjunction, with the alleged intention of arousing lascivious thoughts and degenerate behaviors both private and public. They object, too, to what they take to be Miller's "attitudes" or "beliefs," that is, his cruelty, his indifference to suffering, his immorality, his degradation of women, his homophobia, his lack of patriotism, his anarchism, his fascination with excrement, snot, and other body waste products, his blasphemy, his challenge to such social institutions as law, education, and religion. For many people many of Miller's books (the only ones they care about) are predominantly prurient, patently offensive, and without *any* social value. They should be banned, prohibited, burned, their ashes scattered over enemy territory (wherever that shifting geography happens to be).

Several books may be recommended to those who wish to pursue this aspect of Miller's reputation. E. R. Hutchison's *Tropic of Cancer on Trial: A Case History of Censorship* (New York: Grove Press, 1968) concentrates largely on litigation in Wisconsin, but also takes up the national and international attempts to suppress *Tropic of Cancer*. Charles Rembar's *The End of Obscenity: The Trials of "Lady Chatterley," "Tropic of Cancer" and "Fanny Hill"* (New York: Random House, 1968) has two things in particular to recommend it: the author is the first-rate, clear-speaking lawyer who defended these books for Grove Press, and he includes much actual court testimony (some of it, like Musmanno's fuming, unintentionally amusing). Eleanor Widmer edited

Freedom and Culture: Literary Censorship in the 70s (Belmont, Calif.: Wadsworth Publishing Company, 1970), an instructive anthology that includes several items on *Cancer* and a useful bibliography. Mention should be made too of the substantial section of George Wickes's *Henry Miller and the Critics* (Carbondale: Southern Illinois University Press, 1963) devoted to the legal troubles of *Cancer*. Also worthy of note is the volume edited by Elmer Gertz and Felice Flannery Lewis, *Henry Miller: Years of Trial and Triumph, 1962–1964* (Carbondale: Southern Illinois University Press, 1978). The title index to Lawrence Shifreen's *Henry Miller: A Bibliography of Secondary Sources* provides access to many other relevant newspaper and journal items, including the following especially notable ones. Donovan Bess, "Miller's *Tropic* on Trial," *Evergreen Review* 6 (March–April 1962): 12–37, is an amusing, serious, and day-by-day account of the trial in San Rafael, California (5–15 December 1961): People of California vs. bookdealer Franklin B. Pershina. See Hoke Norris, "*Cancer* in Chicago," *Evergreen Review* 7 (July–August 1962): 40–66, for a vivid and indignant account of one of the most important of the trials. The verbatim testimony of psychiatrist Dr. Sam Irving Stein is one of the highlights of the occasion. Al Katz, "Free Discussion v. Final Decision: Moral and Artistic Controversy and the *Tropic of Cancer* Trials," *Yale Law Journal* 79 (1969): 209–52, provides a detailed study of eight (of the more than sixty) trial transcripts from different regions of the United States. Emil White's *Henry Miller: Between Heaven and Hell: A Symposium* (Big Sur: Emil White, 1961) contains a number of items concerning legal proceedings against Miller's books in Europe. For two thoughtful commentaries on Miller's use of obscenity, see Brian Way, "Sex and Language," *New Left Review* (September–October, 1964): 66–80, and David Lodge, "The Professional Viewpoint," *20th Century Studies* 1 (November 1969): 118–20. Ludwig Marcuse, *Obscene: The History of an Indignation*, translated from the German by Karen Gershon (London: Macgibbon & Kee, 1965), 225–99, offers many shrewd perceptions in a chapter titled "Los Angeles 1962: The Most Obscene Writer in World Literature." Of all this available material, one item seemed especially worthy of reprinting in this volume because it captures and comically deflates the puffed-up self-righteousness (and mindlessness) of those who see ideas as more dangerous than nuclear waste. That item, of course, is John Ciardi's "Concrete Prose and the Cement Mind."

ORPHIC MILLER

Wallace Fowlie was the first critic to locate Miller firmly in the tradition of a visionary company going back to Orpheus and coming forward to Rimbaud and Lawrence. Fowlie, who had first come to Miller's attention through an essay he had written on the Narcissus theme in 1943, was then a professor of French at Yale University specializing in the twentieth century. Fowlie first published his thoughts on Miller in "Shadow of Doom: An Essay on Henry Miller" (1944),[34] but his basic thesis about Miller as "essentially a seer and prophet" is repeated and updated in his Introduction to *Letters of Henry Miller and Wallace Fowlie* (New York: Grove Press, 1975), reproduced in part in this volume. There he argues that Miller is a scapegoat-clown, who, like the boy-prophet Rimbaud, his immediate ancestor, "daily lives the metaphysical problems of his age," and "reassemble[s] in himself all the shattered parts of the world." As Fowlie points out, Paris has been a hospitable location for both native and foreign-born artists, especially in the twentieth century, to defy "the usual contemporary waywardness and bifurcations," an arena for re-membering the dismembered. Fowlie also has perceptive things to say about the way Miller's outlook runs against the grain of "the traditional American treatment of evil" as a force located outside the self. He deals suggestively, moreover, with the interrelations of alimentary, sexual, and spiritual hunger in Miller, implying that Miller's treatment of women as prostitutes is a perversion of Rimbaud's "excessive hate for his mother," a notion further developed by a number of biographers and critics.

At the heart of Fowlie's account of Miller is a commitment to what he takes to be Miller's spiritual innocence—his honesty, integrity, incorruptibility. It is inappropriate, he asserts, to consider Miller as a writer of accepted genres. Rather, he "is a world literary figure who has given us the best confessional writing since Jean-Jacques Rousseau. He has given us the best account of a writer's day-dreaming and reveries that are different from those of the layman."

That Wallace Fowlie wrote the preface to Bertrand Mathieu's *Orpheus in Brooklyn: Orphism, Rimbaud, and Henry Miller* (1976) should hardly be surprising, for Mathieu takes up Fowlie's core notion of Miller as poet-prophet and applies it in a close reading of *The Colossus of Maroussi* (1941), Miller's account of his travels in Greece in 1939. But Mathieu does more than "apply" Fowlie's perception; he greatly extends and enriches it by demonstrating Miller's lifelong interest in Greek myths, his self-conscious identification with the Orpheus myth, his borrowings from the metaphors, imagery, and narrative structures of vatic writings, and the closeness of Miller's affiliation with the French Symbolists and, as the subtitle makes clear, especially with Arthur Rimbaud, to whom Miller devoted an entire book, *The Time of the Assassins: A Study of Rimbaud* (1956).

In any event, Mathieu's book (and the chapters included in this volume) serves most usefully to call attention to another dimension of Miller's oeuvre. Even critics who dislike Miller have approved of *Colossus*. Perhaps attracted by what Ihab Hassan sees as its spirit of resolution, Frank Kermode, for example, names it Miller's best book,[35] and a number of other major critics of Miller have remarked on the curious equability of its mood and the perfection of its writing. Still others, like Leon Lewis,[36] see *Colossus* (as does Norman Mailer) as a deeply flawed book, one in which the absence of an angry hero/narrator robs the narrative of the dynamic tensions that invigorate *Black Spring* and the *Tropics*.

Paul Jackson's essay, "Henry Miller, Emerson, and the Divided Self" (1971), reprinted in this collection, is directed chiefly to Miller's interest in "a complex of Emersonian ideas concerned with the artistic necessity of using autobiographical fact, the relations of fiction to life and the difficulty of understanding the mystery of selfhood basic to autobiographical fiction," but the essay also concerns itself with the visionary qualities of Miller's *Sexus* (1965) and his debt in that book to Emerson's *Journals* and his essay "Manners." It was in Emerson's *Journals* and essays, Jackson proposes, that Miller found that his subject was the divided self of the visionary seer in his long journey of emancipation into life. This direct debt can be most readily observed in Miller's use of Emerson's character Osman, made more masculine and assertive by being renamed Osmanli, a man who is a "desperado of action" as well as a "desperado of love" as he appears variously in the *Tropics* and in *Sexus*.

Miller might also have found warrant for his Orphic ambitions in Emerson's "The Poet,"[37] an essay that seems to predict Miller as well as Whitman (to whom Miller also owes much). Dismissing those who write "at a safe distance from their experience" as "contemporary" rather than "eternal," as having talent but not genius, Emerson remarks that "the experience of every new age requires a new confession." Anticipating both Miller's practice and the response of legions of decency-obsessed censors, Emerson speculates: "The vocabulary of an omniscient man would embrace words and images excluded from polite conversation. What would be base, or even obscene, to the obscene, become illustrious, spoken in a new connection of thought. The poetry of the Hebrew prophets purges their grossness." The Orphic poet, moreover, "turn[s] the world to glass" and sees "the flowing or metamorphosis; perceives that thought is multiform; that within the form of every creature is a force impelling it to ascend into a higher form." One could argue that Miller's career is given over to a scrutiny of the world of himself as he seeks to ascend to a higher form.

Emerson, of course, piously hoped that true poets would lead a moderate and abstinent life, one in which they would be "tipsy with water," and it would be pressing the matter to suggest that the man who urged Whitman to censor himself would have given Miller's *Tropic of Cancer* an enthusiastic review. Even so, if Emerson understood what a poet's duties were, he also understood their frustrations, and surely his example helped Miller to carry on. Perhaps it was this passage from "The Poet" that Miller recalled from time to time, in the decade 1924–1933, as he searched for personal direction and his writing voice, as he pursued with sharklike restlessness sustenance for his body: "Doubt not, O poet, but persist. Say, 'it is in me, and shall out.' Stand there, baulked and dumb, stuttering and stammering, hissed and hooted, stand and strive, until, at last, rage draw out of thee that *dream-*

power which every night shows thee in thine own; a power transcending all limit and privacy, and by virtue of which a man is the conductor of the whole river of electricity" (*Essays, Second Series*, 42).[38]

AMERICAN MILLER

Norman Mailer puts his finger on one of the most puzzling of paradoxes surrounding Henry Miller: "[I]t is as if he is almost not an American author; yet nobody could be more American."[39] This perception reinforces what Miller himself observed: that though he is thoroughly American, he never felt at home in his native land.[40] Many other critics, of course, have also commented on one aspect or another of Miller's "Americanness," and Miller has been associated with a goodly number of American writers. Ihab Hassan, for example, proposes that Miller is distinctive by virtue of his American generosity, violence, and prodigality; Warner Berthoff emphasizes Miller's powerful antinomianism; and J. D. Brown locates Miller in the traditions of American vernacular humor and transcendental autobiography.[41] Kingsley Widmer correctly sees a Thoreauvian strain in Miller (though at every opportunity he characteristically insists on how diminished and distorted the strain is in Miller).[42] Many critics from Orwell on have connected Miller with Whitman (whom Miller often celebrated as the greatest American writer).[43] Herbert Muller was among the first to link Miller with Thomas Wolfe, while Miller's debt to or influence on Sherwood Anderson, e.e. cummings, James Agee, Jack Kerouac, Lawrence Ferlinghetti, J. P. Donleavy, and Phillip Roth among others have also been alleged.[44]

Few critics, however, have offered as detailed (or as favorable) an assessment of Miller's place in American literature as Mailer. "One had to go back to Melville," Mailer asserts in "Status" (included in this volume), "to find a rhetoric which could prove as noble under full sail." At his best, moreover, Miller "wrote a prose grander than Faulkner's and wilder_____." With respect to Miller's influence, Mailer continues, it "is even not unfair to say that Henry Miller has influenced the style of half the good American poets and writers alive today" [1976], an influence apparent in books as different as *Naked Lunch, Portnoy's Complaint, Fear of Flying, Why Are We In Vietnam?* and *The Adventures of Augie March*.[45]

At the center of Miller's Americanness, for Alan Trachtenberg, is Miller's nostalgia for what we might call the pastoral perfect, a "specifically *American* redemption," a redemption "outside of history."[46] Indeed, this "flight from history, from social ties and obligations, is the clearest mark of Miller's underlying commitment to an American dream." For Miller, the urban pastoralist, this ideal state of self-sufficient freedom was associated with that paradise of his childhood in the 14th ward of Brooklyn. Pursuing this notion of displacement in Miller's work, Trachtenberg proposes that

Miller's rediscovery of the idyllic life in the Greece of *The Colossus of Maroussi* may be best understood as his form of participation in the dream of an American frontier peopled with spontaneous, natural, and unattached men. Though Trachtenberg has reservations about Miller's moral self-absorption and stylistic self-indulgence—signs of confusion in his larger vision—he does discern a special feature of Miller's first books: "The excitement in Miller's early work is its authentic emotion of release, its unhindered explorations of the suppressed fringes of middle-class fantasies, where respectability fades into criminality."

John Williams's essay, "Henry Miller: The Success of Failure," also reprinted in this collection, makes a different claim about Miller's Americanness, which he argues is grounded in the ambivalences imposed by the Calvinist strain in American Puritanism, a theology that insisted on "the doctrinal importance of [the] internal life and the practical necessities of [the] external." According to Williams, Miller's life and work embody many of the dilemmas, polarities, and tensions that characterize American life and thought, among them, sentimentality and cynicism, pretension and simplicity, obscenity and tenderness, hypocrisy and honesty, cruelty and kindness. Similarly, he claims, Miller is a compound of failure and success. On the one hand, Miller is prolix and repetitive, given to elephantine diction and gross sentimentalities, formless, incapable of constructing a dramatic scene, inept in developing characters; on the other hand, none of these deficiencies matter because Miller is "an authentic genius" who has given his ordinariness to us with extraordinary skill and honesty. Miller, Williams concludes, is possessed of "vast humanity" and marked by a "vast generosity of spirit"; and in renouncing the dream of worldly (or critical) success he has made a success of failure.

MILLER RECONSIDERED

Art and Outrage is an important small volume consisting primarily of the correspondence in the late 1950s between Lawrence Durrell and Alfred Perlès. Initiated by Durrell, the correspondence had its origins in Durrell's visit to Paris in the mid-1950s, during which he reflected on Miller's journey of self-discovery and on his own sense of injustice that Miller's writings were still essentially unknown to Anglo-American audiences. Durrell had read Perlès's *My Friend, Henry Miller* (1955), but wished now to supplement that biographical memoir with a portrait of the artist "mirrored in his work," drawn from an exchange of letters that "informally and without preciousness" might refine public understanding of Miller's nature and contribution to letters. Two of these letters—and one by Miller in response—are reprinted in this volume.

Perlès's second letter to Durrell in *Art and Outrage* insists on the futility of attempts to essentialize Miller. He is kaleidoscopic, and any attempt to resolve the many Millers into "one rigid picture is as hopeless as trying to gauge the number and scope of all the books that can be written with the 26 letters of the alphabet." Miller can't be reduced to his "intentions," Perlès warns, nor should he be thought of solely from the point of view of his "evolution from the fleshly to the spiritual." Rather, Perlès proposes, if "we want to do him a service I feel we must look at his work through the man and pin him down without any possible literary loopholes." Durrell's reply, also printed in this collection, insists on what he takes to be Miller's "religious and artistic bias of mind," a bias present even in such partially "horripilating" books as *Sexus*. Durrell agrees with Perlès that there are many Millers, the "most endearing . . . of course the childish ones—the clown, the American tourist, the gullible one. . . ." He then makes the provocative suggestion that Miller has provided the best portrait of himself in the words of Sylvia, a character in *Sexus*, who says of the Miller persona: "Because the woman can never give you what you want you make yourself out to be a martyr. . . . You have all the feminine virtues but you are ashamed to acknowledge them to yourself. . . . You will always be trying to dominate yourself; the woman you love will only be an instrument for you to practice on."

Miller's response to these letters is an extraordinary document in self-analysis and critical reflection. "I don't care who the artist is," Miller proposed, "if you study him deeply, sincerely, detachedly, you will find that he and his works are one." The man whom Perlès and Durrell met and knew in Paris when he was in his forties, however, was not the complete man; there was also the Miller in his thirties and the years with June, which climaxed "that fateful day" in 1927 when he mapped out the "whole autobiographical romance—in one sitting." Before that there was the Miller in his early twenties, the "perpetual volcano" furiously composing fiction in his head as he walked to and from his father's tailor's shop. There were, then, the young Miller who wished only to be able to write, the Miller known to Perlès and Durrell who was a writer (certified by the publication of books bearing his name), and now the man and writer who wished simply to be. Reviewing his life and most of his books, particularly those written after his return to America, Miller concludes: "At sixty-six I am more rebellious than I was at 16." He might have said the same thing 20 years later.

In a small book devoted to an "account of the historical character of American writing since the 1940s,"[47] Warner Berthoff devotes a substantial portion of his limited space to Henry Miller and his influence, especially the influence of *Tropic of Cancer*. In one chapter, Miller is even paired with Wallace Stevens as one of the "Old Masters" who anticipated the "central imaginative character" of the writing of the period 1945–75.[48] Pointing out Miller's "classic American . . . antinomianism," Berthoff specifies the attitudes and themes Miller's fiction anticipates: the "apparent withdrawal of any life-serving purpose from normative human relationships, the transformation of the whole institutionalized world into either an absurd farce or an openly murderous global conspiracy."

Berthoff also has some distinctive observations to make about *Tropic of Cancer*, a book he asserts is "engagingly full of other people." These characters—frequently dismissed as flat and underdeveloped—have, in Berthoff's view, a "capacity to occupy real narrative space and impose themselves as speakers and actors on the affirmed progression of events"—something missing in much post–World War II fiction. Perhaps even more unexpected is Berthoff's characterization of Miller's representation of sexuality in *Cancer*: "Miller clearly reveres the beauty and the power of female sexuality, and of ordinary womanly sweetness and practicality as well, and decries the violation of these qualities in the circumstances of modern life." In *Cancer*, he continues, "It is much more commonly the male characters . . . who are ridiculed and despised." In the "Coda" to this brief book, Berthoff suggestively identifies Miller's influence, pointing first to Miller's example as an encouragement to other writers "to take greater expressive risks" and to his role in widening "public tolerance and receptivity." Finally, he identifies nearly a score of writers who may owe some debt to Miller for their subjects, language, metaphors, images, and turns of phrase. Like Freud, Berthoff implies, Miller has in some sense become the very atmosphere of our time.

As the title of her essay prepared for this volume suggests, Mary Kellie Munsil examines three related topics—Henry Miller as person and persona, a variety of social and legal issues surrounding pornographic texts and images (and their relation to behavior), and how earlier and more recent feminist critics and theoreticians have responded to Miller and his writing (especially *Tropic of Cancer*). She also suggests how post-structural theory may contribute to our understanding of pornography in general and specific works as *Tropic of Cancer*, in which communication and the failures of language are central themes. Munsil rejects attempts to essentialize sexuality and gender or to legislate sources of pleasure. At the same time, she points out that Miller the man and the persona often fail to "negotiate the chasm between male and female experience" and are thus "trapped within a misogynist 'prison-house of language.'"

Part of the achievement of James Goodwin's essay "Henry Miller, American Autobiographer," commissioned for this volume, is the elegant economy of its assessment of the relationship between the whole of Miller's life and the whole of his writings. Goodwin locates Miller in the tradition of American autobiography from Benjamin Franklin to the emergence in the last quarter of a century of confessional writing as a dominant American genre. Miller's autobiographical stance, Goodwin argues, is directly related to the discursive mode of Thoreau in *Walden* and of Whitman in *Leaves of Grass*—both of whom situate "subjectivity within the moment of expression"—and opposed to the Franklinian or historical mode, which situates "the subjectivity of the narrator outside the narrative itself." Indeed, in his major works, when Miller (the persona) stays within the "contingent conditions of immediate experience," the fiction is convincing; when he offers accounts of the life from outside (when he invites pity or emulation), the writing suffers.

This fundamental insight makes it possible for Goodwin to illuminate, for example, the extraordinary power and volume of Miller's letters. The writing of letters, he suggests, allows Miller to relocate himself within the contingent, the accidental, the moment-to-moment flow of daily life; the act of writing a letter, with its combination of intimacy and distance, encourages the spontaneously comic monologue at which Miller excels. From this insight it is a short step to a larger and more profound generalization: "The joy of writing is the principal subject of discourse in Miller's life work." Finally, Goodwin suggests Miller's other contributions to American literary history: a modernist sensibility "rooted in sexual and self exploration," important inventions in discursive style, and a precedent for the Beat Movement, the New Journalism, and "other forms of personalist, confessional writings" whether in prose or poetry.

Jeffrey Bartlett's "The Late Modernist," another essay commissioned for this volume, divides its emphasis between the two key words of its title. Miller is "late" in several senses, and one of them emerges from Bartlett's review of Miller as the subject of popular and professional criticism in the 1930s and 1940s, which generally misapprehended Miller because of social, moral, aesthetic, or political preconceptions. Edmund Wilson missed the "feeling" of *Tropic of Cancer* because of his commitment to respectability, to "literature," while George Orwell's angst over the future of Western civilization blinded him to the affirmative, even celebratory impulses in Miller's first books. Partly because Miller came of age late as a writer, literary critics and historians have generally failed to see that Miller "is a full member of the generation of Modernists who flourished from the early years of the century until World War II." More specifically, Bartlett demonstrates in some detail Miller's affiliations with expressionism, dadaism, and surrealism—his interest, respectively, in the non-representational, the playfully expressive, and the unconscious and spontaneous. Insisting on the "unmistakably American" qualities of Miller's style, language, personality, and worldview, Bartlett emphasizes that Miller is an American original, a "Modernist in that he understands himself, however ambivalently, as of his times." Unlike the "high" modernists, Bartlett observes, Miller was never popular, respectable, famous, or fashionable, but he did help to release English literature from certain linguistic, formal, stylistic, and subject-matter restrictions that had come to confine it.

Miller is seen by Welch Everman in "The Anti-Aesthetic of Henry Miller," commissioned for this volume, as not only a "late modernist" but as in some ways a harbinger of postmodernism as well, especially in the sense that Miller, like many postmodernists (regardless of the times in which they emerged), "collapses the distinction between art and life." (As Bartlett notes, Miller pulled art off its pedestal.) More specifically, Miller's "anti-aesthetic rejects the well-crafted novel of coherent characters and a logical cause-and-effect plot in favor of association, digression and contradiction."[49] One of the few critics to have much good to say about *The Rosy Crucifixion* trilogy, Everman proposes that it needs to be seen as anti-art—"seemingly without system, without method, without rigor, without logic." More generally, Everman insists, "Miller wants not beauty but ecstasy, and his aesthetic is an aesthetic of the sublime." For Miller, art is only a symbolic substitute and simulacrum for moments of actual if transient union with the sublime, and it is therefore not surprising that Miller's work should be replete with transcendent experiences of an erotic or religious character. Such ecstatic moments, of course, don't last, but as Emily Dickinson and Henry David Thoreau remind us, "forever is composed of nows."

Richard Kostelanetz's "Henry Miller: On the Centenary of His Birth" is a survey of Miller's writings by a young man who wished to (and did) become a writer himself. This covers a great deal of ground, offering observations about Miller's style and themes, his treatment of sexuality ("definitely low mimetic"), his conception of art and artists, his strength at depicting city life, his weakness as a systematic thinker, and the limits of Miller's literary criticism. Miller nonetheless ranks, Kostelanetz concludes, "among the best writers of his generation," not as great as Eliot and Faulkner but in the same league with Hemingway, Fitzgerald, Dos Passos, and Stein. Miller opened up writing by having the courage to expose himself completely, and the unique contribution his work makes is to insist "that freedom of speech is the essence of liberation—a fundamental right . . . rooted in the body."

MILLER IN RETROSPECT

Jonathan Cott's *Rolling Stone* interview with Miller, reprinted in this volume, offers a sympathetic view of the author as a physically decrepit and intellectually intense man in his eighties, still responding hungrily to ideas, still voluble about the human comedy. Cott also provides a long arm's-length assessment of Miller's total career, an assessment that will strike most favorably disposed readers of Miller as generous, perceptive, and fair. Looking back over Miller's life and oeuvre, Cott proposes that Miller's oeuvre "must be read simply as one enormous evolving work—a perpetual *Bildungsroman*—manifesting the always changing, yet ever the same, awareness and celebration of the recovery of the divinity of man." It is in this context that Cott remarks on the unfortunate reputation Miller has as the author of a few dirty books, "since his work . . . consistently evolves, perfectly exemplifying the ideas of rapturous change, metamorphosis, surrender and growth."

Addressing the Miller-Millett-Mailer issue quite directly, if briefly, Cott believes that Millett distorts Miller's representation of women, particularly in failing to respond to the comic dimension of Miller's treatment of sexuality. He concludes that Anaïs Nin is more perspicacious on Miller's attitudes regarding sex than either Millett or Mailer—or, he might have added, than anyone else, including Miller himself. In response to a question by Cott, Miller characteristically denies that there was "any woman problem" in his mind, that he never had any "evil thoughts" about them or any desire to denigrate them. He quickly shifts to a discussion of the lifelong animosity between him and his mother.

What is most distinctive about Cott's piece, however, is its tone of measured admiration. Without turning Miller into a saint, Cott discerns the ferocious intensity of Miller's hunger for life,[50] his often anguished questing for answers to the persistent riddles of the painful earth, his willingness to keep himself open to the always changing circumstances of individual and collective life.

Cott, in short, sees the mystical and spiritual qualities of Miller's life and work and gives them the foregrounding they deserve but seldom get. Miller was, as he himself once ironically allowed, something higher than a louse.

TRIBUTES AND OTHER RESPONSES TO MILLER

The tributes that conclude this volume are meant to suggest not only the great respect many writers have shown for Miller as a writer but also the affection many have felt toward the many-sided man who wrote all those books. Still others testify to the power Miller had to enter their imaginations—in one way or another. William Carlos Williams thought Miller "a very good influence." For some, like Isaac B. Singer, he was "a mighty good writer" and a courageous fighter for literary freedom. Bern Porter valued the sanity and objectivity Miller brought to sex. For others, like Jerzy Kosinski, Miller has served as "custodian of our innermost equator." Robert Creeley testifies to Miller's usefulness as an alternative to institutionalized writers, and to the value of his joyful, healthy connection to urban realities. Erica Jong was astonished by his generosity and notes his capacity to loosen the inhibitions and anxieties of those with whom he came in touch. At the end of her eulogy, Jong expresses the hope that Miller might be awarded a Nobel prize in heaven. What Henry Miller might say by way of an acceptance speech is most interesting to contemplate. Bob Snyder's grainy reminiscence makes the speech easier to imagine. Whatever else he might say, Diane Miller is no doubt correct in suggesting that he would urge us by his own example not to be afraid of being naked.

Notes

1. The critical response to Miller in English has been ill-assorted, and so odd as to resist a shapely narrative history. With some exceptions noted here, serious scholarly work on Miller in England and the United States has been scarce. Assessments of individual works and of the whole career tend to be polarized for a number of reasons: Miller published his first work relatively late in life; his early and best work was published first in France (and then in many other countries except England and the United States) and was linguistically, stylistically, and philosophically radical; it didn't fit into any familiar genre; it ran against the grain of prevailing critical interests and methods; its author was neither genteelly poor nor conventionally ambitious—indeed was scandalously bohemian and anarchistic; perhaps worst of all, the author was uncompromising about his life and writing. In view of all this, it is not surprising that Miller's chief appreciators have been writers, artists, and the socially and economically marginal.

The best single source of bibliographical information about Henry Miller and his writings is Lawrence J. Shifreen's *Henry Miller: A Bibliography of Secondary Sources* (Metuchen, N.J.: Scarecrow, 1979). This guide undertakes to list and annotate everything written about Miller in all languages through 1977. While inevitably marred by errors of fact and interpretation, this fully indexed, nearly 500-page work is indispensable. Shifreen notes that he was preparing (in 1977) a descriptive bibliography of Miller's publications, a volume that has recently been announced by Roger Jackson (339 Brookside Ave., Ann Arbor, Michigan 48105) as forthcoming soon. Given Miller's productivity, his peripatetic life, and the publication of many of his shorter works by small, obscure, and short-lived presses, the task is daunting. In the meantime, Miller scholars and collectors must make do with the three hopelessly outdated bibliographies of the early 1960s listed by Shifreen.

Jay Martin's *Always Merry and Bright* (Santa Barbara, Calif.: Capra Press, 1978) is the major, pioneering biography, an "unauthorized" work based primarily on the more than 100,000 pages of manuscript material in twenty-three libraries and in individual hands. Martin also takes into account the vast secondary literature, printed personal recollections, and interviews with Miller's friends. Alfred Perlès's *My Friend Henry Miller: An Intimate Biography* (New York: J. Day Co., 1956), written literally under Miller's supervision during a reunion visit by Perlès at Big Sur, is an agreeable—and sometimes freshly informative—memoir by Miller's closest male friend of the 1930s.

There are many other biographical works, and some supply a few useful facts about one period or another of Miller's life, but most lack psychological penetration or critical acumen. See, for example, Sidney Omarr, *Henry Miller: His World of Urania* (London: Villiers, 1960). Kathryn Winslow, *Henry Miller: Full of Life* (Los Angeles: Jeremy P. Tarcher, 1986), supplies some useful details on the last thirty years of Miller's life. The *Diaries of Anaïs Nin* and the many published volumes of Miller's letters to Lawrence Durrell, Anaïs Nin, Michael Fraenkel, Wallace Fowlie, Emil Schnellock, William A. Gordon, Elmer Gertz, J. Rives Child, Hoki Tokuda, and Brenda Venus are all important sources of biographical information. See, too, interviews Miller granted over the years, especially those with George Wickes, Georges Belmont, Barbara Kraft, and Bertrand Wolfe. The living presence of Miller is best captured in Robert Snyder's masterful film portrait *The Henry Miller Odyssey* and in his *Henry Miller: Reflections on Writing*; Snyder's book *This is Henry, Henry Miller from Brooklyn* (Los Angeles:

Nash Publishing Co., 1974) is an engaging compilation of conversations and photographs. The major Miller archive is at UCLA; for details on other holdings, see Martin, *Always Merry and Bright*.

A number of critical studies can be recommended: Annette Kar Baxter, *Henry Miller, Expatriate* (Pittsburgh: University of Pittsburgh Press, 1961); J. D. Brown, *Henry Miller* (New York: Ungar, 1986), one of the best introductions; William A. Gordon, *The Mind and Art of Henry Miller* (Baton Rouge: Louisiana State University Press, 1967); Ihab Hassan, *The Literature of Silence: Henry Miller and Samuel Beckett* (New York: Alfred Knopf, 1967); Leon Lewis, *Henry Miller: The Major Writings* (New York: Schocken Books, 1986); Jane A. Nelson, *Form and Image in the Fiction of Henry Miller* (Detroit: Wayne State University Press, 1970); John Parkin's *Henry Miller, The Modern Rabelais* (Lewiston, N.Y.: Edwin Mellen Press, 1990) makes a persuasive case for the many parallels in form and content of the two authors named in his title. George Wickes, *Henry Miller* (Minneapolis: University of Minnesota Press, 1966), an elegantly concise monograph; Kingsley Widmer, *Henry Miller* (rev. ed.; Boston: Twayne Publishers, 1990), an even more graceless, splenetic, over-written, and self-congratulatory version of his 1963 book, which for all its faults makes a few good points. For a useful review of the major secondary literature on Miller, see the introductory chapter in Leon Lewis's book.

Recent "standard" histories of American literature give Miller short shrift. Wendy Steiner, in the *Columbia Literary History of the United States* (New York: Columbia University Press, 1988), devotes three pages (869–71) to Miller and offers a few ill-assorted generalizations about his work. Nor has Miller fared much better in the recent vast outpouring of books on modernism; J. Hillis Miller is more likely to be found in the indexes of these books than Henry Miller. And it is still the case that with all of the recent movement of the margins to the center, Henry Miller appears only in one major anthology of American literature, vol. 2 of James E. Miller, Jr.'s *Heritage of American Literature* (San Diego: Harcourt Brace Jovanovich, 1991).

One of the few wide-ranging books on modern fiction to take up Henry Miller in the context of feminist literary criticism is Frederick R. Karl's *American Fictions, 1940–1980* (New York: Harper and Row, 1983), 439–43. Sandra M. Gilbert and Susan Gubar's *No Man's Land: The Place of the Woman Writer in the Twentieth Century* (New Haven: Yale University Press, 1988) makes only passing reference to Miller. Perhaps the two most insightful brief treatments of Miller in the context of surveys of the modern novel are to be found in Malcolm Bradbury's *The Modern American Novel* (Oxford: Oxford University Press, 1984), 116–21, and in Brian Lee's *American Fiction: 1865–1940* (London and New York: Longman, 1987), 204–07. Walter Allen's *Tradition and Dream: The English and American Novel from the Twenties to Our Time* (Hogarth: London, 1986), 180–81, is representative of such surveys in being succinctly dismissive of Miller.

2. Earlier anthologies of criticism include: Bern Porter, ed., *The Happy Rock: A Book About Henry Miller* (Berkeley, Calif.: Bern Porter, 1945); Oscar Baradinsky, ed., *Of, By, and About Henry Miller* (Yonkers, N.Y.: Alicat Bookshop Press, 1947); George Wickes, ed., *Henry Miller and the Critics* (Carbondale: Southern Illinois University Press, 1963); and Edward B. Mitchell, ed., *Henry Miller: Three Decades of Criticism* (New York: New York University Press, 1971). There is relatively little overlap among these collections. See Selected Bibliographies in this volume.

3. See Miller's letter in this volume.

4. See Perlès's letter and Mailer's "Status" in this volume.

5. There is no collected American edition of Miller's work. Capra, Grove, and New Directions keep most of his work in print. (See Selected Bibliographies in this volume.) In England, Macgibbon & Kee has published individual works and an excellent two-volume *Selected Prose* (1965). The most readily available collections of Miller are: Lawrence Durrell, ed., *The Henry Miller Reader* (New York: New Directions, 1959), and Norman Mailer, ed., *Genius and Lust: A Journey Through the Major Writing of Henry Miller* (New York: Grove Press,

1976). The former has too little from the early books, the latter too much. *Into the Heart of Life: Henry Miller at One Hundred*, edited and with an introduction by Frederick Turner (New Directions, 1991), is slight and reprints familiar material.

6. *Crazy Cock* was published by Grove Weidenfeld Press in 1991 with a foreword by Erica Jong and an introduction by Mary V. Dearborn. Robert Ferguson's *Henry Miller: A Life* (W. W. Norton) and Mary Dearborn's *The Happiest Man Alive: A Biography of Henry Miller* (Simon & Schuster) appeared in the same year. John Tytell's 1991 *Passionate Lives* (Carol Publishing Group) features a long chapter on "Henry and June and Anaïs."

7. Feminist scholarship of the past two decades has uncovered the manifold and pervasive forms of patriarchal oppression in life and in literature, and sex and gender-conscious cultural theories have helped explain more fully how human sexuality as well as gender have been "constructed" in all of their complexities of relationship. Very little of this sophisticated analysis, however, has been brought to bear on Henry Miller's work.

Andrew Ross's "The Popularity of Pornography" chapter in his *No Respect: Intellectuals and Popular Culture* (New York and London: Routledge, 1989) offers a lively critical review of much of the recent and abundant feminist (and nonfeminist) book and journal literature on pornography. For an illuminating feminist reading of a film director who shares many of the consciously misogynist and unconsciously confused attitudes toward women and sexuality displayed by Miller, see Tania Modleski's *The Women Who Knew Too Much: Hitchcock and Feminist Theory* (New York and London: Methuen, 1988). For an important study of film pornography see Linda Williams's *Hard Core: Power, Pleasure and the "Frenzy of the Visible"* (Berkeley and Los Angeles: University of California Press, 1989).

Pornography, misogyny, and homophobia are not, of course, the only topics that interest feminist and other gender-conscious critics, but in Miller's case the absence of informed criticism around these issues is especially regrettable. It is also unfortunate that other currently dominant theoretical perspectives have largely ignored Miller.

8. See the introduction to George Wickes, *Letters to Emil* (New York: New Directions, 1990), for an account of this remarkable friendship and of the way Miller used Schnellock as a first audience and depository for first-draft versions of material later incorporated into his books. See also Miller's *Semblance of a Devoted Past* (Berkeley: Bern Porter, 1944), a small selection of the letters Miller wrote to Schnellock during the Paris years.

9. For a fascinating compendium of information on Fraenkel (as well as on Walter and Lillian Lowenfels and another Fraenkel friend, Howard McCord), see Walter Lowenfels and Howard McCord, assisted by Lillian Lowenfels and Will Slotnikoff, *The Life of Fraenkel's Death* (Pullman: Washington State University Press, 1970).

10. Terry Southern's "Miller: Only the Beginning," *Nation* (18 November 1961): 391–401, credits Miller with creating a new voice in writing, the "Scrupulously honest mindflow of an adult." See also my discussion of Orwell. Miller was a talker rather than a preacher (though he was often didactic), but he never underestimated the power of the human voice and knew intuitively that the royal road to the human heart was through the ear.

11. See Gunther Stuhlmann's introduction to *A Literate Passion: Letters of Anaïs Nin and Henry Miller, 1932–1953* (San Diego: Harcourt Brace Jovanovich, 1987), v. The quotations in the following paragraph are from Gunther Stuhlmann's edition of *The Diary of Anaïs Nin*, vol. I, 1931–1934.

12. Kate Millett and Norman Mailer (in selections in this volume) both speculate on how much of Miller's animus against women might derive from his "lacerating" experience with his second wife, née June Edith Smerth, later Julia Edith Smith Mansfield).

13. For insight into Miller's dreams—and his literary uses of them—see Jay Martin, *Always Merry and Bright*, 278–96. For a consideration of the theoretical and clinical implications of Miller's "Dream Book," see Martin's essay: "Three Stages of Dreaming: A Clinical Study of Henry Miller's 'Dream Book,' " *Journal of the American Academy of Psychoanalysis* 12 (July 1984): 233–51.

14. Anaïs Nin, Preface to *Tropic of Cancer* (New York: Grove Press, 1961).

15. Each of the critical books listed in note 1 devotes considerable space to *Cancer*. Karl Shapiro's hyperbolic "Introduction" to the Grove Press edition is widely known; dozens of additional reviews and interpretations can be identified by consulting the title index to Shifreen's bibliography. The following items may also be consulted. Maurice Girodias, "Pornography," *Twentieth Century* 174 (Summer 1965): 24–29, is an account of how his father, Jack Kahane, first published *Tropic of Cancer*, how Girodias came to draw the book-jacket picture, and how Barney Rosset eventually published *Cancer* in the United States. Steven Foster's "A Critical Appraisal of Henry Miller's *Tropic of Cancer*," *Twentieth Century Literature* 9 (January 1964): 196–208, offers a negative assessment, chiefly on formal grounds. David Littlejohn's "The Tropics of Miller," *New Republic* 132 (5 March 1962): 478–80, is an essentially negative critique. Don Kleine, "Innocence Forbidden: Henry Miller in the Tropics," *Prairie Schooner* 33 (Summer 1959): 125–30, suggests that Miller's naive, honorable sincerity is his chief claim on our attention. Emile Capouya's "Henry Miller," *Salmagundi* 1 (Fall 1965): 81–87, has much of value to say about *Cancer* and about Miller more generally.

16. An English-language translation is available in Wickes, *Henry Miller and the Critics*, 23–24.

17. Martin, *Always Merry and Bright*, 317.

18. A number of these solicited comments were printed as a promotional piece: "Opinions of This Writer's Work." See Martin, *Always Merry and Bright*, 317.

19. D. D. Paige, ed., *The Letters of Ezra Pound: 1907–1941* (New York: Harcourt, Brace, 1950), 272, 301.

20. Originally published in the *Massachusetts Review* 5 (Spring 1964): 481–91, Lowen-fels's "Unpublished Preface to *Tropic of Cancer*" is reprinted (in part) in Wickes, *Henry Miller and the Critics*, 16–19.

21. Reprinted in Wickes, *Henry Miller and the Critics*, 44–51.

22. Frank Kermode, "Henry Miller and John Betjeman," *Encounter* 16 (March 1966): 69–75; reprinted in Mitchell, *Three Decades of Criticism*, 85–95.

23. Reprinted in Wickes, *Henry Miller and the Critics*, 111–18.

24. Philip Rahv, "Sketches in Criticism: Henry Miller," from *Image and Idea* (New York: New Directions, 1957); reprinted in Wickes, *Henry Miller and the Critics*, 77–85. This essay brings together material written in the early 1940s.

25. This essentially conservative charge will be echoed for many years. See Theodore Solotaroff, " 'All That Cellar-Deep Jazz': Henry Miller and Seymour Krim," *Commentary* 32 (October 1961): 317–24.

26. See Rexroth under author index in Shifreen.

27. Wickes, *Letters to Emil* (New York: New Directions, 1989), 72, 80.

28. See Norman Mailer, "Narcissism" in this volume.

29. See interview with Jonathan Cott in this volume.

30. See Miller's "First Love" from *Stand Still Like the Hummingbird*, 46–49, one of the clearest revelations of Miller's longing for oneness and fear of merger.

31. First published in Peter Neagoe, ed., *Americans Abroad; An Anthology* (The Hague: Servire Press, 1932); reprinted in Henry Miller, *The Wisdom of the Heart*.

32. Norman Mailer takes up Millett's charges most fully in *The Prisoner of Sex* (Boston: Little Brown, 1971). Here he not only defends Miller but attacks Millett. For Mailer, Henry Miller is the leading figure in the sexual "renaissance," that revolt of the 1920s against the "long medieval night of Victorian sex with its perversions, hypocrisies, and brothel dispensations" (77). Miller is to be applauded; he alone had both the literary power and the honesty to reveal his own faults with respect to sexual behavior. Miller is the only writer, Mailer claims, to explore lust as both an ennobling and degrading feature of human experience, as a way of exploring spiritual and metaphysical differences between the sexes. Millett, Mailer

charges, "has a mind like a flatiron, which is to say a totally masculine mind" (88), and her reductive indictment of Miller is flawed by her practice of misquoting Miller, quoting him selectively, quoting him out of context, and by her tendency to treat Miller heavy-handedly for ideological purposes. For a balanced account of Mailer, Miller, and Millett, see Frederick Karl, *American Fictions: 1940–1980* (New York: Harper & Row, 1983), 439–43.

Virtually everyone who has written about Miller has had something to say about his attitudes toward sex and his attitudes toward women in and out of his writings. Recently, for example, Donald Gutierrez's " 'Hypocrite Lecteur': *Tropic of Cancer* as Sexual Comedy" in his *The Maze in the Mind and the World* (Troy, N.Y.: Whitsun, 1985), 75–89, notes that in Miller's works men are individualized, whereas women are reduced to synechdocal body parts; men, he also points out, are also often comic figures in *Cancer* anxious about their ability to perform. Most interestingly, Gutierrez suggests the double-edged character of Miller's sexual comedy: "our responses to Miller's characters indicate our complicity in the comic-tragic anarchy of our sexual drives and relations: they reflect as well the dangerous and vicious attitudes towards women latent in much male sexual comedy."

33.   Quoted in a newspaper article concerning a forthcoming book edited by Fred R. Shapiro, *The Oxford Dictionary of American Legal Quotations*.

34.   Reprinted in Bern Porter, *The Happy Rock*, 102–7.

35.   Hassan, *The Literature of Silence*, 84; for Kermode, see note 22.

36.   Lewis, *Henry Miller*, 132–49.

37.   All references are to this essay as it appeared in Emerson's *Essays, Second Series* (1844), volume III of Edward Waldo Emerson, ed., *The Complete Works of Ralph Waldo Emerson*, 12 volumes, Centenary Edition (Boston and New York: Houghton Mifflin Co., 1903–1904).

38.   Jane A. Nelson's *Form and Image in the Fiction of Henry Miller* (1970) carries the "orphic" idea to an extreme, offering a Jungian psychomythic reading of Miller's life and work. She has provocative things to say about Miller's relationship with women as part of the process of his "individuation." Indeed, though she perhaps pushes her thesis too hard, her work is powerful and stimulating. Nelson understands Miller as spiritual quester as well as anyone who has written about him. Arnold Smithline, in "Henry Miller and the Transcendental Spirit," *Emerson Society Quarterly* 2 (1966): 50–56, most concretely locates Miller within the Emerson-Whitman prophetic tradition, insisting that Miller is at heart a religious writer, one whose mysticism draws on American sources and on Oriental ones that lie behind them. Gordon's *Mind and Art* develops most fully Miller's place in the Anglo-American romantic tradition. Grace D. Yerbury, "Of a City Beside a River: Whitman, Eliot, Thomas, Miller," *Walt Whitman Review* 10 (September 1964): 67–73, locates Miller in the Emerson-Whitman tradition of prophetic spiritually.

39.   See Mailer's "Status" in this volume. Miller has also, of course, been placed in a European tradition running from Petronius to Rabelais, Swift, Dostoyevsky, Nietzsche, Rimbaud, Strindberg, and Spengler, among many others. See Henry Miller, *The Books in My Life* (New York: New Directions, 1969).

40.   For Miller's negative views of America, see his *The Air-Conditioned Nightmare*.

41.   Brown, *Henry Miller*, 107–19.

42.   Widmer, *Henry Miller*, 3–4. Widmer draws attention to parallels between *Walden* and *Cancer*, "curious books of the two American Henrys—libertarian egotists declaiming in elaborate prose their defiant quests for individualistic regeneration—." See Miller's essay "Henry David Thoreau" in the collection *Stand Still Like the Hummingbird*, 111–18.

43.   See especially "Walt Whitman" in *Stand Still Like the Hummingbird*, 107–10.

44.   See Berthoff on the influence of *Tropic of Cancer* in this volume.

45.   Frederick Crews's "Stuttering Giant," *New York Review of Books* 24 (3 March, 1977): 7–9, takes the occasion of a review of Mailer's *Genius and Lust: A Journey Through the Major Writings of Henry Miller* to offer a favorable assessment of early Miller—particularly

Cancer—and to suggest that while Mailer is right "in spirit" about Miller, he uses his subject to run interference for his own ambition. Crews's stress on the powerful and enduring originality of *Cancer* and the tailing off of Miller's achievement after the mid-1930s is made with convincing force. For a tour de force, largely negative, quicksilver review of Miller and Mailer's *Genius and Lust*, see William H. Gass's review in the *New York Times Book Review*, 24 October, 1976, 1–3.

46. See his " 'History on the Side': Henry Miller's American Dream" in this volume.

47. Berthoff, *A Literature Without Qualities: American Writing Since 1945* (Berkeley: University of California Press, 1979), 1.

48. Berthoff might also have argued that between them Miller and Stevens had cornered the market on astonishingly playful and vivid titles for seriously comic literary works.

49. See Edward B. Mitchell's "Artists and Artists: The 'Aesthetics' of Henry Miller" in his *Henry Miller: Three Decades of Criticism*, 155–72. Mitchell examines Miller's views on art in the light of Miller's conception of art as expression and the artist as seer.

50. See Miller's "Uterine Hunger" in *The Wisdom of the Heart*, 187–91.

EARLY MILLER

◆

Just A Brooklyn Boy

Emil Schnellock

I wish I had written about Henry Miller long ago, wish that I had written at every step of the journey. Of course my letters were full of him, and my talk. Every one who knew me was forced to hear of my remarkable friend. People who to this day have never read a line of his always ask on meeting me: "How is Henry? Where is he, what is he doing?"

I must have been about fourteen years old when I first met him. It was in Public School No. 85, on the corner of Covert Street and Evergreen Avenue, in Brooklyn, that the meeting took place. The names Evergreen and Covert are not evocative of the dreary neighborhood which adult eyes encounter; it was easy for us who lived in its street to endow it with enchantment.

I wish, now that I am ageing, that my memories of this period would sharpen. Only a few details emerge. I cannot recapture the appearance of the boy who approached me to ask excited questions as I stood covering the large black-board with murals in colored chalk. Were there spectacles even then? I believe not. I do know that there was a good crop of hair, that it was blonde and fine, almost fluffy in texture. If I attempted to describe him, later memories would obtrude.

What impressed me most was the quality of his interest. It communicated intense enthusiasm, and made what I was doing take on a greater importance to me. There was no way for me to know that this encounter with the fourteen year old boy who watched me with such intense absorption was to ultimately alter the nature of my life. Fifteen years were to elapse before I received the first of his famous letters.

I remember our school song. The opening lines, sung to a quite spirited melody, were—"Dear 85, we'll ever strive to honor thy fair name. . . ." Now, in our fifties, Henry and I still chant it hilariously when we get together. I doubt very much whether "dear 85" has a particularly renowned alumni, or that any of its members know of that singular luminary of the class of 1905. Henry has honored "dear 85" in a manner that will leave its children somewhat flabbergasted.

Excerpted and reprinted from *The Happy Rock: A Book About Henry Miller*, Bern Porter, ed. (Berkeley, CA: Bern Porter, 1945), 7–25. Reprinted by permission of Bern Porter.

After my graduation from public school I lost track of Henry. He had gone to Eastern District High School, in the "old neighborhood" (Williamsburg), which he has written about so movingly in *Black Spring* and elsewhere. Something like twelve years were to pass before I saw him again. In the meantime I had become an advertising artist. It was in my Bedford Avenue studio that Henry made his appearance. He had probably come across my name in the phone book.

It was a short visit but a memorable one. It would be better to describe it as a visitation: an intrusion of values and forces quite outside my dreamy life. There was something that burned in him, something flame-like. I found him the aroused champion of the exploited. He told me of his battles with the higher-ups in the firm he worked for. "I gave it to them straight from the shoulder, and where they don't like it and can't take it." It's a wonder these onslaughts didn't cost him his job. (He had already had so many jobs that I suppose it didn't matter to him if he were fired or not.) "No," he relates, "to my surprise I get a telephone call from the general manager, telling me to take it easy, don't do anything hasty, we'll look into it." He grins and chuckles as he describes their discomfiture.

It is thus I glimpse him already launched on those ferocious attacks which later, in his books, he will direct against all that is false, dead, corrupt. It must have been about this time, or perhaps a little earlier, that through Henry's persuasion his father gave his bewildered consent to abdicate complete ownership of his Fifth Avenue "Tailor Shop" and share it with his employees.

He leaves me a bit dazed. When he's well down the street I suddenly realize that I don't know where to find him. Four years are to go by before I have the good fortune to run into him, a chance encounter on a street corner, which he has described in one of his books. Apparently it was a decisive moment in his life, but at the time I had no idea that the casual description of my travels abroad were to affect him so deeply.

For about three years I had a studio at No. 60 West 50th Street (Radio City has since swallowed it). Here it was I saw Henry most; here he tackled his first book. He had been writing before this, it's true—short stories, essays, diatribes and dithyrambs, as well as articles on the most diverse subjects, such as the making of chewing gum, for example. The book was begun on a three weeks' vacation from the "Cos[mo]demonic Telegraph Company." Every day and all day long he was hard at it. I remember his habit of sitting quite erect, and the muscular energy with which he thumped away at the keyboard. In the *Tropic of Capricorn* he tells us about this book. It seems that the vice-president of this same "cosmococcic" company had once made a suggestion which stuck in Henry's crop. He had said he would like to see some one write a sort of Horatio Alger book about the messenger boy.

"I'll give you an Horatio Alger book, you bastard, you just wait. . . ." I saw the Horatio Alger hero, the dream of a sick America, mounting higher and higher, first messenger, then operator, then manager, then chief, then superintendent, then vice-president, then trust magnate, the Lord of all the Americas, the money god, the god of gods, the clay of clay, nullity on high, zero with ninety-seven decimals fore and aft . . . I took three weeks' vacation instead of two and I wrote the book about the twelve little men. I wrote it straight off, five, seven, sometimes eight thousand words a day. I thought that a man, to be a writer, must do at least five thousand words a day. I thought he must say everything all at once, in one book, and collapse afterwards. I didn't know a thing about writing. I was scared—but I was determined to wipe Horatio Alger out of the North American consciousness. I suppose it was the worst book any man has ever written. It was a colossal tome and faulty from start to finish. But it was my first book and I was in love with it. . . . Everybody I showed it to said it was terrible. I wanted to give up the idea of writing. I had to learn, as did Balzac, that one must write volumes before signing one's own name. I had to learn, as I soon did, that one must give up everything and not do anything else but write, that one must write and write and write, even if everybody in the world advises you against it, even if nobody believes in you. Perhaps one does it just because nobody believes; perhaps the real secret lies in making people believe. That the book was faulty, bad, terrible, as they said, was only natural. I was attempting at the start what a man of genius would have undertaken at the end. I wanted to say the last word at the beginning. It was absurd and pathetic. It was a crushing defeat, but it put iron in my backbone and sulphur in my blood. I knew at least what it was to fail.

He was disproportionately grateful for the use of my studio. It meant more to him than I guessed. I keep going through old letters as I write this outline. Only the other day I came upon this:

Just a note to let you know how deeply I have appreciated your kindness and hospitality these æons past. It may have seemed on occasion that my conduct was reprehensible and transgressed the limits of friendship. I hope it only *seems* so. You are the one individual among all my friends whom I would least injure—in any way. . . . I shall try to give you a vacation for a few days, which will doubtless appeal to you. Frankly, I hate to do it. Living with you has been a rare luxury for me. The atmosphere which your presence always succeeds in creating has done more to restore my spiritual ease and poise than any influence I know. I would that I had given you the same solace; instead, I fear I have been a disruptive force.

The date of the letter shows that he was thirty-two and I thirty-three, and that we took our age with grave seriousness. I remember how we spoke of being mellowed now. I chuckle as I read these lines by the man who as yet had not crossed the Atlantic. "We have had our fling, you and I. Let us look forward to the 'still waters running deep.' "

It never seemed to occur to him how much his visits meant. Just now, as I write, I suddenly recall the words he often used when I opened the door to him: "Is it all right?" Meaning—*was it all right for him to come in.* "Of course, Henry, of course. Come in. Come any time!" That still goes! People who thought him crude, vulgar and aggressive never knew to what lengths his consideration for others could go.

He has just galloped up the three flights. (He always ran up and down stairs; his gait was always springy, jaunty, alive.) I remember a battered felt hat he wore, cocked at a rakish angle. I think one of the very first drawings he made was of that hat. I had placed it so that he saw it in profile, but he drew it as though he were looking at it from above. He drew it the way he felt about it, disregarding the laws of optics. I remember that he wore then a tight-fitting overcoat and an army shirt. Frequently a worn suit would be replaced by one of imported cloth from his father's shop. He could have dressed like a millionaire in those days, but he was always giving his clothes away to those in need. At any rate, no matter how old or new his clothes, he was always neat and tidy, always bathed and sparkling with health and good humor.

The steel-rimmed spectacles which he wore were set very close to his eyes; the whole eye structure seemed to come out to meet them, creating a bland, Chinese flatness about the contours. His eyes, though a cold blue, more often suggested the warmth of quick interest, of lively response—until his gaze followed his thoughts outside the room. Then he gave the illusion of being completely out of the body, a man rapt to another world. These trances came upon him now and then, often at the most unusual, unexpected moments. Suddenly he was "gone". . . .

His body was well developed, but gave a deceptive appearance of frailty; it matched his intense, quick, volatile nature. It suited him, so to speak, and made you feel that he was one with himself. He kept in good shape without any ritual of calisthenics. The days of athleticism were over, though I believe he still used a racing wheel now and then. But he was always agile, and would remain so always. When he chose to he could caper like a goat.

One day when he, Randolph Scott and I reached the street, after sampling some apricot brandy, he bounded to the top of a coupé in two leaps; the first carried him easily to the tonneau, the second to the top of the car which was slippery with rain. There he slithered, pumping his arms and jerking his knees, until he caught his balance. He was in a fever of ecstasy and gave quite a performance before he leapt to the sidewalk.

In attempting to describe him I can manage only a few details—the full lower lip, the pliant, distended nostrils, the two distinct protuberances at the projection of the cheek bone, and the somewhat hemispherical contours where the forehead bulged. There was something of the priest about the fleshiness of the lower face contrasted to the tautness of the brow.

As I said elsewhere, and will say again, the nights of his visits were nights apart. With his appearance the atmosphere changed at once. No moping, no introspection now. Time to dust away the cobwebs of apathy and doubt. Something was sure to happen when he showed up. "Something is bound to happen, even if I have to make it happen myself," he would say. "Wherever I go there is drama." And so it was.

Yes, we're glad he has come, though perhaps not revealing our full joy. It's even possible that we're a bit "patronizing" (unconsciously, of course) in our safer, more limited world . . . in our "solvency." We move in the "sophisticated milieu of the advertising louts." Even though we do nothing but promote the sales of pickles and automobiles, cosmetics and cigarettes, or paint the ivory smiles of the sweet and vacuous glorification of American womanhood, we take our talent and our fat checks seriously. Perhaps our air of slight condescension was due more to Henry's open, child-like trust and the rapt attention he gave to everything we had to say. (This is the moment to emphasize that any attempt to describe Henry Miller must include this attentiveness.) How he could listen! This attention became a thing in itself, almost obliterating his own personality. It was as though he were all ears and eyes. Only once did I encounter anything similar to it. It was on a night when I went to see Thomas Wolfe, expecting to meet a man who would dominate the company, who would talk down to us from the heights of his newly acquired fame. What I found instead was a man who questioned *me*. Shy, sensitive, probing questions. In the presence of such individuals it seems that *you* are the one who is to do the talking, and while you do you are being studied, drawn out, egged on. Suddenly you remember their penetrating character studies, and you realize that you are in the presence of a painter observing his model.

To go back. . . . We relished this attention we got from Henry. Because of his comments and queries, which were endless, our experiences became more significant to us in the telling. It was a little frightening, though, because you always told him more than you wanted to, or meant to. There would be some awkward explaining to do if these stories appeared in print— though that possibility then seemed quite remote. Moreover, it was all very well to be the focus of this remarkable attentiveness if it weren't for his disconcerting habit of occasionally laughing right in your face. Any inanity or insincerity would provoke this laugh. One didn't like to hear it. I can tell you. I would leave many a thought unuttered rather than hear that devastating chortle.

What we all wanted, of course, was to get *him* started. Usually we didn't have to wait long, unless there were a lot of strangers present. If there were, he seemed to be out of it and would remain silent, apparently submerged by the smooth, conventional patter of a world foreign to his experience. Once, after every one had left, I reproached him about this. "Let anybody come here and speak in faultless English, refer to his travels or his yacht, and what do you do? You stand there like an oaf, you shut up like a clam."

To this he retorted vehemently: "Why, God damn you, don't you know what that means? *That's totem and taboo!*" That reply floored me.

But it was not often he permitted himself to be snowed under. For a while he might be conspicuous by his awkward silence, but something would be working in him. One remembers, perhaps, how in the *Tropic of Cancer* he relates how he had been sent out to buy the wine, how he had heard that loose laugh of Mrs. Wren (complications ahead), and how on his way to get the liquor he was already intoxicated by "the grand speech inside me that's gurgling like Mrs. Wren's loose laugh. . . . a bubble and splash of a thousand crazy things that gush out of me pell-mell." Well, it would be something like that, especially if the crowd were large or if one or more of the women present had captured his interest. Fed up with the sluggish vanity about him, surfeited with the crawling pedestrianism of the mob, he'd suddenly sweep away all barriers and take the company by storm. Off he'd soar—on a flight that swept us along with him, to a level that dizzied us. Fiery, glowing talk that set the shores wider, that pushed back constricting walls; utterances that tore and ripped through the foggy veils of our apathy. He himself has described better than any one (in his books) this kind of talk which came over him at moments, a sort of seizure in which he spoke all languages at once. In that fierce torrent which rushed from his lips the words and phrases he used flashed like jewels; they were magnificent, life-giving words, words that seemed to restore us to what life had robbed us of. Truth, lies, fantasy, dreams, invention—and a side-splitting humor. Sometimes we couldn't contain ourselves. We'd laugh so hard that often we rolled on the floor in agony. No strangers here now; we are all caught up in this vital tide, every one looking at each other with new interest, with the light and glow of mutual discovery. After such evenings I am always besieged . . . "Can you get hold of Miller again?" "*When* will you get him?" "Where can one find him?"

On my wall there was a map of Europe. Under his scrutiny it takes on new significance. It becomes a *living* continent, an organism which breathes, vibrates, speaks. To him the mountains, lakes, rivers, the frontiers natural and artificial, were all part of a pattern which was as mysterious and awe-inspiring as the divine order is in the life of human creatures. It is the map of Paris, however, that obsesses him. I can still see a maple desk, a cone of light, a dark, bent figure with glitter of spectacles, poring over the illumined map of that city which he is later to explore inch by inch and absorb into his very being.

It's easy to indulge this queer child-like fellow who understands so much more than we do. We watch that focused intentness from which a light crackles with puzzled amusement; we answer as best we can the prying, probing questions. It was a great lesson to observe his curiosity at work. "The questioning faculty"! He had it to the nth degree. Why in the world, you said to yourself, hadn't you opened your eyes? You had thought they were open, but they were only half open. The answers he received seemed to satisfy him, but you were left with deep misgivings as to what you had really seen and felt. His questions implied so much more than any answers we were capable of giving could yield. You could feel whatever it was you told him seeping in, adhering, nourishing him, and stimulating him to further explorations and inquiries. Though you could never tell him enough, everything seemed to satisfy him. He'd come back to that map again and again.

One wondered, of course, why this tremendous avidity, why this tremendous curiosity. One wanted to say: "Hold on there, Henry! Take it easy! How in hell are you going to get to Paris? How will you get breakfast tomorrow?" Idle questions, to be sure, for when did Henry ever take thought of the morrow? If he was going to Paris—or Timbuctoo—or Tibet—nothing on earth could stop him. Money? Of course you had to have money. But before money there had to be something else, and that he always had. Call it hunger, desire, tenacity, vision, illusion, enchantment—no matter what name it goes by, and it is probably all of these, he possessed it. Or it possessed him. But whatever he wanted, wherever he wanted to go, the miracle always happened. He has always believed in the miraculous and he has always made use of it.

We watch him leave, descend the stairs, with feelings of affection. Perhaps there still lingers a trace of complacent superiority in us; this does not prevent us, however, from wondering when we will see him again. No social calendar for him, no patterned days. You see him when you're lucky enough to see him. "Done with appointments. Done with pleasantries." He knows how to "ditch" us. He may have had enough advice and patronage for one night. That day—Knut Hamsun was much in his mind then—he may have been Glahn the Hunter, likening his ups and downs, his vicissitudes, and the intrusions of sudden drama, to his Hamsun hero's plights. But tonight he is The Cabinet Minister. Against our admonitions and banter, waving his cigar, maybe shaking his fist too, he shouts back to us: "Cabinet Minister! Cabinet Minister!" and races down the remaining flights of stairs with sustained falsetto laughter. Aye, Henry, Cabinet Minister indeed! And with what a portfolio! And where did we think you were headed for, and why didn't we know?

They were great days in that old Fiftieth Street studio. Books and pictures were not our only interest. I have not mentioned a word, I notice, about the books he read, the books he flung at us, the books we read, in our negligent way, only years later when he had forgotten them, or denied them, or buried them as a dog buries a bone, only to resuscitate them at some incongruous moment and make them live again in a new light. No, to describe those evenings when he came round on the trot, panting like a dog, spilling over with his latest find—a book that none of us had ever heard of, or whose existence we doubted, so much had it already become a part of him—to describe such an evening, I say, would require a book in itself.

No, there were other evenings besides these, and having a totally different ambiance or lustre. Waiting for the girls to come, he'd lean over the banister straining to catch the rustle and patter that marked their approach. Once they arrived, he was expert in breaking the ice. While I was attempting the chivalrous and romantic he'd somehow get them to turning somersaults on the floor. Stroking the tweed that covered a lush thigh, he'd say—"Just the tailor in me that's coming out."

He introduced me to one girl whose skin had the deep tone of languorous days at the seashore. She had delicate features, shapely hands. I was always disturbed, however, by two things—the violent colors she wore (one turban seemed made of a cockatoo's plumage) and the way diners would stare at us when we entered a restaurant. When I mentioned this to Henry he said: "Why, do you mean to tell me you didn't know she was a Negress?" *Always merry and bright!*

I had visits, too, of a more serious nature. His first wife, the mother of his only child, came one day to ask me whether "all was hopeless." Another time his father called on me to ask if I knew of any way to make Henry take a more sensible attitude. Often his friends came to discuss "the case" with me. To be with him, however, one would never suspect what trouble was brewing all about him. A trail of disasters seemed to follow in his wake, but he was always innocent and starry-eyed, always mystified that things should go wrong, always ready to assume the blame for any unpleasantness, any mishap, any tragic happening. That is one of the things I shall always ponder over—his complete innocence and his readiness to assume full guilt. And the way he could switch from abject sorrow to ringing laughter, the way he could forget and abandon himself to fresh experience. It is this virtue, if I may call it such, which some people deeply misunderstood. They called it "irresponsibility." Perhaps it was, but he was never "unresponsive." And of the two, I think perhaps it is better to be responsive than responsible.

Through his studio and those I occupied later, in the Village, there marched a parade of characters who never dreamed, I am sure, that they would be immortalized in his books: Blackie, Kronski, MacGregor, O'Mara, Stanley, Valeska, Mona. . . . Even some of the characters in *Tropic of Cancer* were to make their way to me and tell me of him, of the experiences they had shared in Paris—such as Boris (with a young Negress in tow), Fillmore, Collins, Mandra, and the young Hindu whom he pilloried in the chapter dealing with the brothel. We spoke of our hopes for him and our fears, since he seemed determined to estrange publisher and public alike. I would dig out his letters and manuscripts, read them aloud amidst gales of hilarious laughter.

Newer friends are now arriving. I am warned that there will be many more visitors yet to come. In my diary I recently made this entry: "I turn from the walls I am painting. A slight, sensitive man confronts me. Be careful! No accident, this. One comes in so innocently—and then there is change, disruption, upheaval. Who is this spirit with a flaming red shirt? He is, it turns out, Bern Porter—painter, physicist, writer, biographer and publisher. I offer him what courtesies I may—a bed, all of Henry's books, his manuscripts and letters. From then on there is no cessation to his labors; his notes cover every sheet of paper I have. When he is not questioning me about Henry and his work a deep absorption claims him." It is a strange story he tells me. "I am just an example," he said, "of what is to follow. There will be others, many . . . many. Young men from college . . ." (What young men? I want to ask. Why? What do they want of *me*?) I learn that my collection of Millerana is priceless; he implores me to safeguard it, it must fall into the right hands at my death. And so on. Rather disturbing, all this. I have lived so long with these treasures of Henry's—and now I realize they belong to the world. When I tried to give people these riches they spurned them. I was obliged to ram them down my friends' throats. Now suddenly all is changed. . . .

It was as a man of tremendous gusto that we always thought of Henry. His energy, his ardor, his fever of communication were but aspects of his many-sided nature. We did not see the shadows this bright light cast. In his darker hours he remained alone. If, as we sensed, he was so quiveringly receptive to every delicate vibration, why did we not realize that there were periods of torture and anguish too? "I feel such a wall of silence about me I could weep . . . I have been a misfit all my life." This from the man who could write such joyous books as *Black Spring* and *The Colossus of Maroussi*.

We were blinded, I suppose, because he was so alive; we saw only his riches, never thinking of the processes which led to their creation: the vigils, the privations, the tortures he endured. Only once did I find him really sunk. He was being defeated in a strange, triangular conflict in which the woman of many names—Mona, Mara, Alraune—played a singular rôle. The fleshy, priestly look was gone. He was haggard, gaunt, skeletal. I remember that I had to run from the room, his anguish in relating the experience was so great. Revisiting Columbia Heights with him years later I heard him groan, actually saw him shudder, as we passed through the street where that struggle had taken place. I mentioned how, in thinking of him, I remembered only his gusto, his ecstasies. He muttered something about the sides of a man's nature which not even the closest friend can glimpse.

It must have been about this time that everything proved too much for him. He went to a friend, a Jewish doctor who figures in the *Tropic of Capricorn* (and even more in *The Rosy Crucifixion*). He asked him to give him something that would gently ease him out. His friend promised solemnly that he would. He went to bed, took the dose which had been prescribed, and opened the windows wide. It was a bitterly cold night and he had thrown himself on the bed naked. Should the drug fail, he reasoned, he would die of exposure. Twelve hours later he awoke, feeling fine. His friend had given him an opiate.

I have a huge cupboard desk of whorled maple. It was over this desk that Henry used to study the map of Paris. Now he is there, and the huge trunk-like drawers begin to bulge with manuscripts, theatre bills, curiosa of all descriptions . . . and with "The Letters." Here they are to slumber for many a year before starting their journey.

The first of these letters was written in 1921. In them the masterful writing to come is often foreshadowed, just as the first crude strokes of Van Gogh's charcoal revealed the man's potential genius. One of the early letters is blithely addressed to "Emil, Stanley and Posterity." Of course he never dreamt—or did he?—that it would reach its destination. Another time he writes: "Let me make it clear that this is no request for alms but an outburst in introspective vein. Perhaps a sly leaf inserted into my future memoirs." All right, Henry, we'll insert part of that sly leaf right here.

Many of his letters were on violet tinted paper. As I would sit reading page after page I discovered a curious phenomenon, one that I later learned Delacroix had discovered years ago. My maple desk would become more yellow still—with an added tinge of green—and my hands would take on this greenish yellow tinge. Staring at the violet paper caused me to see its complementary color.

Those letters! How far does one have to go to find their equal? A cascade, a river, an ocean of words. Stories, prophecies, dreams, ideas, travels, plans, outlines of coming books, adventures, intrigues, expositions of books he is reading, dialogues with new characters he meets up with, reveries, longings, philosophical and metaphysical speculations, descriptions of banquets—everything is in them. Large fragments, too, from books in the making—on Lawrence, Proust, Joyce, Spengler, Balzac—and big slices from the "Tropics" as they took on growth. How could I tell him what these letters meant to me? Just to acknowledge them was a task. To have answered in any fullness, to be able to answer in any full sense of the word, would have required genius. I had a desperate time getting a trickle back to him. I tried my best to tell him what that avalanche meant to me. It was something that swept me off my feet, a tide in which I floundered and almost foundered. If I disappeared, as it seemed sometimes, I always came up like a pearl diver. I was literally suffocated with riches. At times the power and scope was too much for my understanding. (Which reminds me how one night he shouted: "I am too strong for you!") Once I even had the effrontery to tell him that I preferred my own simplicity. I think I even tried to uphold stupidity. Sometimes I just had to run down into the street to gaze at what is called "average humanity" in order to regain my balance. I began to feel inhibited, paralyzed. Even to-day I can write a better letter to anybody than I can to Henry.

"You don't know what a letter from you means," he would write. (Perhaps the only word he got from America was from me.) I couldn't believe, however, that my letters could mean so much to a man whose life was so rich. Had I realized his need I would have written more often, made a greater effort.

Let me not give the impression that the pages he sent me caused only bewilderment. On the contrary, the greater part of this huge collection is made up of warm, intimate letters, letters full of encouragement and guidance—never advice. Letters of two pages, twenty, forty—evoking every phase of his life in Paris. The life of the streets and the river, of the characters he encounters in the cafés, studios and brothels. Behind all this his own self-portrait emerges: his autobiography. Half of his life is in these pages.

It would be rash for me to profess to understand all he has written even now. Perhaps few realize the voyage he has made. To understand him completely would mean to be aware of another order of reality . . . and to live in the light of it. However, one could not read these messages without something happening. Weeks, months, even years later, an amazing insight is suddenly granted you. A phrase of his comes to mind and lo! an immense vista opens before you.

I take these letters wherever I go. I have some here now in the Hatfield McCoy country, near the Kentucky line. I crammed them *all* into a huge duffle bag once and brought them to Henry when he was staying at Caresse Crosby's place in Bowling Green, Virginia. I could see by the expression on his face that he hadn't guessed how huge a bulk they made. He shook his head slowly several times. "Emil," he said, "I must have been a friend of yours!"

In all the crowd that passed through my studio, and they were not our worst nit-wits by any means, I do not remember one who sought to return and read or discuss this astonishing literature. Not one. ("No one to whom I can communicate even a fraction of my feelings," he wrote somewhere, reflecting on this period of his life. No wonder he has railed so against his own country, his friends, his neighbors, his associates. No, there was no one who appreciated his real worth.) Among my visitors were writers for the popular magazines—"The Great Megaphones." Men I hoped to excite, men I stormed at. I pushed Henry's manuscripts under their noses. They would look into that huge drawer which contained almost everything he had written and pronounce it "a psychological"—or sometimes "pathological"—"discharge." I wonder what kind of discharge their writing was. Or were they permitted discharges of *any* kind?

The most attentive reader was Joe Gould. (How I wish my heart had opened even more to him! Instead, I gave him a special bell-ring which he faithfully adhered to and which I'd disregard sometimes.) At any rate, he read quietly and attentively, and what's more, he'd chuckle and cackle. That was something, for a change. That this writing affected the man who claimed Saroyan as disciple I know, but not to what extent. Joe always excelled in witticisms. ("I have delusions of grandeur—I believe that I am Joe Gould.") When finishing a heap of Henry's manuscripts which had kept him agog he would say quite simply: "Christian humility . . . Classic restraint." Or— "an embrace in Paris has a cosmic significance which obtains nowhere else in the world." Or again, when he read: "*Ici mourut Henry Miller*," he would say: "Yes, here *died* Henry Miller." You see, Joe was something of a writer himself.

I used to play chess with Henry in many different places. Often we played on Columbia Heights where at night we looked out on the harbor traffic, the air filled with the piping and shrilling of tugs. I had a number of chess sets and so did he. I remember him pawning a Chinese set once for almost a hundred dollars. I remember too that his Japanese friend, Tori Takekawa, had attempted to teach us the Chinese game. Henry had learned to play chess as a boy of seven when he went to stay with his little friends in the country, Joey and Tony Imhof. He made no attempt to become a good player; he merely wanted to enjoy himself.

The evolution of the game, its history and philosophy, had not been neglected in his devouring researches. In those bulging envelopes which carried excerpts from the works of Whitman, Proust, Spengler, Lawrence, Faure, Nietzsche and dozens of other writers, together with annotations and exegeses, there would now and then be included records of famous championship games or a few problems. Sometimes he would steal a rare book on the subject from the public library and lend it to me. Or he would drag me to a museum to show me some extraordinary boards which had been used in the Middle Ages.

I was always happy to play chess with him. In the first place, the nights which marked a visit from him were, as I said before, nights apart, and, since at that time I played to win, I felt cheered at the prospect of a not too difficult victory. I won frequently and plumed myself on these victories. I shouldn't have. It's taken me a long time to realize that I won for all the wrong reasons. My game was based on caution and vigilance, and a determination to grab at any prop in order to stave off defeat. Henry exposed himself constantly, leaving out-posts unguarded. Ready to sacrifice piece after piece to create a poetic game, or win by a stroke of brilliance, as he sometimes did, his bizarre and reckless manoeuvres often left me dumb-founded.

One night, after I had captured a number of his pieces, he shouted: "Damn it all, it's a war of attrition!" I wondered why it shouldn't be, if my men were to win. But he had probably been facing a war of attrition on all fronts.

Our respective games revealed our attitude toward life. Henry open, credulous, exposed, as in his life: always out on the open board, always believing that there were others who would play the game as he did. I can still see the look of good-natured scorn and contempt he had for those captured pawns I so eagerly put to one side. If he had played a good game and lost he was just as pleased as if he had won. Victory or defeat meant nothing to him—it was how you played that counted with him. He despised the modern game, as played by the masters. His idol was Paul Morphy. He was a romantic, even in chess, some would say. But I prefer to think that he was a poet—in everything.

Then there were the water-color festivals, so to speak. I have been making water-colors nearly all my life—it was my profession. But when Henry and I make them together it's an altogether different experience. When I am alone I work with my whole being, with a feeling in which joy and anguish are oddly combined: a peculiar inner torture. I have yet to make them in gayety—when alone.

Yes, it's an altogether different experience when we go at it together. To begin with, the very atmosphere of the room seems to change. There is an uncomplicated sense of livingness. (If I stress this life-giving quality so often it is only because my words so far have failed to evoke it.) As he examines them, the homely tubes of color take on the magic they have in the art store show window. "What's this, Emil? *Prussian blue?* Say-ay, that's a wonderful color. And indigo, eh? *What?* Here, squeeze it out on this! Ah, that's it, is it? I see! I see! And what's this, gamboge? Ah ha! *Gamboge!* The word itself is marvelous. *Gamboge.* . . . Oh-ho!" It would seem that gamboge is indeed a remarkable color. I only used to think so before, but now I *know* it is. I look with new interest at the nodules of squeezed-out color on the clean white enamel tray, at the brushes, the little pot of water, the sheen of the still virgin paper.

Calmly enough we apply our first washes. But with the first explosive blobs of vibrant color this calm vanishes. The interblendings, the penetrations of one color into another, the juxtapositions and watery suffusions, the clear shine of untouched white paper, all this arouses him to a state of excitement. He takes his brush and goes at it with vim, in a joyful frenzy that is still controlled. But suddenly, if he feels that the experiment is getting out of hand, he shouts: "Away with caution! To hell with it! Let's see what happens!" Then he begins in real earnest, jumping up and down, dancing, singing, shouting, stabbing at the paper with right or left hand, spitting on it, grinding his heel into it, anything, anything at all, anything that his impulse dictates.

If the result is too chaotic there is always the opacity of Chinese white to fall back on. The pen, the charcoal, the crayon—the cleaver, if need be. Or, suddenly perceiving something seductive in the scratch sheet, he will set to work on that, this time with great pains, great deliberation, almost like a jeweler. Finally there comes the business of naming these productions. He will set them out on the floor, or hang them about the room, walking about, whistling to himself, humming, coaxing the title he wants out of the very floor or walls. Here are a few titles he invented at Beverly Glen during a particularly prolific period (1943):

Sea Cow and Foetus

Morgenrot Himmelweiss

Paysage Chinois

Sub-tropical Heat Wave

The Strange Colloquy between the Pheasant and the Woodchuck

Anxiety Complex and the Octopus

Dream of Dr. Cowen's Dental Laboratory

Polar Aquamarine

The Pope Joanna

Tipsy Englishwoman with Lascivious Mind

Madame Blavatsky Dematerialized

Sunday After the War

The Oceanographer

Aries—Saturn Retrograde

The Prisoner of Koutsaftis (reproduced in *Semblance of a Devoted Past*)

"I have none of that small regard for polite conversation which distinguishes the gentleman from the ordinary biped."

This remark of his reminds me of a strange evening we once spent together in the Village. I had a friend there, a woman painter, who was something of a lion hunter, or perhaps it would be fairer to say that famous writers, painters, critics gravitated toward her. She is a person I hold in great esteem. I include this anecdote, in which she certainly does not appear at her best, only because it is one more example of Henry's presence acting as a catalyst, of that uncanny quality in him which so often made the false give way to the real.

Blanche wanted to meet him and he agreed to my proposal to visit her. Her impressive studio apartment was handsomely furnished; an impeccable butler served the martinis and the hors d'oeuvre. The first thing that went wrong was the smoke from the fireplace; it filled the room and caused our eyes to water. Henry, having glimpsed a huge bedroom through the open door, suggested that we sit in there. Our hostess consented, but her manner indicated that she preferred more conventional behavior. Having, as I've said, little use for amenities or pleasantries, for anything artificial or superficial, for that matter, Henry's share of the conversation had a direct honesty that made the sparks fly. The talk was so far removed from polite drawing-room formalities that the uneasiness grew by the minute. At the table, when our hostess inquired which we would prefer, red or white wine, Henry blithely said: "Why not have both? Tell your man to bring them both in." As if that were not enough of a faux pas, before very long Henry asked her if she couldn't dispense with the butler, said it made him uneasy to have the fellow dodging around behind us, we could get along quite well without him—*or*, why not let him sit down and eat with us? I did my best to pass this off as one of Henry's little jokes, knowing full well of course that he was utterly serious, but trying my best to disabuse Blanche of the idea that he was an utter barbarian. That incident over, I remember the next thunderbolt which came just as the butler was pouring out the red wine, Henry having decided that he didn't care for the white wine. In an effort to be over-gracious, Blanche inquired if we wouldn't like to meet some of her distinguished friends some evening. She wanted to know if we had any preference among the various authors, critics, scholars and publishers she apparently could summon by waving her magic wand. "Oh, get us some girls instead," said Henry. "*Pretty ones*, mind you!" That hit her between the eyes. In icy tones she made it clear that never in her life had any one implied that her own presence was insufficient. Henry, of course, in his naïve way, had intended no slight. He was being absolutely sincere, that was all. If you wanted to make him a gift and you asked him what he liked, he told you straight out and no mincing about it. He could ask for caviar, a roll of toilet paper, or an ex-Follies girl with equal sincerity. Of course the situation might have been different had Blanche been younger and prettier.

By that time he was a bit in his cups and anything might spill out. I had the devil's own time trying to explain his blunt quips. Yet, despite all the bantering, she was obliged now and then to guffaw. He actually succeeded in making her laugh at herself, which relieved me enormously because I had been on the verge of exploding ever since we crossed the threshold. Later the talk turned to psychoanalysis. I heard my hostess say that although many of her friends were now parading their complexes and wooing one analyst after another she, thank heaven, did not feel the need of an analyst.

"But you do," said Henry bluntly. "You need it more than any one I know. You haven't uttered a sincere word since we entered."

With that she began to sob. It was a prolonged, hysterical weeping and there was nothing to do but let her have it out. At that point we were all three seated on a divan and before us, on a tabouret, was an assortment of whiskies and cognac and liqueurs. Henry nonchalantly filled the glasses and, handing us each one, took a good gulp. Then a broad smile came over his face and he began to talk to Blanche in a low, soothing voice, a sort of cooing I would call it. He made Blanche take a few deep draughts and then he put his arm around her and continued in that same low, soothing voice to restore her to her senses. It was amazing to observe how this man whom she feared, and perhaps hated, gained possession over her. She began to smile, a wan, thin smile at first, which gradually broadened into a laugh. "That's it," he said, purring in her ear and stroking her like a cat, "that's it . . ." In a few minutes he had not only placated her but had lifted her to the seventh heaven. She positively beamed at him now and hung on his every word, turning to me now and then with a look of dumb gratitude, as though to say—"He's really a wonderful fellow, your friend; forgive me if I seemed to be offended with him."

What followed I unfortunately cannot relate here. Suffice it to say that I have never spent such a strange evening in my life. Never did so many things happen at once, and such contradictory things. When we left we stood outside and fell into each other's arms laughing hysterically. In fact, we had to duck into a nearby bar and rehearse the whole skein of events immediately. When we parted we were still shaking with laughter. I remember that when I tumbled into bed I had another laughing fit which lasted for an hour or more.

Henry often made appeals for help by letter, telephone and telegram. He had the peculiar quirk of sending circular telegrams "to all and sundry." So fantastically eloquent were these appeals that they were put down to eccentricity rather than dire want. Of course, if you don't want to help, any reason will do. I often responded, but never with the open-hearted generosity he was capable of. He loved to give things away. You could get anything he had, and if he didn't have what you wanted, if he thought you needed it badly, he would beg it of some one or steal it for you.

I gave him eight dollars once. He returned with an armful of brand-new clothes from his father's shop: flannel trousers, knickerbockers, sport coats, an overcoat, all of the finest imported material and just my size. They must have been worth a pretty sum!

I was glad to take Henry to dinner whenever I had the chance—perhaps for selfish reasons. No one who bought him a meal was apt to forget the experience. Often when we dined together, especially if it were in a foreign restaurant, people came over to our table and asked if they could join us. He never tried to draw attention to himself but it was inevitable, when he was in high spirits, that people would be magnetized and insist on sharing our company. Sometimes it would be the proprietor and his wife who would join us; then there would be choice wines and liqueurs to sample, always at the host's expense. I remember a French restaurant we dined at one evening rather late and how, as we were leaving, the *patrone* invited us to the bar downstairs and insisted on buying several rounds for us. Henry himself was amazed at this.

I know we could have helped him more than we did. Why in the world didn't we? We would have been the better for it. Most often he came to help rather than ask help. Then, too, no matter how desperate he was, he was always gay and cheerful. It seemed sometimes as if he were just pretending he was in need. I know now, however, that sometimes he came to me intending to borrow something for a meal—it might be four in the afternoon or one in the morning—and he would leave on an empty stomach and walk all the way home to Brooklyn, too shy to ask even for carfare. After a while it became the usual thing for me to ask on meeting him—"Tell me, Henry, have you eaten?"

Our caution very nearly estranged him. Once he wrote:

As for you and myself, listen . . . I have often referred to you as a son-of-a-bitch, when talking to June, and that stands, as far as your cautious nature goes. *But*—you never got under my skin; I felt always that I understood you and I always forgave you immediately, though it often pained me and nettled me. What you gave me I was grateful for, and that was enough, all that mattered. Why should we expect of one another the things which we are unable to give?

I wanted freedom too, I must say here. Freedom from the advertising agencies and the art directors. But I could only see that freedom in terms of money. Freedom for me was fixed at the arbitrary sum of three thousand dollars. With that behind me I'd begin to breathe easy: I'd leave the telephone unanswered, or go to Canada or some other place to paint. It takes a long time for some of us to learn the economics of the spirit.

Rereading some of his old letters causes me some regrets. One indicates that I refused a request which Henry is abashed to have made. . . .

Your reply makes me contrite . . . In my own extremity I forget sometimes that here are others who are equally bad off, perhaps worse. For, after all, I always have my health, my *savoir vivre*. Seriously, your letter gives me a secret pang. The Mezzotints arrive in the mail, subscription or no subscription. And not only Mezzotints but letters, clippings, book reviews, prints, theatre tickets, pornographic incunabula, hippogriffs and land unicorns.

That promise has been kept. From that day to this, for twenty years, the flow of gifts continues. Even now, despite an item filched here and there, the accumulation is staggering and priceless. The money which the postage cost him must have deprived him of many a meal.

I am not unaware that to some people, and perhaps with reason, this slender sketch seems extravagantly one-sided. How should I explain the aggressiveness, the inexplicable fury of the attacks which suddenly and without warning he would hurl at some bewildered neighbor or friend for whom he felt an instinctive antagonism? Or the viciousness, the monstrous cruelty, of those delineations of people who thought themselves his friend? Where literary genius is concerned this is hardly a new story. It was as though no note on the keyboard was to be left untouched, no facet of the self left unexposed, on the path toward realization. A marriage of light and shadow, of good and evil; a partnership of angel and demon, but with the angel in the ascendancy. He fought off everything that was in conflict with his purpose with a selfishness which genius alone knows how to employ in striving for that ultimate unselfishness which will enrich others.

Whoever reads the *Tropic of Cancer* with discernment will find, along with its obscenity, its howling honesty, behind the curses and excoriations, that the author of the "greatest underground book," "the more than Rabelaisian Henry Miller," "Henry Miller the Desperado," has gentleness and tenderness, and above all an overwhelming compassion for the sufferings of men and women in a dislocated world. Of this book he says:

> The great importance of it, as I now see it, lies in the fact that it summed up (alas, all too incompletely for my satisfaction) a whole period of the past. I suppose, nay, I am quite sure, I shall never write another book like it. It was like a surgical operation. And out of it I emerged whole again. Though when I embarked on it, it was with no intention of curing myself of anything—rather to rid, to divest myself, of the horrible wounds I had allowed to fester in me.

Many of our best writers have written about the dilemma of the artist in America. Henry has written of it anew in that collection of "Open Letters" entitled: *The Plight of the Creative Artist in the United States of America*. His own story is a success story that dwarfs all tales of the bright boy who "brings home the bacon" (Local Boy Makes Good). "Just a Brooklyn boy," he says of himself in *The Colossus of Maroussi*, in one of those extravagant passages of which no Brooklyn boy ever dreamed. (I wonder, in the years to come, if Brooklyn will disown her prodigal son, or will she proudly erect a monument to him in one of those quaint, woe-begone public squares which are like no place on earth.)

No spiritual cripple here, but a whole man, as more than one writer has testified. "A free spirit," Keyserling calls him. Yes, his is a success story such as our captains of push and hustle have no conception of. The man who only the other day wrote me, "It's either make water-colors or die," knows a success of which he will see only the opening phases. It is a cumulative success which will fecundate the oncoming generations.

A friend of mine once asked me if I thought the ordeal Henry had gone through had undermined his health. I said I'd be more concerned over the state of his physical and spiritual being if he had been protected, had led the routine life of the "successful American." (Can you imagine *him* commuting to "a large property"?) It's true he had work for a while, an essential job for him, one might say. Nothing could have given him a deeper insight into life's problems than this position which he held for almost five years. Another man would have cracked in six months under the strain. People from every walk of life, every country, every race almost, came to him for succor. I saw some of those derelicts with my own eyes, and I saw too what he did for them. It's a job that he has immortalized in the *Tropic of Capricorn*. (Don't, for God's sake, miss this description of the "Cosmodemonic-Cosmococcic Telegraph Co!") It was a destined task, a phase in his evolution as creative artist. I honestly don't see how he could have become the man we know him to be today had he not accepted this strange rôle of employment manager, father confessor, and benefactor at large to all sorts and conditions of men.

And here I must say another thing . . . He did not go to Paris because he failed to gain recognition here, as has been said. Had he been able to, he would have gone there long before—or to Zanzibar and Samarkand, and all those strange-sounding places he loves to list. He went where his desires beckoned—to ordeals and orgies, to famines followed by feasts, to strange cities and stranger experiences, but always toward a maximum of living and, above all, a maximum of being. He found it good to make the world his home.

What would we have if Henry had been cared for, I ask? Would there have been the pangs of death and re-birth? How often has he had to cast off dead experience to emerge at another level? How often has he been forced to confront all that we dread? A man who has been face to face with direct extremes, and who has lived through them, is free from that terror. And being free, he is another man, a man inhabiting a larger cosmos and belonging to a definite hierarchy of the spirit.

Thus he writes me,

There is nothing I can't have, if I want it. My problem, I have discovered recently, is to be very careful about what I desire. I seem to have an Aladdin's Lamp in my hand all the time. The frustration from without is almost nil now. I have lost practically all my fears. And the fear of evil is almost non-existent. Ditto, of course, the fear of death. On the contrary, I look forward to death eagerly. This life has been so wonderful, I am sure the next will be even more so. Because, believe me, I am making it so. I can't possibly be cheated. Experience quickly transforms itself into significance. I see everything as metamorphosis. Endless being and becoming. I can't imagine what could be disappointing, disillusioning, or "bad."

The Genesis of the *Tropic of Cancer*

Michael Fraenkel

In the beginning was Henry Miller, and in the beginning was chaos . . . It was *circa* 1930–1931. In England the pound was falling, and a Lord Ellsworth or other was calling on the City to carry on as if uncertainty were the rule, the natural, normal thing. In Spain Alfonso XIII had abdicated, and the Spanish Republic was founded, the same Republic that was later to be murdered in cold blood by Hitler and Mussolini while the democracies looked on and talked neutrality. In China flood and famine raged over the valleys of the Yangtse and Hwai, much as usual perhaps, but Jap thunder rumbled in Manchukuo, and Chapei tossed fitfully in a nightmare of terror and rape, while the League of Nations regaled itself with the latest statistics on the dope traffic. Hoover just announced the Moratorium on German debts, the pocket battleship *Deutschland* was launched, and Hitler and his Storm Troopers were beginning to march through the streets with a curse upon their tongues. The Burning of the Books was not far off. In America it was the day after the Great Crash and the October Suicides, and on the eve of the Bank Holidays. In Russia dekulakization was in full swing, and hunger and famine stalked the plains and the cities. In Italy the trains were coming in on time, and in France there was Doumerque and paralysis and dumb despair. Our little world that the statesmen and politicians had put together with a paste and pasteboard of words at Versailles was falling apart again. Everywhere there was uncertainty, confusion, fear. *And utter incomprehension.* This was just another economic crisis, people said. There were crises, all kinds of crises, political, economic, social and what not, and this was just another economic crisis we were going through. It would pass, like all the other economic crises in the past; it would pass—with time. The breadlines growing longer and longer day by day, the public soup kitchens swelling, the factories closing, the currencies breaking, the spirit breaking, the world breaking—they were things that would pass, if not today, then tomorrow or the day after tomorrow, or the day after that, but they would pass. This was an economic dislocation simply. The understructure, the underpinnings were sound . . . So they thought! And all the while the

Excerpted and reprinted from *The Happy Rock: A Book About Henry Miller*, Bern Porter, ed. (Berkeley, CA: Bern Porter, 1945), 38–56. Reprinted by permission of Bern Porter.

uncertainty, the apprehension and fear grew and deepened and spread. It reached out everywhere, left nothing untouched. It was like a mist, a fog, a condition of the weather; the air was thick with it. It fell, a stain or rust, a gentle dew from heaven, and settled over people's lives and homes, over their thoughts and feelings, words and acts; over everything they touched or handled, the clothing they wore, the food they ate, the books they read, the pictures they saw. It left its mark on their bodies, their faces. You could see it every morning in the face of the baker across the street who turned out the fresh morning's *croissants*, or the little Bourse operator who had just placed his latest "put and call," or the broker who had just rounded up another private loan to finance another bombing plane for the defence of *La Belle France*. It was seen everywhere, in the faces of all—the politician, the business man, the workman, the clerk, the waiter, the maid, the tart. It was seen in the faces of the émigrés, the Russians, the Germans, the Poles, the Roumanians and Hungarians, the Italians. It was seen in the faces of the last of the expatriates who had fled the America that refused to be born à la Whitman, and now, stranded in the city of eternal light, their money run dry at the source, warmed themselves in the charcoal glow of the brasiers in the Café Dôme. And always there was the same incomprehension. This was just another economic crisis we were going through, it would pass—in time. The fear and uncertainty would pass . . . the stain and rust would pass, the air would clear—in time. They did not know what was behind these crises, what lay behind this stain and rust, the putrefaction that lay behind them and found its way to the surface again and again, like the putrefaction of a silent, secret wound. They did not know that this rust was the same rust that lay on the surface in 1914, and before that, and before that. A rust that lay on the surface for many years now, many generations, a rust that no blood from the living or the dead could wipe or wash away, as they secretly and naïvely, in their great desperateness, sometimes thought and feared and wished. They did not know that this rust was only the merest visible sign of a rust, a malaise below, in the silent depths of their being. A rust of the soul, a blight of the spirit, a death, a spiritual devastation within, of the mind and heart and soul, which no blood of the living or dead could wash away, so long as the death underneath remained. They did not know that only by washing away this death would the stain be washed away, and the blood cease to flow, the blood drawn again and again to wash away the stain.

It was *circa* 1930–1931, and I had just published *Werther's Younger Brother*, my first book. It dealt with this stain and this death. The outer stain; the inner death. The inner spiritual devastation that left the gaping hole inside, the unfilled void; the outer frenzy of activity that turned the whole world into a chaos in a desperate effort to fill up the void. In the spiritual suicide of a single individual, Alfred, counterpointed against the older and more familiar physical suicide of Werther, it traced the progress of this death, step by step and stage by stage, from the loss of *Body* (body-wholeness) to the emergence of *Will* (will-dispersedness). From an end in himself, self-contained and self-sufficient unto himself, image and symbol of nothing but himself, man is transformed into a means to an end, a tool, an instrument in the service of Will. Vital, living, meaningful activity is replaced by the volitional furor of force for the sake of force, motion for the sake of motion, activity for the sake of activity. In the person of Alfred, the book set up the ultimate image of modern man's spiritual death.

The book took its stance in a whole metaphysical compost of ideas relating to The Death—to its mode of expression, the awareness of it, the way to resolve it, etc., etc.

It was difficult for people to understand the book or the larger ideas behind it, just as it was difficult for them to understand the meaning of the recurring crises, the uncertainty and fear, the outer stain which they thought they could wash away with this or that political or economic solution, nostrum, panacea, or, when everything else failed, with war. It was difficult for them to see the inner death which lay below, the inner putrescence and heart-rot, of which these crises, this uncertainty and fear, this outer stain were but surface manifestations. How could they see this inner death? How could they understand the meaning of this outer stain? It was difficult for people to see and understand who had lost the power to see and understand. For what, after all, was this death that they had known? What was it that had fallen, broken, deep inside them? The soul! The soul: precisely the source of this power! They had known a soul-death; they had lost their soul. So now, without it, how could they see this inner death or understand the meaning of this outer stain? How could people who had lost their soul, now without it, know that they had lost it? And yet it was precisely this power to see and understand what was lost, this knowledge and awareness of death, that made all the difference between being alive and being dead. In the awareness lay whatever possibilities there still were for experiencing a sense of life. Unawareness meant apathy, insouciance, death.

Awareness, then, was primary. But it was not enough. It was not enough to be aware of The Death. Awareness gave a sense of life, but only vicariously, by proxy, as it were. There had to be something more: the active confrontation and resolution of The Death. One had to recover life itself, the real living thing itself, and that was possible only by clearing away The Death, liquidating it, living it out: by *dying*. "What is spirit?" asks Kierke-gaard in his *Journals*. "Spirit," he replies, "is to live as though dead." And by "dead" he means of course dead to the world: the world within and without us that has gone dead and now stands between us and life. To recover life or spirit, then, you have to kill off this world, die to it, that is, die to it again and again and again.

It was no political or economic or social solution. It was really no solution at all. But what was there to solve? We were at the end of an age, a whole culture; a way of life, an historical past, was coming to a close: we were caught up in a process, a cyclical or organic process, and a process spends itself, completes and fulfills itself, *resolves*. It was not a question of solution but of resolution. We simply had to face and accept The Death, squarely and resolutely, take it inside, as it were, into our blood stream, consciously, deliberately, face it and accept it in the inmost depths of our being, and—live it out. There was no other way of getting rid of it, scotching it. One had to meet and face and accept it and live it out. Live it out, and you set up at once the new rhythm of life, the life rhythm. Live out The Death, and the new life asserts itself at once.

It was not a way out for all and sundry, to be sure. One had to be ready for it, one had to have a special temperament and genius for it, one had to stand in a very special relation to oneself and the time for it. It was no salvation for all those up to their ears in death, and unaware of it—the man in the street, the politician, the statesman, the so-called man of action, etc. This was a way out for the truly exceptional or creative individual accustomed to working with himself, profoundly aware of the dead end we had reached, and determined to strike out on fresh ground at all costs. The individual, in other words, who, at this extreme point, moves not with the times, to effect a change in the times, but with himself, to effect a change within himself. *To come alive to himself.* Precisely the individual in whom a moribund age has always had the greatest stake. For, at this point, it is not the movers and shakers of the world with their death formulas and death cures who point the way to the future, to the new life, but the solitary, the "still one," as Keyserling calls him, who has withdrawn to himself and in the purity and single-mindedness of his purpose found life within himself. Having found life within himself, he can point the way to life to others. By the force of his example, by the vitality he radiates, the emotional release he effects, he serves as a leaven to stir to life the inert mass of humanity.

I was seeing a good deal of my friend Walter Lowenfels at this time. When I first met him the year before, in the winter of 1929, he was already at work on his *Apollinaire*, an elegy, and he mourned the poet's death in lines like these:

> This day we mourn this man
>   because the world
>   and our world
> is less one possibility
> still unlisted
> in the tables of insured certainty

but he was still on old, familiar ground. He was dealing with death, but it was still in the old terms; it was a physical death, not the spiritual death with which I was concerned. The physical death of the French symbolist poet remained unrelated to the larger spiritual death of the world. The *Death Theme* was opened up to him later as a result of the talks I had with him and the veritable labor in exegesis I had to perform to render *Werther's Younger Brother* comprehensible to him; it launched him into the new universe of death. With *Werther's Younger Brother*, a friendship grew up between us, revolving around the *Death Theme*. It informed all our meetings and talks and invested them with a kind of secret understanding, a freemasonry. A death school grew up—just between the two of us! And then one day Walter told me about a strange man he had run across in Montparnasse, a fellow called Miller. He was described as one of tremendous vitality, zest, enthusiasm, an amazing talker, without visible means of support, a kind of derelict, but gay and happy withal, alive. "Not alive exactly," he said, "but certainly not dead. Alive in a kind of confused, old-fashioned way. An interesting chap. Why not drop him a line, a *pneu*? He is down and out and maybe he can do some typing for you." And then with a twinkle in his eye: "Take him on. Just your meat." Did he perhaps see a possible disciple in him? . . .

Anyway, the next day I dropped him a note. And the day following he called. Looking back on that first meeting now, if I ask myself what it was that drew me to him the moment he entered the room and began to talk, I can only think of this: the man's absolute simplicity. He was a complete stranger to me, I didn't know a thing about him except for the few oblique remarks my friend Walter had dropped, and yet I felt perfectly at home and at ease with him the moment he entered the room and began to talk. You are likely to feel that way sometimes with someone simple, an idiot or a half-wit or—possibly a saint. But this man was no simpleton or idiot, to be sure, nor did he strike me exactly as being a saint. But there he was, absolutely himself, open, natural, artless, and no bluff about it, no "putting on," no play-acting. It was the real thing if ever I saw it. We moved in an atmosphere of perfect ease, there was nothing of the nervousness, reserve, constraint, that prevails so often between two people who have met for the first time. I felt I could say anything and everything to him without the slightest hesitation. In fact, I felt that precisely because I felt that that way we would get along. I felt as if I stood in the presence of a friend, a good old friend whom one hasn't seen for a very long time who now suddenly turns up from somewhere at the other end of the earth; a most welcome find. With this man, I said to myself, you can go the whole hog, you can deliver the whole package, all of yourself, and without the wrappings or the strings. And I did; you couldn't do otherwise, even if you wanted to. For this was not a one-way affair. The man gave, gave of himself, freely, generously, without forethought or afterthought. And so, like him, you gave—it was a contagion. That afternoon saw the beginning of our friendship. When he left, I presented him with a copy of *Werther's Younger Brother*.

Passed a few days, and then a long letter from him in which he wrote:

Dear Mr. Fraenkel:

I started writing this letter in a café the other night, after reading your book. I was interrupted and had to lay it aside. Then I planned to go upstairs after work to the editorial room and dash it off without delay, but again circumstances intervened as I was requested to work overtime, and then when I had partaken of my food and drink at a *bistrot* I fell into a conversation with an Algerian girl and she took me up to her room to show me her paintings. Which was five a.m. So here I am, sitting down to transcribe the feverish notes I had started.

As a matter of fact, I had not quite finished the book when I began the note. I could not wait. To be utterly matter of fact, the very first paragraph made me jump to attention. It won me. I was standing at the proof-desk, snatching a glance at it now and then, shoving it out of sight when the boss hove in view, etc. I simply couldn't put it aside. And as I read I began exclaiming. I felt that I had made a great discovery.

But let me set down the first few words, as I put them on paper, and you will see more precisely what were my feelings then . . . I said: Dear Mr. Fraenkel: "I don't know where to begin, concerning my emotions upon reading your book. I find myself thinking only in superlatives, and I am waiting, biding my time, so that I may cool off and see it all more clearly. And yet, that is precisely what I do not want. I want you to know first and foremost that I am in a fever about it . . . Between you and the whole American scene there is a gulf, and it is glorious to contemplate . . . You say things that no one in America is saying—that I would dearly love to say myself. You give a whole panorama of the interior individual without a single compromise or concession . . . I applaud you humbly, sincerely, I never dreamed that you could put in my hand such a treasure."

(Petit filet)

And now in sober retrospect—what shall I say? I repeat all that I have said above. You wanted my criticism. Alas, I am only too well aware that I have no critical faculty. I have only the creative instinct . . . violent passions, hates, aversions, etc. What I would write about your book would not be criticism. It would be only a register of my emotions. And they are still strong. They prejudice me—in favor of you. I accept you with all the flaws, aye, for the flaws, perhaps, though where they are I cannot say, since I am still in a state of prostration. Yes, I am extravagant. I have a distorted vision of things. Nevertheless . . .

In the book there were phrases, lines, images . . . on every page they were . . . not gems, but living bits of you, with the roots and fibres still clinging to them. It was that which moved me so much. It was as though you had performed some fourth dimensional trick with your body, had turned it inside out for me, and though in totality it was so strange as to be literally unrecognizable, still upon examination, or perhaps, not upon examination, but just resting back, listening, feeling it, touching it, I saw all the component elements of you . . . People had said to me that it was morbid, chaotic, disgusting, etc . . . But I found everything touched with a wild beauty, and if there were disorder, then it was, as Bergson said, an order of disorder which is another order. And in truth, I do not care so much about order or disorder. When I think of painting and what the moderns are attempting, or even music, I can express myself better, because (I don't know why it should be so) in literature I do not perceive so clearly what is transpiring. To put it in my feeble way, I should say that you gave me, as few men ever did, the feeling that you were making alive again all those forces and elements which are in danger of getting killed through the sheer necessity of movement from mind to paper. Certain phrases, due to this orientation, struck me with the force of explosives. There was always a fear, as I read, that if you were just a little more insistent, you would drive me mad. How marvelous it would be to go mad reading a book!

So then I must disagree with you about this being a skeleton. Rather is this a corpus, not even a foetus, of human essences. It is complete and unrelated. It is of life most living yet taking neither the form of man, beast or angel. It is Werther's younger brother who was never born and therefore has never died. It is like an Alraune snoozing in the sod, an Alraune midway between plasma and consciousness. On the eighth day the body jumping its axis . . . the middle eye . . . crucifixion without nails, vinegar, holy Mary. What am I saying? You have said it all . . . violently, terribly, beautifully. I salute you.

Time passed, we got better and better acquainted. I learned about the life he had led in the United States, the life he was leading in Paris. He had been a vagabond, a tramp, a ranch-hand, an athlete, a reporter, a typist, a clerk, a grave digger, a garbage collector, a panhandler. He had tried everything and anything, only to drop it soon after. And now he was in Paris, trying to make a go of it here. But still he seemed no nearer to his goal. He was now in his fortieth year, and still there seemed to be no end to this restless searching and groping. What was it he was looking for? What did he want? Throughout that whole fantastic pattern of apparent shiftlessness there ran a bright thread which belied the shiftlessness at once. No, this was not shiftlessness, but something else. It was an immense restlessness in the man: a deep, terrible impatience with everything and anything within himself and in the world that sought to disperse him: a hectic, frenzied desire to stay himself, absolutely, inviolably, himself: a rock bottom integrity. With all the powers of his being, he would resist any and every effort to get him to fall in line, "to belong." He simply would not "belong." He would stick to himself at all costs. If he was not sure about anything else—and he was not sure—he was dead sure about this: he would stick to himself, come hell and high water. He would insist on preserving his personal freedom, his personal integrity. He would insist on staying Henry Miller. That was the meaning of his flight from America. He came to Paris, and would stay in Paris, because he was determined now more than ever to gather and integrate and fuse round that in himself which he recognized as truly his, Henry Miller's, his very own; he would make a fresh start, make a life for himself round that. He wanted to write, to be a writer. He saw in writing a way to this integration, this realization. But he was very much confused about it, and a little discouraged. He had done a lot of writing in his life but he considered it worthless. He showed me one of his manuscripts—he had piles of them—a big fat book called *Crazy Cock*. He wanted me to tell him what was the matter with it. I told him. The matter with it was that he was trying to write to order, to write what the American editors and public want—the slick, smooth, dead American fiction that sells in the thousands, in the hundreds of thousands. He was trying to do, in other words, what most writers in the United States try to do, and in the end, with persistence, succeed in doing. *Trying*, mind you, for actually *Crazy Cock* was still a pretty far cry from the real stuff. It ran frightfully off the line, into a language, style, etc., all its own, against all known rules. Henry Miller was still in evidence, that bright thread of integrity shone dimly through: he couldn't quite kill him off, no more than he could in actual life. Between the long dreary stretches of inexecrably flat, insipid, sterile writing, there were passages here and there of amazing directness and power: certain lines, phrases, passages, exploded like rockets. *Crazy Cock* was the queerest mixture of bad and good writing I had ever seen. I told him to tear it up, and forget it. I told him to be himself, to stop trying to be Henry Miller the successful writer and robot. By this time I knew the sort of person he was, impulsive, erratic, anarchic, a mass of contradictory moods, ideas, feelings, and I told him to sit down before the machine and white paper and write anything and everything that came to his mind, as it came, red-hot, and to hell with the editors and the public. Write as you talk, I told him. Write as you live. Write as you feel and think. Just sit down before the machine and let go— tell everything you are going through now; you've got all the material you want right in this, in what you are thinking and feeling and going through *now*. Forget the fancy stories and novels and that sort of thing. Write about yourself, your life. Get all this pent-up emotion out of your system. Evacuate the trenches! A writer's first duty now is to himself—to liberate himself, to come clean of his past, his death, to come alive. A personal record. No time for anything else. Anything else is literature—with a bad smell!

And so we talked and talked, for days on end, weeks, months. Our friendship had ripened. And always at the center of the talks there was the same theme: The Death. The Death which *Werther's Younger Brother* probed and plumbed and sounded. We talked about The Death. We were exploring ourselves, our lives, our experiences, in relation to the larger life, the larger experience on the outside. We tackled The Death from every possible standpoint, laid it open from every angle, explored it as no explorer ever explored a new country, north, south, east and west, from all the points of the compass. We sang about it, we revelled in it, we mourned and cursed it— it was a festival, The Death Festival, as Miller called it. And all the while something was going on in him, some change was taking place; I could see it in the isolate gesture, the word, the expression of recognition that would suddenly light up his face, the expression of a man in whom a deep responsive chord has been struck. He was moving, gathering, fusing round something with all the weight of his body and blood; coalescing, hardening, forming. An emotional and mental stance, an emotional and mental attitude was being fixed and set. The meaning of a whole life-time of drift and flux, of inchoate thoughts, feelings, emotions, ideas, moods, was being fixed and set. The meaning of a whole world of inner chaos, of confusion and darkness was being fixed and set. It was a great turning over and settling down of a load in him, in his blood and guts; the sun of his being turning over, moving and settling down, in its proper orbit, on its proper axis. All his innermost thoughts and emotions, his fears, doubts, loves, hates, hopes, despairs, were moving and gathering and integrating and coalescing into a mighty mass and settling down at the center of him, at the solar plexus from which he moved and felt and thought and lived. He had glimpsed an attitude, a direction; the meaning of his life, of his searching and groping.

He had discovered the vantage point from which he could see all around him, see the road ahead. He had only to take it. On this road, stripped and shorn as he already was of everything, of home, family, children, money, possessions, accustomed as he already was to being naked, on this road he needed no other baggage than himself, Henry Miller the naked suffering man. He did not have to be a philosopher or thinker, he had only to be himself, the man with deep urgent emotions, deep urgent loves and hates, who saw and felt and understood from the blood, with the heart and sympathetic nerves, who had known life first-hand and knew what a terrible and lovely thing it was, a knife that cut both ways. Death, death—he saw his life-long relation to it, his life-long meaning to it. The *Death Theme* had struck home. He leaped from the physical death to the spiritual death. It answered to something within him for which he had been groping all these years, bending and straining with all the powers of his heart and will and mind. He found it now. He found the axis of his being. He was a sun on his own axis. He had found himself at last.

In the beginning was Henry Miller, and in the beginning was chaos . . . Henry Miller would speak out of this chaos—this death within himself, this larger death in the world. He would not seek to interpret and define this chaos; he would seek only to give it utterance. In this utterance lay his salvation; in this utterance was life. He would leave it to others to reveal the meaning of this chaos—this death. He would stick to the task. His was not to understand and reflect, but to witness and report. His life was chaos and the world was chaos, and he would reflect the chaos of his life and the chaos of the world. He was ready for his task. He was ready for the *Tropic of Cancer*.

It was a task for which he was eminently fitted by temperament and circumstance. Never could the conditions, inner and outer, within the man himself and in the world on the outside, never could they have been more favorable; they were playing into his hands. "I was born under a lucky star," Miller is fond of saying. Yes, indeed, he was born under a lucky star. Born under the conjunction of Pluto and Neptune, the farthest stars from the earth, the latest to be discovered by science. The conjunction with its back to the past and its face turned toward the future. The conjunction that says: *Corruptio est generatio*. In the old corruption lies the seed of the new life. The conjunction that leads you straight to the heart of the chaos and brings you out again at the other end, at a new and flaming life . . . Was the world full of darkness, of corruption and death? Was he right in the thick of it, in the center of it, at the festering heart of it? Wonderful! Did he know all the humiliation, the degradation, the disgust, the bitterness which one knows who is without money, home, wife, children, family, friends? Did he know what it means to sleep in flop-houses or in doorways or on the banks of the Seine? Did he know what it means to have to beg a few pennies to buy himself a piece of bread? Wonderful! Did he know all the physical and moral tension such a life would breed? Wonderful! Did he carry a consuming hatred in him that seared and burnt and ate into his bowels? Did he have a natural, a born flair for smelling out all the secret places within himself and in the world where all the helpless, dumb misery and pain gather and lie rotting? All grist for his task! A lucky fellow, Miller, good fortune and bad fortune serve him alike! The mass of corruption and death that is the world, the image of it in his own soul; the dire circumstances of his life; the nature of the man himself, impulsive, compulsive, explosive, given to deep passions, loves and hates; his amazing power of speech, his nose that led him straight to the festering heart of things, etc., etc.: they all conduced and conspired to make the *Tropic of Cancer*. Now he could batten on the chaos in the world and the chaos in his own soul:

> The world around me is dissolving, leaving here and there spots of time. The world is a cancer eating itself away . . . It is why I sing.*

Now he could tear his hair, rave and screech in ecstasy, yell at the top of his voice:

> I am crying for more and more disasters, for bigger calamities, for greater failures. I want the whole world to be out of whack. I want everyone to scratch himself to death.

Now he could rejoice in his poverty and want, in his suffering and anguish, he could dance over it, he could shriek in joy and gladness over it, he could spit on it:

*This and all succeeding quotations not otherwise identified are from *Tropic of Cancer*.

I have no money, no resources, no hope, I am the happiest man alive.

Yes, indeed, the very manner of his life, the way he had to live it day by day, never sure of a roof over his head, never knowing where his next meal would come from or the next bit of change, the hectic uncertainty and tension all this produced—something which would have broken and rendered inarticulate and frustrate almost any other man—only made and appointed him. It gave the style of the *Tropic of Cancer* its deep, terrible immediacy, its dynamism, its tension, its desperate swing and beat. For never was a line written, a phrase, a word, without the fear accompanying it that maybe the next moment the chair would be taken from under his behind, and he'd have to move, finish the line elsewhere. *Elsewhere!* Was there an elsewhere? One was never sure. So he had to terminate the line now; he had to terminate it, come what will, happen what will. He had to terminate it now, this moment, even if he had to pay for it with his very life. *One writes as if this moment were the last.*

Or then again, take that power of his of speech. It was something that bowled you over completely the first time you heard it. It was extraordinary, amazing, incredible. A compulsion mechanism, a kind of sickness, if you like, something pathological. Miller himself refers to it in just these terms in the *Tropic of Cancer*. A disease, a neurosis, he calls it. *Echolalia.* It was especially noticeable in those moments when he was completely rested, collected, at ease, when he had thrown off the weight of something or other that had lain upon him and oppressed him, when he'd wake up from a long and sound sleep, for example. He'd wake up, and before you could so much as catch his eye or say anything, it'd begin, just like that, suddenly, impulsively, as in a dream, with anything at all that happened to strike him at the moment—the subject was of no importance whatever. He'd wake up and it'd begin, this flow and rush of words, this wild, mad, fantastic talk that swelled and grew and gathered momentum—a stream, a torrent, a flood. It was just as if he had begun and carried it on in his sleep, as if he had begun and carried it on before that, when the umbilical cord was snapped and he emerged into the light, as if he had begun and carried it on even further back, when man suddenly discovered he could talk and began to talk and talked and the wonder and marvel of it swept him out of himself and rendered him absolutely unconscious. The man was in the grip of a power that set not so much his tongue, the word, in motion, as his whole body, the whole effective spirit of the man; his whole body worked with the force of it. A purely physiological phenomenon.

Today I awoke from a sound sleep with curses of joy on my lips, with gibberish on my tongue, repeating to myself, like a litany—Fay ce que tu voudras! Fay ce que tu voudras!—Do anything but let it produce joy! Do anything but let it produce ecstasy!

It was the kind of wild, uncontrolled, passionate chant or pæan to life, to the powers of life, of joy and gladness, that primitive man might have known. A welling-up, an outpouring from hidden, subterranean depths of the unconscious such as we find in Dostoevsky, in Mishkin in *The Idiot*, for example, or Stavrogin in *The Possessed*. It was talk of the highest order I have ever heard. Talk such as only Henry Miller has succeeded in recapturing here and there in the pages of the *Tropic of Cancer*. For between this talk, this compulsive rushing forth of the living word and the printed page, there is still the machine, the machine which is a barrier, which stands between the living man and the expression. It was talk that made the whole universe, all of animate and inanimate life its province, that ranged for its symbols far and wide, in the skies, over the earth, in the earth, in the waters under the earth, among stars, planets, nebulæ, living and dead suns, living and extinct animals, birds, reptiles, insects, trees, plants, flowers, lichens, stones, rocks, minerals, fishes, corals, shells, what not. It was free, unconscious expression, yet with a solid core of feeling to it. It didn't have a specific object or purpose, it wasn't bound anywhere, didn't try to clarify or demonstrate or prove anything. It just was . . . It began when the impulse began and ended when the impulse ended; when the impulse exhausted itself, the solid core of hot feeling or emotion informing it, holding it together as by some secret gravitational law, burnt itself out. It was expression in the truest sense of the word—*consummation*. The kind of expression that entered into the making of the *Tropic of Cancer* and gave it that extraordinary quality of *talk*, of the voice keeping time with the pulse, the rise and fall of the blood, the rhythm of the heart; that living throbbing quality which only the spoken word, formed out of the living breath with the warm blood still clinging to it, can possibly give. I have heard people say that sometimes a phrase, a line or word will come floating up to the mind long after the book itself has been forgotten, and that is true, for the spoken word has a power of evocation greater than the power of the word as such.

Or then again, take that extraordinary nose of his for putrefaction, for the dark, hidden, concealed sources of the putrefaction, the dark, secret, unmentionable places of the body—"the drains clogged with strangled embryos," "the gangrened ducts which compose the urinary system," "the stitched wound," etc. etc. An attraction for, a pre-occupation, an obsession almost, with all that suggested the visceral, the shut-in and confined, the interstitial and infundibular—the gizzards, the intestines, the bowels, the entrails, the guts, etc., all subsumed under the figure of the belly of the whale. It invested the *Tropic of Cancer* with something more than the crude element of shock inherent in it; gave it its frightening *moral* implication. Informed and illumined by the *Death Theme*, it ceases to be the mere coprophilic strain that some have seen in it, or the expression of irresponsibility— of an unconscious desire to wash one's hands of the world and its problems and return to the womb—that still others have seen in it, and enters on another plane. The physical element of shock yields to the moral. A whole intricate, complex and dynamic system of double relations is set in motion. On the one hand, the figure of time and space shut in, confined, trapped in the gut of the whale—"dead mastoid," "varicose," "hungry seething mouths," "hidden chromosphere of pain"; on the other hand, the figure of time and space open, free, flowing—"orgasm," "issue," "dissolution," "falling away into the Pacific." Always the double rhythm, the double movement, inner and outer, the descent into the body of the whale and the ascent into the light. With the fœtal, always birth; with arrest, always release; with paralysis, always resolution, liberation. We are witnessing here something related to the inmost meaning of his life, to that long bloody struggle for self-liberation in which his whole life had been caught up. Miller who pries into these orifices, openings, crevices, Miller in the symbolic belly of the whale, is not simply the scatophage or the irresponsible, but Miller the suffering man who has entered the "festering wound" to cleanse it, to be cleansed, to come clean of the past, to be born. He situates himself here because he knows that it's here where human beings retreat with all their stifled suffering anguish, their frustrate loneliness and lack; and that it's precisely here therefore, at this dead quick, where the cleansing must begin, the opening up, the flow, if we are ever to throw off our death and emerge into the light. Open up these silent, secret, festering wounds, these "hungry seeing mouths" within ourselves, Miller is saying, open them up and let all the pus and sickness and fever out. Restore the life-flow that has been stopped and dammed up! Get born!

As I ruminated, it began to grow clear to me, the mystery of his pilgrimage, the flight which the poet makes over the face of the earth, and then, as if he had been ordained to re-enact a lost drama, the heroic descent into the very bowels of the earth, the dark, fearsome sojourn in the belly of the whale, the bloody struggle to liberate himself, to emerge clean of the past, a bright, gory sun-god cast up on an alien shore.

If anyone knew what it meant to read the riddle of that thing which today is called a "crack" or a "hole"; if anyone had the least feeling of mystery about the phenomena which are labelled obscene, this world would crack asunder. It is the obscene horror, the dry,————aspect of things which makes this crazy civilization look like a crater. It is the great yawning gulf of nothingness which the creative spirits and mothers of the race carry between their legs. . . . It is no use putting on rubber gloves: all that can be coolly and intellectually handled belongs to the carapace, and a man who is intent on creation always dives beneath, to the open wound, to the festering obscene horror. He hitches his dynamo to the tenderest parts; if only blood and pus gush forth it is something. The dry,————crater is obscene. More obscene than anything is inertia. More blasphemous than the bloodiest oath is paralysis.

Here is the dark terrible symbol, the deep frightening meaning of that "open wound," that "yawning gulf," which our prescribed language, long accustomed to indirection and concealment and deceit, prevents us from calling by the right name, to which human beings escape with all their thwarted, mangled longings, desires, feelings, hopes, dreams. Here is Miller the suffering man at the very center, at the very plexus and dead quick of our dumb frustrate being, wailing and tearing his hair in rage and consternation at our physical and moral cowardice before life, at our refusal and fear to be born. Is all this shocking? It *is* shocking. It is meant to be shocking. It is precisely this element of shock that lifts the *Tropic of Cancer* out of the realm of mere literature—the weak, measly, picayune, prissy and snooty thing so many of us understand by literature today—and makes it a flaming, desperate challenge to physical and moral restoration which, as things go in the world, must necessarily be an act of violence: a bombshell thrown in our midst.

Thus fitted and appointed by nature and circumstance, Miller sat down and began the *Tropic of Cancer*. He did not begin a book, in the ordinary sense of the word. He began *Henry Miller*: Henry Miller the living man *talking*, giving expression to the chaos within himself and the chaos in the world, speaking out of the death in the world and the death within himself. The book is unfinished, will not be finished until his life is finished. It is a big chunk out of his life, at a certain period, in a certain time and place. Had he remained in that time and place, perhaps the book would still go on, because Henry Miller is still going on, will continue to go on until his life is finished. If he has turned his face in another direction, to another kind of book—as he apparently has done—it's because he's moved into a new time and place, into a new dimension, a new constellation of himself. But the book is capable of going on indefinitely, that is to say, as long as Henry Miller goes on, as I once wrote him, which he unfortunately mistook at the time as a slur or reflection on the book, whereas in fact I was paying him the greatest compliment anyone could possibly pay an author, namely, that his book is capable of going on because he, the living man, is capable of going on. The book is the author, the living man going on. It is not artifact, contrivance, manufacture, like a piece of furniture, finished and complete in itself, separate and apart from the hand that made it. It is the living plasma itself, inseparable from the living man. In this sense all essential literature, every *real* book, is unfinished. In this sense Petronius' book is unfinished, the Bible, the earliest sagas and folk tales. In this sense Whitman spoke of his *Leaves of Grass*—who touches this touches not a book but a man—and Emerson and Nietzsche advised writers to stop writing books and begin living them.

Before sitting down to write this, I re-read the *Tropic of Cancer*. The last time I read it was in manuscript, in 1931, and I wanted to refresh my reactions. Lots of people say there is a good deal of dirt in the book. There is a good deal of dirt in the book, as the reader might have already gathered from what I have said about it. But the book is not a dirty book. And it is not a dirty book for the very simple reason that Miller is not a dirty man.

The average man might not think so, but the average man thinks a lot of things which are not so. The average man has a peculiar conception of what constitutes cleanliness. He thinks a thing is clean simply because it's been scrubbed and washed; it's clean outside and inside, and so, it's clean, and that's all there is to it. According to this, the pimp who has just stepped out of his morning's bath is clean too. Or the shady business man. Or the crooked politician. All clean because they are washed and scrubbed, they look clean. The average man looks at the appearance of things, inside and out, what meets the naked eye, and there he stops, he doesn't bother to go any further. He doesn't trouble to ask himself what's behind a thing, the relation, that is, in which it stands to itself and all the other things in its circle or ambiance. He doesn't stop, in a word, to make relations, the relations of things which determine everything, whether a thing is clean or not. For example: if I stand in a false relationship to you, I can soak and drench it in all the rose-water of polite manners and polite words in the world, it'll still stink. It'll stink though outwardly it may appear perfectly clean. It'll stink because the relation in which I stand to you is false. In the same way, sexual prostitution is what it is because the order of relations in which it moves is false. When two people meet to make love they don't meet to buy and sell over the counter. Everything in its proper place and time. Likewise, marriage is often the mean, niggardly, dirty thing it is because the relations, the order of relations in which the two people stand to each other and to themselves, is false. Likewise, too, social contact sometimes gives off the bad smell it does, because it moves in a false order of relations. It's all a question of relations. A dry-goods business, for instance, may be clean or it may not be. It's not clean if it purports to sell culture, when in fact all it sells is dry-goods. The advertisement in this morning's paper stinks to heaven because it pretends to shed blood with the rest of the boys when the truth is that all it sheds is dollars. The filing cabinet in my room is clean or not clean. It's clean not simply because it's just received a fresh coat of varnish; it's clean because it stands in the right order of relations to itself and everything else in the room. And so it goes, from the biggest thing to the smallest. The relations in which things stand determine everything, whether a thing is clean or not.

The other day I saw a French film, I think it was called *Tourbillon*. To all outward appearances, to the naked eye, that is, it looked perfectly clean, there wasn't a single dirty crack or a single dirty scene in it. And yet it was positively the filthiest, foulest movie I ever saw. It told the story of a man and woman on their honeymoon, and how it was suddenly cut short by an automobile accident, which left the man a cripple for life. And for the rest of the picture you weren't allowed to forget it for a single instant—*the man was left a cripple for life*. The crude, cold, brutal fact of the man's sexual inadequacy stuck out of the picture like an eyesore. It was a terrible finger pointing all the time. The whole relationship between man and wife was reduced and compressed into the one single fact of sex, physical sex . . . and the terrible finger pointing all the time . . . It was repulsive, sordid, foul; and it was *false*. It was false because you can't reduce the relationship between man and wife to the physical fact of sex nohow, no matter how much you try; there is something else. In the same way a *Saturday Evening Post* story may be clean enough as far as meets the naked eye, but be foul just the same.

Miller's cleanliness is of another order. It is a cleanliness that recognizes relations, that moves in relations. It's not the cleanliness that sees only the things that are dirty to the naked eye, and overlooks all the others. It sees *both*: the things that are manifestly dirty and the dirty things that are manifestly clean. It's a cleanliness that doesn't shrink or recoil from dirt, whether seen or unseen, patent or concealed. It's not afraid of being contaminated. It accepts dirt as a part of life, a fact of life, like all the other facts of life, pleasant or unpleasant. It accepts life for what it is, dirty and clean. It is a natural, a rock-bottom kind of cleanliness that doesn't hold itself aloof because it knows that it cannot be soiled. It is beyond soiling, inviolable. It is purity. Purity which moves in the relations of things, sees the relations of things, and not merely appearances. Children have this sense of purity naturally; you might say they are born with it; it's in nature. They do not have to see or make relations consciously the way grown-ups have to. Their vision is unspoiled. Everything falls into the proper relations spontaneously, automatically, in a kind of completed order and harmony as old as life and nature itself. They are the little sainted ones to whom the Christs make their first appeal. They lose this sense of purity of course later, as they grow up, as they enter the world with its false system of relations: its morality, standards, values, its ideas and ideals of good and bad, success and failure, truth and falsehood, etc. Then, as grown-ups, they have to recover or recapture it, and when they do, it's no longer of course quite the same thing. It's a little more conscious, a little less spontaneous, whole, pure, but it's still purity. Grown-ups recapture this sense of purity by going through a kind of little death: by dying to the world and to themselves and being born again *in a new vision*. They see then with different eyes, as different from their old ones as the child's are from the adult's. They have entered into a new order of relations. These are the people the world usually calls mad or dangerous, a menace to the existing order. There are never very many of them in the world at any time. Miller is one of them.

The *Tropic of Cancer* is not so much a clean book as a *pure* book. Those who read it for the dirt in it are not clean, just as those who read it for the non-dirt are not clean. In either case, what is lacking in the reader is purity.

One contaminates, the other is afraid of being contaminated. It is the same thing in the end—lack of purity.

There are those who would take a book like the *Tropic of Cancer* and draw an imaginary line, like the line of the equator in geography books, between what they consider dirty in it and what they consider not. It's like drawing an imaginary line in Henry Miller himself, and saying: "This part of him is clean, this part dirty." A man is clean or he is not. The *Tropic of Cancer* is a dirty book or it is not. No one part of it can be said to be clean and another part unclean. You accept the whole thing, or you reject it. I have no patience with those who have written about the *Tropic of Cancer* and declare it in one breath literature and in another breath pornography. It's one or the other. Let us not confuse the issue. The so-called pornography is as much a part of it as the rest of it. They are one whole, one organic thing, and must be considered as such. The book is either dirty or clean, literature or pornography. And to decide that question we do not have to run to the law courts, to the jurists and lawyers. We can decide that question quite simply among ourselves. We decide it on the strength of the man; not the evidence, but the man, the writer. A writer is a man who talks, talks to himself or to others. Who is he talking to? Who is he talking to in himself or in others? Is he talking to the pander in him or the man? There's the crux of the whole matter. If he is talking to the pander, he is talking dirt, obscenity, no matter what he's talking about, whether about love, beauty, God or the angels. Is he talking to the man? Then he may talk about cabbages, unpaid gas bills, hairpins, stick-ups, bed bugs, fornication, rape, murder or anything else: it'll be purity itself. Let our lawyers and judges rack their heads with definitions in fact. The definition of the *Tropic of Cancer* is a definition of spirit.

To charge a book like the *Tropic of Cancer* with pornography is like charging life itself with pornography. Is there anything pornographic about a man defecating? Anything pornographic about the sexual act? Anything pornographic about the sexual organs? All such processes and things just are . . . Life is . . . Twist and distort it to some special end or aim outside and beyond itself, and you have something else—in life: insanity, neurosis, disease, prostitution: all foulnesses, uncleanlinesses, falsehoods; in literature: pornography. The *Tropic of Cancer* is . . . It is Henry Miller the living man reflecting life as he knew it and felt it and lived it. Over and beyond this it has no aim or purpose whatever. If there is dirt in it, there is also hate and beauty and wonder and despair and suffering and loneliness and heartbreak and sickness and death. Blame life for the one as for the other. But don't blame Henry Miller!

Life is that which flows . . . The sentiment is from Miller. With the *Tropic of Cancer* Miller in his fortieth year comes full cycle. "For forty years he had been sound asleep and thrashing about with furious activity," and now he awoke, now he was born. This is a long time to be born, but it's more than most of us can say about ourselves; most of us remain dead to the very end. With the *Tropic of Cancer* Miller emerges from the darkness and death, the inertia and paralysis in which the world held him as in a vise, a prisoner within himself, and all that was pent up in him all these years, all that lay hidden and buried in the inmost places of his being, all the loneliness and lack, the suffering and anguish, the love, hate, despair, hope, come surging up to the surface. "I had found a voice," he declares. "I was whole again." He expresses himself, he flows, he is alive. Having found his voice, he has found life itself. Life which had been denied him all this time because, in truth, he had denied himself. He had sought a way which was not his, which was alien to him: he had sought the world's way of seeing and saying. It was not his and so he groped and stumbled and failed. For with him it was always all or nothing; it was an instinct in him which made all half-measures impossible. He had to be Henry Miller, indubitably, absolutely himself, right down to the very core of him, or be nothing. "All or nothing," a favorite phrase of his. And so he blundered and groped and failed because he failed himself, he failed to go the dead limit, to strike out for Henry Miller at his dead limit and plant himself there and stay there. *And see and say from there.* From Henry Miller at the dead limit, at the deadmost reach of himself. There are natures which catch fire only when struck at their extremes; strike them anywhere else, at some neutral point, and they remain cold, unresponsive. It's as if the essence of them has to catch fire before the whole man can catch fire; as if the final irreducible element, the quintessential element in them, must be touched off before all the other elements can come into play. Such a nature is Miller. The whole of him had to respond before any part of him could respond, and no part of him could respond before the quintessential element in him was aroused. With the *Tropic of Cancer* Miller catches fire, and the whole of him is caught up in a blaze of life. He expresses himself, he flows . . . Gone now, dissipated and dispersed, are all the hobgoblins of fear, the shadows and phantoms we breed within ourselves in our self-denial, our holding-down and damming-up of ourselves. Where now are the problems, the difficulties, the obstacles, the hindrances, all those things in which we tie ourselves up in a knot because we are afraid, all those things which are there *because* we are afraid? One flows, one is in life, in the naked throbbing present, in the moment stripped of past and future, and they are not of this moment, they are somewhere beyond, in a world beyond, not now, not here. *Here, now*, in this living pulsing moment, you are in the present, in the moment's sharp awareness, in the quick of the moment's life, and there are no problems, no difficulties, no obstacles, no hindrances: there is no thought of past or future: there is no fear, fear which means arrest, paralysis: you flow, you express yourself: you are alive. Free of fear, you have attained the only freedom that really means anything: the freedom to live now, this moment. You have attained peace, the only peace that really means anything: peace with yourself. You have attained security, the only security that really means anything: security within yourself. Now you need no protection from society or governments or people or ideals or love or God or what not. You can throw off that armour of property, possession, place, name, into which people hustle themselves in order to feel secure. You can stand naked. You need no protection. Protection against what? There is simply nothing to fear. You flow, you express yourself, you live: you have thrown yourself wide open to all of life, to the whole world.

Flow. . . . "*I love everything that flows,*" declares Miller. The *Tropic of Cancer* ends as it should end—on this note, a calm, subdued, reflective note, full of peace and hope, after all the horror and violence of the book. For a moment there, as he stands watching the Seine flow quietly past him, the thought occurs to him that perhaps he might return to the States.

> I asked myself—"do you want to go?" There was no answer. My thoughts drifted towards the sea, towards the other side, where, taking a last look back I had seen the skyscrapers fading out in a flurry of snow flakes. I saw them loom up again in the same ghastly way as when I left. Saw the lights creeping through the ribs. I saw the whole city spread out, from Harlem to the Battery, the streets choked with ants, the elevated rushing by, the theatres emptying.

—No, he will not go back; that way lies death. He will stay where he belongs, in life. And then follows what is perhaps the tenderest passage of the book, with which the book closes:

> So quietly flows the Seine that one hardly notices its presence. It is always there, quiet and unobtrusive, like a great artery running through the human body. In the wonderful peace that fell over me it seemed as if I had climbed to the top of a high mountain: for a little while I would be able to look around me, to take in the full meaning of the landscape . . .
>
> The sun is setting. I feel this river flowing through me—its past, its ancient soil, the changing climate. The hills gently girdle it about, its course is fixed.

Miller chose life.

"The joys of birth" . . . Miller never tires of speaking of them. And the greatest birth of all is self-discovery. And the greatest joys of all are the joys of self-discovery. What joy and gladness, what happiness, must have been his when he finally discovered himself, his true path, his true voice, as the pages of the *Tropic of Cancer* came winging off the machine! Something of this happiness the reader may glean from the letter he sent me to China when the book finally appeared in 1934 and he held the first copy of it in his hands—the first copy: the first true, authentic image of himself:

Dear Fraenkel:

The first floor left, here I am! Today I am mailing you a copy of the *Tropic of Cancer*—the first copy! What was begun is ended and all's well. Dear old Fraenkel, you don't know with what pleasure, with what gayety, with what affection, with what hope I send you this copy . . . When you return to Paris may it be a day like today, with the sun out strong, and a light wind blowing from the east, and the colors running red, and no dust in the eye . . .

Have just fried a pork chop and inscribed a few copies of my book to those few old friends like yourself, for whom everything has been worth while. I feel like a king. I feel the sun in my bones and the wine in my marrow. I put *Werther's Younger Brother* on the shelf, in the front row. I read it again and I weep . . . Now in this silent studio, the machine clattering, the birds chirping, the walls a bright spanking sienna, Walter coming and going, the half-wits coming and going, I feel right. I feel as though I shall stay here a long while. I feel as though fortune is with me—at last!

All morning I have been singing—*Old Black Joe, Way Down Upon the Swanee River, My Old Kentucky Home*. I am singing, do you hear? The voice vibrates, it reverberates, it carries way out into the back yard and beyond where the woodsheds rise. It began this morning with the *Sacre du Printemps*, and Walter says "Why don't you put on a soft needle?" Why the soft needle? I am singing and I want the neighbors to hear. Here comes a glad man. I am moving in, my neighbors. Moving in to the Villa Seurat. I am the last man alive. They say these are bad times. Perhaps they be. But they are good times for me. I move with the changing climate. I move with the sun and the light. With the birds. With the wild flowers.

Dear Fraenkel, I don't know what to say to you, I am so happy . . .

The Last Book

JAY MARTIN

The new book. The first book. In dismissing *Crazy Cock*, Fraenkel had urged him: "Write as you talk. Write as you live. Write as you feel and think. Just sit down before the machine and let go . . . Evacuate the trenches!" That was good advice and Henry followed it. He decided to find out how he did live and think and feel. Inspired now by the mere existence of Anaïs's *Journal intime* (which he had not yet read in its entirety), and accepting the logic of the confessional impulse from which her book had sprung, he decided to compose his own autobiography as a diary. He called it "The Last Book." Later he called it "The Tropic of Capricorn" and finally *The Tropic of Cancer*.

Probably to conserve paper, but with a nice gesture of dismissal for his previous work, he turned over the sheets of his original Tony Bring manuscript and rolled the clean side upward into the typewriter. Osborn was on his mind, and he began the logbook of his desperate life with the story of Osborn, himself, and Irene, the Russian princess. This was an account of a woman who lived with them and preyed on the two of them, especially upon Dick, while assuring them of the truth of the most outlandish tales of her past and keeping them away from her by claiming that she had a dose.

At once the line between fiction and reportage broke down. Whatever Henry said was true *was* true, at least for that moment. The only rule that remained was the drive to digress. Soon, everything was going into the diary, all the stories of his Paris years. "It's like a big, public garbage can," he wrote to Ned Schnellock. "Only the mangy cats are missing. But I'll get them in yet." In they went. He pillaged his notebooks for additional material, observations, quotations, questions. Some he even pasted in, along with newspaper clippings and menus. A description of Wambly Bald's room went in along with a catalogue of the labels and brand names of the liquors from which Bald distilled his column. One day while he was writing, the voice of a woman singing "Never wanted to . . . What am I to do?" drifted into his room. The song and her rich, dark voice went into the book. He wrote to Bertha, hoping to put some of his love letters in the book. They didn't go in: she replied that on the day that his actions had ceased to correspond

Excerpted and reprinted from *Always Merry and Bright* (Santa Barbara, CA: Co. Press, 1918), 250–64. Copyright © by Jay Martin. Reprinted by permission of the author.

with his words she had destroyed his letters. *The bitch*, he growled as he castigated her in his diary. From "Bezeque" he extracted the story of the prostitute with the dying mother. The Cirque Medrano was revisited. That went in. George Grosz's paintings, as well as Grosz's and Spengler's ideas about "the late-city man," were inserted. Herbert Wilkie of Valier, Montana, and Marseilles appeared, a "confessed pederast." Nanavati, Eugene, Fred, Germaine, Putnam, Zadkine, Claude, Fraenkel, and Lowenfels appeared, each pursuing his own identity, illumined by his own mania. The higher mathematics of the gospel of death were formularized. The whole Dijon episode was spun out with high humor. For good seasoning, Papini, Duhamel's *Salavin*, Rabelais, Proust, Whitman, Annie Besant's *The Ancient Wisdom*, and Keyserling's *Creative Understanding* were stirred in. Henry had given up any desire to defend himself. Defenseless, his single motto now was *fais ce que voudras*: do anything—so long as it yields ecstasy.

Certainly, there were many presences here, but Miller was finding his own voice among theirs as he pounded his typewriter in the Hôtel Central in a room next to Fred's. He radiated the excitement of his self-discovery. In those days, as Perlès has beautifully said, his friends walked in his shadow, "and even his shadow was warm." He expanded in every direction: everything he did took on a new dimension. He was up every morning at six. With mountains of books piled high on his worktable, enormous charts tacked to the walls, Beethoven or jazz or an African laughing record blaring at full volume from the victrola (a present from Anaïs), his typewriter racing over the speed limit, the gargantuan became commonplace and it almost seemed as if the tiny hotel room could not contain him.

As a matter of practical fact, it was obvious to Henry and Fred that they would save money and live more pleasantly by renting an apartment together; not only would they be able to divide the rent, they would be able to prepare their own meals, as they could not do in the hotel. Fred's affections settled upon a flat in a recently built row of apartment buildings at 4 Avenue Anatole France in Clichy, just on the outskirts of Paris. It did not particularly appeal to Henry for it was like being transported back 3,000 miles and twenty years to the apartment rows put up above Central Park. Henry would have preferred a studio or grand, old-fashioned Parisian hotel apartment. At the Clichy place the look was functional modern, the architecture was undistinguished; the interiors were plain and angular, unmarked by time or human use. Much as in some tough areas of New York, there was a spot on the way to the apartment that was dangerous to cross at night, along the junkyards between the Porte Clichy, with its trolley terminals and garages, and the beginning of Clichy itself. But the kitchen and bathroom decided the issue: to Fred's eyes these were glorious. The fixtures were new, the faucets didn't drip, the toilet seat was intact, and the bowl didn't run all night. In addition, there were two bedrooms separated by a hallway, which made it possible for Henry and Fred to come and go quite separately or entertain friends privately. (Fred had a young woman named Paulette living with him.)

The French would have said that Henry had at last established a *domicile fixe*. But after years of transience Henry could not dare to call the Clichy flat more than "pseudo-permanent." For Fred, so long relegated to the shabby and second hand, the bourgeois modernity of the place was marvellous. For Henry it was a simple financial arrangement, based on the fact that the rent was far below ordinary hotel rates. At 5,100 francs plus the tax at the end of the year, they could afford to agree that if either one lost his job the other would support him.

Before the middle of March 1932 they moved their few belongings into Avenue Anatole France. Henry, of course, promptly lost his job—though not directly as the result of any calculation of his own. As early as the second of March, the accounting office at the *Tribune* had asked him to put his Work Permit on file. Since arriving in Paris he had never registered for employment. Now, when he did so, he was refused a permit. For this reason, before the middle of March he received a notice of termination from the *Tribune* and two weeks later, on the twenty-fifth, his dismissal came in a letter from Jules Frantz, the managing editor. When Henry accused Jules of injustice—for there were a number of Americans who were working at the *Tribune* without permits—Frantz hung his head and muttered some excuses about "economy" and promised to allow Henry to go downstairs as a proofreader again for the vacation period. But though he excoriated Frantz, in truth Henry was secretly gratified. Again, he told himself, he owed his salvation to the French. Nothing, he felt, could be lower than the depths to which he had fallen at Nanavati's or the Cinéma Vanves so how could he concern himself over the mere loss of a newspaper job? Everything that happened was exactly what was meant to happen. To convert defeats into triumphs—that was as much as he could ask. For the first time, Henry was thoroughly convinced that he had lived out his fate and had a destiny to fulfill.

Besides, he was working at such a pace now that the extra four and a half hours that he had gained by his dismissal from the paper were put to immediate and good use. He was so full of energy that he hardly seemed to need sleep—no more than five hours. He slept, he claimed, only for the pleasure of dreaming. He dreamed constantly: of the books he would read (loaned by Anaïs or filched from the American library), of the watercolors he would make (influenced by Klee, Chagall, and Picasso), and, above all, of the books he would write. There was a depression all over the world; literary men, like the economy, had diminished expectations. Miller was one of the few American writers who by 1932 still preserved the grandiloquent hope of the twenties: to compose works as great as any that had ever been written. Many others wanted only to compose something "proletarian," something superior to Gorki. Henry was ready to take on the *Iliad*, Rabelais, Joyce, Proust—and the Holy Ghost, if need be. At this moment he was sure about his destiny. He *had* to write a certain number of pages each day, he told Alf, "for the sake of posterity."

Now he arranged his life like pieces on a chess board—in little ordered graduated rows, so much space for everything and everything having a place. He lived as he had wished to live in Remsen Street (without the disorder introduced by June), a simple, bare, Japanese life. Each morning he arose, washed thoroughly and straightened up after himself, raised the curtains, and, though naked, inspected the doings in the courtyard, then dressed and made his bed. His Teutonic habits of orderliness prevailed until the matter of work came up—then he'd explode. Sometimes as he began to prepare his morning meal he'd notice a book he had left unfinished the night before. Then he'd forget breakfast altogether. Instead of clearing a place for his plate, he'd pick up an enormous tome by Rank, Jung, or Keyserling and start in reading. This was a promising sign. Soon there'd be a pencil in his hand and he'd be annotating the margins, at first sparsely, then copiously. From that stage to the next required only a jump to the typewriter, usually to copy out a particularly meaty passage. Then he'd toss the book aside in order to start right into squeezing the juices out of it, possibly in a letter to Emil or Anaïs. By now his fingers would be flying over the keys, as if he had leaped with hardly a transition from the "Moonlight Sonata" to the "Minute Waltz." He went like lightning once he turned to work on his novel. The associations that had begun in his reading would accumulate and bubble into new blendings which went far beyond their origin. Those were the days when writing was as easy as singing—no wonder that even as he was typing he'd occasionally burst into song. Ten or more sheets might easily roll in and out of his typewriter before he was ready, having missed breakfast, to stop for lunch. He didn't worry any more about losing an idea. For the first time in his life, to begin writing seemed no harder than turning on a tap. Like running water, the stream of recollections, words, and ideas was always there—he had only to turn on the faucet to have the flow begin or snap it off to give the illusion that it had ceased.

After lunch, which would sometimes be washed down with a fresh Vouvray or a Muscadet, he'd arrange everything neatly and go through his daily ceremony: he'd undress completely, put on his pajamas, and tuck himself into bed for a nice nap. This seemed to his friends to be an incredibly self-indulgent luxury—but it was a necessity of his routine: his sleep not only, as he claimed, put "velvet in his vertebrae," it was a deliberate dam-ming of the stream until, on its own, it overflowed its banks. His dreams, which he cultivated, were also part of his work, imparting new angles and different directions to the thoughts of the morning. The nap was also, clearly, a beautiful return to his childhood, whose bourgeois tranquillity the Clichy flat recalled. He was like a child tucked into his bed for his afternoon nap, a good boy. So much of his adult life had destroyed his dreams, he was committed now to dreaming his way backward to childhood, and forward to art, again.

Upon awakening, he might even hold back the headwaters a little longer while he took an excursion on his bicycle or by foot. By the time he sat down at the typewriter again his fingers were itching to slaughter the machine, like a drummer. The flood would rumble along for several hours of the late afternoon. On this work schedule, twenty, thirty, forty, and—on one day—forty-five pages (with two carbons) would be stacked up beside the laboring typewriter before dinner. He would have been playing music all day, keeping time to the music, and by the end, a triumphal column of records would be piled next to the victrola. All the ashtrays would be filled with Gauloises Bleues. A visitor could count the stubs and figure that there would be one burnt-out Bleu for each page he had produced. And, far from being tired, Henry would be full of vinegar, ready to reach for a bottle—of a velvety Nuits St. Georges, say—when Fred sat down at the kitchen table for a chat.

Fred was working on a novel of his own in just the opposite way from Henry's volcanic outpourings. As Paulette put it: "Monseiur Henri can type much faster than you, and when he sits at his typewriter he goes on for hours without a stop." Henry was unconcerned about his productivity because he produced so much, while Fred avoided that concern by deliberately limiting his writing to no more than two pages a day. If he reached the bottom of that second page (and most often he didn't reach it) he'd stop abruptly, even in the middle of a sentence. To Fred this procedure was eminently clear and perfectly rational. As he often explained it: "Two pages a day, 365 days in the year, that makes 730 pages. If I can do 250 in a year I'll be satisfied. I'm not writing a *roman fleuve*." He was in fact writing a book in French called *Sentiments limitrophes*—a book of "peripheral feelings," a work about the fragments of his memory and the streams of association flowing between memories. Although these memories went back to his childhood, they also included recent ones and involved portraits of Henry, June, and Anaïs Nin. Henry was certain that he himself could not match the delicate power and transparency, like that of a perfect watercolor, of Alf's book. Fred's writing he thought of as a "subtle distillation" and declared that he liked it better than anything he could do himself. But though their methods of composition were different, the books shared a similar view of the flexibility and rapidity of the faculty of memory, were influenced by Proust's treatment of recollection, and had some of the same materials—their mutual acquaintances. And finally, they were, as Henry wrote to Alf after both volumes were published, "companion books in misery and loneliness."

In the evening, then, Henry and Fred were likely to loaf over a bottle of wine and talk about their work of the day, add up their funds, and discuss the women upon the horizon. If they lingered long enough to open a second bottle of wine and both started to feel euphoric, Fred might suddenly stop the conversation and seize Henry by the arm, begging him to take him along to America should he ever return. Then he'd urge Henry to give him an account of his travels in that fabulous place, America. Once Henry got started on the subject of places in the United States, no natural end to his monologue was foreseeable: it was like mentioning the decline of the western world, painting, sex, or the role of the artist to him. Just ask him for a good description of Miami or mention Santa Fe and he'd be on the wing. He had his own especially favorite places, such as Mobile Bay and Big Sur, and concerning these places he had never seen he could spin dazzling improvisations. But no matter how long he rambled on, at the end Alf would always pipe up with the demand: "*Now* tell me about Arizona." It was not one of Henry's specialties, and he'd sometimes growl: "The hell with Arizona. I'm going to bed. I've told you all I know." "Then tell me again," Fred would ask in a tone of blissful expectation. They'd both have had a skinful of wine and Fred's eyes would be shining with tears of joy. Almost invariably, Henry would start in again, inventing freely. Very likely, he'd become newly interested in the subject and begin to talk about the places he wanted to visit before he died—Mexico, India, Greece, the land of Saladin, Tibet. From the last he expected to go to Devechan; but before that time came, Henry would ruminate, there'd be time to see Fillmore Place once again as well as the bayous at the mouth of the Mississippi. When he finished, perhaps an hour later, Fred would gratefully raise a ruby glass of Porto *sec* to him and say: "Now tell me about *Arizona!*"

Such epic expressions of their *sentiments limitrophes* were reserved for special occasions and demanded Fred's night off from work for proper elaboration. Occasionally, one of Miller's friends would arrive. Fraenkel, still deep in the writing of his gospels of anonymity and death, often came to mull over his ideas. Start him anywhere and soon Fraenkel would be in the cemetery and battlefield, tallying up the corpses. At this point, Fred was likely to take himself off to the Restaurant de l'Escargot if he had any cash, or, if he didn't, to Giolotte's on the Rue Lamartine, where the staff of the *Tribune*—housed just across the street—could run up tabs. Henry and Michael would monumentally occupy the apartment, jabbering about "creative suicide" to their heart's content. But if he had ever been, Henry was no longer on Fraenkel's side. Fraenkel was right in every particular but one: everyone was dead—everyone but Henry himself. For him, the gospel of death became a measure of his own triumph. As Michael became more and more convincing, Henry became more and more justified. All the people he wrote about—Bertha, Bald, Fred, and even Fraenkel—were like so many cold corpses in transparent caskets. He, Henry, danced alone in the graveyard, picking flowers.

For Michael, that was a definite and unwelcome compromise. But it was just as he had feared. Even before Henry left for Dijon. Fraenkel had cautioned him: "The reason I wanted you to commit suicide that evening at the Lowenfels' . . . I was afraid, terribly afraid, that some day you'd go back on me; die on my hands. And I would be left high and dry with my idea of you simply, and nothing to sustain it. I should never forgive you for that." He meant that he wanted Henry to commit creative suicide by admitting that his life was a death. By the spring of 1932, however, Henry came alive for himself. Now, Michael's once-respected letter was inserted into "The Last Book" as an instance of the gospel of mumbo-jumbo.

Richard Osborn actually did threaten to die on their hands. During the winter while Henry was in Dijon, Dick experienced a complete mental breakdown with paranoiac delusions. The hospital on the outskirts of Paris in which he was incarcerated was literally nightmarish and at least part of Osborn's fears had real basis. He had been living with a younger French girl named Jeanne who had become pregnant—or at least he *thought* she was pregnant and he believed he was the father. He'd knocked her up—he kept mumbling to himself as if even biology was persecuting him. None of his Paris friends would have predicted the next development. His Bridgeport morals reasserted themselves: he *wanted* to marry her, the woman he had ruined. He was preparing to die, hoping to die—and his mind was dying— but he was determined to "do the right thing" first.

In the asylum Osborn was raving: his mind was shooting fragments in every direction. He suspected that while he was out during the day Jeanne had had men up to the apartment. He had gotten the clap and given it to her, he said with tears streaming down his face. But the next moment he'd claim that it was Jeanne, the little slut, who'd given him the dose and pretended to have gotten it from him. He couldn't bear to leave her, he wailed. But then, he'd say, he was desperate to escape from her but had no chance, she'd track him down and claw his eyes out if he tried to defect. He wanted to marry the poor girl. But as soon as he said that he'd turn around and curse his fate: now he'd be stuck in a provincial town forever. Christ!— all he had wanted was a fling in Paris before settling down to a practice in corporation law, with a nice house in Bridgeport and an office in Wall Street. His mind had collapsed: he was paralyzed by fears of others and accusations of himself.

Henry vowed to save the poor devil, no matter how desperate the required measures might be. He tried to penetrate the fogs of Osborn's paranoia to discover what had actually happened. Henry talked to some of Jeanne's friends and neighbors and concluded that she was not pregnant, only growing fat from indolence. After a while he simply gave up and decided that the truth was irrelevant. The main thing was to save Dick. Some time later, when Osborn was released from the hospital and allowed to return to Paris, Henry determined that he should light out, abandon Jeanne, and return to America. There was nowhere in France that he could hide from Jeanne if in fact she decided to track him down. Certainly, as soon as Dick got back to Paris, she seized him like a spider; she didn't quite devour him, but she wouldn't let him out of her sight. One day in late July, Henry ran into him on the Right Bank. "I'm just on my way to the bank to draw out some money," he said uneasily. "I've got to be back in a half-hour. I don't know what to do." It was a sunny, breezy Paris day. Outwardly Osborn looked like a healthy American—well-dressed, bareheaded, with a little paunch. But there was a dizziness in his eyes. "You've got to help me out of this," he suddenly urged Henry with desperation in his voice. "I don't belong here. I wish I were home." He started to blubber and go to pieces. He groaned about his disgust with the cruelty and sterility of the French, a people he once adored. It even drove him crazy, he said, to have to speak incessantly in French.

Henry's thoughts were going fast and he took Dick's arm. He formed a crazy scheme—crazy enough to work. Henry decided to break his plan easily to Osborn—otherwise sheer panic might follow. "I'm going to help you," he said. "Let's have a drink." Dick looked at him with horror. Hysteria danced behind his eyes. To have a drink, to invite Jeanne's displeasure, to be late returning from his errand, to put his trust in this irresponsible Henry Miller—sounded crazy to Osborn. "Relax, sit down. Let's have a whiskey, an American whiskey," Henry said. The whiskey did it. As the American liquor arrived, looking velvety and golden brown, his eyes brimmed with tears. He seized Henry as if he were his last friend and sang the praises of their native land, which he said he dared not hope to see again. The garçon arrived with a second drink. "Bottoms up!" Henry commanded. Dick downed it at once. "Listen," Henry said, "if I were in your boots, I'd go— I'd go to America, without hesitation, today." Osborn glanced about, as if the mere whispering of such an idea would be enough to bring Jeanne down on his head. "How much do you have in the bank? Is it yours or Jeanne's father's?" Henry asked. Getting satisfactory answers to both questions, he outlined his plan. He gave his voice the air of command and authority. The plan was insanely simple. At once—hatless—lacking a cane—abandoning his mackintosh, his manuscripts, and even his Yale diploma—without returning to his apartment to pick up a toothbrush—Osborn was to board a boat to his native land. In hardly more than a week, Henry reminded him, he'd be back in Bridgeport. The slapstick plan was so preposterous that Osborn went right along with it. Henry had never acted decisively in any of his own crises, but he had become desperate enough to learn to be resourceful. "Jesus, Osborn," Henry said to buck him up, "why by tonight you'll be in London up to your ears in English."

Henry shepherded him through the ordeals of the bank, the British consulate, and American Express, with a pause at a fine restaurant and a farewell bottle of wine, the finest on the menu. With Dick's money stuffed into his pockets he was pretty exhilarated by the events himself. By the time they were on their way to the Gare du Nord in a cab, he had changed all but about 2,500 francs of Dick's money into traveler's checks and pounds. In great confusion Osborn tried to explain how to break the news to Jeanne and was getting muddled and feeling responsible and preparing to collapse on Henry's hands. But now Henry was determined to see it through. "Never mind that," he told Dick. "How much dough do you want to give her?— that's all!" Osborn looked ready to faint: "How much do you have?" "About 2,000 francs, more than she deserves," Henry replied. "I don't know . . ." Osborn said weakly, wanting to go and wanting to stay. "All right, I'll give her all this French money," Henry said, holding up the two-thousand.

So it was settled. Henry pocketed the dough and promised to see Jeanne the very next day, and he pushed the tottering wreck onto the boat train, and Dick was off toward America.

America!—how much Henry himself had wanted to return to his country. Once, he had begged his friends and his wife to send him the funds to come home, fearful that he would starve to death in France. He had been as desperate to get out as Osborn was. So, as he sat in a café on the Place Lafayette, he counted Osborn's money up to a total of 2,800 francs—$125. That was enough for a ticket to America. Who would ever know if Jeanne never got the money at all? Even if Osborn did write to her, who would believe him, a crazy fellow who had performed the kind of act unthinkable to the French—boarding a boat for London without picking up his reversible or planting his hat firmly on his head! If Henry wanted to follow Dick to America, then, he had but to take a train to Le Havre or Cherbourg and wait for a departure. It was the first time since he had been in Paris that he had any choice about his own fate. He sat in the Place Lafayette and let his thoughts drift. All the defects that Osborn found in French life were there all right—the selfishness and indifference, the insistence on the reasonable and restrained, the petty severity and mean puritanism—there for Frenchmen at least. But for an American, like himself, who had not caved in, an American who knew where his next meal was coming from, France was just fine, he could ask no more. The way the colored awnings were gently flapping in the breeze, the chestnut trees spilling gold sequins in blond beer, the clock ringing in a church tower—these all seemed to be a part of the flow of the seasons, the sweep of time, and yet for the very same reason to be unchanging. It was not the whiskey or the wine or the last Pernod he shared with Dick that flowed through him—it was the golden stream of the life about him gliding by and then through him and becoming his life. Now that it came to a choice about returning to America, he discovered that the Paris which he had never chosen had chosen him. It was like his first Sunday in Paris: he would stay and live and write—he felt that same conviction again, only now it was born from experience and not innocence and was likely to last. He and Dick, that day, both made their way home.

This did not imply that Henry wasn't pleased with the escape plan which he had led Osborn to execute. He decided at once to vote himself a sizeable commission of eight hundred francs. He sent an even 2,000 francs to Jeanne by postal check that very afternoon. He enclosed a note written with his left hand, shakily, like Osborn's writing, saying: "*Chère Jeanne. Je suis parti pour l'Amerique, O.*" His haste could have been an error of a major sort, since Jeanne rapidly checked the schedules of French departures and was on a train that very evening to Le Havre where she kept her eye upon the departing steamship *Rochambeau* until it sailed. Fortunately Dick was departing that same day from Cherbourg for London on the *Olympic*.

Henry put his story into "The Last Book" even before Osborn landed in America. By this time the book was far enough advanced for him to take the chance of showing it to Lowenfels. Walter sensed its importance after reading the first fifty pages and wrote out eight pages of commentary on them. "He is careful to surround himself with dead people," Lowenfels remarked, "Naturally he adores Fraenkel. . . . Miller recognizes Fraenkel's death as the real thing, and so idolizes it. The others, the living dead, he had only to annihilate by—what? It's not contempt. It's that he is so alive nothing else can exist. It's like being close to the sun." "This book should be called," Lowenfels announced, "I am the only man in the world that's alive." For a while Henry actually thought of calling the novel "Cockeyed in Paris." At the end of the month he proposed two more titles to Anaïs: "I Sing the Equator" and "Tropic of Cancer." The first was an apt allusion to Whitman, but Anaïs' interests in astrology predisposed her to prefer the second. The title had several associations for Henry. Into his notebook he had copied an excerpt from the *Satyricon*: "I was born myself under Cancer, and therefore stand on my feet, as having large possessions both by Sea and Land!" Cancer is the crab, a creature who can move in many directions, the fabulous beast of the Chinese sagas. Cancer is the sign of the poet who observes and exposes the disease of a civilization which is proceeding in the wrong direction. Cancer is also the sign of death in life, with affinities to Nietzsche's doctrine of eternal recurrence as well as to Buddhist Doctrine.

Tropic of Cancer is about the critical early period of Miller's poverty and personal despair in Paris. He uses his encounters with Bertha, Eugene Pachoutinsky, Fraenkel, Nanavati, Perlès, Osborn, and others as symbols of the fragments into which his life had fallen. Death and nausea hover about him. He begins as he had begun the book in his earliest draft (though the real names were finally eliminated):

> I am living in the Villa Borghese. There is not a crumb of dirt anywhere, nor a chair misplaced. We are all alone here and we are dead.

But though death is the prison house about which he writes, it is the living artist who is writing the book. Surely he was right: in his worst days in Paris Henry Val Miller had really died from failure of the heart. But a new desperado had been reborn:

I have no money, no resources, no hopes. I am the happiest man alive . . .

To sing you must first open your mouth. You must have a pair of lungs, and a little knowledge of music. It is not necessary to have an accordion, or a guitar. The essential thing is to *want* to sing. This then is a song. I am singing.

Song, food, words, physical sensations of sex and many other kinds, the lunacy of acceptance, these bubble to the surface of the narrative even as Miller recounts his dark days—of hunger, decay, pain, cold, and the sense of personal extinction. The story he is telling, of course, is fundamentally an explanation of the book in which the story is told. How did such a book come to be written?—a book that is "a gob of spit in the face of Art, a kick in the pants to God, Man, Destiny, Time, Love, Beauty"? Such a book, he implies, could have been accomplished only through the death of the conventional artist and his resurrection into a new man who sees with new eyes and tells his tale in accordance with a new compact with the world. At the time of his writing the main character of the book and Miller were not at all identical. He had come out of his desperation in order to write—but he wrote from the point of view gained through his harrowing experiences.

This, then, is not an autobiography in the usual sense, though filled with chunks of the actual. It is an autobiography of Miller's present perspective on his past experience, which he changes freely to suit his present mood. The most brilliantly achieved instance of this kind of autobiographic transmutation occurs in the closing scene. Here, Henry Miller tells of how Val Miller saved Osborn (Fillmore) from the clutches of his French fiancée. In fact, Henry had delivered most of the francs left by Osborn to the girl. But in the autobiographic romance of *Tropic of Cancer* he pockets all the dough, since that is what such an artist as he now sees himself to be would do. And in the book the money turns into a radiant symbol, a warm comforting bulge in his pocket. Under the spell of his money, he understands for the first time how joyous Paris is. He sits by the Seine and feels the river swelling and flowing through him with its burst of new freedom: "In the wonderful peace that fell over me it seemed as if I had climbed to the top of a high mountain; for a little while I would be able to look around me, to take in the meaning of the landscape." His first look, of course, will be at the spiritual geography of his life in Paris. At the end of the book the man who can write the book is born.

Although he had not quite completed *Tropic of Cancer*, Miller was already trying to find a publisher for it. Michael Fraenkel had openly asserted his belief that Henry was "doing something greater than *Ulysses*," and he proposed to have the type set in Bruges and issue the book under his own Carrefour imprint. But Michael was in a bad state emotionally. Arguments with Lowenfels and domestic problems had rendered him almost as ineffectual as Osborn; all day long he sat in a cold room too broken and helpless to be able even to make up his mind to go out. Henry hesitated to entrust the book to him; he made up a list of other "little presses." First, however, Anaïs encouraged him to try for commercial publication. She asked her friend Dr. Krans (through whom Henry had been placed at the Lycée Carnot) to recommend Miller to a Paris literary agent named William Aspenwall Bradley. Wambly Bald had mentioned Bradley in the same column in which he reviewed "Mademoiselle Claude," asserting that Bradley "has encouraged and assisted more buds than any other angel we know." Soon, Henry received a cordial letter in which the agent requested that he bring his books around to his office on the Rue Saint-Louis in the Île de la Cité.

Henry left the manuscripts of *Crazy Cock* and *Tropic of Cancer* and waited—not too patiently. Bradley answered within a week: "I have been through both the books now, and should like very much to talk them over with you—especially the *Tropic of Cancer*, which is magnificent." Could Henry come to see him by the end of the week? he inquired. In their first talk, Bradley was discouraging about *Crazy Cock*, but he softened his criticism by persuading Henry that the novel suffered terribly through comparison with the later, richer book: he dismissed *Crazy Cock* in about two minutes. But what would Henry think of seeing *Tropic of Cancer* published in a limited edition of 500 copies at 500 francs apiece by the Obelisk Press? Miller's first reaction was revealing. Though Anaïs was with him, he cried out: "If only June could have been here to enjoy this with me. To think that all we dreamed of is happening and she doesn't even know about it." His second reaction was curious—a kind of backpedalling loss of confidence exactly at the moment of his triumph. Out of some deep-seated need for self-justification, Henry wanted to force *Crazy Cock* down their throats. *Tropic of Cancer* was not the book he wanted to write, he crazily asserted, not the story he really wanted to tell. He had promised himself in 1927 that he would dedicate himself to writing the story of his life with June. And like a pilgrim of little faith who settles for the first shrine he sees, he had merely written a book recounting his own miserable history. *Crazy Cock* was the story he wanted to tell. If they wanted *Tropic of Cancer* they must take *Crazy Cock* too!

Just when this defiant mood was fully upon him, Henry received a letter from Samuel Putnam, who was in New York. On behalf of Covici-Friede, Publishers he inquired if Henry had any work to submit; Covici had read and liked "Mademoiselle Claude." Now, stubbornly, Henry was enraged that interest should be taken in such a "weak" story, a *jeu d'esprit* done with his left hand. It was humiliating, he decided, to be admired by such buggers. In letters to Lowenfels, Anaïs, Putnam, and Emil he ranted and raved. If Americans wanted a book by him now, they would have to take *Crazy Cock*. He wanted it to be a big success in the United States, he said, so that he could take down his pants and show his ass to his countrymen and say: "I'm crapping on it, disowning it. So much for you, America, of thee I sing! That's just the kind of shit you've been eating for the last fifteen years!"

Having said all of this, he went on outrageously to propose that either Lowenfels or Putnam should undertake the publication of *Crazy Cock*. Wouldn't it be an apt gesture of the New Instinctivism for him to bring out a book which its author would publicly castigate just as the public began to praise it? To Henry's surprise Putnam actually read the manuscript and said he believed it to be "a Covici-Friede book." ("I think he's crazy," Miller told Schnellock—but he did send the book to the Covici-Friede editors.) Typed on the title page was a one-sentence foreword ("Apologies to Michael Fraenkel") and a Preface only slightly longer ("Good-bye to the novel, sanity, and good health. Hello angels!"). It was another man, he told Emil, who had written *Crazy Cock*, a man whom Henry now saw as an imposter; and he was defecating on that man too, the hollow American puppet he had left behind.

His fury over American interest in his writing also worked its way into *Tropic of Cancer*, which he expanded now that its publication by Obelisk Press seemed guaranteed. At around the same time *Crazy Cock* was being considered by Covici-Friede, Henry was excising everything but the "fire and dynamite" from *Tropic of Cancer*. Determined to affront readers and to make his book completely unacceptable to the public taste, he added several new sections whose frankness would be almost certain to offend. He also added a contentious preface in which he connected his own world-view of contemporary disease with the surrealist savagery of Luis Buñuel and with Duhamel's violent attack upon American values in *Salavin*. Such a prefatory critical *tour de force*, he felt, would throw the critics overboard or sink their ship. He ruthlessly followed Fraenkel's logic, signed his book "Henry Miller, Pseudonym," and then went one step further and typed a new title page: " 'Tropic of Cancer' by Anonymous." Last, he vowed that the fact of publication being merely an incidental occasion in his expression of himself, he would not revise in order to please the public, mollify the censors, or perfect his art. Only his own integrity, he decided, mattered to him. He was even willing, if need be, to accept expulsion from France as a consequence of the publication of *Cancer* and to wander the earth like an untouchable.

Jack Kahane might have been dismayed had he known of these resolutions; for as editor and owner of the Obelisk Press, he was drawing up a contract for the publication of *Tropic of Cancer*. By the terms of this document, Miller agreed to give Obelisk Press world rights to publish his book in English in return for a 10% royalty and an option on his succeeding two books. That last provision of the contract was far from being an empty gesture. From Kahane's side it indicated faith in this new writer. From Miller's it promised at least a reading for future books. Indeed, as he signed the contract he had already written sixty pages of his next production, a book which he was inevitably calling *Tropic of Capricorn*.

[Letter, August 1935]

LAWRENCE DURRELL

C/o The British Consul, Villa Agazini, Perama, Corfu   [August 1935]

Dear Mr. Miller:

I have just read *Tropic of Cancer* again and feel I'd like to write you a line about it. It strikes me as being the only really man-size piece of work which this century can really boast of. It's a howling triumph from the word go; and not only is it a literary and artistic smack on the bell for everyone, but it really gets down on paper the blood and bowels of our time. I have never read anything like it. I did not imagine anything like it could be written; and yet, curiously, reading it I seemed to recognise it as something which I knew we were all ready for. The space was all cleared for it. *Tropic* turns the corner into a new life which has regained its bowels. In the face of it eulogy becomes platitude; so for Godsake don't blame me if this sounds like the bleat of an antique reviewer, or a cold-cream ad. God knows, I weigh the words as well as I am able, but the damn book has rocked the scales like a quake and muddled up all my normal weights and measures. I love its guts. I love to see the canons of oblique and pretty emotion mopped up; to see every whim-wham and baga-telle of your contemporaries from Eliot to Joyce dunged under. God give us young men the guts to plant the daisies on top and finish the job.

Tropic is something they've been trying to do since the war. It's the final copy of all those feeble, smudgy rough drafts—*Chatterley, Ulysses, Tarr* etc. It not only goes back, but (which none of them have done) goes forward as well.

It finds the way out of the latrines at last. Funny that no one should have thought of slipping out via the pan during a flush, instead of crowding the door. I salute *Tropic* as the copy-book for my generation. It's man-size, and goes straight up among those books (and they are precious few) which men have built out of their own guts. God save me, that sounds pompous, but what can one say?

Perish the Rahuists!* Skoal to the stanchless flux!

Yours Sincerely,
Lawrence Durrell

---

*Rahu, a tribal god in northern India, is supposed to become incarnate in priests who then walk on hot embers and cure diseases and barrenness. Perhaps Durrell sees them as hidebound traditionalists.

[Review of *Tropic of Cancer*]

Ezra Pound

The bawdy will welcome this bawdy book with guffaws of appreciation, but the harassed and over-serious critic (over-serious as measured by the reviewing trade) will be glad of deliverance from a difficult situation. For twenty years is has been necessary to praise Joyce and Wyndham Lewis (author of *The Apes of God*) not in an attempt to measure them, but in a desperate fight to impose their superiority, as against the ruck of third rate stuff tolerated through the era dominated by Wells, Shaw and the late cash-register Arnold Bennett. D. H. Lawrence held an intermediate position, that is, an almost solitary writer in the second category, *between* Joyce, Lewis, a few writers of high quality but not of very great dynamism, and the definitely THIRD rate authors welcomed by the trade, inventors of nothing, adapters and diluters of everything according to the demands of laziness, popular hang-over and the grossness of standards.

Non-agreement with the mob and snob, as Porson in the Imaginary Dialog remarked, being the reason for a critic's uttering an opinion at all.

Thirty years ago H. James, W. H. Hudson, Cunninghame Graham, F. Madox Ford maintained a literature which took count of a fairly full gamut of values. The slump toward the impoverishment of values, toward the cheapening of every mental activity whatsoever can be best illustrated by Mr. G. B. Shaw's Ersatz. When I say that Shaw is the best illustration I mean that other writers of the abasement were probably subject to enthusiasms and illusions, or got excited by their personal wants. Shaw would have defiled and cheapened Ibsen, Butler, Nietszche whether there had been any economic pressure or not.

Joyce and Lewis in 1913/14 surged up against the pauperization of letters, the two full bodied prose writers with any sort of amplitude and abundance. Lawrence was, to state it quite bluntly, very stupid. He had a magnificent gift for words, discovered by F. Madox Ford without whom Lawrence would have remained unknown for a decade. Lawrence's borders

*This review, published here for the first time, was probably written in 1935. See the Introduction to this volume.

Printed by permission of the Yale Collection of American Literature, Beinecke Rare Book and Manuscript Library, Yale University.

marched with these of his two greater contemporaries, but he was not their intellectual equal. There was need of critical insistence on up-jutting and out-jutting qualities of Joyce and W. Lewis, and until these were established at least in the mind of that limited public which possesses the organ, one could neglect the nuances.

The appearance of a full sized 300 page volume that can be set beside Joyce and Lewis gives one a chance and right to mention their limitations, and to be glad that all question of verbal licence can be left out of the estimate (for that also has been an impediment to criticism). Naturally no foreign nation will consider England adult with six books explaining a book (*Ulysses*) which is not admitted to England, though the baboon law has been emended in her uncouth ex-colony.

As against Joyce's kinks and Lewis's ill-humour we have at last a book of low life "incurably healthy." Bawdy the book is, and is so proclaimed by its publishers who probably would have been blind to its other dimensions. But if an obscene book is obscene because of any vileness in the author's mind, this book is certainly not obscene. It is a picaresque novel of life little above that depicted by Smollett; but the author adds nothing whatever to [the] odour of life as he has seen it, valet to a Hindoo in Paris, aide for a few hours to a Russian emigre engaged in delivering disinfectants, assistant to a "photographer," but all from human necessity, not a searcher for low life, but plunged into it by the destiny of our epoch, namely the monetary system. The milieu of La Cupole seen from somewhere near its nadir, but thereby limited, the circle of reference considerably wider than that of Joyce's foetid Dublin, or the much more special inferno of *The Apes*. Miller's Americans are very American, his orientals, very oriental and his Russians, oh quite so. The sense of the sphericality of the planet presides. The book takes shape with an excursion to Havre, sailor's bordello, and by perfect contrast to [the] Lycee in Dijon, the grim greyness whereof balances both the jincrawl and the lights of Paris.

For a hundred and fifty pages the reader not having started to think very hard, might suppose the book is amoral, its ethical discrimination seems about that of a healthy pup nosing succulent "poubelles," but that estimate can't really hold. Miller has, and has very strongly a hierarchy of values. And in the present chaos this question of hierarchy has become almost as important as having values at all.

The return toward (I say toward, not to) catholicism is imposed by the grossness of the protestant value-scale. To choose between good and evil will never be unimportant, but the penal scale is a necessity only secondary to the main division. The degree of responsibility varies, and no moral scheme is valid which does not sort out the venal from the deadly.

Miller's sense of good and evil is probably sounder than that of either Joyce or Lewis. La chair est triste? Perhaps, but not till it begins to give way to wear and tear. The lack of Dantescan top floors is, I admit, apparent in certain chapters, but the gamut of values goes up at least to the finest burst of praise and appreciation of Matisse, and a better evaluation of Matisse's particular gift, than I have found anywhere else. Throughout the whole book there is an undercurrent of comfort in Miller's eminent fairness. He paints in honest colours life of the cafe international strata as seen by a man with no money, whose chief preoccupation is FOOD, with a capital F and all the other letters in majuscule.

Twilight of the Expatriates

EDMUND WILSON

The *Tropic of Cancer*, by Henry Miller, was published in Paris four years ago, but nobody, so far as I know, has ever reviewed it in the United States, and it seems to me to deserve some notice.

Every phase of literary opinion is responsible for its critical injustices. During the twenties, this book would have been discussed in the *Little Review*, the *Dial* and *Broom*. Today the conventional critics are evidently too much shocked by it to be able to bring themselves to deal with it—though their neglect of it cannot wholly have been determined by the reflex reactions of squeamishness. A book bound in paper and published in Paris has no chance against a book bound in cloth and brought out by a New York publisher, who will buy space to announce its appearance. The conservative literary reviews have not been so easily outraged that they would not give respectful attention to John O'Hara's *Butterfield 8* or squander space on the inferior Hemingway of *To Have and Have Not*. As for the Left-Wingers, they have ignored *The Tropic of Cancer* on the ground that it is merely a product of the decadent expatriate culture and can be of no interest to the socially minded and forward-looking present.

Expatriate Mr. Miller certainly is: he is the spokesman, par excellence, for the Left Bank; but he has produced the most remarkable book which, as far as my reading goes, has come from it in many years. *The Tropic of Cancer* is a good piece of writing; and it has also a sort of historical importance. It is the epitaph for the whole generation of American writers and artists that migrated to Paris after the war. The theme of *The Tropic of Cancer* is the lives of a group of Americans who have all more or less come to Paris with the intention of occupying themselves with literature but who have actually subsided easily into an existence almost exclusively preoccupied with drinking and fornication, varied occasionally by the reading of a book or a visit to a picture exhibition—an existence for which they muster the resources by such expedients as pimping for travellers, playing gigolo to rich old ladies and sponging on one another. The tone of the book is undoubtedly low; *The*

Reprinted from *Shores of Light* (New York: Farrar, Straus and Giroux, 1952), 705–10. Copyright © 1952 by Edmund Wilson. Renewal copyright © 1980 by Helen Miranda Wilson. Reprinted by permission of Farrar, Straus and Giroux, Inc. By permission of Random Century Ltd. on behalf of Edmund Wilson and Chatto and Windus, publishers.

Tropic of Cancer, in fact, from the point of view both of its happenings and of the language in which they are conveyed, is the lowest book of any real literary merit that I ever remember to have read; it makes Defoe's Newgate Calendar look like Plutarch. But if you can stand it, it is sometimes quite funny; for Mr. Miller has discovered and exploits a new field of the picaresque.

The disreputable adventures of Mr. Miller's rogues are varied from time to time with phosphorescent flights of reverie devoted to the ecstasies of art or the doom of European civilization. These passages, though old-fashioned and rhetorical in a vein of late romantic fantasy reminiscent of *Les Chants de Maldoror*, have a youthful and even ingenuous sound in queer contrast to the cynicism of the story. And there is a strange amenity of temper and style which bathes the whole composition even when it is disgusting or tiresome. It has frequently been characteristic of the American writers in Paris that they have treated pretentious subjects with incompetent style and sordid feeling. Mr. Miller has done the opposite: he has treated an ignoble subject with a sure hand at color and rhythm. He is not self-conscious and not amateurish. And he has somehow managed to be low without being really sordid.

The last episode of *The Tropic of Cancer* has a deadly ironic value. A friend of the narrator called Fillmore, who is unique among these cadgers and spongers in enjoying a small regular income, becomes entangled in an affair with a French girl, who is pregnant and declares him responsible. Poor Fillmore first drinks himself into an insane asylum; then, emerging, falls straight into the clutches of the girl and her peasant family. They reduce him to utter abjection: he is to marry her, set her father up in business. The girl quarrels with him every night over dinner. The narrator suggests to Fillmore that he run away and go back home. For the latter, the glamor is all off Paris: he has been up against the French as they really are (in general these émigrés see nobody but one another); he realizes at last that the French regard Americans as romantic idiots; and he is weepily homesick for America. He allows himself to be sent off on a train, leaving the narrator a sum of money to provide for the girl's accouchement.

But as soon as Fillmore is gone, the helpful hero, left to himself, with the money for the girl in his pocket, decides that good old Paris, after all, is a wonderful place to be. "Certainly never before," he thinks, "had I had so much in my fist at one time. It was a treat to break a thousand-franc note. I held it up to the light to look at the beautiful watermark. Beautiful money! One of the few things the French make on a grand scale. Artistically done, too, as if they cherished a deep affection even for the symbol." Ginette need never know about it; and, after all, suppose her pregnancy was all a bluff. He goes for a drive in the Bois. Does he want to take the money, he asks himself, and return to America too? It is the first opportunity he has had. No: a great peace comes over him now. He knows that for half an hour he has money to throw away. He buys himself an excellent dinner and muses on the Seine in the setting sun. He feels it flowing quietly through him: "its past, its ancient soil, the changing climate." It is only when they are looked at close-to that human beings repel one by their ugliness; they become negligible when one can put them at a distance. A deep feeling of well-being fills him.

In retelling this incident from *The Tropic of Cancer*, have I made it more comic than it is meant to be? Perhaps: because Mr. Miller evidently attaches some importance to the vaporings of his hero on the banks of the Seine. But he presents him as he really lives, and not merely in his vaporings or his poses. He gives us the genuine American bum come to lead the beautiful life in Paris; and he lays him away forever in his dope of Pernod and dreams.

March 9, 1938

Mr. Miller, in reply to this review, wrote the *New Republic* the following letter, which appeared in the issue of May 18. I regret that I am unable to restore a passage cut by the editors.

Sir: There are several inaccuracies in Mr. Wilson's review of *Tropic of Cancer* . . .

First of all, I should like it to be known that the book has been reviewed before, by Professor Herbert West. It has been mentioned numerous times in a sensational manner by so-called reputable magazines in America. . . . The theme of the book, moreover, is not at all what Mr. Wilson describes: the theme is myself, and the narrator, or the hero, as your critic puts it, is also myself. I am not clear whether, in the last paragraph of his review, Mr. Wilson meant to imply that Fillmore is the genuine American bum, or myself. If he means the narrator, then it is me, because I have painstakingly indicated throughout the book that the hero is myself. I don't use "heroes," incidentally, nor do I write novels. I am the hero, and the book is myself. . . .

Perhaps the worst mistake which the eminent critic makes in his review is to say that because a book is bound in paper and published in Paris, it has no chance against a book bound in cloth and sold in New York. This is the very contrary of the truth. Without any hocus-pocus of the American publicity agents, almost entirely by word-of-mouth recommendations, *Tropic of Cancer* has already gone into several editions at a price which for Europe is prohibitive. It is now being translated into three languages. It may be procured at leading bookstores in practically every important city of the world excepting those of America, England, Germany and Russia. It has been reviewed enthusiastically by some of the foremost critics of Europe. If it has not yet brought me riches, it has at any rate brought me fame and recognition. And, whether it is given notice by American reviewers or not, Americans coming to Europe buy it, as they once bought *Ulysses* and *Lady Chatterley's Lover*.

A conspiracy of silence, like censorship, can defeat its own ends. Sometimes it pays *not* to advertise. Sometimes the most effective, realistic thing to do is to be impractical, to fly in the face of the wind. The Obelisk Press took my book on faith, against all commercial wisdom. The results have been gratifying in every way. I should like to add that the Obelisk Press will publish any book of quality which the ordinary commercial publisher refuses, for one reason or another, to handle. Any writer with guts who is unable to get a hearing in America might do well to look to Paris. And damn all the critics anyway! The best publicity for a man who has anything to say is silence.

Henry Miller

Paris, France

The Reality of Henry Miller

KENNETH REXROTH

It is a wonderful thing that some of Henry Miller's work at last is coming out in a popular edition in the United States. Henry Miller is a really popular writer, a writer of and for real people, who, in other countries, is read, not just by highbrows, or just by the wider public which reads novels, but by common people, by the people who, in the United States, read comic books. As the Southern mountain woman said of her hero son, dead in Korea, "Mister, he was sure a great reader, always settin' in the corner with a piece of cold bread and one of them funny books." In Czech and Japanese, this is the bulk of Miller's public. In the United States he has been kept away from a popular public and his great novels have been banned; therefore only highbrows who could import them from France have read him.

I once crossed the Atlantic—eighteen days in a Compagnie Générale Transatlantique freighter—with a cabin mate, a French African Negro, who was only partially literate, but who was able to talk for hours on the comparative merits of *Black Spring* and the *Tropic of Cancer* and the *Tropic of Capricorn*. When he found out I came from California and knew Miller, he started treating me as if I were an archangel newly descended, and never tired of questions about *le Beeg Sur* and *les camarades de M'sieu Millaire*. He had a mental picture of poor Henry living on a mountaintop, surrounded by devoted handmaids and a bevy of zoot-suited existentialist jitterbugs.

This picture, I have discovered, is quite commonly believed in by people who should have better sense. Miners in the Pyrenees, camel drivers in Tlemcen, gondoliers in Venice, and certainly every *poule* in Paris, when they hear you're from California, ask, first thing, in one voice, "Do you know M'sieu Millaire?" This doesn't mean he isn't read by the intellectuals, the cultured people over there. He is. In fact, I should say he has become part of the standard repertory of reading matter everywhere but in England and the United States. If you have read Balzac, or Baudelaire, or Goethe, you are also expected to have read Miller. He is certainly one of the most widely read American writers, along with Upton Sinclair, Jack London, Fenimore Cooper, William Faulkner and Erskine Caldwell.

Reprinted from *World Outside the Window* (New York: New Directions, 1947), 154–67. Copyright 1947 by New Directions Publishing corporation. Reprinted by permission of New Directions Publishing Corporation.

This is the way it should be. Nothing was sadder than the "proletarian novelist" of a few years back, the product of a sociology course and a subscription to a butcher-paper weekly, eked out with a terrified visit to a beer parlor on the other side of the tracks and a hasty scurry past a picket line. Nobody read him but other Greenwich Village aesthetes like himself. The people Henry Miller writes about read him. They read him because he gives them something they cannot find elsewhere in print. It may not be precisely the real world, but it is nearer to it than most other writing, and it is certainly nearer than most so-called realistic writing.

Once the written word was the privilege of priests and priestly scribes. Although thousands of years have passed, vestiges of that special privilege and caste artificiality still cling to it. It has been said that literature is a class phenomenon. Can you remember when you first started to read? Doubtless you thought that some day you would find in books the truth, the answer to the very puzzling life you were discovering around you. But you never did. If you were alert, you discovered that books were conventions, as unlike life as a game of chess. The written word is a sieve. Only so much of reality gets through as fits the size and shape of the screen, and in some ways that is never enough. This is only partly due to the necessary conventions of speech, writing, communication generally. Partly it is due to the structure of language. With us, in our Western European civilization, this takes the form of Indo-European grammar crystallized in what we call Aristotelian logic. But most of the real difficulty of communication comes from social convention, from a vast conspiracy to agree to accept the world as something it really isn't at all. Even the realistic novels of a writer like Zola are not much closer to the real thing than the documents written in Egyptian hieroglyphics. They are just a different, most complex distortion.

Literature is a social defense mechanism. Remember again when you were a child. You thought that some day you would grow up and find a world of real adults—the people who really made things run—and understood how and why things ran. People like the Martian aristocrats in science fiction. Your father and mother were pretty silly, and the other grownups were even worse—but somewhere, some day, you'd find the real grownups and possibly even be admitted to their ranks. Then, as the years went on, you learned, through more or less bitter experience, that there aren't and never have been, any such people, anywhere. Life is just a mess, full of tall children, grown stupider, less alert and resilient, and nobody knows what makes it go—as a whole, or any part of it. *But nobody ever tells.*

Henry Miller tells. Andersen told *about* the little boy and the Emperor's new clothes. Miller is the little boy himself. He tells about the Emperor, about the pimples on his behind, and the warts on his private parts, and the dirt between his toes. Other writers in the past have done this, of course, and they are the great ones, the real classics. But they have done it within the conventions of literature. They have used the forms of the Great Lie to expose the truth. Some of this literature is comic, with a terrifying laughter—Cervantes' *Don Quixote*, Jonson's *Volpone*, Machiavelli's *Mandragola*, Shakespeare's *King Lear*. Some of it is tragic, in the ordinary sense, like the *Iliad*, or Thucydides' history, or *Macbeth*. In the last analysis it is all tragic, even Rabelais, because life itself is tragic. With very few exceptions, however, it is all conventional. It disguises itself in the garments of harmless artistic literature. It sneaks in and betrays the complacent and deluded. A great work of art is a kind of Trojan Horse. There are those who believe that this is all there is to the art of poetry—sugar-coating the pills of prussic acid with which the poet doses the Enemy.

It is hard to tell sometimes when Miller is being ironic and when he is being naïve. He is the master of a deadpan style, just as he has a public personality that alternates between quiet gentleness—"like a dentist," he describes it—and a sort of deadpan buffoonery. This has led some critics to consider him a naïve writer, a "modern primitive," like the painter Rousseau. In a sense this is true.

Miller is a very unliterary writer. He writes as if he had just invented the alphabet. When he writes about a book, he writes as if he were the first and only man who had ever read it—and, furthermore, as if it weren't a book but a piece of the living meat whacked off Balzac or Rimbaud or whoever. Rousseau was one of the finest painters of modern times. But he was absolutely impervious to the ordinary devices of his craft. This was not because he was not exposed to other artists. He spent hours every week in the Louvre, and he was, from the 1880s to the eve of the First World War, the intimate of all the best painters and writers, the leading intellectuals of Paris. It didn't make any difference. He just went his way, being Henri Rousseau, a very great artist. But when he talked or wrote, he spouted terrible nonsense. He wasn't just a crank, but quite off his rocker in an amiable sort of way. This is not true of Miller.

In some mysterious way, Miller has preserved an innocence of the practice of Literature-with-a-capital-L which is almost unique in history. Likewise he has preserved an innocence of heart. But he is not unsophisticated. In the first place, he writes a muscular, active prose in which something is always going on and which is always under control. True, he often rambles and gets windy, but only because he likes to ramble and hear his head roar. When he wants to tell you something straight from the shoulder, he makes you reel.

Now the writer most like Miller in some ways, the eighteenth-century naïf, Restif de la Bretonne, is certainly direct from the innocent heart, but he can be as tedious as a year's mail of a Lonely Hearts Club, with the same terrible verisimilitude of a "Mature woman, broadminded, likes books and music" writing to "Bachelor, fifty-two, steady job, interested in finer things." And, in addition, Restif is full of arrant nonsense, every variety of crackpot notion. If you want the common man of the eighteenth century, with his heart laid bare, you will find him in Restif. But you will also find thousands of pages of sheer boredom, and hundreds of pages of quite loony and obviously invented pornography. Miller too is likely at times to go off the deep end about the lost continent of Mu or astrology or the "occult," but it is for a different reason. If the whole shebang is a lie anyway, certainly the amusing lies, the lies of the charlatans who have never been able to get the guillotine in their hands, are better than the official lie, the deadly one. Since Hiroshima, this attitude needs little apology. Some of our best people prefer alchemy to physics today.

There aren't many people like Miller in all literature. The only ones I can think of are Petronius, Casanova, and Restif. They all tried to be absolutely honest. Their books give an overwhelming feeling of being true, the real thing, completely uncooked. They are all intensely masculine writers. They are all great comic writers. They all convey, in every case very powerfully, a constant sense of the utter tragedy of life. I can think of no more chilling, scalp-raising passages in literature than the tolling of the bell from the very beginning of Casanova's *Memoirs*: the comments and asides of the aged man writing of his splendid youth, an old, sick, friendless pauper in a drafty castle in the backwoods of Bohemia. And last, and most important, they were all what the English call "spivs." Courtier of Nero or Parisian typesetter, they were absolutely uninvolved; they just didn't give a damn whether school kept or not.

The French like to compare Miller with Sade. But nowadays they like to compare everybody with Sade. It is the currently fashionable form of Babbitt-baiting over there. The comparison is frivolous. Sade is unbelievably tedious; Diderot stood on his head, a bigot without power, an unemployed Robespierre. In the eighteenth century the French writers most like Miller are the "primitive" Restif, and Mirabeau when, in some of his personal writings, he really works up a lather.

Miller has often been compared with Céline, but I don't think the comparison is apposite. Céline is a man with a thesis; furthermore, he is a litterateur. In *Journey to the End of the Night*, he set out to write the epic of a Robinson Crusoe of the modern soul, the utterly alienated man. He did it, very successfully. Céline and his friends stumble through the fog, over the muddy ruts with the body of Robinson, in a denouement as monumental as the *Nibelungenlied*. But it is all a work of art. I have been in the neighborhoods Céline describes. They simply aren't that awful. I am sure, on internal evidence of the story itself, that his family wasn't that bad. And, like Malraux and some others, he is obsessed with certain marginal sexual activities which he drags in all the time, willy-nilly.

Céline makes a sociological judgment on Robinson. Miller is Robinson, and, on the whole, he finds it a bearable role, even enjoyable in its way. The modern French writers who most resemble Miller are Carco, without the formulas, Mac Orlan, if he weren't so slick, Artaud, if he weren't crazy, and Blaise Cendrars. Cendrars is a good European and Miller is only an amateur European, but Europe has been going on so long that the insights of the amateur are often much more enlightening.

Henry Miller is often spoken of as a religious writer. To some this just seems silly, because Miller is not especially profound. People expect religion to come to them vested in miracle, mystery, and authority, as Dostoevski said. The founders of the major religions are pretty well hidden from us by the accumulation of centuries of interpretation, the dirt of history—the lie you prefer to believe. Perhaps originally they weren't so mysterious and miraculous and authoritarian. Mohammed lived in the light of history. We can form a pretty close idea of what he was like, and he wasn't very prepossessing in some ways. He was just naïvely direct. With the simple-mindedness of a camel driver he cut through the welter of metaphysics and mystification in the Near East of his time. Blake dressed his message up in sonorous and mysterious language; but the message itself is simple enough. D. H. Lawrence likewise. You could write it all on a postage stamp: "Mene, mene, tekel, upharsin. Your official reality is a lie. We must love one another or die." I suppose any writer who transcends conventional literature is religious insofar as he does transcend it. That is why you can never actually base an educational system on the "Hundred Best Books." A hundred of the truest insights into life as it is would destroy any educational system and its society along with it.

Certainly Miller is almost completely untouched by what is called religion in England and America and northern Europe. He is completely pagan. This is why his book on Greece, *The Colossus of Maroussi*, is a book of self-discovery as well as a very true interpretation of Greece. It is thoroughly classic. Although he never mentions Homer and dismisses the Parthenon, he did discover the life of Greece: the common, real life of peasants and fishermen, going on, just as it has gone on ever since the Doric invasions. A world of uncompromised people, of people if not like Miller himself, at least like the man he knew he wanted to be.

His absolute freedom from the Christian or Jewish anguish of conscience, the sense of guilt, implication, and compromise, makes Miller humane, maybe even humanistic, but it effectively keeps him from being humanitarian. He might cry over a pet dog who had been run over, or even punch the guilty driver in the nose. He might have assassinated Hitler if he had had the chance. He would never join the Society for the Prevention of Cruelty to Animals or the Friends' Service Committee. He is not involved in the guilt, and so in no way is he involved in the penance. This comes out in everything he writes, and it offends lots of people. Others may go to bullfights and write novels preaching the brotherhood of man. Miller just doesn't go to the bullfight in the first place. So, although he often raves, he never preaches. People have been taught to expect preaching, practically unadulterated, in even the slick fiction of the women's magazines, and they are offended now if they don't find it.

Fifty per cent of the people in this country don't vote. They simply don't want to be implicated in organized society. With, in most cases, a kind of animal instinct, they know that they cannot really do anything about it, that the participation offered them is a hoax. And even if it weren't, they know that if they don't participate, they aren't implicated, at least not voluntarily. It is for these people, the submerged fifty percent, that Miller speaks. As the newspapers never tire of pointing out, this is a very American attitude. Miller says, "I am a patriot—of the Fourteenth Ward of Brooklyn, where I was raised." For him life has never lost that simplicity and immediacy. Politics is the deal in the saloon back room. Law is the cop on the beat, shaking down whores and helping himself to apples. Religion is Father Maguire and Rabbi Goldstein, and their actual congregations. Civilization is the Telegraph Company in *Tropic of Capricorn*. All this is a quite different story to the art critics and the literary critics and those strange people the newspapers call "pundits" and "solons."

I am sure the editors of our butcher-paper liberal magazines have never sat in the back room of a sawdust saloon and listened to the politicians divide up the take from the brothels that line the boundary streets of their wards. If they did, they would be outraged and want to bring pressure to bear in the State Capitol. With Miller, that is just the way things are, and what of it?

So there isn't any social message in Miller, except an absolute one. When you get through reading the realistic novels of James Farrell or Nelson Algren, you have a nasty suspicion that the message of the author is: "More playgrounds and properly guided social activities will reduce crime and vice." There is nothing especially frightful about Miller's Brooklyn; like Farrell's South Side, it is just life in the lower middle class and upper working class section of a big American city. It certainly isn't what queasy reviewers call it, "the slums." It's just the life the reviewers themselves led before they became reviewers. What outrages them is that Miller accepts it, just as do the people who still live there. Accepting it, how he can write about it? He can bring back the whole pre-World War I America—the bunny hug, tunes from *The Pink Lady*, Battling Nelson, Dempsey the Nonpareil, Pop Anson and Pearl White, a little boy rushing the growler with a bucket of suds and a sack of six-inch pretzels in the smoky twilight of a Brooklyn Sunday evening.

I think that is what Miller found in Paris. Not the city of Art, Letters, and Fashion—but prewar Brooklyn. It is certainly what I like best about Paris, and it is what I get out of Miller's writing about Paris. He is best about Paris where it is still most like 1910 Brooklyn. He doesn't write about the Latin Quarter, but about the dim-lit streets and dusty little squares which lie between the Latin Quarter and the Jardin des Plantes, where men sit drinking beer in their shirt sleeves in front of dirty little bars in another smoky Sunday twilight. He is better about the jumble of streets between Montrouge and Montparnasse with its polyglot and polychrome population of the very poor than he is about Montparnasse itself and its artists' life. He practically ignores Montmartre; apparently he concludes that only suckers go there. But he writes very convincingly about that most Brooklyn-like of all the quarters of Paris, the district near the Military Academy on the Place du Champs de Mars, now filling up with Algerians and Negroes, where the subway becomes an elevated, tall tenements mingle with small bankrupt factories and people sit on the doorsteps fanning themselves in the Brooklyn-like summer heat, and sleep and couple on the summer roofs.

So his intellectuals in Paris are assimilated to Brooklyn. They may talk about Nietzsche and Dostoevski, but they talk like hall-room boys, rooming together, working at odd jobs, picking up girls in dance halls and parks. "Batching" is the word. Over the most impassioned arguments and the bawdiest conversations lingers an odor of unwashed socks. The light is the light of Welsbach mantles on detachable cuffs and unmade beds. Of course that is the way they really talked, still do for that matter.

There is a rank, old-fashioned masculinity about this world which shocks the tender-minded and self-deluded. It is far removed from the Momism of the contemporary young American male. This is why Miller is accused of writing about all women as though they were whores, never treating them as "real persons," as equals. This is why he is said to lack any sense of familial love. On the whole, I think this is true. Most of the sexual encounters in the *Tropics* and *The Rosy Crucifixion* are comic accidents, as impersonal as a pratfall. The woman never emerges at all. He characteristically writes of his wives as bad boys talk of their schoolteachers. When he takes his sexual relations seriously, the woman disappears in a sort of marshy cyclone. She becomes an erotic giantess, a perambulating orgy. Although Miller writes a lot about his kinship with D. H. Lawrence, he has very little of Lawrence's abiding sense of the erotic couple, of man and woman as the two equal parts of a polarity which takes up all of life. This again is Brooklyn, pre-suffragette Brooklyn. And I must admit that it is true, at least for almost everybody. A real wedding of equals, a truly sacramental marriage in which every bit of both personalities, and all the world with them, is transmuted and glorified, may exist; in fact, some people may have a sort of talent for it; but it certainly isn't very common. And the Great Lie, the social hoax in which we live, has taken the vision of this transcendent state and turned it into its cheapest hoax and its most powerful lie. I don't see why Miller should be blamed if he has never found it. Hardly anybody ever does, and those who do usually lose it in some sordid fashion. This, of course, is the point, the message, if you want a message, of all his encounters in parks and telephone booths and brothels. Better this than the lie. Better the flesh than the World and the

Devil. And this is why these passages are not pornographic, but comic like *King Lear* and tragic like *Don Quixote*.

At least once, Miller makes up for this lack. The tale of the *Cosmodemonic Telegraph Company* in *Tropic of Capricorn* is a perfect portrait of our insane and evil society. It says the same thing others have said, writing on primitive accumulation or on the condition of the working class, and it says if far more convincingly. This is human self-alienation at its uttermost, and not just theoretically, or even realistically. It is an orgy of human self-alienation, a cesspool of it, and Miller rubs your nose in it. Unless you are a prig and a rascal, when you get through, you know, once and for all, what is the matter. And through it all, like Beatrice, if Beatrice had guided Dante through the Inferno, moves the figure of Valeska, who had Negro blood and who kills herself at the end—one of the most real women in fiction, if you want to call it fiction.

Once Miller used to have pinned on his bedroom door a scrap of paper. Written on it was "S'agapo"—the Greek for "I love you." In *The Alcoholic Veteran* he says, "The human heart cannot be broken."

Henry Miller: Down and Out in Paris

George Wickes

On March 4, 1930, a slight, bald middle-aged American arrived in Paris. Mild-mannered and bespectacled, he had the air of a college professor. Café waiters often took him for a German or a Scandinavian. "I lack that carefree, audacious air of the average American," he wrote in a letter at the time. "Even the Americans ignore me. They talk English at my elbow with that freedom which one employs only when he is certain his neighbor does not understand." Like so many Americans during the previous decade he had come to write, but his circumstances were altogether different. They came mostly from families which could afford to support their idleness. They usually sowed a very small crop of unpublishable literary oats and indulged in mild libertinage with their own kind along the Boulevard Montparnasse: got drunk in the American cafés for a season or two, mastered a few dozen French clichés, read a little, wrote a little, then went home to bourgeois respectability. They were the university wits of their day, following the pleasant fashion of their class, but their creative impulses were largely wishful and soon dissipated.

Henry Miller came from another world. An outcast from the lower middle class, a dropout after two months of college twenty years before, an outsider in his native land, he had worked at a succession of odd jobs and seen more of life than most men. He had no desire to associate with his compatriots in Montparnasse when he first arrived, referring to them scornfully as "the insufferable idiots at the Dôme and the Coupole." And this was more than the usual reflex of the American abroad, to whom all other Americans were a source of embarrassment. Miller had a deep-seated hatred of all things American. For him the United States represented "the air-conditioned nightmare" of technology without a soul. He had come to Europe to get away from America and to find a way of life that would answer to his psychic needs. Like most Montparnasse Americans he was a sentimental expatriate. Unlike them he found what he wanted and succeeded as a writer.

Miller had been to London and was on his way to Madrid, according to his later accounts, when he ran out of money. But the letters he wrote at

Reprinted from *American in Paris* (Garden City, New York: Doubleday, 1969), 239–76. Reprinted courtesy of DeCapo Press.

the time reveal no intention to travel any farther. On his first Sunday in Paris he wondered, "Will I ever get to really understand the true spirit of this people?"—not a question asked by the casual transient. A few weeks later he wrote, "I love it here, I want to stay forever." Paris was the destination toward which he had been moving for years, ever since his friend Emil Schnellock had described it to him. Schnellock, whom Miller had known as a schoolboy, had lived abroad and become a painter. To Miller it was incredible that his friend, "just a Brooklyn boy" like himself, should have been magically transformed into an artist and cosmopolite. No doubt his example more than anything else affected Miller's decision to become a writer at all costs. Years later in *Tropic of Capricorn* Miller was to write: "Even now, years and years since, even now, when I know Paris like a book, his picture of Paris is still before my eyes, still vivid, still real. Sometimes, after a rain, riding swiftly through the city in a taxi, I catch fleeting glimpses of this Paris he described; just momentary snatches, as in passing the Tuileries, perhaps, or a glimpse of Montmartre, of the Sacré Coeur, through the Rue Laffitte, in the last flush of twilight. . . . Those nights in Prospect Park with my old friend Ulric are responsible, more than anything else, for my being here today."

Miller's wife June also played a crucial role. As Mona or Mara she appears in *Tropic of Capricorn* and other autobiographical romances, an enigmatic figure who entered his life in the early twenties, a Broadway taxi dancer with literary aspirations. Their love was often tempestuous, but through it all she was determined that he would become a writer. She persuaded him to quit his job at Western Union, she worked so that he could write, she found patrons for his work among her admirers by passing herself off as the author. Thus she raised money for a trip to Europe, convinced that he would be able to write there. They went together in 1928, but only on a tour. In 1930 she found the money to send him alone, intending to join him when she had more. As she knew better than Miller, he had reached a dead end in New York.

In one of his first letters from Paris in 1930 he voiced his deep sense of frustration: "I can't understand my failure. . . . Why does nobody want what I write? Jesus, when I think of being 38, and poor, and unknown, I get furious." By the time he landed in Paris he had been writing for eight years. He had completed four books and countless stories and articles. Only three articles had ever been published. Discouraged by poverty, debts, and the fact that his wife had to work so that he could lead "the true life of the artist," he still yearned for the comforts of bourgeois life. These contradictory feelings of guilt and self-pity, the compulsion to succeed and the interpretation of success as money, were all neuroses of Protestant America, with its gospel of work and wealth. In Paris Miller was never troubled by such worries. Though he lived more parasitically and marginally than ever, he was psychologically liberated as he had never been in New York. Hence the euphoric mood that marks all his writing during the decade he spent in Paris. There at last he was able to write, on the first page of *Tropic of Cancer*: "I have no money, no resources, no hopes. I am the happiest man alive. A year ago, six months ago, I thought that I was an artist. I no longer think about it, I *am*."

Miller's first impressions of Paris—and the most reliable account of his first eighteen months there—are to be found in the letters he wrote to Emil Schnellock at the time. His first letter, written three days after his arrival, announces: "I will write here. I will live quietly and quite alone. And each day I will see a little more of Paris, study it, learn it as I would a book. It is worth the effort. To know Paris is to know a great deal. How vastly different from New York! What eloquent surprises at every turn of the street. To get lost here is the adventure extraordinary. The streets sing, the stones talk. The houses drip history, glory, romance." From the start he liked everything about the city, its cosmopolitan atmosphere, the variety of people, their nonconformity. "Here is the greatest congregation of bizarre types. People do dress as they please, wear beards if they like, and shave if they choose. You don't feel that lifeless pressure of dull regimentation as in N. Y. and London."

The letters written within a month of his arrival are full of wonder and delight. Everything is new and charming, the language, the way of counting, the procedure in the restaurants, the tipping. The police are allowed to smoke on duty. Gourmet meals are cheap. The writing in the newspapers and magazines is intelligent and sophisticated. Miller was prepared to see good in everything, from the fifty thousand artists of Paris selling their work to an appreciative public to the custodian in the underground toilet writing a love letter, happy with her lot, unlike the silly stenographer in a New York skyscraper. As on his previous visit he was overcome by the setting, particularly at night. "I am on the verge of tears. The beauty of it all is suffocating me. . . . I am fairly intoxicated with the glamour of the city." His second letter, sixteen pages long, describes that emotion peculiar to the place, *la nostalgie de Paris*, nostalgia that can be experienced at the moment itself.

At the same time Paris gave him an inexhaustible supply of material and the urge to write. Within three weeks of his arrival he reported, "I have added a hundred pages to my book and done excellent revision work also. No water colors. I am overwhelmed yet by the multifarious, quotidien, anonymous, communal, etc. etc. *life*!" The program announced in his first letter of exploring the city and writing about it was carried out in a number of long letters written during his first two months or so. Actually these were not letters at all, but feature articles for circulation to magazine editors and for eventual use in a book on Paris Miller planned to write. Bearing such titles as "Spring on the Trottoirs" and "With the Wine Merchants," they usually described itineraries in quest of local color.

Paris was always a great city for walkers, and Miller was one of its most tireless pedestrians, covering enormous distances in his search for the picturesque. The paintings he had seen colored his vision so that wherever he went he found scenes from Monet, Pissarro, Seurat. In painting even more than literature Paris has always drawn its lovers back toward the past. Miller was particularly susceptible to this nostalgia for a city he had never known, regretting that he had been born too late. Many years later, in *Big Sur and the Oranges of Hieronymus Bosch*, he was still wishing he had been there as a young man: "What would I not give to have been the comrade or bosom friend of such figures as Apollinaire, Douanier Rousseau, George Moore, Max Jacob, Vlaminck, Utrillo, Derain, Cendrars, Gauguin, Modigliani, Cingria, Picabia, Maurice Magre, Léon Daudet, and such like. How much greater would have been the thrill to cycle along the Seine, cross and recross her bridges, race through towns like Bougival, Châtou, Argenteuil, Marly-le-roi, Puteaux, Rambouillet, Issy-les-Moulineaux and similar environs circa 1910 rather than the year 1932 or 1933!" Actually the world he yearned for was older than 1910; it was the impressionists' Arcadia painted in that string of sparkling villages along the Seine before they were industrialized into grimy suburbs.

Although somewhat self-conscious as literary compositions, the Paris letters marked an important stage in Miller's writing. They were good exercises, and they provided him with plenty of material that he was soon to use in his own way. Miller thought he was writing a book on Paris to match Paul Morand's slick guided tour of New York, which he had been reading with considerable envy at its success. He hoped his impressions might amount to "something popular, saleable, palatable." Unwittingly he was already at work on *Tropic of Cancer*. The letters contain the earliest writing that was to go into that book. One of them in particular, entitled "Bistre and Pigeon Dung," contains several passages that Miller saved and later wove into the fabric of his book. Here is one that reappears on one of the opening pages of *Tropic of Cancer*, only slightly revised:

Twilight hour, Indian blue, water of glass, trees glistening and liquescent. Juares station itself gives me a kick. The rails fall away into the canal, the long caterpillar with sides lacquered in Chinese red dips like a roller-coaster. It is not Paris, it is not Coney Island—it is crepuscular melange of all the cities of Europe and Central America. Railroad yards spread out below me, the tracks looking black, webby, not ordered by engineers but cataclysmic in design, like those gaunt fissures in the Polar ice which the camera registers in degrees of black.

Another passage in the same letter describes a nude by Dufresne with "all the secondary characteristics and a few of the primary," likening it to a thirteenth-century *déjeuner intime*, a vibrant still life, the table so heavy with food that it is sliding out of its frame—exactly as it appears at the beginning of the second chapter of *Tropic of Cancer*. Still another passage describes the animated street market in the rue de Buci on a Sunday morning, then moves on to the quiet Square de Furstenberg nearby, providing a page at the beginning of the third chapter of the book. Here is Miller's original description of the Square de Furstenberg, a spot that particularly appealed to him:

> A deserted spot, bleak, spectral at night, containing in the center four black trees which have not yet begun to blossom. These four bare trees have the poetry of T. S. Eliot. They are intellectual trees, nourished by the stones, swaying with a rhythm cerebral, the lines punctuated by dots and dashes, by asterisks and exclamation points. Here, if Marie Laurencin ever brought her Lesbians out into the open, would be the place for them to commune. It is very, very Lesbienne here, very sterile, hybrid, full of forbidden longings.

When he incorporated this passage into *Tropic of Cancer*, Miller revised for economy and sharpness of outline, but kept the imagery unchanged. The original, written in April 1930, shows his particular vision of the city; he had yet to discover how to use it.

"Bistre and Pigeon Dung" was probably rattled off in one day, like other fifteen-or twenty-page letters. Under the stimulation of Paris Miller was indefatigable: "I feel that I could turn out a book a month here. If I could get a stenographer to go to bed with me I could carry on twenty-four hours a day." Walking in the city was a creative act in itself. He was forever composing in his head as he walked, the writing as vivid to him as if he had put it down on paper. Sometimes he could not remember what he had actually written and had to ask Schnellock. His books of the thirties were all to be written in this state of exaltation, as he walked around Paris in the present tense.

Other letters anticipate *Tropic of Cancer* even more in spirit. Miller lost no time in getting acquainted with the most squalid sights. He had always been attracted to the ghetto and the slums; now he often painted the ugliest street scenes.

> I looked around and there stood a brazen wench, leaning against her door like a lazy slut, cigarette between her lips, sadly roughed and frizzled, old, seamed, scarred, cracked, evil greedy eyes. She jerked her head a few times inviting me to come back and inspect her place, but my eyes were set on a strange figure tugging away at some bales. An old man with enormous goitres completely circling his neck, standing out below the hairline like huge polyps, from under his chin hanging loosely, joggling, purplish, veined, like gourds of wine—transparent gourds. Here the breed is degenerate and diseased. Old

women with white hair, mangy, red lips, demented, prowl about in carpet slippers, their clothes in tatters, soiled with garbage and filth of the gutters.

This was Quasimodo's Paris, he pointed out, visible from the towers of Notre Dame, the inhabitants no different from those in the Middle Ages. But there was nothing romantic about the way he saw them. "They have bed-bugs, cockroaches and fleas running all over them, they are syphilitic, cancerous, dropsical, they are halt and blind, paralyzed, and their brains are soft."

Picturesque and sordid, this is Miller's Paris. Here even more than in the passages he actually used can *Tropic of Cancer* be anticipated. Again and again he dwelt with relish on the cancerous street scenes he found in the old quarters. He also explored the uglier regions of the modern industrial city, walking through endless dead stretches of suburb, bleak neighborhoods like those of his native Yorkville or Brooklyn. Paris provided local color of the particular kind that appealed to his imagination. Some six or seven weeks after his arrival he listed the topics he wanted to write about, including in addition to such standard items as the flea market, the six-day bicycle races, and the Grand Guignol, some that appealed to his rather special tastes: the slaughterhouses, the mummies at the Trocadéro, the Moslem cemetery, sexual perversions, the pissoirs, a comparative study of toilets on the Left Bank and toilets on the Right Bank. As this list suggests, Miller took particular delight in all that was unappetizing and macabre.

Miller's accounts of his first two months in Paris are full of enthusiasm. His feelings never changed, but the idyll soon ended. The troubles recorded in *Tropic of Cancer* were just beginning: the long walks to American Express for the check that never arrived, the constant change of address, the search for cheap hotels, soon followed by homelessness and hunger. He had arrived with enough money to last him till the middle of April and with expectations that his wife would send more. By the latter part of April his money had run out, and he had to go without food for five days. Then he received a small amount, not enough to last long, for in early May he was penniless again and desperate enough to think of looking for a job. A week later he was solvent again, quoting prices and urging Schnellock to come to Paris where he would show him how to live on less than twenty-five dollars a week. Miller's standards were still fairly grand.

As his circumstances grew progressively worse, his notions of poverty became more realistic. In August he was living with Monsieur Nanavati, the Hindu he calls Mr. Nonentity in *Tropic of Cancer*, and complaining of his lot as a servant: "Life is very hard for me—very. I live with bed-bugs and cockroaches. I sweep the dirty carpets, wash the dishes, eat stale bread without butter. Terrible life. Honest!" After that his friend Alfred Perlès took care of Miller off and on, sneaking him past his concierge and hiding him in his hotel room; Perlès worked at night, so Miller could sleep in his bed then.

He became well acquainted with hunger and vagrancy and discovered that the climate was miserable most of the year. October was rainy and cold. June came for a visit, but she brought no money and stayed only three weeks under wretched circumstances. Miller began to realize that he could not live on hopes indefinitely and resigned himself to leaving before long. Several letters mentioned plans to return to New York. But he managed to hang on till December, when he found a friend who took him in for the winter. Then his constant obsession was food: "What we artists need is food—and lots more of it. No art without food." Phagomania, his chronic complaint, is as prominent as lust in *Tropic of Cancer*.

He spent the winter months in a studio with a view of the Eiffel Tower. Ten years later he dedicated *The Wisdom of the Heart* to the man who took him in, Richard Galen Osborn, "who rescued me from starvation in Paris and set my feet in the right direction." Osborn was a Connecticut Yankee who worked in a bank by day and indulged his fondness for French culture in all its forms by night. He liked to talk with Miller about modern French writers, he liked to drink Anjou, and he had a weakness for the ladies. One day he added a third member of the household, the Russian princess who appears in *Tropic of Cancer* as Masha. The book presents a fairly faithful portrait of their absurd *ménage à trois* based on a letter Miller wrote to Schnellock at the time: "Irene has the clap, Osborn has bronchitis, and I have the piles." The letter records Irene's dialogue for four pages, later reproduced almost verbatim when the episode was expanded into half a chapter. Osborn wrote his own story about their life together, "No. 2 Rue Auguste Bartholdi," presenting the same basic circumstances from another point of view and rather unexpectedly portraying Miller as a man who worked all the time.

In the same letter Miller described the full beard he grew that winter, a shaggy, dark red beard that would soon make him look like Dostoevsky. According to *Tropic of Cancer*, he grew the beard at the request of a painter, who then did his portrait with his typewriter in the foreground and the Eiffel Tower in the background. The painter was John Nichols, a great talker who regaled Miller with anecdotes about the artists he knew and who accompanied him to that favorite resort of painters, the Cirque Médrano, where they had "a fine Seurat night." Miller, who always sought the company of painters, acquired many artist friends in Paris. When Osborn had to give up the studio, Miller went off to stay with a sculptor, Fred Kann, who lived near the Montparnasse cemetery.

Nichols' portrait had vanished along with the beard, but a verbal portrait survives from about the same period in an article that appeared in the Paris edition of the *Chicago Tribune* with a caricature of Miller by the Hungarian artist Brassaï. The writer was an American newspaperman with the unlikely name of Wambly Bald who wrote a weekly column called "*La Vie de Bohème*." What he had to say was not particularly memorable, except as evidence that Miller was already a notorious character who in his daily life enacted the role he was about to turn into literature. The role came to him naturally; he was simply acting himself as a *clochard*, a Paris bum. He was of course fully aware of the impression he created and capable of exploiting it. He could even have ghost-written the article himself, for he often wrote Bald's weekly column; and certainly the man who wrote *Tropic of Cancer* was not above self-portraiture. Miller returned the compliment by depicting Bald—probably without the least malice—as his most scabrous character.

After a year in Paris Miller calculated that he could live on six dollars a week, if only he had it, but actually he was living on nothing at all. How he managed is explained by Alfred Perlès in *My Friend Henry Miller*: "Henry was always to be seen at one or the other of the terraces, the Dôme or the Coupole, surrounded by people he had just met or was just meeting. Impossible to say how he picked them up and where and why." After his first few months in Paris Miller had overcome his prejudices against the Montparnasse cafés, finding them good places to cadge food and drink. He had a great talent for making friends, and as he explains in *Tropic of Cancer*, "It's not hard to make friends when you squat on a *terrasse* twelve hours a day. You get to know every sot in Montparnasse. They cling to you like lice, even if you have nothing to offer them but your ears." Eventually he worked out a rotating dinner schedule with his friends, dining with a different friend every evening of the week. Sometimes he performed small services in exchange, giving English lessons or walking a child in the Luxembourg Gardens. But usually his friends were only too willing to feed him for the pleasure of his company. He was a most ingratiating person, a spellbinding talker, and a man of completely unaffected charm. Perlès observed that people loved to watch him eat and drink.

Miller did not begin writing *Tropic of Cancer* until the end of August 1931, but everything he experienced during that first year and a half in Paris went into the book as substance or style, the world's rottenness or his crazy hallucinated vision of it, that particular combination of "cancer and delirium" which gives the book its own very special atmosphere. By the time he began writing the book he had thoroughly explored the lower depths. What he had seen and heard would have depressed any other man beyond words; Miller was fully alive to it but buoyed up by his sense of humor, and because he had gone to rock bottom himself, elated that he had survived, more alive than ever. Then at last he succeeded in writing what had been bottled up inside him for so many years.

Toward the end of his first year in Paris he took stock of himself and his writing. To Schnellock he reported the opinions of friends who urged him to stay on: "I'm supposed to be a guy with promise. Besides that, I'm supposed to be a *romantic*. People wonder and shake their heads. How is it that things happen to that guy the way they do? Always in the midst of exciting things, adventures, confessions, etc. But the question in my mind is: what am I doing for literature?" He was still trying to finish the manu-script he had brought with him from New York, probably the novel called "Crazy Cock," but was disgusted with it, unable to express his true feelings, boxed in by too much careful plotting and form. When he finished he wanted to burst through all such barriers. "I will explode in the Paris book. The hell with form, style, expression and all those pseudo-paramount things which beguile the critics. I want to get myself across this time—and direct as a knife thrust." In another letter written about the same time he gloried in the life he was leading: "Great days—full of missing meals—but rich in paint, verbiage and local scenery. Getting into such a bummy condition that people everywhere nudge one another and point me out." Despite hunger and hardship he felt he had lived more richly during one year in Paris than in all the rest of his life. Here is the protagonist of *Tropic of Cancer*: "I feel now exactly as all the great vagabond artists must have felt—absolutely reckless, childish, irresponsible, unscrupulous, and overflowing with carnal vitality, vigor, ginger, etc. Always on the border of insanity, due to worry, hunger, etc. But shoving along, day after day." Finally on August 24, 1931, having finished his novel at last, he announced that he was ready to go to work on the book he had been wanting to write: "I start tomorrow on the Paris book: first person, uncensored, formless—fuck everything!"

At the end of his second summer in Paris, Miller worked for a time as a proofreader for the Paris edition of the *Chicago Tribune*. His friend Perlès, who earned his small income as a proofreader, got him the job. Miller disapproved of jobs on principle but liked this one. He enjoyed the atmo-sphere of the newspaper office, the noise of the machinery, and the company of his fellow workers, especially the typesetters who were all like characters out of a French novel. Working at night had a charm all its own. Every evening he, Perlès, and Wambly Bald would make their long walk across Paris to the newspaper office. After work they would eat in a nearby bistro, the favorite haunt of pimps, whores, newspapermen, and others who worked by night. Then in the early morning hours, when all Paris was deserted, they would walk home again. Though Miller worked only a short time for the newspaper, the impressions of that time remained among the most vivid of his Paris years. Of the many writers and would-be writers who worked on the *Tribune* or the Paris edition of the *New York Herald*, only Miller and Bravig Imbs have given any sense of the atmosphere. Most of the journalists' accounts are full of sophomoric clichés.

Although Miller preferred the subterranean drudgery of proofreading to the more exalted editorial work upstairs, he was only too willing to be published in a newspaper, even anonymously or pseudonymously. Long before he was employed by the *Tribune* he wrote feature articles for that paper's Sunday edition. Only employees were supposed to contribute such articles, so Perlès submitted them as his own. In his biography Perlès reprints one of these articles, "Rue Lourmel in Fog," which is very much like the impressionistic compositions Miller had sent to Schnellock when he first arrived in Paris. Other articles appeared in the *Tribune* or in the *Herald* during his first year in Paris: "The Cirque Médrano," "The Six-Day Bike Race," "Paris in *Ut Mineur*." The usual rate was fifty francs, and once Miller received three hundred and fifty francs, but the important thing was that he was getting his work published readily for the first time in his life. He had tried to write for newspapers and popular magazines in the past, but with no success.

During his second year in Paris Miller's work also appeared in a literary magazine for the first time, Samuel Putnam's recently founded *New Review*. Putnam was a scholarly newspaper correspondent who had come to Paris in 1926 to translate Rabelais. Besides the standard modern translation of that difficult author, he produced translations of contemporary authors ranging from François Mauriac to Kiki. For all his mastery of the written language, Putnam spoke French with such an abominable accent as to be almost unintelligible. He was a steady customer of the Montparnasse bars, where Miller probably met him about the time he quit as associate editor of *This Quarter* and decided to found his own quarterly. Miller appeared twice in the *New Review* and edited one issue with Perlès. Putnam made the mistake of asking them to see the magazine through the press when he had to go to America for a visit. They promptly threw out some of the contents they found boring, including a long article by Putnam, and put in material they thought livelier, including a story by Miller. They also decided to add a supplement, a bawdy, vituperative, nonsensical parody of all manifestoes called "The New Instinctivism," denouncing everything: "A proclamation of rebellion against the puerilities of art and literature, a manifesto of disgust, a gob of spit in the cuspidor of post-war conceits, a healthy crap in the cradle of still-born dieties." When the printers sent proofs to Putnam, he quashed the supplement, but the review appeared with the contents Miller and Perlès had chosen.

Miller first appeared in the *New Review* as a film critic. The second number, which came out in the summer of 1931, included his review entitled "Buñuel or Thus Cometh to an End Everywhere the Golden Age." Miller, who had been a cineast since childhood, was delighted to be in Paris where he could see avant-garde films that were never shown in New York. On the first Sunday after his arrival he had made a pilgrimage to Studio 28 in Montmartre to see one of the great surrealist films, *Un Chien Andalou*, made by Buñuel in collaboration with Dali the previous year. A week or so later he went to a ciné club meeting and was impressed by the brilliant discussion. By October 1930 he had made friends with the film maker Germaine Dulac, who promised June an important role in a talkie that was to be made in two or three months; nothing ever came of this proposal, and Madame Dulac, whom Miller described as "one of the celebrated Lesbiennes of Paris and all Europe," may have had only a passing interest in June. Toward the end of

October he saw the new Buñuel-Dali film, *L'Age d'Or*, and in December he sent Schnellock a draft of his article for the *New Review*. His admiration for Buñuel never diminished. In the mid-thirties he paid tribute to him again in a long article on the cinematic art entitled "The Golden Age." Less explicit but even more pervasive is the influence of Buñuel's films on certain surrealist sequences in Miller's writing, particularly "Into the Night Life" in *Black Spring*.

Miller's first published story, "Mademoiselle Claude," appeared in the third number of the *New Review* in the fall of 1931. That story marks the actual beginning of his literary career, announcing all the characteristics of the *Tropics*—the first person monologue, the progressive narrative moving into the present tense, with events happening and time passing as the story unfurls. Here too are the tropical moral values—the generous whore who is almost an angel, the narrator-*maquereau* who wants to be a saint. He finds her customers to keep her from being sad, and they end up going to the clinic together every day, more in love than ever. Even the imagery is here: "Paris looks to me like a big, ugly chancre. The streets are gangrened. Everybody has it—if it isn't clap it's syphilis. All Europe is diseased, and it's France who's made it diseased."

The style anticipates *Tropic of Cancer* with its flowing rhythms: "The idea, though, of waking up in the morning, the sun streaming in the windows and a good, faithful whore beside you who loves you, who loves the guts out of you, the birds singing and the table all spread, and while she's washing up and combing her hair, all the men she's been with and now you, just you, and barges going by, masts and hulls, the whole damned current of life flowing through you, through her, through all the guys before you and maybe after, the flowers and the birds and the sun streaming in and the fragrance of it choking you, annihilating you. O Christ! Give me a whore always, all the time!" Miller liked that long sentence well enough to quote part of it in *Tropic of Cancer*.

Miller was fascinated by the Paris whores. On his first Sunday in Paris he had noted with surprise: "Montmartre is simply lousy with whores. Little bars, hardly bigger than a coffin, are jammed with them." The imagery is typical, if not the reaction. "Wow! they make you shiver those dolled-up spectres. They sit in the cafés and beckon to you from the window, or bunk smack up against you on the street, and invite you to come along." By May he had found his first girl friend, a whore named Germaine. In December he wrote, "And who is Mlle. Claude? Ah, the prettiest, juiciest, cleverest little cocotte in Montparnasse. Osborn and I share her once in a while. Such taste, such discretion, such politesse." He found her intelligent, well-read, animated, and refined. He recommended her to Schnellock, who could address her in care of the Coupole. Though the letter ends half-humorously, sounding like an advertisement, Claude is described in similar terms in *Tropic of Cancer*, but compared unfavorably with that ordinary hustler Germaine, who according to the book, served as the real model for the story. "She was a whore all the way through," Miller concludes, "and that was her virtue!"

By the time "Mademoiselle Claude" appeared in print Miller had started writing *Tropic of Cancer*. He had already met most of the characters and had most of the experiences that went into the narrative. But there is more to that book than mere storytelling; *Tropic of Cancer* dramatizes a particular outlook, a satiric blend of humor and iconoclasm, a fiercely critical view of the world. In the fall of 1931 Miller was being exposed to some of the ideas that gave the book its philosophical bias. He then lived for a time with Michael Fraenkel, a prophet of doom whose theories appear in the first two chapters and elsewhere. On the opening page Miller summarizes Fraenkel's death philosophy, complete with Fraenkel's favorite weather metaphor.

> Boris has just given me a summary of his views. He is a weather prophet. The weather will continue bad, he says. There will be more calamities, more death, more despair. Not the slightest indication of a change anywhere. The cancer of time is eating us away. Our heroes have killed themselves, or are killing themselves. The hero, then, is not Time, but Timelessness. We must get in step, a lock step, toward the prison of death. There is no escape. The weather will not change.

There is usually a note of ridicule in Miller's treatment of Fraenkel's ideas, but he also admits that Fraenkel is one of the two writers he respects, the other being Perlés. The reason he takes them seriously is that, unlike other writers he knows, these two have fervor. "They are possessed. They glow inwardly with a white flame. They are mad and tone deaf. They are sufferers."

Fraenkel was a small intense man with a goatee who bore a marked resemblance to Trotsky. Born in Russia and brought to the United States as a boy, he became the greatest book salesman in America and saved enough money to retire at the age of thirty in 1926. He had always wanted to write, and Paris seemed the best place for a writer to go. His writing was the product of a philosophical mind obsessed with one subject, the spiritual death of modern man as symbolized by the millions of deaths of the Great War. His friend Walter Lowenfels plays upon the central paradox of Fraenkel's life in an unpublished biographical sketch, "The Life of Fraenkel's Death," pointing out that Fraenkel earned his living in America so that he could retire in Europe to write about death.

Lowenfels himself followed a similar pattern. He too had been in business in America, the family butter business which he later treated as something of a joke, contrasting butter with poetry, and which he quit at the age of twenty-nine, having decided to go to Europe to write. His ideas were akin to Fraenkel's, though not nearly so extreme. At the time they became friends he had just finished an elegy on Apollinaire. Under the influence of Fraenkel he then took death as his central theme and wrote a sequence of elegies called

Some Deaths, lamenting the suicides of poets such as Hart Crane and Harry Crosby, René Crevel and Jacques Rigaut. Fraenkel and Lowenfels also formed what they called an anonymous school, writing books together anonymously in the spirit of French writers and painters before them. In *Tropic of Cancer* Miller jokes about an anonymous collaboration proposed by Fraenkel, to be called "The Last Book," and some years later Miller and Fraenkel actually did collaborate on a book, the *Hamlet* correspondence, which was published by Fraenkel's Carrefour Press.

Miller became acquainted with Fraenkel about the time he started writing *Tropic of Cancer*. Lowenfels and Fraenkel had already been in league for two years or more. Now the three of them formed what Lowenfels calls "the avant-garde of death." Neither he nor Miller took Fraenkel's monomania altogether seriously. "Henry and I really joked about Fraenkel's death business—turning it into something else, something we could use in our business, which was, say what you like, writing." Fraenkel was useful to Miller in more immediate ways, for he owned an apartment building at 18 Villa Seurat and was better off than Miller's other friends. A number of people have claimed an influence on Miller when he was still unknown, but their most important contribution at this time was keeping him alive. This was Lowenfels' motive in bringing Miller and Fraenkel together, this and Fraenkel's need for an intelligent audience, which was as great as Miller's need for bed and board.

The Miller-Fraenkel relationship was a strange and amusing one, founded on phagomania and the death obsession and kept alive by talk. Both men were prodigious talkers. Miller remembers that Fraenkel used to drop in at breakfast time, stay through lunch, through dinner, and far into the evening, talking, talking all the time, leaving Miller exhausted. Fraenkel in turn was overwhelmed by Miller's talk. "It was extraordinary, amazing, incredible. A compulsion mechanism, a kind of sickness, if you like, something pathological." But he also adds, "It was talk of the highest order I ever heard." Though by nature stingy and indifferent to food, Fraenkel would occasionally buy Miller a meal just to be able to keep talking. In *Tropic of Cancer* Miller complains that there is not a scrap of food in the house. He also registers a feeling of impermanence, fearing his chair will be pulled out from under him as he types. Fraenkel, ever the businessman, rented out apartments and soon evicted Miller by renting the room he occupied. Miller liked the Villa Seurat and returned there to live three years later; meanwhile his discussions with Fraenkel continued and turned into correspondence when Fraenkel traveled about the world.

Years later, in an article entitled "The Genesis of the *Tropic of Cancer*," Fraenkel reminisced about the beginning of their acquaintance: "And then one day Walter told me about a strange man he had run across in Montparnasse, a fellow called Miller. He was described as one of tremendous vitality, zest, enthusiasm, an amazing talker, without visible means of support, a kind of derelict, but gay and happy withal, alive. 'Not alive exactly,' he said, 'but certainly not dead. Alive in a kind of confused, old-fashioned way. An interesting chap. Why not drop him a line, a *pneu*? He is down and out and maybe he can do some typing for you.' And then with a twinkle in his eye: 'Take him on. Just your meat.' Did he perhaps see a possible disciple in him?" According to Fraenkel there were no preliminaries between them, no reservations; they immediately talked to each other like old friends. Fraenkel gave Miller his book *Werther's Younger Brother*, a self-portrait ending in suicide. Miller responded with a long enthusiastic fan letter which Fraenkel quotes: "You say things that no one in America is saying—that I would dearly love to say myself." Miller, who had been told that Fraenkel's book was pessimistic and confused, "found everything touched with a wild beauty, and if there were disorder, then it was, as Bergson said, an order of disorder which is another order."

Though Fraenkel claims too much credit for his influence on *Tropic of Cancer*, he gives the best explanation on record of Miller's state of mind at the time. And though he was only the latest in a series of friends to advise Miller to write spontaneously, his insight may have been the clearest. Certainly his advice was most timely. Beneath Miller's restless confusion Fraenkel detected a determination to be himself. Miller had come to Paris to make a new start but had not yet found himself. When Fraenkel read Miller's novel in manuscript, "Crazy Cock," he immediately saw that Miller was trying to write for the publishers, not for himself. "By this time I knew the sort of person he was, impulsive, erratic, anarchic, a mass of contradictory moods, ideas, feelings, and I told him to sit down before the machine and white paper and write anything and everything that came to his mind, as it came, red-hot, and to hell with the editors and the public. Write as you talk, I told him. Write as you live. Write as you feel and think. Just sit down before the machine and let go—tell everything you are going through now; you've got all the material you want right in this, in what you are thinking and feeling and going through *now*."

As they talked endlessly of death, Miller found the theme that could integrate his creative impulses and give him the direction he lacked. His obscenity, his violence, his inner chaos, and love of corruption are all expressions of "The Death Theme." So Fraenkel thought at any rate, though at times his disciples may have had their little joke at his expense. Lowenfels wonders whether the Fraenkel they remember is not a creature of their imagination. He feels that Fraenkel did not come through very well in his own writing. A greater thinker than writer, he left more of himself in the writings of others, in Miller's early work and Lowenfels' poems written between 1929 and 1934. Lowenfels also remarks that Fraenkel was at his best when writing under the stimulus of Miller. No doubt they inspired each other, but long before he met Fraenkel, Miller was steeped in the thinking of Oswald Spengler, whose apocalyptic view he had taken as his own. Miller had in fact reread the first volume of *The Decline of the West* since coming to Paris and in doing so had concluded that Spengler was the greatest of contemporary writers, greater than Joyce, Mann, or even Proust. "There is great music, great literature, great ideas." Surely his thinking in *Tropic of Cancer* was fired by Spengler, though Fraenkel undoubtedly fanned the flames.

The book that most immediately anticipated *Tropic of Cancer* was Louis-Ferdinand Céline's first novel, *Voyage au Bout de la Nuit*. Not only the Spenglerian sense of doom is there, but the very idiom and tone, the picaresque narrative and the gallows humor that Miller adopted. Céline's *Voyage* is another episodic autobiographical novel that dwells on all that is vicious, treacherous, sadistic, obscene, diseased, and repulsive in human nature. The central character is an underdog adventurer who lives by luck and by his wits. Céline's favorite setting is the ugly, working-class Paris where he was born and where he practiced medicine, though he also traveled about the world like Candide, finding inhumanity wherever he went. His experience eventually drove him to bitter misanthropy, but his first book achieved a balance between laughter and pessimism that is much the same as Miller's comic treatment of inherently tragic matter. After reading *Voyage au Bout de la Nuit* it is easier to understand *Tropic of Cancer*, for Céline's war experience exposes the "civilization" that both writers attacked. Céline lost his innocence in the Great War, suffered shell shock, was cured of his illusions, learned to distrust all ideals and to place the law of self-preservation above all others. Miller, despite his imagery of trench warfare and poison gas, had no direct experience to compare with Céline's, yet he had gone through the same process of disenchantment, emerging with even fewer scruples. He too had become a militant anarchist, declaring war on society.

Despite the many striking parallels between the two books, Céline and Miller produced their works quite independently. Miller had finished the first draft of *Tropic of Cancer* before the publication of *Voyage au Bout de la .Nuit* in November 1932. He read the book soon after it appeared and was overwhelmed, although he found it difficult reading and had to spend a week isolated in a hotel room with a dictionary to decipher its colloquial French. During the next two years he was to revise his own book three times before it appeared in print, so conceivably Céline could have influenced the rewriting. But the letters to Schnellock reveal that Miller had found his style and subject matter before he had ever heard of Céline. It was simply another case of two writers responding to their time and place with the same perceptions.

Like Céline's novel, *Tropic of Cancer* is autobiographical, but it is not to be taken as documentary. Although Miller protests that he is writing the plain unvarnished truth, this gambit is one of the oldest in fiction. He is closer to fact than most novelists, but his method is theirs, his powerful imagination producing a metamorphosis as it colors and heightens the original circumstances. Miller has confessed that he has difficulty remembering what he imagined and what actually happened.

Tropic of Cancer gives a more or less fictionalized account, then, of the adventures of a character named Henry Miller who explored the lower depths in Paris during the depression. The book is a jumble of sensations, reflections, conversations, encounters, and hallucinations, all filtered through the consciousness of its narrator in the first person, present tense. The chaos is deliberate, for Miller wanted to put down impressions and thoughts as they occurred to him, to depict a man "in the grip of delirium." He also wanted "to get off the gold standard of literature," to write without revising, and to record "all that which is omitted in books."

Tropic of Cancer is sometimes compared to *The Sun Also Rises*, not for the similarities but for the differences between them. The comparison is absurd yet apt, for it shows how much the world had changed between the mid-twenties and the early thirties. Henry Miller's adventures in Paris present a burlesque of the expatriate romance. Instead of a potentially tragic hero, the protagonist is a clown whose escapades mock all sense of human dignity. Instead of investing his characters with a glamour that excuses their faults, Miller caricatures his friends, bringing out all that is grotesque, ludicrous, or contemptible in their private lives. He also sees his surroundings in a jaundiced light and thereby makes more meaningful use of his Paris scenery. For Hemingway Montparnasse provided an appropriate backdrop, a likely setting for the lost generation, but his characters stayed on the surface and could just as well have dissipated elsewhere. Miller penetrated far deeper into Paris than any other American writer and projected a vision of the city that was altogether different. He succeeded only as Céline had done in making its ugliness symbolic of private and universal anguish, a sordid modern-day inferno, a labyrinth of cancer and despair.

Much of *Tropic of Cancer* is lived in cafés and hotels, the usual setting of the expatriate life. But the book also has a more permanent background in certain neighborhoods. During his first year in Paris Miller found his natural habitat in the Fourteenth *Arrondissement*, the district back of the Boulevard Montparnasse where many artists lived. The location was handy to the American cafés when he had to scout for meals and small loans; Perlès, who was always ready to put him up, lived in a hotel there; Fraenkel and Lowenfels also lived in the vicinity, as did others who fed him regularly. Miller often went to other sections of Paris for food and lodging, but he always returned to the *Quatorzième*.

This lower-middle-class quarter was the Parisian equivalent of the Fourteenth Ward of Brooklyn, where he had lived as a boy. Completely off the beaten track, it has none of the glamour usually associated with Paris, though most of the city is in fact like the Fourteenth *Arrondissement*, commonplace, monotonous, rather ugly. To Miller it was "an awfully genuine, homely neighborhood," as he wrote to Schnellock during his first year in Paris, and he felt at ease among its inhabitants. "Everyone knows me, likes me, treats me like a Prince. Drinks are cheap, life flows leisurely, no intellectual slush, just kind honest folk." This was always to be the Paris of Miller and his friends, a provincial backwater somewhat removed from Montparnasse and the bright lights. Better than any other Americans, they knew the everyday life of the petit bourgeois and the proletariat. Being poor themselves, they wanted a cheap place to live and a quiet place to work.

Actually Miller's first real home in Paris was across the city at the foot of Montmartre. During his first two years he had no fixed abode but lived with one friend after another. He spent the first two months of 1932 in Dijon as an English teacher at the Lycée Carnot. The job provided room and board but no salary and no comforts; in *Tropic of Cancer* Miller describes the institution in terms that suggest Cummings' Enormous Room rather than a boarding school. Once again Perlès bailed him out, finding him another job at the *Tribune*, and in March 1932, shortly after Miller's return to Paris both moved into a small apartment at 4 Avenue Anatole France in Clichy. Perlès evidently paid the rent, for Miller's job at the *Tribune* did not last long. Anaïs Nin, who visited them when they had just moved in, described the apartment in her diary: "A few pans, unmatched dishes from the flea market, old shirts for kitchen towels. Tacked on the walls, a list of books to get, a list of menus to eat in the future, clippings, reproductions, and water colors of Henry's. Henry keeps house like a Dutch housekeeper. He is very neat and clean. No dirty dishes about. It is all monastic, really, with no trimmings, no decorations." The apartment was plain and bare, but it was home. The neighborhood was a grimmer version of the Fourteenth *Arrondissement*, a working-class quarter with plenty of sordid bars, yet it suited them perfectly.

Miller still remembers the two years he lived in Clichy as the best in his life. "When I think about this period," he wrote in *Quiet Days in Clichy*, "it seems like a stretch in Paradise. . . . even though the world was busy digging its grave, there was still time to enjoy life, to be merry, carefree, to work or not to work." With his living problem solved, he was free to write, and he went at it with prodigious energy. Perlès remembers the clatter he made, typing at high speed, and Miller himself recalls that one day he turned out forty-five pages. In a furious creative outburst he began working on four or five books at once, finishing *Tropic of Cancer*, beginning *Black Spring*, *Tropic of Capricorn*, a book on Lawrence that he never completed, and enough shorter pieces to fill at least one volume. At the same time he was painting water colors to illustrate his writings. These and other activities are outlined in his wall charts for the period. Miller liked to pin lists and memoranda on the walls: "Get old manifestoes of Dada and Surrealism, Steal Good Books from American Library, Write Automatically." His charts outlined works in progress, enumerating themes and topics to be written about and further research to be done. They admonished him to follow a daily work schedule and to carry out his projects in a disciplined way. Some of his eleven commandments seem rather contradictory:

3. Don't be nervous. Work calmly, joyously, recklessly on whatever is in hand.

4. Work according to Program and not according to mood. Stop at the appointed time!

7. Keep human! See people, go places, drink if you feel like it.

11. Write first and always. Painting, music, friends, cinema, all these come afterwards.

Miller's wall charts suggest that he worked all the time, while his writings create the impression that he did nothing but play. In Clichy he was somehow able to do both.

Those who claim to have influenced Miller in the thirties tend to speak slightingly of Alfred Perlès, dismissing him as a hanger-on. Miller himself has always given Perlès a central role in his Paris years. Perlès was not only his benefactor, sharing whatever he had, and his greatest friend, with whom he found most in common, but also an insidious influence. "He is right under my skin," Miller wrote many years later in his notes to *The Henry Miller Reader*, and elsewhere in the same collection he commented that Perlès "had quite a hand" in the final draft of *Tropic of Cancer*. In the book itself he went even further, stating on one of its opening pages, "I am writing this for my friend Carl," that being the name he gave Perlès in his fictionalized narratives.

As a writer no one could have been further removed from Miller. "Fred has a finesse which I lack, the quality of an Anatole France," Miller once remarked to Anaïs Nin, who understood Miller's gifts better than he did at the time, and who contrasted the two writers in her diary. Perlès was a subtle ironist who wrote in three languages, but it was not his writing that influenced Miller. Rather it was his character that provided Miller with a point of view that he could use in his writings, a mixture of cynicism, bravado, and buffoonery. Perlès was born to be a Miller character, a rogue and clown who lived marginally by his wits. A castaway of the Austro-Hungarian Empire, the bearer of a Czechoslovakian passport, he had managed to save his skin during the war—evidently by some discreditable ruse—and afterward had gravitated to Paris via all the capitals of Europe. In his portrait of Perlès in "Remember to Remember" Miller notes that his friend seldom talked about his past. Nevertheless the sense of futility engendered by the war played a large part in his outlook. Fundamentally Perlès was a dadaist.

Another writer who played a major role in Miller's life at this time was Anaïs Nin. Like Perlès she came from another world. A cultivated cosmopolite, she had much to teach him but much to learn as well. They met through Richard Osborn in the fall of 1931, began by exchanging works in manuscript, soon became more involved when Miller's histrionic wife June appeared on the scene, entangling them in a feverish romance *à trois*, and started corresponding intensively when Miller went to Dijon. In the opening pages of her published diary, which begins that winter, Anaïs Nin presents herself as a kind of Emma Bovary living in a romantic village outside of Paris. Fond of role-playing, she led a triple life as the gracious lady of Louveciennes, the Bohemian writer, and the psychoanalyst's apprentice. Fond of intrigue, she was fascinated by June, whom she found "the most beautiful woman on earth," but in the long run found more to admire in Miller. In December 1932, when June returned to Paris, rendering Miller's life impossible, it was Anaïs Nin who provided him with the money to make his escape to England an experience he recounted in one of his funniest narratives, "Via Dieppe-Newhaven."

Married to an American banker, Anaïs Nin could afford to be Miller's patroness. She frequently helped him out with small gifts, later underwrote the publication of *Tropic of Cancer*, and eventually rented an apartment for him in the Villa Seurat. Miller admired her as a writer and as a clairvoyante— "*un être étoilique*," as he called her in an article about her voluminous diary, using her own word, coined by analogy to "*lunatique*." He was enormously impressed by her diary, an endless labyrinth which he compared to the writings of Proust, and he regarded the diary as a form that would replace the novel—like his own autobiographical narratives. Miller's letters to Anaïs Nin also show how much he relied on her for advice and criticism. Humble and anxious to learn, he turned to her as his chief literary mentor.

Better than any other source, his letters to her record the everyday facts about the most creative period of his life. His letters from Dijon, for example, not only describe the circumstances behind two chapters in *Tropic of Cancer* but register his response to French culture. Miller had long been in love with the language, but this was the first time he had lived completely in French. At the same time he was reading Proust, which she had lent him, and falling under the spell of the written language. "Proust is going to my head," he wrote. "I am nearing the end of the first volume and have deliberately stopped reading because I want to ration my enjoyment and my suffering." He was reading in a big café with an orchestra playing and people talking all around him, yet he had no trouble concentrating on the involuted style. Proust was one of the authors he absorbed with the sense that the writing was addressed directly to him. "The man seems to take the words out of my mouth, to rob me of my very own experiences, sensations, reflections, introspections, suspicions, sadness, torture, etc. etc. etc."

After Miller's return from Dijon, Anaïs Nin noted in her diary, "With me he explores the symphonies of Proust, the intelligence of Gide, Cocteau's fantasies, Valéry's silences, the illuminations of Rimbaud." With the exception of Rimbaud, Miller was already acquainted with these writers, for he had introduced Osborn to them the year before. But it was one thing to read French authors in translation, as Miller had done in New York during the twenties, and another to examine their subtleties with a woman who was thoroughly at home with the language and culture. For an autodidact who read avidly but erratically, such a teacher could fill in the gaps from her more sophisticated background. Under her tutelage he deepened his understanding of French literature. It was already broad, and critics have cited Rabelais, Villon, Rousseau, Sade, Restif de la Bretonne, Rimbaud, Lautréamont, and others as sources for *Tropic of Cancer*. Disconcertingly, Miller has announced that he had not read most of his sources before writing the book, but the critics could reply that he wrote in the tradition of the *poètes maudits*, whether he had read them or not. Miller's reading remains full of surprises. In the fifties he confessed that he had not yet read Restif de la Bretonne or managed to "wade through" Rousseau's *Confessions*, though he had tried several times. He feels a particular affinity for Balzac, Rimbaud, Cendrars, and Giono, none of whom had any significant influence on his own writing. To this day he admits that he cannot read the Marquis de Sade.

Apart from Céline and Proust, the French writers Miller most resembles are the dadaists and surrealists. But here again influence appears dubious. "I was writing Surrealistically in America before I had ever heard the word," Miller declares in "An Open Letter to Surrealists Everywhere," and in *Tropic of Capricorn*, which chronicles his life in the early twenties, he states, "I was perhaps the unique Dadaist in America, and I didn't know it." Nevertheless he became more immediately aware of surrealism upon his arrival in Paris, and more susceptible in the presence of Anaïs Nin. Her diary reflects a preoccupation with dreams and fantasies, analyzed in the light of surrealism, psychoanalysis, and astrology—the kind of thinking that increasingly fascinated Miller. An entry for April 1932 records that she has begun writing surrealistically under the influence of *Transition*, Breton, and Rimbaud. The work she wrote was her autobiographical *House of Incest*, which "directly inspired" Miller's "Scenario," according to his own prefatory acknowledgment. The resemblance is hard to find, but both writers were concerned with the problem of adapting film techniques in writing dream scenarios, and both works present a sequence of surrealistic visions.

Although Anaïs Nin frequently contrasted her dreams and illusions with Miller's harshly realistic writing, she also saw that he had a great deal in common with the surrealists. In her diary she observed that like Breton he believed in freedom from all restraints, "to write as one thinks, in the order and disorder in which one feels and thinks, to follow sensations and absurd correlations of events and images." He too believed in the cult of the marvelous, of mystery, of the unconscious, in "an effort to transcend the rigidities and patterns made by the rational mind." Along with her he was attracted to the improvisation, madness, and chaos of the dadaists and surrealists. At the same time he was living on an all too realistic plane. He took her out of her enchanted garden down into the streets, introducing her to a life which she had only read about in *Bubu de Montparnasse*. While she never escaped from her introspection, Miller made the best of both worlds in his writing, allowing his imagination to rampage, yet remaining firmly anchored in reality.

Black Spring, dedicated to Anaïs Nin and datelined "Louveciennes;—Clichy;—Villa Seurat. 1934–1935," was his major work of the Clichy period. While obviously written by the same hand, this book is quite different from *Tropic of Cancer*, less violent and obscene, more euphoric. Though the materials are basically autobiographical, the method is not narrative; instead of character and episode, Miller presents a series of monologues, meditations, reminiscences, dreams, and visions, shifting back and forth from his Paris surroundings to his early years in Brooklyn and New York. Composed in ten independent sections, the book was nonetheless conceived as a whole and developed through a process of organic growth. Underlying its chaotic variety in style and technique is a coherence of theme and symbol. Organization, structure, discipline was always Miller's biggest problem. His wall charts for the early thirties show how he labored to organize his materials; most of his "Major Program" is a detailed outline of the multifarious elements that went into *Black Spring*.

Miller began writing that book about the beginning of May 1932 and was absorbed in it during the next two years. He may have originally thought of it as an autobiography, for its title was to be "Self-Portrait." In June 1933 he decided to incorporate a "dream book" he had been keeping, and in February 1934 he decided to make this section the climax of the entire work, using the dreams to recapitulate its major themes. By April 1934 he had finished a version of the book, still called "Self-Portrait," which Anaïs Nin took to London when she went in search of a publisher for his books. But he went on adding, rearranging, and revising long after. During the thirties he was forever rewriting and reorganizing, never satisfied with his work.

Black Spring reveals none of his labor. The writing seems completely spontaneous, the language prodigal and exuberant, the imagination rampant, giving the impression that Miller was elated all the time he worked. This euphoria seems to be the mood of Clichy, and the book is full of local scenery: Sacré Coeur up on the hill, the Gare Saint-Lazare, the cemetery, the red-light district. Clichy is Céline country, but the book has none of Céline's ferocity or disgust. Miller lists plenty of horrors, only to forget them immediately, so that the theme of impending doom in the title is never taken seriously. Miller is in a mellow mood, sitting in the Place Clichy in the sunshine or cycling along the Seine on the outskirts of Paris. He is closer to Proust in his vivid recollections of childhood and to the surrealists in his dreams and "grand obsessional walks" around Montmartre.

Two sections of the book are particularly surrealistic, "The Angel Is

My Watermark" and "Into the Night Life." The first begins with "the dictation," a demonic seizure that possesses Miller so that he becomes merely a passive instrument, a hand that writes down what is transmitted. Like the surrealists Miller believes that the best writing comes from such subconscious outpouring, the source of his most inspired virtuoso passages. In painting too he demonstrates the role of improvisation, retracing the steps in producing a water color. The process illustrates surrealist theory and practice: creation on impulse, the element of chance, the proximity between art and madness. "Into the Night Life" deals with the dream world. Miller had been recording his dreams for some time when he realized that he could use them in *Black Spring*. In this instance he made a deliberate decision to write surrealistically, as the subject demanded, and to produce a scenario, since the cinema was the best medium for surrealism.

Miller was really a self-made surrealist, a primitive who had been working in the same vein before he came upon Breton's movement. In "An Open Letter to Surrealists Everywhere," he wrote, "Scarcely anything has been as stimulating to me as the theories and the products of the surrealists." Yet he instinctively distrusted the sterile dogmatism of the surrealist movement and always showed a marked preference for dada. *Black Spring* is full of parodies and puns, zany free associations and digressions, anarchy and irreverence. Miller in a comic mood is constantly running off the rails.

> To prognosticate this reality is to be off either by a millimeter or by a million light years. The difference is a quantum formed by the intersection of streets. A quantum is a functional disorder created by trying to squeeze oneself into a frame of reference. A reference is a discharge from an old employer, that is to say, a mucopus from an old disease.

"Jabberwhorl Cronstadt" is dadaistic from start to drunken finish, a parody of nonsensical language that begins: "He lives in the back of a sunken garden, a sort of bosky glade shaded by whiffletrees and spinozas, by deodars and baobabs, a sort of queasy Buxtehude diapered with elytras and feluccas." "Burlesk" is a ragout of phrases and styles taken from a sign in a bar, a Dutchman's letter, a Negro church service, the pitchman's spiel at Minsky's, and all kinds of learned jargon. Miller's gift for pedantic nonsense later reached its highest expression in *Money and How It Gets That Way*, a treatise written in such impeccable jargon that economists have been known to take it seriously. This dada masterpiece was dedicated to Ezra Pound, who in the thirties became obsessed with economic theories. In a postcard commending *Tropic of Cancer* Pound had remarked that Miller had not pondered the question: "What IS money? who makes it/ how does it get that way?////"

Miller left Clichy early in February 1934 and spent the next seven months at various addresses. Then on September 1, 1934, he moved into an apartment at 18 Villa Seurat that was to be his home for the remainder of his stay in Paris. Though surrounded by a rather slummy neighborhood, the Villa Seurat was more like a prosperous suburban street, a quiet impasse with plenty of light and air between the houses. The residents were mostly successful artists who liked their comfort. Anaïs Nin rented a top-floor studio apartment for Miller in Fraenkel's old house at the end of the street.

Here, she remarked, he had begun writing *Tropic of Cancer*, and now at last, four years later, the book appeared in print on the day he returned. During the next few months Miller kept busy sending the book around to various writers, nervously awaiting their response, watching for reviews, checking the bookstores to see how it was selling. On the whole the writers received it favorably, the book sold slowly but steadily, and Miller gradually became known. The most gratifying response came from Blaise Cendrars, who not only gave the book its first review but came to call, treated Miller to a feast, and praised him publicly, insisting that the book must be translated into French since it belonged to the great Catholic and Rabelaisian tradition of France. Miller was speechless for once in his life, embarrassed in the presence of this writer he so admired. Cendrars's review, written about Christmas, begins, "Unto us is born an American writer," shows a hearty appreciation of Miller's Paris, and concludes that "this book springs from our soil, and Henry Miller is one of us, in spirit, in style, in his power and in his gifts, a universal writer like all those who have been able to put into a book their own vision of Paris."

The Villa Seurat became the headquarters for a circle of friends who gathered around Miller, most of them writers or painters. Besides Fraenkel, Perlès, and Anaïs Nin, the group included Betty Ryan, an American painter who lived downstairs; David Edgar, "the most lovable neurotic America ever produced," who specialized in a mixture of psychology and theosophy; the German painter Hans Reichel, described in "The Cosmological Eye" as a mad visionary; and Conrad Moricand, an impoverished Swiss astrologer. Another friend was the Hungarian photographer Brassaï, who appears anonymously in *Tropic of Cancer* as Miller's guide to some of the most sordid neighborhoods, and whom Miller celebrated in "The Eye of Paris." Lawrence Durrell, the English writer living in Greece, had begun an enormous correspondence with Miller in 1935 and became a member of the circle in 1937. All in all, they represented an odd assortment, the flotsam and jetsam of international society, with neither a true Frenchman nor an orthodox American among them.

During the later thirties the Villa Seurat became the headquarters for several publishing ventures. Perlès, who had been editing a monthly bulletin called *The Booster* for the American Country Club of Paris, found himself out of a job and in possession of the magazine one day. Without changing its name he altered its character entirely by recruiting Miller and Durrell as associate editors and chief contributors along with himself. The result was the zaniest of all little magazines, with dada manifestoes and mastheads, "boosts" for all and sundry, some serious writing, but mostly bawdy nonsense. The president of the country club soon disassociated himself from the magazine, but the editors managed to keep it going for six issues between September 1937 and Easter 1939, the last three appearing as *Delta*. A more serious venture was the Villa Seurat Library, a series of books edited by Miller. Only three titles were published: Durrell's *Black Book*, Miller's *Max and the White Phagocytes*, and Anaïs Nin's *Winter of Artifice*.

During the latter thirties Miller began to discover that his work as editor and literary agent could be a full-time job. As he became better known, the demands on his time increased, and much of his energy went into correspondence about various schemes, often to help others. His life was more stable now than it had been during his earlier years in Paris, and he had the satisfaction of being a writer at last, but he found that he had far less time for writing. His major project during these years was *Tropic of Capricorn*, a book he had been struggling with since 1932. In his letters to Durrell he frequently mentioned it but only to say it was not yet finished. Finally in August 1938 he announced that he had reached the end, though the revising remained to be done. Miller was always a digressive writer, but *Tropic of Capricorn* is more disconnected than most of his books, creating the impression that he was constantly distracted during the writing. The book contains some brilliant passages, which by their discontinuity indicate where he sat down to write and where he left off. In *Big Sur and the Oranges of Hieronymus Bosch* he gives an amusing account of "the dictation" of *Tropic of Capricorn*, protesting that the most obscene passages were not his idea at all, that he had no choice but to set them down as dictated. "I didn't have to think up so much as a comma or a semicolon; it was all given, straight from the celestial recording room. Weary, I would beg for a break, an intermission, time enough, let's say, to go to the toilet or take a breath of fresh air on the balcony. Nothing doing! I had to take it in one fell swoop or risk the penalty: excommunication."

Memories of those years in the Villa Seurat are scattered throughout *Big Sur and the Oranges of Hieronymus Bosch*. Written twenty lears later, this is in part an account of Conrad Moricand's disastrous visit to Big Sur, an event which naturally reminded Miller of their earlier encounters. He looked back on his years in Paris as the best of his life and those in the Villa Seurat as the most serene. Under Moricand's influence perhaps, he dwelt on the astrologic side of experience, his dreams, his chance encounters, his horoscope, his nature as a Capricorn. Among other things, the Capricorn is an ambulatory paranoiac, as Miller demonstrates once again in describing his walks around the outlying regions beyond the Fourteenth *Arrondissement*. These morning constitutionals, which were supposed to relax him for the long hours of typing, usually stimulated him to the point that he saw hallucinatory sights. "Goats from the *banlieue*, gangplanks, douche bags, safety belts, iron trusses, *passerelles* and *sauterelles* floated before my glazed eyeballs, together with headless fowl, beribboned antlers, rusty sewing machines, dripping ikons and other unbelievable phenomena." Apart from the modern junk this could be the surrealistic world of Hieronymus Bosch.

Big Sur and the Oranges of Hieronymus Bosch also tells of his last evening in Paris, his farewell dinner with Moricand and his final, solitary visit to Montparnasse. In the drizzling rain he stopped off for a drink, alone again as he had been so many years before when he first arrived. His departure seems an anticlimax, but he intended to return. He was going off to Greece to visit Durrell, who had been inviting him for two years, but Miller had constantly postponed the trip, content with his routine in the Villa Seurat and determined to finish *Tropic of Capricorn*. When it was published at last, in May 1939, he felt free to take a "sabbatical year," left Paris the following month, and sailed from Marseilles on July 14, 1939. When the war broke out, he was forced to return to America.

As Perlès says in his biography, "Paris never wore off." Back in his native land Miller became a permanent expatriate. Not only did he loathe America as much as ever, but wherever he went, whatever he saw and did, reminded him of Paris and left him terribly homesick. Memories of France turn up constantly in his later writings. In 1946, with the war over but the postwar prospect none too bright, he sat down to write "Remember to Remember," a long evocative essay about the French provinces and their capital. Here he dwells lovingly on the flavor, the ambiance, the wealth and variety of the garden of France, and the inexhaustible charm of the city.

In 1946 he saw clearly what he had not seen at the time, how much those first two years there had meant to him. "I was so desperately hungry not only for the physical and the sensual, for human warmth and understanding, but also for inspiration and illumination. During the dark years in Paris all these needs were answered. I was never lonely, no matter how miserable my condition. To be a prisoner of the streets, as I was for a long time, was a perpetual recreation. I did not need an address as long as the streets were there free to be roamed. There are scarcely any streets in Paris I did not get to know. On every one of them I could erect a tablet commemorating in letters of gold some rich new experience, some deep realization, some moment of illumination."

He remembered the little everyday details, the look of an ordinary street in the morning, the faded façades of houses, the sparrows chirping, the smell of fresh bread. Most of the time during "those ten glorious years" was spent in unexciting ways, yet he found an extraordinary satisfaction in the commonplace. "I treasured the little menus written out by hand each day. I liked the waitresses even though they were slatternly often and bad tempered. To see the bicycle cops patrolling in pairs at night always gave me a thrill. I adored the patches in the old carpets which covered the worn stairs in the cheap hotels. The way the street cleaner went about his task fascinated me. The faces of the people in the Metro never ceased to intrigue me, as did also their gestures, their conversation."

Above all Paris was a city of writers and artists. Bookshops, art galleries, the very streets told of a creative past and present. "One needs no artificial stimulation, in Paris, to create. The atmosphere is saturated with creation. One has to make an effort to avoid being over-stimulated." The Villa Seurat, where he lived for almost five years, was named after an artist of the past and provided an ideal setting for those of the present. "The whole street is given up to quiet, joyous work. Every house contains a writer, painter, musician, sculptor, dancer, or actor. It is such a quiet street and yet there is such activity going on, silently, becomingly, should I not say reverently too? This is how it is on my street, but there are hundreds of such streets in Paris. There is a constant army of artists at work, the largest of any city in the world. This is what makes Paris, this vast group of men and women devoted to the things of the spirit. This is what animates the city, makes it the magnet of the cultural world."

PHALLIC MILLER

◆

Narcissism

Norman Mailer

The gusto of Miller's relation to sex is so outside the clam-like formulations of conventional psychoanalysis that it is probably incumbent to make a pass at the psychology of his sexual patterns. Some possible psychology, at any rate. Who can conceive today of a man without a psychology? On the other hand, let it be done in modesty. To analyze the sexuality of another person, any other person, is unattractive; it is not even a question of taste but philosophy. The implicit assumption is that the person who performs the analysis is sexually superior to the subject. One is equal at such times to a writer for *Time* who assigns objectivity to himself.

To analyze anyone's sexuality assumes we know what sex is about; even the assumption is offensive. But to suggest we know the psychological patterns of a great writer is doubly irritating. As soon talk about the real secret in the reflexes of a great athlete. Nonetheless, by the style of this apology, it is obvious some attempt is going to be made. There is a modern vanity which thrusts us into the dissection of our betters. Besides, in the case of Henry Miller, a species of cop-out exists. To the degree we come to know Miller's psychic apparatus, we can claim sympathy with the difficulty of what he managed to achieve.

Told often enough by the victim, Miller comes from a mother from whom he admits to receiving no love. In his childhood he is, so far as his parents have influence, hermetically sealed against sexuality. Whatever sex is, it is on the other side of the wall. His first and fundamental relation to a woman is detestation. A grand beginning! To it he adds the formative logic of an eight-year-old. To anyone familiar with Miller, the next scene is peculiarly subdued in the writing. If he is telling the truth (and on reflection we can hardly be certain he is), then he killed a boy in a gang fight at the age of eight by hitting him in the temple with a stone.

I'm thinking now about the rock fight one summer's afternoon long long ago when I was staying with my Aunt Caroline up near Hell Gate. My cousin Gene and I had been corralled by a gang of boys while we were playing in the

park. We didn't know which side we were fighting for but we were fighting
in dead earnest amidst the rock pile by the river bank. We had to show even
more courage than the other boys because we were suspected of being sissies.
That's how it happened that we killed one of the rival gang. Just as they were
charging us my cousin Gene let go at the ringleader and caught him in the
guts with a handsome-sized rock. I let go almost at the same instant and my
rock caught him in the temple and when he went down he lay there for good
and not a peep out of him. A few minutes later the cops came and the boy
was found dead. He was eight or nine years old, about the same age as us.
What they would have done to us if they had caught us I don't know. Anyway,
so as not to arouse any suspicion we hurried home; we had cleaned up a bit
on the way and had combed our hair. We walked in looking almost as
immaculate as when we had left the house. Aunt Caroline gave us our usual
two big slices of sour rye with fresh butter and a little sugar over it and we
sat there at the kitchen table listening to her with an angelic smile. It was an
extremely hot day and she thought we had better stay in the house, in the big
front room where the blinds had been pulled down, and play marbles with
our little friend Joey Kasselbaum. Joey had the reputation of being a little
backward and ordinarily we would have trimmed him, but that afternoon, by
a sort of mute understanding, Gene and I allowed him to win everything we
had. Joey was so happy that he took us down to his cellar later and made his
sister pull up her dress and show us what was underneath. Weesie, they called
her, and I remember that she was stuck on me instantly. I came from another
part of the city, so far away it seemed to them, that it was almost like coming
from another country. They even seemed to think that I talked differently
from them. Whereas the other urchins used to pay to make Weesie lift her
dress, for us it was done with love. After a while we persuaded her not to do
it any more for the other boys—we were in love with her and we wanted her
to go straight.

Tropic of Capricorn

After war and good chow comes this natural readiness for love. The
story offers a bit of help in accounting for the good humor in the murderous
cold accounts he will later give of women's reactions as he is tooling them,
a good Brooklyn substitute for fornication. Three-quarters of the women to
whom he makes love are tooled quicker than they are fucked. Miller comes
after all out of a milieu where sex has something wrong with it if it is not
sordid. The last contractive spasm of the Victorian age may have been
throttling the sexuality of Miller's parents and the parents of everyone around
him (as if every late Victorian working-class and middle-class Brooklyn
parent had a nightmarish vision of a disordered sexual chaos to come), but
the children were loose. Sex was stinky-pinky back in Brooklyn at the turn
of the century (and for a good part of the next forty years). Sex and filth were
components of the same equation, as related as mass and energy—tender sex
was a flower you shoved up a girl's ass. Sex was a function of filth; filth was

a function of sex—no surprise that sex was getting ready for the automobile, and the smell of gasoline would prove the new aphrodisiac. Henry Miller's milieu was incapable of experiencing sex without the power relation of sex. In a fight one man may beat another man's head against the ground. In sex, in dirty sex, the tastes are ground into the other's mouth and cowardice is expiated by going down. Beyond dirt is karma.

They weren't thinking of karma, however, in Miller's Brooklyn. Sex was hunting season. "How far did you get with her?" went the question. "Hit a triple." Which is to say my hand got into her wet pussy. Needless to say, in the land of the filthy fuck, all pussies are wet. Sexuality was a river of grease in the crack of the taboo.

That was his environment. With a sexy loving mother, he would still have seen sex as dirty. With his own home-grown family strictures against sexuality, a part of Miller had to see sex as equal to disembowelling a garbage can. It is his achievement that he didn't end as a rapist, a suicide, or a monk. Instead he made what moves he could to extricate himself from a doomed relation to sexuality. If he never succeeded altogether in being able to love a woman, or at least never so deeply that he could enter the literary lists against Lawrence (whom he tried to write about for years), he did pry himself out of a sexual pit and it was a true climb up the inside of a chimney: he proceeded to have his first serious affair with that woman old enough to be his mother. All the while he was still feeling love for the blonde blue-eyed near-mythical girl he could not have and never touched. At least he has forged an ideal of love. Of course, he will never reach that love and on the consequence will never cease in some classic part of himself to pine for the girl.

From the rear windows of the flat we occupied, my mistress and I, I could look into the bedroom of the one I loved, the one I swore to love forever. She was married and had a child. At the time I was ignorant of the fact that she was living in this house across the yard; I never dreamed that it was *she* whose silhouette loomed before my eyes, and *me* filled with blackest misery. If only I had known, how grateful I would have been to sit forever before the window, aye, even in muck and filth. No, never once during those agonizing sessions did I suspect that she was there, less than a stone's throw away, almost within my grasp. *Almost!* If only, when calling her name in vain, I had thought to open the window! She would have heard. She might have answered.

Crawling into bed with the other I would pass heart-breaking hours wondering about the one who was lost to me. Exhausted, I would fall back into the deep pit. What an abominable form of suicide! I not only destroyed myself and the love that devoured me, I destroyed everything that came my way, including the one who clung to me desperately in sleep. I had to annihilate the world which had made me its victim.

The World of Sex

Still, he has moved from his family's detestation of sex to some sense of sexual pleasure however full of misery. After a few years he will marry a woman he never fails to describe as a prissy and/or puritanical bitch.

With this one the war of the sexes began in earnest. Her musical talent, which was the magnet of attraction, soon took second place. She was an hysterical, lascivious, puritanical bitch whose crack was hidden beneath a tangled mat of hair that looked for all the world like a sporran. The first time my fingers came in contact with it was of an evening during the early days of our courtship. She had stretched herself out on the radiator to warm up. She had nothing on but a silk dressing gown. The tuft of hair between her legs stood out so prominently that it almost looked as if she had a head of cauliflower hidden beneath her wrap. To her horror and amazement I made a grab for it. She was that startled I thought she would jump out of her skin. There was nothing for it but to grab my hat and coat and—bolt. In the hallway, at the head of the stairs, she caught up with me; she was still trembling, still dazed, but obviously unwilling to let me depart in such precipitate fashion. Under a flickering gas jet I held her in my arms and did my best to soothe her ruffled feelings. She responded with warm embraces. I concluded that everything was okey-dokey again. (A few more minutes, thought I to myself, and we'll be back in her snug little room making honey.) Unbuttoning my overcoat as discreetly as possible, I opened my fly. Then I gently took her hand and closed it around my pecker. That was the climax! With a shudder she let go of it and burst into a spasm of tears. I left her there in the hallway and, scampering down the long flight of stairs, I fled into the street. The following day I received a letter saying that she hoped never to see me again.

A few days later, however, I was back. Again she stretched out on the radiator, clad only in the silk dressing gown. This time I was a little more tactful. Casually, as it were, I ran my fingers lightly over the dressing gown. Her thick bush seemed to be full of electricity; the hair stood up stiff and crackly, like a wire sponge. It was necessary, in this approach, to maintain a running stream of chatter about music and other lofty subjects, while stroking her in absent-minded fashion. By resorting to this dodge I enabled her, or so I surmised, to tell herself that there was no harm in such deportment. In the kitchen later she showed me a few stunts she had learned in boarding school; these acrobatic enticements served, of course, to reveal her figure to full advantage. Every time her dressing sack fell open it disclosed the rich growth of fungus which was her secret pride. Tantalizing, to say the least.

Things went on this way for several weeks before she forgot herself. Even then she didn't abandon herself completely. The first time she lay down for it she insisted that I try to do it through her night gown. Not only was she mortally afraid of being knocked up, she wanted to test me. Should I give in to her whims and caprices, she would be able and willing to trust me all the way. That was her logic.

Gradually, very gradually, she began to react like a normal human being. Occasionally I would pay her a call in the middle of the day. I always had to proffer the excuse that I came to hear her play. It would never do to walk in and grab hold of her immediately. If I took a seat in the corner and listened to her attentively she might stop half way through a sonata and come over to me of her own accord, let me run my hand up her leg, and finally straddle me. With the orgasm she would sometimes have a weeping fit. Doing it in broad daylight always awakened her sense of guilt. (The way she voiced it was that it deteriorated her keyboard technique.) Anyway, the better the fuck the worse she felt afterwards. "You don't really care for *me*," she would say. "All you're after is sex." By dint of repeating it a thousand times it became a fact. I was already fed up with her by the time we legalized the relationship.

The World of Sex

It remains a curious relation. He detests his wife but loves to fuck her. There is nothing in literature to compare to the accounts he gives in *Tropic of Capricorn* and *Sexus* of making love to other women—they read like round by round AP wire stories. Returning to his wife, he will have a predictable itch to make love to her even if she is asleep. Then he meets June, and a short time later leaves his wife. By every one of his descriptions he is altogether in love with June (who is first called Mara, then Mona, in *Tropic of Cancer, Capricorn* and *The Rosy Crucifixion*). Still he continues to fuck his ex-wife. He enjoys her more than ever. It is as if every man must have in addition to everything else a sexy statue—some embodiment (here prissy) of all the non-sexuality and anti-sexuality imbibed from all the cold and disinterested women of childhood, and yet succeed somehow in converting that cold marble to flesh sweet and happy at room temperature. So he makes love to his ex-wife like a pirate opening a chest or a terrorist blowing up a factory, a sex murderer whose weapon is his phallus. It is social artifice he would slay first, and hypocrisy, and all the cancers of bourgeois suffocation. "Take that, you cunt," is his war cry. Yet the enigma of woman's nature (if she has, that is, a nature, and is not merely a person altogether equal, hoof to human hoof, with man), the enigma, if it exists, is that women respond to him, of course they do, it is the simple knowledge of the street that murderers are even sexier than athletes. Something in a woman wishes to be killed went the old wisdom before Women's Liberation wiped that out, something in a woman wishes to be killed, and it is obvious what does— she would like to lose the weakest part of herself, have it ploughed under, ground under, kneaded, tortured, squashed, sliced, banished, and finally immolated. Burn out my dross is the unspoken cry of his girls—in every whore is an angel burning her old rags.

It is a pure period of his life. He is in sex for the kill and will later write about it better than anyone ever has. (The kill.) But we are far from arriving at the truth of him. He is not Henry Miller who can sublimate murder into sex, and nothing more. No, he is Henry Miller, the man of metamorphoses. The first of the lovers in him, and it will never leave him altogether, is the stud with a rock for a cock and a rock for a heart—so he will present himself. That is the first manifest of himself as a lover. Others are to follow.

June (Mona) has been met in a dancehall in 1923. She is to prove the love of his life. In writing about that love, he begins an infatuation with the number seven equal to Mann's in *The Magic Mountain*. He speaks of the first seven days of their meeting, and the seven years of their relation (which came to an end of sorts in 1930 when he went off to Europe alone—although they were to live together on and off for another few years). He must bring himself up to the point of trying to write about her at least seven times. In *Tropic of Cancer* he is about to begin more than once, and *Tropic of Capricorn* could be described as a book written entirely around the difficulty of trying to write about her. Forget the number seven—it will still take six years from the time of their divorce in 1934 before he can undertake to describe their affair and marriage in anything like novelistic fashion, and *The Rosy Crucifixion*, which just about covers the day-to-day movement of their five years of excursions and capers together in New York is a novel of 1600 pages. If the first book *Sexus* was begun in 1940 it was not finished until 1945, and *Plexus* took from 1947 to 1949. *Nexus*, the final volume, was not even started until 1952 nor done until 1959. He has spent close to twenty years on his magnum opus! Of course, he has written other books in the same time, *The Air-Conditioned Nightmare, The Time of the Assassins, The Books in My Life, Big Sur and The Oranges of Hieronymus Bosch* plus some smaller works, but in comparison to the prodigies of talent he exhibited in the thirties with *Tropic of Cancer, Black Spring* and *Tropic of Capricorn*, he is something like half the writer stretched out to twice the length.

He is also, of course, now old for a writer. His work on *The Rosy Crucifixion* corresponds almost exactly to his fifties and his sixties. He is not far from seventy when he is done, yet the mysteries of his relation with Mona have so beguiled him that he has spent thirty-six obsessive years living with her and writing about her and never succeeds, never quite, in making her real to us, as novelistically real as Anna Karenina or Emma Bovary. She hovers in that space between the actual and the fictional where everything is just out of focus. Indeed Anaïs Nin in one page of her diary succeeds in making Mona as vivid as Miller ever can. (Yet, no more real.)

> Henry came to Louveciennes with June.
> As June walked toward me from the darkness of the garden into the light of the door, I saw for the first time the most beautiful woman on earth. A startlingly white face, burning dark eyes, a face so alive I felt it would consume itself before my eyes. Years ago I tried to imagine a true beauty; I created in my mind an image of just such a woman. I had never seen her until last night. Yet I knew long ago the phosphorescent color of her skin, her huntress profile, the evenness of her teeth. She is bizarre, fantastic, nervous, like someone in a high fever. Her beauty drowned me. As I sat before her, I felt I would do

anything she asked of me. Henry suddenly faded. She was color and brilliance and strangeness. By the end of the evening I had extricated myself from her power. She killed my admiration by her talk. Her talk. The enormous ego, false, weak, posturing. She lacks the courage of her personality, which is sensual, heavy with experience. Her role alone preoccupies her. She invents drama in which she always stars. I am sure she creates genuine dramas, genuine chaos and whirlpools of feelings, but I feel that her share in it is a pose. That night, in spite of my response to her, she sought to be whatever she felt I wanted her to be. She is an actress every moment. I cannot grasp the core of June. Everything Henry had said about her is true.

By the end of the evening I felt as Henry did, fascinated with her face and body which promises so much, but hating her invented self which hides the true one.

The Diary of Anaïs Nin

Curious! If we fix on Miller's mind rather than June's beauty, Nin could be giving a description of his talent: *startling, burning, phosphorescent, bizarre, fantastic, nervous, in high fever*, full of *color, brilliance* and *strangeness* but possessed of an *enormous ego, false, weak, posturing* and finally *lacking the courage of its personality*, leaving behind *chaos* and *whirlpools of feeling*. Yet it may be all a *pose*. One *cannot grasp the core* of Henry Miller, and one can come near to *hating* (his) *invented self which hides the true one*.

It works. If one is to judge Miller's talent by the vices of his mind, the result is not unequal to the flaws in June's beauty. No wonder they have seven years together. It is a relation which proves obsessive but consistently changeable; fixed in compulsion yet stripped of roots; emotional as blood and yet as insecure as emotion itself. She will take him a long way in seven good and bad years from the cold mean calculating street-fucker, the hard-nosed Brooklyn hard-on by which he was still picturing himself when they met. He is one stud who has met more than his equal. She is more enterprising than he, wiser about the world, more subtly aggressive, a better hustler. Before a year is out, she has convinced him to quit work and try to write while she will make their living. If ever there is an inner movement in his life, it is here, indeed we are witness to his first metamorphosis. He shifts from an intelligent and second-rate promoter of bad debts, and some riotous Brooklyn nights, to a faithful and tortured young writer helplessly in love with a Junoesque woman whose maddening lack of center leads him into an intuition of his own lack of identity. He comes to discover all those modern themes which revolve around the discovery of oneself. Soon he will dive into the pit of recognizing that there may not be a geological fundament in the psyche one can call identity. Like June, he will have to re-create himself each morning, and soon realizes he has been doing it all his life. He has never looked back in moral guilt because whatever act he committed yesterday, and it could have been atrocious, heinous, or incommensurately disloyal to what he thought he believed or loved, it hardly mattered. He could look yesterday's act in the eye because the man who did it was no longer himself. In the act of doing it, he became another man, free to go in another direction. It can be 180° away from yesterday's attempt. Tomorrow he may be close again to the man he was day before yesterday, but never the same. He has passed from the sublimation of murder (by way of a sullen intent cock) to the liberation of the self from every cancer-habit of the past. Since he has a life full of adventure, debts, mishaps and constant on-coming lack of funds, since June brings in their living as irregularly as changes in the weather, so there is no nicety to his liberation, no, Miller's psychic life is equal to a scatback scampering upfield on a punt return. He can lose ten yards as easily as gain them. And his head is forever ringing from the last concussion.

His confusion, however, is great; his passivity feels pervasive. He has changed from a stand-up hallway-fucker to a somewhat indolent husband-pimp. His wife is having the adventures, and he is home doing the writing, sometimes the cooking. He is in the untidy situation of a man who lives with a Brooklyn moral code for sex, "If she won't screw, she's frigid; if she does, she's a whore," yet the wife is a consummate liar, and makes money off men to the tune of hundred dollar bills dropped in from the sky, never tells him how, a woman even more changeable than himself and vastly more bisexual—their love will crash finally when she brings home a girl to live with them, and becomes hooked on the girl. Sixteen hundred pages of *The Rosy Crucifixion* will founder on Miller's inability to penetrate these depths, or even come near them. He was brought up by a moral code which taught that love was attached to the living room; one's family was one's house. The living room carpet was one's rock. Now he floats in a fluid as limitless as amniotic fluid. He has no limbs and his feet are over his head, his eyes smell sounds and his nose hears colors, he is living with a woman even more incredible than himself. All the while he is becoming an artist. He is moving away from the use of himself as a skilled and stealthy sex murderer who can instill small deaths into every hot and humping fornication. Now, he is emerging as a narcissist at loose in the uncategorizability of his own experience.

It is too simple to think of the narcissist as someone in love with himself. One can detest oneself intimately and still be a narcissist. What characterizes narcissism is the fundamental relation. It is with oneself. The same dialectic of love and hate that mates feel for one another is experienced within the self. But then a special kind of insanity calls to the narcissist. The inner dialogue hardly ever ceases. Like animals are each half of themselves and forever scrutinizing the other. So two narcissists in love are the opposite of two mates who may feel a bond powerful as the valence holding the atoms of a molecule together. Narcissists, in contrast, are linked up into themselves. They do not join each other so much as approach one another like crystals brought into juxtaposition. They have a passionate affair to the degree each allows the other to resonate more fully than when alone. Two narcissists might live together for fifty years in every appearance of matrimonial solidity (although it probably helps if money is present) but essentially, no matter how considerate they may be of one another, the courtesies come more from a decision to be good to the other than issuing from a love which will go forth whether one wills it or not. The narcissistic relation insists that the other continue to be good for one's own resonance. In the profoundest sense, one narcissist is never ready to die for the other. It is not love we may encounter so much as fine tuning. Small wonder that the coming together of narcissists is the natural matrimony of the Technological Century. Small wonder that Henry Miller, the last great American pioneer, is first to boff and bang his way across this last psychological frontier, there first with the most. No love in literature is so long recounted as his 1600-page affair and marriage and separation from his Mona. *The Rosy Crucifixion* becomes one of the greatest failures in the history of the novel, a literary cake large as the Himalayas which fails to rise. And across half at least of its sixteen hundred pages are peaks and avenues and haunches and battlements and arêtes and basins and summits and valleys of writing so good one shakes one's head. Pity the poor aspiring mediocrity of a writer who reads Miller without protection—he will never write another word if he has any decency left. Pity for that matter the good writer. At times Miller is too good.

Yet *The Rosy Crucifixion* is one of the monumental failures of world literature. For those sixteen hundred pages, Miller knocks on the door of ultimate meaning and it never opens a crack. By the end he is where he was at the beginning at least so far as sexual satori is concerned. I-got-laid-and-it-was-wondrous is the opening theme of the book, and by the end not one new philosophical connection has been laid onto that first lay. Miller and the reader know no more of the intimate wonders beneath the first wonder after the book is done.

An obvious critical impulse is to decide the work is too long. But on examination it cannot be cut. Rather, as it stands, it is too fragmentary. Perhaps it should be a novel of four thousand pages. What Miller has bogged into (precisely because he is the first American to make the attempt) is the uncharted negotiations of the psyche when two narcissists take the vow of love. Yet it is finally his own novelistic terrain. Since he has always eschewed politics as a literary subject (he merely issues calumnies against it), since he therefore has also eschewed the incomparably finicky and invaluable literary task of trying to place people in society, he never really writes about society except through metaphor. Since he is a great writer, his metaphors occasionally produce the whole and entire machine of society until it passes over one's brain like an incubus. He does this with his vision of the Cosmodemonic Telegraph Company and the unforgettable metaphor in *Tropic of Cancer* when Miller and Van Norden are exhaustedly fucking a worn-out whore like men standing up in the trenches.

His preference, however, is to create his literary world through the visions of dreams and the tides of whatever myths he finds appropriate to his use. Since that has to be a perfumed and farty literary game unless there is real novelistic meat on each mythic tendon, Miller naturally goes to sex for his meat. He is not a social writer, but a sexual writer. Even Lawrence never let go of the idea that through sex he could still delineate society; Miller, however, went further. Sex, he assumed, was a natural literary field for the novel, as clear and free and open to a land-grab as any social panorama. One could capture the sex-life of two people in all its profundity and have quite as much to say about the cosmos as any literary plot laid out the other way with its bankers and beggars, ladies and whores, clerks and killers. The real novel, went Miller's assumption, could short-circuit society. Give us the cosmos head on. Give it to us by way of a cunt impaled on a cock.

That is a herculean assumption. Because you need the phallus of Hercules to bring it off (and conceivably the brain of Einstein). A writer works with what he is given, and in Miller's case, for cosmic blast-off, he had a narcissistic cunt on a narcissistic cock and thirty-six years of bewilderment from the day of meeting his love to the hour he finished writing of her. She was so changeable went his everlasting lament.

It is hard enough for a man twisting a pencil through the traps and loops of his handwriting to get a character onto an empty page, but to create someone who shifts all the time! As soon teach one's spine to wind like a snake. The narcissist is always playing roles, and if there is any character harder for an author to create than that writer greater than himself, it may be a great actor. We do not even begin to comprehend the psychology of actors.

The narcissist suffers from too much inner dialogue. The eye of one's consciousness is forever looking at one's own action. Yet these words turn us away from the psychic reality. The narcissist is not self-absorbed so much as one self is absorbed in studying the other. The narcissist is the scientist and the experiment in one. Other people exist for their ability to excite one presence or another in oneself. And are valued for that. Are even loved for that. Of course, they are loved as an actor loves an audience.

Since the amount of stimulation we may offer ourselves is obviously limited, the underlying problem of the narcissist is boredom. So there are feverish and/or violent attempts to shift the given, to alter the context in which one self is forever regarding the other. It is a reason why narcissists are forever falling in and out of love, jobs, places and addictions. Promiscuity is the happy opportunity to try a new role. Vanity is the antidote to claustrophobia. Miller complains bitterly of June's lack of center, her incapacity to tell the truth or even recognize it. "I want the key," he says once to Anaïs Nin, "the key to the lies." As if necessarily blind to himself (for every artist lives in a self-induced blindness which establishes a foundation for his shifting effort) Miller never wants to recognize that the key may be simple. Every day is a scenario for June. On the best of days she creates a life into which she can fit for a few hours. She can feel real love and real hate for strangers, and leave the circle of her own self-absorption. Through scenarios, she can in an hour arrive at depths of emotion other people voyage toward for years, but the scenario once concluded, so, too, is the love for that day. The passing actor she was playing with is again a stranger. It is useless to speak of whether she loves or does not love Miller. It depends on whether he is a part of her scenario that day. So is it also useless to speak of her lives. They are no more real to her than last year's role for an actor. It is the scenario that is her truth and her life. That is her liberty from the prison cell of the narcissist.

Indeed, part of Miller's continuing literary obsession with his second wife for close to thirty more years is due to the variety of her roles. Each offered a new role for Miller to play opposite. To be living as a detective one day and as a criminal the next is to keep one's interest in one's own personality alive.

Narcissists, after all, do not hand emotion back and forth through their bodies so much as they induce emotion in one another through their minds. It is not their own flesh nor the other's which is felt so quickly as the vibrancy of the role. Their relations are at once more electric and more empty, more perfect and more hollow. So it is possible that narcissism is a true disease, a biological displacement of the impulse to develop which could bear the same relation to love that onanism does to copulation, or cancer to the natural growth of tissue. As we come a little nearer to the recognition that the base beneath all disease, the ultimate disease, is insanity or cancer, and other illnesses may even be bulwarks against some irreversible revolt of the flesh or the mind once they have determined to grow in ways and into places flesh and mind have never grown before, so to the narcissist, there is always the unconscious terror that isolation, if unrelieved, must end in one arm or the other of the ultimate disease.

The paradox is that no love can prove so intense, therefore, as the love of two narcissists for each other. So much depends on it. Each—the paradox turns upon itself—is capable of offering deliverance to the other. To the degree that they tune each other superbly well they begin to create what had before been impossible—they begin to have a skill which enables them to enter the world. (For it is not love of the self but dread at the world outside the self which is the seed of narcissism.) So narcissists can end by having a real need of each other. That is, of course, hardly the characteristic relation. The love of most narcissists tends to become comic, since seen from the outside, their suffering manages to be equalled only by the rapidity with which they recover from suffering.

Of course, the reality is considerably more painful. Given the delicacy of every narcissist and the timidity which created their detachment, we can recognize that the intensity of their relations has to be with themselves. They need an excess of control over external events for their own self-protection. Not too removed in analogy is that excess of control which technology is forever trying to exact from nature, even as the love affairs of technology give back in recollection their own comic atrocity: defoliation of the land in Vietnam, or computerized dating services.

To the degree, however, that narcissism is an affliction of the talented, the stakes are not small, and the victims are playing their own serious game in the midst of the scenarios. If one can only break out of the penitentiary of self-absorption, there are artistic wonders, conceivably, to achieve. Indeed, for a narcissist to stay in love with someone else for a long period is to speak of the fine art of the beloved. They can tune, after all, the unspeakably complex machine of oneself.

Miller may have been playing, therefore, for the highest stakes we can conceive. He had the energy, the vision, the talent, and the outrageous individuality to have some chance of becoming the greatest writer in America's history, a figure equal to Shakespeare. (For Americans.) Of course, to invoke such contrasts is to mock them. A writer cannot live too seriously with the idea that he will or will not beat Tolstoy—he has rather some sense of a huge and not impossible literary destiny in the reverberations of his own ambition; he feels his talent, perhaps, as a trust, so he sees his loves as evil when they balk him. He is living, after all, with his own secret plot. He knows that a writer of the largest dimension can alter the nerves and marrow of a nation: no one, in fact, can measure what collective loss of inner life would have come to English people if Shakespeare had failed to write.

In those seven years with June, Miller was shaping the talent with which he would go out into the world. It is part of the total ambiguity with which he has surrounded himself (despite the ten thousand intimate details he offers of his life) that we do not know by the end of *The Rosy Crucifixion* whether she breathed a greater life into his talent or exploited him. We do not know if Mona was a Great Ice Lady who chilled a part of him forever, or a beautiful much-abused piece of earth-mother. We do not know if Miller could have become something like an American Shakespeare capable of writing about tyrants and tycoons (instead, repetitively, of his own liberation) if he had never met Mona, whether, that is, she left him frozen in obsession, and *The Rosy Crucifixion* could have become the most important American novel ever written if not for her; or—we are left wide open—the contrary is the true possibility and he might never have written at all if he had not met her, certainly never become a writer of the major dimension he achieved. All we know is that after seven years of living with her, he went off to Paris alone and learned to live by himself. He had escaped his mother, the blonde with the blue eyes, the reproachful widow, his first wife, and even could work after separation from Mona. He had come into that magical confluence of his life where he could extract a clean and unforgettable esthetic from ogres and sewers. And June after their separation, and divorce in 1934, sinks from view. The last we hear of her is by way of a line in a one-page letter full of news to Anaïs Nin somewhere in the winter of 1954–55. "June, by the way," he writes, "was taken to a mental institution some months ago. Must stop—mailman due any minute, Henry."

We will not know if brutality or stoicism is the foundation of the line, nor will we have a clue to whether he weakened her in their seven years or if she would have been considerably more damaged without him. In *The Diary of Anaïs Nin* (1931–1935) there is a heartbreaking comment made by June after she has read some of what Miller has finally written about her. "I expected Henry to do wonderful things with my life," she says. "But instead he reduced it all, vulgarized it, made it shabby and ugly." It is the cry of everyone who has ever been written about when the author failed to share the inner eye of the model. In another place, Anaïs Nin will write of June,

> She died in Paris. She died the night she read Henry's book (the manuscript version of *Tropic of Cancer*) because of his brutality. She wept and repeated over and over again, "It is not me, it is not me he is writing about. It's a distortion. He says I live in delusions, but it is he, it is he who does not see me, or anyone as I am, as they are. He makes everything ugly."
>
> *The Diary of Anaïs Nin*

Yet even Anaïs Nin, firm as a countess in her percipience, veers first to one side of the marriage in her sympathy, then the other,

> June, having no core of strength, can only prove it by her power to destroy others. Henry, until he knew me, could only assert his strength by attacking June. He caricatured her; she weakened him by protecting him. They devoured each other. And when they succeed in destroying each other, they weep. June wanted Henry to be a Dostoevsky, but she did all she could to make it impossible. She really wanted him to sing her praises, to paint her as an admirable character. It is only in the light of this that she judges Henry's book a failure. It failed to aggrandize June.
>
> *The Diary of Anaïs Nin*

Each evaluation overthrows the consistency of the previous one. A clue to the endless mirrors of Miller's relation to June shimmers through this earlier extract from the same diary.

> Yesterday Henry came to Louveciennes. A new Henry, or, rather, the Henry I sensed behind the one generally known, the Henry behind the one he has written down. This Henry can understand: he is sentient.
>
> He looked so serious. His violence has burnt itself out. The coarseness, in the alchemy, became strength. He had received a letter from June, in pencil, irregular, mad, like a child's moving, simple cries, of her love for him. "Such a letter blots out everything." I felt the moment had come to expose the June I knew, to give him June, "because it will make you love her more. It's a

beautiful June. Other days I felt you might laugh at my portrait, jeer at its naïveté. Today I know you won't."

I let him read all I had written about June.

What is happening? He is deeply moved, torn apart. He believes.

"It is in this way that I should have written about June." he says. "The other is incomplete, superficial. You have got her."

"You leave softness, tenderness out of your work, you write down only the hatred, the rebellions, the violence. I have only inserted what you leave out. What you leave out is not because you don't feel it, or know it, or understand, as you think. It is left out only because it is more difficult to express, and so far, your writing has come out of violence and anger."

I confide in him completely, in the profound Henry. He is won over. He says, "Such love is wonderful. I do not hate or despise that. I see what you give each other. I see it so well. Let me read on. This is a revelation to me." I tremble while he is reading. He understands too well. Suddenly he says, "Anaïs, I have just realized that what I give is something coarse and plain, compared to that. I realize that when June returns. . . ."

I stop him. "You don't know what you have given me! It is not coarse and plain." And then I add, "You see a beautiful June now."

"No, I hate her."

"You hate her?"

"Yes, I hate her," Henry says, "because I see by your notes that we are her dupes, that you are duped, that there is a pernicious, destructive direction to her lies. Insidiously, they are meant to deform me in your eyes, and you in my eyes. If June returns, she will poison us against each other. I fear that."

"There is a friendship between us, Henry, which is not possible for June to understand."

"For that she will hate us, and she will combat us with her own tools."

"What can she use against our understanding of each other?"

"Lies," said Henry.

The Diary of Anaïs Nin

He is speaking like a man who is now in love with Anaïs Nin. It is a worthy Jamesian dialogue. He has come a long way from the boy who has no relation to his mother. But as we shall see in the sections on Mona which follow (and they were written ten years after these entries from Anaïs Nin's diary) a part of Miller has been amputated forever from any comfort in the idea that woman has a character as large as man. No matter.* We will not know all of Mona, but we will live through enough to stimulate any knowledge we have acquired already about the dimensions of a heroine.

---

*In compensation, he will see Woman with a nature large as Nature itself.

Henry Miller

KATE MILLETT

Certain writers are persistently misunderstood. Henry Miller is surely one of the major figures of American literature living today, yet academic pedantry still dismisses him as beneath scholarly attention. He is likely to be one of the most important influences on our contemporary writing, but official criticism perseveres in its scandalous and systematic neglect of his work.[1] To exacerbate matters, Miller has come to represent the much acclaimed "sexual freedom" of the last few decades. One finds eloquent expression of this point of view in a glowing essay by Karl Shapiro: "Miller's achievement is miraculous: he is screamingly funny without making fun of sex . . . accurate and poetic in the highest degree; there is not a smirk anywhere in his writings."[2] Shapiro is confident that Miller can do more to expunge the "obscenities" of the national scene than a "full-scale social revolution."[3] Lawrence Durrell exclaims over "how nice it is for once to dispense with the puritans and with pagans," since Miller's books, unlike those of his contemporaries, are "not due to puritanical shock."[4] Shapiro assures us that Miller is "the first writer outside the Orient who has succeeded in writing as naturally about sex on a large scale as novelists ordinarily write about the dinner table or the battlefield."[5] Significant analogies. Comparing the *Tropic of Cancer* with Joyce's *Ulysses*, Shapiro gives Miller the advantage, for while Joyce, warped by the constraints of his religious background, is prurient or "aphrodisiac," Miller is "no aphrodisiac at all, because religious or so-called moral tension does not exist for him."[6] Shapiro is convinced that "Joyce actually prevents himself from experiencing the beauty of sex or lust, while Miller is freed at the outset to deal with the overpowering mysteries and glories of love and copulation."[7]

However attractive our current popular image of Henry Miller the liberated man may appear, it is very far from being the truth. Actually, Miller is a compendium of American sexual neuroses, and his value lies not in freeing us from such afflictions, but in having had the honesty to express and dramatize them. There *is* a kind of culturally cathartic release in Miller's writing, but it is really a result of the fact that he first gave voice to the

Reprinted from *Sexual Politics* (Garden City, New York: Doubleday, 1970), 294–313, Copyright © 1969, 1970, 1990 by Kate Millett.

unutterable. This is no easy matter of four-letter words; they had been printed already in a variety of places. What Miller did articulate was the disgust, the contempt, the hostility, the violence, and the sense of filth with which our culture, or more specifically, its masculine sensibility, surrounds sexuality. And women too; for somehow it is women upon whom this onerous burden of sexuality falls. There is plenty of evidence that Miller himself is fleetingly conscious of these things, and his "naive, sexual heroics" would be far better if, as one critic suggests, they had been carried all the way to "self-parody."[8] But the major flaw in his oeuvre—too close an identification with the persona, "Henry Miller"—always operates insidiously against the likelihood of persuading us that Miller the man is any wiser than Miller the character.[9]

And with *this* Miller; though one has every reason to doubt the strict veracity of those sexual exploits he so laboriously chronicles in the first person, though one has every reason to suspect that much of this "fucking" is sheer fantasy—there is never reason to question the sincerity of the emotion which infuses such accounts; their exploitative character; their air of juvenile egotism. Miller's genuine originality consists in revealing and recording a group of related sexual attitudes which, despite their enormous prevalence and power, had never (or never so explicitly) been given literary expression before. Of course, these attitudes are no more the whole truth than chivalry, or courtly, or romantic love were—but Miller's attitudes do constitute a kind of cultural data heretofore carefully concealed beneath our traditional sanctities. Nor is it irrelevant that the sociological type Miller's impressions represent is that of a brutalized adolescence. The sympathy they elicit is hardly confined to that group but strikes a chord of identification in men of all ages and classes, and constitute an unofficial masculine version of both sexuality and the female which—however it appears to be at variance with them—is still vitally dependent on the official pieties of love: mother, wife, virgin, and matron. The anxiety and contempt which Miller registers toward the female sex is at least as important and generally felt as the more diplomatic or "respectful" version presented to us in conventional writing.[10] In fact, to hear Miller bragging of having "broken down" a "piece of tail" is as bracing as the sound of honest bigotry in a redneck after hours of Senator Eastland's unctuous paternalism.

Miller regards himself as a disciple of Lawrence, a suggestion certain to have outraged the master had he lived to be so affronted. The liturgical pomp with which Lawrence surrounded sexuality bears no resemblance to Miller's determined profanity. The Lawrentian hero sets about his mission with notorious gravity and "makes love" by an elaborate political protocol. In the process, by dint of careful diplomacy and expert psychological manipulation, he effects the subjection of the woman in question. But Miller and his confederates—for Miller is a gang—just "fuck" women and discard them, much as one might avail oneself of sanitary facilities—Kleenex or toilet paper, for example. Just "fucking," the Miller hero is merely a huckster and a con man, unimpeded by pretension, with no priestly role to uphold. Lawrence did much to kill off the traditional attitudes of romantic love. At first glance, Miller seems to have started up blissfully ignorant of their existence altogether. Actually, his cold-blooded procedure is intended as sacrilege to the tenderness of romantic love, a tenderness Lawrence was never willing to forgo. In his brusque way, Miller demonstrates the "love fraud" (a species of power play disguised as eroticism) to be a process no more complex than a mugging. The formula is rather simple: you meet her, cheat her into letting you have "a piece of ass," and then take off. Miller's hunt is a primitive find, fuck, and forget.

Among other things, it was a shared dislike for the sexual revolution that sparked Miller's admiration and drove him to undertake a long essay on Lawrence:

> It seems significant that, with all the power that was in him, Lawrence strove to put woman back in her rightful place . . . The masculine world . . . deeply and shamefully feminized, is . . . inclined to distrust and despise Lawrence's ideas . . . what he railed against and fought tooth and nail . . . the sickly ideal love world of depolarized sex! The world based on a fusion of the sexes instead of an antagonism . . . [for] the eternal battle with woman sharpens our resistance, develops our strength, enlarges the scope of our cultural achievements: through her . . . we build . . . our religions, philosophies and sciences.[11]

There is a similarity of purpose here, but what Miller fails to recognize, or at least to comment upon, is the total disparity of their methods. Lawrence had turned back the feminist claims to human recognition and a fuller social participation by distorting them into a vegetative passivity calling itself fulfillment. His success prepared the way for Miller's escalation to open contempt. Lawrence had still to deal with persons; Miller already feels free to speak of objects. Miller simply converts woman to "cunt"—thing, commodity, matter. There is no personality to recognize or encounter, so there is none to tame or break by the psychological subtleties of Lawrence's Freudian wisdom.

While both writers enlist the fantastic into the service of sexual politics, Lawrence's use seems pragmatically political, its end is to compel the emotional surrender of an actual woman, generally a person of considerable strength and intelligence. Miller confronts nothing more challenging than the undifferentiated genital that exists in masturbatory revery. In the case of the two actual women, Maude and Mara, who appear in Miller's world amidst its thousand floozie caricatures, personality and sexual behavior are so completely unrelated that, in the sexual episodes where they appear, any other names might have been conveniently substituted. For the purpose of every bout is the same: a demonstration of the hero's self-conscious detachment before the manifestations of a lower order of life. During an epic encounter with Mara, the only woman he ever loved, Miller is as clinical as he was toward Ida; Mara just as grotesque:

> And on this bright and slippery gadget Mara twisted like an eel. She wasn't any longer a woman in heat, she wasn't even a woman; she was just a mass of indefinable contours wriggling and squirming like a piece of fresh bait seen upside down through a convex mirror in a rough sea.
>
> I had long ceased to be interested in her contortions; except for the part of me that was in her I was cool as a cucumber and remote as the Dog Star . . .
>
> Towards dawn, Eastern Standard Time, I saw by that frozen condensed-milk expression about the jaw that it was happening. Her face went through all the metamorphoses of early uterine life, only in reverse. With the last dying spark it collapsed like a punctured bag, the eyes and nostrils smoking like toasted acorns in a slightly wrinkled lake of pale skin.[12]

The Victorians, or some of them, revealed themselves in their slang expression for the orgasm—"to spend"—a term freighted with economic insecurity and limited resources, perhaps a reflection of capitalist thrift implying that if semen is money (or time or energy) it should be preciously hoarded.[13] Miller is no such cheapskate, but in his mind, too, sex is linked in a curious way with money. By the ethos of American financial morality, Miller was a downright "failure" until the age of forty; a writer unable to produce, living a seedy outcast existence, jobless and dependent on handouts. Before exile in Paris granted him reprieve, Miller felt himself the captive of circumstances in a philistine milieu where artistic or intellectual work was despised, and the only approved avenues of masculine achievement were confined to money or sex. Of course, Miller is a maverick and a rebel, but much as he hates the money mentality, it is so ingrained in him that he is capable only of replacing it with sex—a transference of acquisitive impulse. By converting the female to commodity, he too can enjoy the esteem of "success." If he can't make money, he can make women—if need be on borrowed cash, pulling the biggest coup of all by getting something for nothing. And while his better "adjusted" contemporaries swindle in commerce, Miller preserves his "masculinity" by swindling in cunt. By shining in a parallel system of pointless avarice whose real rewards are also tangential to actual needs and likewise surpassed by the greater gains run up for powerful egotism, his manly reputation is still assured with his friends.

When reporting on the civilized superiority of French sex, his best proof is its better business method. The whore's client is "permitted to examine and handle merchandise before buying," a practice he congratulates as "fair and square."[14] Not only is the patron spared any argument from the "owner of the commodity," overseas trade is so benevolent that there is nothing "to hinder you should you decide to take a half-dozen women with you to a hotel

room, provided you made no fuss about the extra charge for soap and towels."[15] As long as you can pay, he explains, full of the complacency of dollar
culture, no other human considerations exist. "At the hotel I rang for women
like you would ring for whiskey and soda,"[16] he boasts once in a pipe-dream
of riches, inebriated with the omnipotence of money and the yanqui Playboy's
conviction that the foreigners do these things better.

During his tenure as personnel manager for Western Union, Miller was
happily placed to exercise a perfect combination of sexual and economic
power over the women applying to him for jobs: "The game was to keep
them on the string, to promise them a job but to get a free fuck first. Usually
it was only necessary to throw a feed into them, in order to bring them back
to the office at night and lay them out on the zinc-covered table in the dressing
room."[17] As all Americans know, the commercial world is a battlefield. When
executives are "fucked" by the company, they can retaliate by "fucking"
their secretaries. Miller's is "part-nigger" and "so damned pleased to have
someone fuck her without blushing,"[18] that she can be shared out to the
boss's pal Curley. She commits suicide eventually, but in business, "it's fuck
or be fucked,"[19] Miller observes, providing some splendid insight into the
many meanings we attach to the word.

One memorable example of sex as a war of attrition waged upon economic grounds is the fifteen-franc whore whom Miller and his friend Van
Norden hire in the Paris night and from whom, despite their own utter lack
of appetite and her exhaustion from hunger, it is still necessary to extort the
price.[20] As sex, or rather "cunt," is not only merchandise but a monetary
specie, Miller's adventures read like so many victories for sharp practice,
carry the excitement of a full ledger, and operate on the flat premise that
quantity is quality. As with any merchant whose sole concern is profit, the
"goods" themselves grow dull and contemptible, and even the amassing of
capital pales beside the power it becomes. So enervating is the addiction to
sex that Miller and his friends frequently renounce it: "Just cunt Hen . . .
just cunt," MacGregor sighs.[21] Van Norden is ashamed of his own obsessive
weakness, glad to make do from time to time with an apple, cutting out the
core and adding cold cream.[22] Sensually or emotionally, such a surrogate
involves no special hardship, since one has so little sense of actual women in
Miller's accounts of intercourse. Apples, however, offer no resistance, and
the enterprise of conquest, the fun of "breaking her down," is lost thereby.[23]

In the surfeit of Miller's pervfervid "fucking," it is surprising how much
of sexuality is actually omitted: intimacy, for example, or the aesthetic
pleasures of nudity. A very occasional pair of "huge teats" or "haunches" are
poor and infrequent spare parts for the missing erotic form of woman. Save
for the genitals—the star performers cock and balls—not a word is wasted
on the male body. It is not even bodies who copulate here, let alone persons.
Miller's fantasy drama is sternly restricted to the dissociated adventures of
cunt and prick: "The body is hers, but the cunt's yours. The cunt and the

prick, they're married," he lectures, after having demonstrated how life has so divorced the couple that "the bodies are going different ways."[24] In so stipulating on a contingent and momentary union, Miller has succeeded in isolating sexuality from the rest of life to an appalling degree. Its participants take on the idiot kinetics of machinery—piston and valve.

The perfect Miller "fuck" is a biological event between organs, its hallmark—its utter impersonality. Of course perfect strangers are best, chance passengers on subways molested without the exchange of word or signal. Paradoxically, this attempt to so isolate sex only loads the act with the most negative connotations. Miller has gone beyond even the empty situations one frequently encounters in professional pornography, blue movies, etc., to freight his incidents with cruelty and contempt. While seeming to remove sexuality from any social or personal context into the gray abstraction of "organ grinding,"[25] he carefully includes just enough information on the victim to make her activity humiliating and degrading, and his own an assertion of sadistic will.

Miller boasts, perhaps one should say confesses, that the "best fuck" he "ever had" was with a creature nearly devoid of sense, the "simpleton" who lived upstairs.[26] "Everything was anonymous and unformulated . . . Above the belt, as I say, she was batty. Yes, absolutely cuckoo, though still aboard and afloat. Perhaps that was what made her cunt so marvelously impersonal. It was one cunt out of a million . . . Meeting her in the daytime, watching her slowly going daft, it was like trapping a weasel when night came on. All I had to do was to lie down in the dark with my fly open and wait."[27] Throughout the description one not only observes a vulgar opportunistic use of Lawrence's hocus pocus about blanking out the mind in order to attain "blood consciousness," but one also intuits how both versions of the idea are haunted by a pathological fear of having to deal with another and complete human personality. Happily, Miller's "pecker" is sufficient to "mesmerize" his prey in the dark: "Come here, you bitch," I kept saying to myself, "come in here and spread that cunt over me . . . I didn't say a word, I didn't make a move, I just kept my mind riveted on her cunt moving quietly in the dark like a crab."[28] One is made very aware here that in the author's scheme the male is represented not only by his telepathic instrument, but by mind, whereas the perfect female is a floating metonomy, pure cunt, completely unsullied by human mentality.

Things are not always this good. To achieve a properly "impersonal fuck" with his despised wife Maude (she persists in the folly of "carnal love" in opposition to her husband's wiser taste for "cold fuck") Miller is put to the trouble of waiting until she sleeps: "Get her half asleep, her blinders off [29] . . . sneak up on her, slip it to her while she's dreaming."[30] The method recommended here is "back-scuttling," preferable for eliminating all superfluous contact and never obliging him to look at her face. Not until his betrayal and imminent departure madden her with grief and fear will she drop her annoying habit (the cause of their incompatibility) of desiring he recognize her as a person, and settle for being a "blind fuck." Earlier she had the gall to protest, "You never had any respect for me—as a human being,"[31] but finally, in a repetitious series of scenes, Miller can play upon her hysteria, put her on the "fucking block" and go at it "with cold-blooded fury."[32] After that it's all "fast, clean work . . . no tears, no love business" until the "ax" falls—a quaint trope which presumably represents his orgasm and her execution.

During a really busy day (Maude, Valeska, Valeska's cousin), Miller awakens from a nap on a West Side pier to discover he has an erection. One must not let such providence go to waste so he hurries to the apartment of a young woman to whom he had been introduced that day at lunch. She opens the door half-asleep and Miller seizes his opportunity: "I unbuttoned my fly and got my pecker out and into position. She was so drugged with sleep that it was almost like working on an automaton."[33] So much the better. More attractive still is the exotic detail, an infringement of several taboos, that she is Jewish passing for Egyptian: "I kept saying to myself— 'an Egyptian fuck . . . an Egyptian fuck' . . . It was one of the most wonderful fucks I ever had in my life."[34] Best of all, he manages to escape from her apartment fast enough to avoid the expense of any communication. This is really something for nothing, a free fuck: "I hadn't a word to say to her; the only thought in my head to get out . . . without wasting any words."[35] To complete his satisfaction, Miller's old friend Kronsky has arrived at the door of the apartment, and standing silently outside, is overhearing the entire scene, a crestfallen witness to the conquest.

Miller's ideal woman is a whore. Lawrence regarded prostitution as a profanation of the temple, but with Miller the commercialization of sexuality is not only a gratifying convenience for the male (since it is easier to pay than persuade) but the perfection of feminine existence, efficiently confining it to the function of absolute cunt. To illustrate this he calls upon Germaine, the archetypal French prostitute of American tourism: "a whore from the cradle; she was thoroughly satisfied with her role, enjoyed it in fact."[36] Launching into a thorough exposition of the subject, Miller explains that Germaine's "twat" is her "glory," her "sense of connection," her "sense of life" because "that was the only place where she experienced any life . . . down there between her legs where women ought to."[37] "Germaine had the right idea: she was ignorant and lusty, she put her heart and soul into her work. She was a whore all the way through—and that was her virtue."[38] Miller states categorically, "I could no more think of loving Germaine than I could think of loving a spider," but he does wish to impress upon us her superiority to another prostitute, Claude, whom he castigates as "delicate" and blames for her "refinement," claiming she offends in having "a soul and a conscience."[39] Most unedifying of all, Claude's evident but unspoken grief is proof she fails to relish her life and even dislikes its active hustle after custom. Such an attitude is inappropriate, morally and aesthetically outrageous: "a whore, it seemed to me, had no right to be sitting there like a lady, waiting . . . for someone to approach."[40]

Since "whores are whores," Miller is also capable of reviling them as "vultures," "buzzards," "rapacious devils," and "bitches"—his righteous scorn as trite as his sentimentality. He is anxious, however, to elevate their function to an "idea"—the Life Force. As with electrical conductors, to plug into them gives a fellow "that circuit which makes one feel the earth under his legs again."[41] Prostitutes themselves speak of their work as "servicing," and Miller's gratified egotism would not only seek to surround the recharge with mystification, but convert the whore into a curious vessel of intermasculine communication—rhapsodizing: "All the men she's been with and now you . . . the whole damned current of life flowing through you, through her, through all the guys behind you and after you."[42] What is striking here is not only the total abstraction Miller makes of sexuality (what could be less solid, less plastic than electricity?) but also the peculiar (yet hardly uncommon) thought of hunting other men's semen in the vagina of a whore, the random conduit of this brotherly vitality.

There is a men's-house atmosphere in Miller's work. His boyhood chums remain the friends of his youth, his maturity, even his old age. Johnny Paul and the street-gang heroes of adolescence continue as the idols of adulthood, strange companions for Miller's literary gods: Spengler, Nietzsche, Dostoievski. The six volumes of autobiography, and even the essays, are one endless, frequently self-pitying threnody for the lost paradise of his youth.

As a result, the sexual attitudes of the "undisputed monarch" of the "Land of Fuck,"[43] as Miller chooses to call himself, are those of an arrested adolescence where sex is clandestine, difficult to come by,[44] each experience constituting a victory of masculine diligence and wit over females either stupidly compliant or sagely unco-operative. There's one girl on the block who will take on the whole boy's club, but most are mean numbers who require working over; "good girls" whom parents and religion have corrupted into tough lays. The first afford the easy exultation of superiority, a feeling of utter and absolute contempt, the second, harder to make, provoke the animosity always reserved for the intransigent. The more difficult the assault, the greater the glory, but any victory is pointless if it cannot be boasted of and sniggered over. Just as Kronsky is said to hover behind the door, the reader is given the impression that sex is no good unless duly observed and applauded by an ubiquitous peer-group jury. And so Miller's prose has always the flavor of speech, the inflection of telling the boys: "And then I had to get over her again and shove it in, up to the hilt. She squirmed around like an eel, so help me God."[45] His strenuous heterosexuality depends, to a considerable degree, on a homosexual sharing. Not without reason, his love story, *The Rosy Crucifixion,* is one long exegesis of the simple admission "I had lost the power to love."[46] All the sentiment of his being, meanly withheld from "cunt," is lavished on the unattractive souls who make up the gang Miller never outgrew or deserted. What we observe in his work is a compulsive heterosexual activity in sharp distinction (but not opposed to) the kind of cultural homosexuality which has ruled that love, friendship, affection— all forms of companionship, emotional or intellectual—are restricted exclusively to males.

Miller's sexual humor is the humor of the men's house, more specifically, the men's room. Like the humor of any in-group, it depends on a whole series of shared assumptions, attitudes and responses, which constitute bonds in themselves. Here sex is a game whose pleasures lie in a demanding strategic deception and manipulation of a dupe. Its object is less the satisfaction of libido than ego, for the joys of sense are largely forgotten in the fun of making a fool of the victim. But unless sex is hard to get, comic, secretive, and "cunt" transparently stupid and contemptible, the joke disappears in air. As with racist humor or bigot fun in general, failure to agree upon the presumed fundamentals turns the comedy into puerile tedium. The point of Miller's game is to get as much as you can while giving nothing. The "much" in question is not sexual experience, for that might imply depth of feeling: the answer appears to be as much "cunt" or as many "cunts" as possible. In standard English the approximate phrase is probably Kinsey's uninviting "number of sexual outlets."

To love is to lose. In his one honest book, *Nexus,* Miller reveals that he lost very badly. His beloved Mara turned out to be a lesbian who inflicted her mistress upon him in a nightmarish ménage à trois, a female variant of the rigged triangle Lawrence aspired to but never achieved. It would be fascinating to speculate on how much of Miller's arrogance toward "cunt" in general is the product of this one lacerating experience.

For those convinced of the merits of the game, nearly any occasion can be exploited. Here is the redoubtable Henry paying a visit of condolence to a widow he once foolishly reverenced and admired, stammering and blushing before her, fatuously imagining she couldn't be "had." Scrupulously, he first sets the scene, welcoming his comrades to the setting of his triumph: "a low sofa," "soft lights"; the drink is catalogued and then the dress—"a beautiful low-cut morning gown."[47] Halfway through a eulogy of her late husband, Miller is suddenly inspired: "Without saying a word I raised her dress and slipped it into her."[48] The moment of truth is at hand; will the widow balk? As in a dream, this surprise attack meets with instantaneous success: "As I got it into her and began to work it around she took to moaning like . . . sort of delirious . . . with gasps and little shrieks of joy and anguish."[49] Finally the moral: "I thought to myself what a sap you've been to wait so long. She was so wet and juicy down there . . . why, anybody could have come along and had what's what. She was a pushover."[50] So are they all, and the joke is that such opportunities are missed only for lack of enterprise or through adherence to false ideals.

They are not only pushovers, they are puppets. Speaking boy to boy about another "fuck," Miller remarks, "I moved her around like one of those legless toys which illustrate the principle of gravity."[51] Total victory is gratuitous insult; the pleasure of humiliating the sexual object appears to be far more intoxicating than sex itself. Miller's protégé, Curley, is an expert at inflicting this sort of punishment, in this instance, on a woman whom both men regard as criminally overambitious, disgracefully unaware she is only cunt:

> He took pleasure in degrading her. I could scarcely blame him for it, she was such a prim, priggish bitch in her street clothes. You'd swear she didn't own a cunt the way she carried herself in the street. Naturally, when he got her alone, he made her pay for her highfallutin' ways. He went at it cold-bloodedly. "Fish it out!" he'd say, opening his fly a little. "Fish it out with your tongue!" . . . once she got the taste of it in her mouth you could do anything with her. Sometimes he'd stand her on her hands and push her around the room that way, like a wheelbarrow. Or else he'd do it dog fashion, and while she groaned and squirmed he'd nonchalantly light a cigarette and blow the smoke between her legs. Once he played her a dirty trick doing it that way. He had worked her up to such a state that she was beside herself. Anyway, after he had almost polished the ass off her with his back-scuttling he pulled out for a second, as though to cool his cock off . . . and shoved a big long carrot up her twat.[52]

One recalls Shapiro's enthusiasm for the "overpowering mysteries of love and copulation."

Even the orgies which Miller presents to us as lessons in a free and happy sensuality, far removed from the constraints of American puritanism, are really only authoritarian arrangements where male will is given absolute license. One of these events takes place at Ulric's studio. But the brilliant surface of the occasion is marred by the hero's cupidity in wishing to enjoy both women, though insanely anxious that Ulric stay away from his own Mara. Here, just as in legendary suburbia, the women take no active part in the arrangements whereby they are swapped. Usually Miller and his friends are magnanimous; they offer each other some "cunt" whenever they can, an offer casually made in front of the property herself. Several unforeseen occurrences trouble the moment's serenity. Ulric's "blind date," because mulatto, is "rather difficult to handle, at least in the preliminary stages."[53] Moreover, she begins to menstruate: "What's a little blood between bouts?" Ulric giggles, alarmed enough to rush to the bathroom and scrub himself "assiduously," unable to cover a primitive fright which infects the whole gang—Miller himself takes twenty pages to fret over the possibility that contact with menstrual discharge has given him "the syph." In their omnipotence, Miller and his cohorts can do anything to women whose only revenge is venereal disease—a major reason for the continual masculine anxiety on this score.

Another group event takes place between Miller, his estranged wife Maude, and a visitor who stopped in for a drink. On this occasion things begin amiably enough, Miller providing an ecstatic running commentary on the ideal freedom from jealousy, ill will, and guilt, and each of the two female robots behaving splendidly. Finally the hero, tried by the exertion of some five consecutive orgasms, summons his last ounce of strength for neighbor Elsie, who has been most enthusiastic till now: " 'Go on, fuck, fuck,' she cried," etc.[54] Suddenly the evening's pleasant ambiance is shattered and Elsie is in pain. Miller's powerful prose renders this " 'Oh, oh! Don't. Please don't. It hurts!' she yelled."[55] The hero is outraged. He appears to reason that, in consenting, the woman had waived all rights and must be kept to the bargain regardless:

"Shut up, you bitch you!" I said. "It hurts does it? You wanted it, didn't you?" I held her tightly, raised myself a little higher to get it into the hilt, and pushed until I thought her womb would give way. Then I came—right into that snaillike mouth which was wide open. She went into a convulsion, delirious with joy and pain. Then her legs slid off my shoulders and fell to the floor with a thud. She lay there like a dead one, completely fucked out."[56]

The spirit of this sort of evening is incomprehensible, both in its frenzy and in its violence, unless one takes into account the full power of the conventional morality it is written against and depends upon so parasitically—every fear, shame, and thou shalt not. Were there not so much to deny, resist, overcome, and befoul, the operator and his feminine machines would hardly require their belabored promiscuity, nor the hero his righteous brutality.

Miller is very far from having escaped his Puritan origin: it is in the smut of his pals; in the frenzy of his partners; in the violence and contempt of his "fucking." We are never allowed to forget that this is forbidden and the sweeter for being so; that lust has greater excitements than love; that women degrade themselves by participation in sexuality, and that all but a few "pure" ones are no more than cunt and outrageous if they forget it. "The dirty bitches—they like it," he apprises us; clinical, fastidious, horrified and amused to record how one responded "squealing like a pig"; another "like a crazed animal"; one "gibbered"; another "crouched on all fours like a she-animal, quivering and whinnying"; while still another specimen was "so deep in heat" she was like "a bright voracious animal . . . an elephant walking the ball."[57]

The very brutality with which he handles the language of sex, the iconographic four-letter words, soiled by centuries of prurience and shame, is an indication of Miller's certainty of how really filthy all this is. His defense against censorship is incontrovertible—"there was no other idiom possible" to express the "obscenity" he wished to convey.[58] His diction is, quite as he claims, a "technical device"[59] depending on the associations of dirt, violence, and scorn, in which a sexually distressed culture has steeped the words which also denominate the sexual organs and the sexual act. Miller is completely opposed to dissipating the extrasexual connotations of such diction, but wishes to preserve their force as "magical terms"[60] whose power is imminent in their quality of mana and taboo. Under this sacramental cloak a truly obscene ruthlessness toward other human beings is passed over unnoticed, or even defended. "Obscenity" is analogous to the "uses of the miraculous in the Masters," Miller announces pretentiously.[61] He and the censor have linguistic and sexual attitudes in common: ritual use of the "obscene" is, of course, pointless, unless agreement exists that the sexual is, in fact, obscene.[62] Furthermore, as Miller reminds us again and again, obscenity is a form of violence, a manner of conveying male hostility, both toward the female (who is sex) and toward sexuality itself (which is her fault). Yet, for all his disgust, indeed because of it, Miller must return over and over to the ordure; steel himself again and again by confronting what his own imagination (powerfully assisted by his cultural heritage and experience) has made horrible. The egotism called manhood requires such proof of courage. This is reality, Miller would persuade us: cunt stinks, as Curley says, and cunt is sex.

With regard to the male anatomy, things are very different, since "prick" is power. While urinating in a pissoir or even emptying the garbage, Miller may be smitten with a painful awareness of his own noble destiny. In the "Land of Fuck" the "spermatozoon reigns supreme." God is the "summation of all the spermatozoa." Miller himself is divine: "My name? Why just call me God."[63] Actually, he's even a bit more than this—"something beyond God Almighty. . . . *I am a man.* That seems to me sufficient."[64] Probably, but just in case, it is safer to develop a theology and know one's catechism: "Before me always the image of the body, our triune god of penis and testicles. On the right, God the Father; on the left and hanging a little lower, God the Son; and between them and above them, the Holy Ghost. I can never forget that this holy trinity is man-made."[65]

Cunt is scarcely this inspiring: a "crack"; a "gash"; a "wound"; a "slimy hole"—but really only emptiness, nothingness, zero. This is no less true of Mara than of the run-of-the-mill female, the taxi-dancer Miller dismisses as a "minus sign" of "absolute vacuity."[66] Gazing at his love, the egoist reports he "finds nothing, nothing except my own image wavering in a bottomless well," admitting at last he is "unable to form the slightest image of her being."[67] In the *Tropic of Cancer* both Miller and Van Norden explore the frightening enigma of "cunt." Sickened, even before he begins, by the very sight of this "dead clam," Van Norden fortifies himself with technology: "I made her hold it open and I trained the flashlight on it . . . I never in my life looked at cunt so seriously . . . And the more I looked at it the less interesting it became. It only goes to show you there's nothing to it after all."[68] Still shaken at the sight, he cannot help exclaiming over the bitter cheat:

> When you look at them with their clothes on you imagine all sorts of things; you give them an individuality like, which they haven't got, of course. There's just a crack there between the legs . . . It's an illusion! . . . It's so absolutely meaningless . . . All that mystery about sex and then you discover that it's nothing—just a blank . . . there's nothing there . . . nothing at all. It's disgusting.[69]

Later on in the book Miller hires a whore himself to have a try at dredging some meaning out of the unfathomable vacuum of the female. Like his fellow investigator, he finds only a "great gulf of nothingness," an "ugly gash" and "the wound that never heals."[70] But he is determined to do better than his buddy. He is also extremely self-conscious about the artist's lofty role in the areas of myth and vision. It is not very far from this to "mystery;" so, doing the best he can, Miller converts the "fucked out cunt of a whore" into a grand "riddle," hoping to convince himself that the planet earth is "but a great sprawling female . . . in the violet light of the stars." After all, he reasons, "out of that dark unstitched wound, that sink of abomination," man is born; part clown; part angel, a thought which leaves him "face to face with the Absolute." And out of this unworthy "zero" derive the "endless mathematical worlds" of masculine civilization, even the holy writ of Dostoievski. There must, therefore, be something to this "festering obscene horror" after all.[71] A false Xavier touching leprosy on a dare, Miller finds it impossible to smother his disgust. There is perhaps a certain unintended irony too, in the fact that Mara, his apotheosis of the eternal and mysterious "female principle," is also a pathological liar.

Miller has a rather morbid fear of excreta. The only woman whom he actually fails to "fuck" lived in an apartment with a faulty toilet and, in some two-thousand pages, his "most embarrassing moment" (to adopt his own interesting phrase) occurred when it overflowed, a generous amount of his feces along with it. Miller abandons the siege and ducks out, leaving her in charge of his remains. In general, he has irreversibly associated sexuality with the process of waste and elimination, and since his responses to the latter are extraordinarily negative, it is significant that, when he intends to be particularly insulting, he carries on his amours in the "shithouse" as, on one occasion, when he happens upon "an American cunt" in a French restroom. Standing her "slap up against the wall," he finds he can't "get it into her." With his never-failing ingenuity, he next tries sitting on the toilet seat. This won't do either, so, in a burst of hostility posing as passion, he reports: "I come all over her beautiful gown and she's sore as hell about it."[72] In the *Tropic of Capricorn* he repeats the stunt; in *Sexus* too. It is a performance which nicely combines defecation with orgasm and clarifies the sense of defilement in sexuality which is the puritan bedrock of Miller's response to women. The unconscious logic appears to be that, since sex defiles the female, females who consent to sexuality deserve to be defiled as completely as possible.[73] What he really wants to do is shit on her.

The men's room has schooled Miller in the belief that sex is inescapably dirty. Meditating there upon some graffiti, "the walls crowded with sketches and epithets, all of them jocosely obscene," he speculates on "what an impression it would make on those swell dames . . . I wondered if they would carry their tails so high if they could see what was thought of an ass here."[74] Since his mission is to inform "cunt" just how it's ridiculed and despised in the men's house, women perhaps owe Miller some gratitude for letting them know.

In a great many respects Miller is avant-garde and a highly inventive artist, but his most original contribution to sexual attitudes is confined to giving the first full expression to an ancient sentiment of contempt. The remainder of his sexual ethos is remarkably conventional. Reading, again in the toilet, he converts his own syndrome into a "great tradition" and fancies himself one of the illustrious company of Rabelais, Boccaccio, and Petronius, "the fine lusty genuine spirits who recognized dung for dung and angels for angels," observing with them the ancient distinctions between good and evil, whore and lady, adamant about the virtues of a "world where the vagina is represented by a crude, honest slit."[75] Under the brash American novelty is the old story: guilt, fear, a reverence for "purity" in the female; and a deep moral outrage whenever the "lascivious bitch" in woman is exposed. Despite the fact that Don Juan's success lies in proving "they all like it—the dirty bitches," Miller seems each time disappointed that they should, shocked and unsettled by the discovery. Somehow he wishes they wouldn't, is sure they shouldn't. Yet, most do and it appears that it is just to unmask this very hypocrisy that he carries on so many campaigns. Disillusion sets in early. Giving piano lessons, the stripling discovered that his pupil's mother is "a slut, a tramp and a trollop if ever there was one." Worse still, she lives "with a nigger . . . seems she couldn't get a prick big enough to satisfy her." Now the first rule of his code is that no opportunity should be wasted—anyway, "what the hell are you going to do when a hot bitch like that plasters her cunt up against you"—yet Miller seems shocked nevertheless.[76] He has a hygienic preference for the daughter, who is "fresh cunt," clean as "new-mown hay." When she is "knocked up" he finds a "Jewboy," coughs up a very modest contribution toward the cost of an abortion and lights out for the Adirondacks. Off on a jaunt to the Catskills he meets a pair of girls who, in the manner of medieval "types," represent Dishonesty and Integrity. Agnes is a "dumb Irish Catholic" and consequently, a prude; she "likes it," but is afraid to admit as much. In splendid contrast stands Francie—"one of those girls who are born to fuck. She had no aims, no great desires . . . held no grievances, was constantly cheerful."[77] She is so exemplary she even relishes a beating: "it makes me feel good inside . . . maybe a woman ought to get beaten up once in a while," she volunteers, and Miller marvels that "It isn't often you get a cunt who'll admit such things—I mean a regular cunt and not a moron."[78]

In the experience of the American manchild sex and violence, exploitation and sentimentality, are strangely, even wonderfully, intermingled. Miller relates how, on one climactic day of his childhood, he murdered a boy in a gang fight, then slicked his hair and returned to the welcoming arms of unsuspecting Aunt Caroline, to bask in the maternal solicitude of her homemade bread—"Mothers had time in those days to make good bread with their own hands, and still do the thousand and one things which motherhood demands of a woman."[79] The same afternoon brings sexual initiation: "Joey was so happy that he took us down to his cellar later and made his sister pull up her dress and show what was underneath . . . Whereas the other urchins used to pay to make Weesie lift her dress up, for us it was done with love. After a while we persuaded her not to do it anymore for the other boys—we were in love with her and we wanted her to go straight."[80] The model of the adult world already shines through the boy's excitement: violence, a male prerogative; sexuality, a secret and shameful province of the female, regulated by the cash nexus. And the pieties are neatly arranged: Weesie shall be saved and isolated into "decency" through "love" and will mellow in time into Aunt Caroline's handy ignorant nurturance.

Through all his exhausting experiences with enthusiastic "bitches," Miller never abandons the icons of his "pure," early loves, immaculate creatures about whom, he is pleased to announce, he "never had an impure thought." Four decades later his chivalrous ardor toward Una Gifford can still gush forth at the remembered echo of a pop tune: ". . . a thousand times beyond any reach of mine. 'Kiss me, kiss me *again!*' How the words pierced me! And not a soul in that boisterous, merrymaking group was aware of my agony. . . . Sounds of revelry filled the empty street . . . It was for me they were giving the party. And she was there, my beloved, snow-blonde, starry-eyed, forever unattainable Queen of the Arctic."[81] Miller, in love, reverts to all the sentimental tokens of "respect" appropriate to a Victorian suitor. Floundering in a sentimentality largely narcissistic, full of a sludgey "idealism" that complements his cynicism, he sends flowers and writes long letters full of regressive daydreams. Rich in pathos as it is, Miller's long, frustrating attachment to Mara is less a love story than the case history of a neurotic dependence.

Part of Miller's conventionality is to insist on a rigid split between body and mind, sense and soul. Van Norden puts it on the line: "You can get something out of a book, even a bad book . . . but a cunt, it's just sheer loss of time."[82] Miller has plenty of time to waste but is just as careful to preserve an obstinate separation between sex and the "higher" life of books and ideas, which can only be experienced alone or in masculine company. His interpretation of the separate spheres is that woman is no more than "cunt," though she is occasionally said to redeem herself by having babies while men write books. Even this uterine mystique is no good unless an abstraction; he has no interest in parenthood, and his compliments to maternity are scanty and without feeling.

Ambivalent about money, Miller is unmoved by the claims of extreme virility, war, and militarism. Yet this hardly makes him any less determined to maintain male hegemony throughout every phase of life. As Lawrence and other prophets have tried to teach us, this can only be done by preserving traditional sexual polarity, the one way to offset the decline of the West and redeem the horrors of the twentieth century. In what must be, beyond question, the most novel analysis of World War I, Miller traces the catastrophe to the loss of sexual polarity, e.g., the feminist movement: "The loss of sex polarity is part and parcel of the larger disintegration, the reflex of the soul's death, and coincident with the disappearance of great men, great causes, great wars."[83]

Miller's scheme of sexual polarity relegates the female to "cunt," an exclusively sexual being, crudely biological. Though he shares this lower nature, the male is also capable of culture and intellect. The sexes are two warring camps between whom understanding is impossible since one is human and animal (according to Miller's perception, intellectual and sexual)—the other, simply animal. Together, as mind and matter, male and female, they encompass the breadth of possible experience. The male, part angel, part animal, enjoys yet suffers too from his divided nature. His appetite for "cunt," recurrent and shameful as it is, is, nevertheless, his way of staying in touch with his animal origins. It keeps him "real." Miller staves off the threat of an actual sexual revolution—woman's transcendence of the mindless material capacity he would assign her—through the fiat of declaring her cunt and trafficking with her only in the utopian fantasies of his "fucks." That this is but whistling in the dark is demonstrated by his own defeating experience with Mara, and, even more persuasively by the paralyzing fear which drives him to pretend—so that he may deal with them at all—that women are things.[84]

In *The World of Sex* Miller explains that most of his writing on sex was simply an attempt at "self-liberation."[85] What he has furnished us is an excellent guide to his dungeon but it provides no clue to the world into which he was emancipated. Delivered from the Brahmin eminence of his old age, the following pronunciamento is woefully shaky: "Perhaps a cunt, smelly though it may be, is one of the prime symbols for the connection between all things"[86]—the possibility might exist, but the stench you may be sure of. There are times when Miller seems to catch a glimpse of what chaos is made of human life through the brutality of the sexual ethic he represents: and at one point, profoundly unconscious of patronization, he serves up this staggering naïveté: "No matter how attached I become to a 'cunt,' I was more interested in the person who owned it. A cunt doesn't live a separate independent existence."[87]

The impulse to see even women as human beings may occur momentarily—a fleeting urge—but the terrible needs of adolescent narcissism are much greater, the cheap dream of endlessly fucking impersonal matter, mindless tissue endlessly compliant, is so much more compelling. And the thrills of egotism are always there: the high of the con game, the excitement of lying, wheedling, acting, cheating, deliberately degrading, then issuing orders and directing the gull in a performance whose "bestiality" only confirms his detached superiority. All these comforts make up for the disgust of the act itself.

Finally, there is the satisfaction of evacuation—a general release of tensions, hostilities, frustrations, even thoughts. "During intercourse they passed out of me, as though I were emptying refuse in a sewer."[88] Americans never underestimate the virtues of indoor plumbing. Miller looks on woman in a surrealist dream and sees "a knot with a mask between her legs" and knows "one crack is as good as another and over every sewer there's a grating."[89] "Cunt" may be lobotomized earthenware, but "behind every slit"[90] is danger, death, the unknown, the exhilarations of the chase, and in Miller's "genito-urinary"[91] system, the sexual comfort-station is a pay toilet whose expense is great enough to constitute its own reward.

Miller has given voice to certain sentiments which masculine culture had long experienced but always rather carefully suppressed: the yearning to effect a complete depersonalization of woman into cunt, a game-sexuality of cheap exploitation, a childish fantasy of power untroubled by the reality of persons or the complexity of dealing with fellow human beings and, finally, a crude species of evacuation hardly better than anal in character.

While the release of such inhibited emotion, however poisonous, is beyond question advantageous, the very expression of such lavish contempt and disgust, as Miller has unleashed and made fashionable, can come to be an end in itself, eventually harmful, perhaps even malignant. To provide unlimited scope for masculine aggression, although it may finally bring the situation out into the open, will hardly solve the dilemma of our sexual politics. Miller does have something highly important to tell us; his virulent sexism is beyond question an honest contribution to social and psychological understanding which we can hardly afford to ignore. But to confuse this neurotic hostility, this frank abuse, with sanity is pitiable. To confuse it with freedom were vicious, were it not so very sad.

Notes

1. It may be that his own eccentricity in granting permission is also a factor: Miller regards permission to quote as a personal endorsement of the critic's views. Unfortunately space does not permit me to pay tribute to Henry Miller's considerable achievement as an essayist, autobiographer and surrealist; my remarks are restricted to an examination of Miller's sexual ethos.

2. Karl Shapiro, "The Greatest Living Author," reprinted as an introduction to the Grove Press edition of *Tropic of Cancer* (New York: Grove Press, 1961), p. xvi.

3. *Ibid.*, p. xviii.

4. Bern Porter, *The Happy Rock* (Berkeley, Packard Press, 1945), pp. 2–4.

5. Shapiro, *op. cit.*, pp. xvi–xvii.

6. *Ibid.*, p. xvii.

7. *Ibid.*, pp. xvii–xviii.

8. Ihab Hassan, *The Literature of Silence, Henry Miller and Samuel Beckett* (New York: Knopf, 1967), p. 10.

9. I am pleased to find that Hassan agrees with me here.

10. I have in mind not only traditional courtly, romantic, and Victorian sentiment, but even that of other moderns. Conrad, Joyce, even Faulkner never approach the sexual hostility one finds in Miller.

11. Henry Miller, "Shadowy Monomania," *Sunday After the War* (New Directions, New York, 1944), pp. 259–61.

12. Henry Miller, *Sexus* (New York: Grove Press, 1965), p. 143.

13. See Steven Marcus, *The Other Victorians* (New York: Basic Books, 1966).

14. Henry Miller, *The World of Sex* (New York: Grove Press, 1965), p. 101.

15. *Ibid.*, pp. 101–2.

16. Henry Miller, *Tropic of Capricorn* (New York: Grove Press, 1961), p. 202.

17. *Ibid.*, p. 29.

18. *Ibid.*, p. 57, p. 180.

19. *Ibid.*, p. 30. This is the sense of the passage.

20. Henry Miller, *Tropic of Cancer* (New York: Grove Press, 1961), p. 141 ff.

21. Henry Miller, *Plexus* (New York: Grove Press, 1965), p. 475.

22. Miller, *Tropic of Cancer*, pp. 291–92.

23. Henry Miller, *Nexus* (New York: Grove Press, 1965), p. 275 and passim. The expression is used often in this book and elsewhere.

24. *Sexus*, p. 83.

25. Steven Marcus attributes this happy expression to Philip Rahv.

26. Henry Miller, *Tropic of Capricorn*, pp. 181–82.

27. *Ibid.*, p. 183.

28. *Ibid.*, p. 182.

29. *Sexus*, p. 83.

30. *Ibid.*

31. *Ibid.*, p. 97.

32. *Ibid.*, p. 100.

33. *Tropic of Capricorn*, p. 82.

34. *Ibid.*, p. 83.

35. *Ibid.*, pp. 83–84.

36. *Tropic of Cancer*, p. 45.

37. *Ibid.*, pp. 45 and 47.

38. *Ibid.*, p. 47.

39. *Ibid.*, pp. 44 and 46.

40. *Ibid.*, p. 46.

41. *Ibid.*, p. 47.

42. *Ibid.*, p. 46.

43. *The World of Sex*, p. 114.

44. It is important to bear in mind that Miller was fifty-eight when *Sexus* was published. The scarcity ethic of callow youth—"Did you get to first base?" "Did you get her to go all the way?"—probably accounts for the sheer quantity, the cloying plenty of Miller's escapades.

45. *Tropic of Capricorn*, p. 214.

46. *Nexus*, p. 37.

47. Henry Miller, *Black Spring* (New York: Grove Press, 1963), p. 96.

48. *Ibid.*

49. *Ibid.*

50. *Ibid.*

51. *Sexus*, p. 94. The legless toy in question is Mara.

52. *Tropic of Capricorn*, pp. 1180–81.

53. *Sexus*, p. 91. Miller has a certain faltering sympathy for blacks which does not extend itself to black women, about whom he makes remarks so outrageously racist that (as expressions of the author's own sentiment) they are difficult to match in serious writing. "Try a piece of dark meat now and then. It's tastier, and it costs less," etc. (*Nexus*, p. 261).

54. *Ibid.*, p. 384.

55. *Ibid.*

56. *Ibid.*

57. Chosen at random: see *Sexus*, p. 227, *Capricorn*, p. 213, and *Sexus*, p. 101, and 377 and 378.

58. Henry Miller, *Remember to Remember* (New York: New Directions, 1947), p. 280.

59. *Ibid.*, p. 287.

60. *Ibid.*, p. 288.

61. *Ibid.*, p. 287.

62. Unfortunately for the religiously inclined of every persuasion, from Miller to the censors to the Church, fuck is losing its aura of the nefarious and in time may, while meaning all things to all people, mean just what it does mean and cease to function as a synonym for hurt, humble, or exploit. In *Eros Denied* Wayland Young has already demonstrated that it is surely the best English word to convey "sexual intercourse," "coitus," and other pretentious locutions to which expository prose is still confined.

63. *Tropic of Capricorn*, pp. 203–4.

64. *Black Spring*, p. 24. Italics Miller's.

65. *Ibid.*, pp. 24–25.

66. *Tropic of Capricorn*, pp. 120–21.

67. *Ibid.*, p. 343.

68. *Tropic of Cancer*, pp. 139–40.

69. *Ibid.*, p. 140.

70. *Ibid.*, p. 249.

71. *Ibid.*, pp. 248, 9, 50.

72. *Ibid.*, p. 18.

73. E.g. Women are dirty because they are sex; "pure" women are those who deny this. Some few of these are admirable (mothers, childhood sweethearts, etc.); most, however, are only hypocrites to be punished and exposed.

74. *Tropic of Cancer*, pp. 174–75.

75. *Black Spring*, pp. 48, 50.

76. *Tropic of Capricorn*, pp. 255–56.

77. *Ibid.*, p. 261.

78. *Ibid.*, p. 263.

79. *Remember to Remember* (New York: New Directions, 1947), p. 40. The homily, delivered with absolute gravity, echoed by (and echoing) popular magazines, soap opera, etc., is an object lesson in how interrelated the various levels of American media can be.

80. *Tropic of Capricorn*, p. 125.

81. *Nexus*, p. 303.

82. *Tropic of Cancer*, p. 140.

83. Henry Miller, *The Cosmological Eye* (New York: New Directions, 1939), p. 120.

84. Miller's respect for the work of Anaïs Nin appears to be the single exception to the rule, perhaps in itself a reason for his enthusiasm over her productions.

85. *The World of Sex*, p. 16. This short essay veers between aspiring to be a "serious message" on the subject and its more pressing need to sell the title.

86. *Ibid.*, p. 44.

87. *Ibid.*

88. *Ibid.*, p. 51.

89. *Black Spring*, p. 164.

90. *Ibid.*

91. Miller is fond of this term and uses it often.

Beyond Ideology: Kate Millett and the Case for Henry Miller

MICHAEL WOOLF

Fundamentally he intended to undermine, if possible, the whole structure of the Puritan ethos which would open the way for correct loving, real loving and consequently art; sensuality, sensibility go hand in hand.

Lawrence Durrell[1]

When he deals with sex he seems to me to achieve a crudity unsurpassed except by the graffiti on the walls of public urinals. . . . In my view, Tropic of Cancer *is obscene in the simplest sense.*

Walter Allen[2]

No writer has caused greater controversy in the twentieth century than Henry Miller. For Lawrence Durrell, Miller is an inspiration. Norman Mailer sees within him a paradox out of which artistic genius is formed: "It is as if Henry Miller contains the unadvertised mystery of how much of a monster a great writer must be."[3]

There are, though, many alternative notions. Walter Allen's sense of a pornographic crudity in Miller's fiction is echoed by Richard Hoggart, who says that Miller's men "are alone even when they are fornicating."[4] Kenneth Rexroth relegates Miller's work to the status of naughty-boy scribbling: "Most of the sexual encounters in *The Tropics* and *The Rosy Crucifixion* are comic accidents, as impersonal as a pratfall. The woman never emerges at all. He characteristically writes of his wives as bad boys talk of their schoolteachers."[5]

However, the most sustained assault on Miller has come from feminist critics, especially Kate Millett in *Sexual Politics*. She argues that his work expresses a "neurotic hostility"[6] towards women, "the yearning to effect a complete depersonalisation"[7]; in his prose "Miller simply converts woman to 'cunt'—thing, commodity, matter."[8] Yet at the same time there is an oblique admiration in Millett's view that Miller offers "a compendium of

Reprinted from *Perspectives on Pornography: Sexuality in Film and Literature*, Gary Day and Clive Bloom, eds. (London: The Macmillan Press, Ltd., copyright © 1989; and New York: St. Martin's Press, Inc., copyright © 1989), 113–28.

sexual neuroses, and his value lies not in freeing us from such afflictions, but in having the honesty to express and dramatise them."[9]

At the heart of Millett's view is an ideological rejection of Miller's representation of women. There is, though, a sense of distance between ideology and art in Millett's writing. Politics and creativity are seen as strangely separate areas of consciousness that make vastly different kinds of demands. Millett is torn between a political and ideological alienation from Miller's work, and a responsiveness to his creative method and artistic vision. In this respect, her autobiographical work dramatises the supremacy of art over ideology.

In *Sita* and *Flying* she reveals a profound sympathy for many of Miller's attitudes and narrative strategies.[10] Essentially, *Flying* owes much to *Tropic of Cancer* in both method and ideas.[11] Both books occupy a place in the study of the relationship between sex and introspection in American culture. They belong within a tradition of fiction that uses sexual action to assert an anti-Puritan position, and that further sees sexuality as a means of liberating an essential self from social restraints and conventions. The ideological and historical distinctions between these books obscure the underlying correspondences. Millett's understanding of Miller is best expressed not in the conventional perspectives of *Sexual Politics* but in the complex and contradictory field of consciousness that constitutes *Flying*.

A central concept in *Flying* is the pursuit of a version of liberation expressed as freedom from social and political obligation. This is seen as a necessary prerequisite of an independent existence, of the discovery of the real self: "I will do it then, live my life, my own now maybe. I will be who I am. I must get that first, learn not through words but through feeling what that means. Then later I can go on, live for other people. If I have felt it enough. Lived it myself" (pp. 236–7). Ideology is, thus, concerned with the world of words; liberation (and art) is made from "feeling what that means." Political idealism is set against, and is a barrier to, the discovery of an essential instinctive self.

Miller and Millett are profoundly related by a sense that the drama of self-liberation is the essential material of creative expression. Millett's political sympathies are not vastly different from the kind of rage expressed in *Tropic of Capricorn*, where Miller exhibits a clear political sympathy for the dispossessed.[12] However, the real relationship in their work is based on a shared, paradoxical assumption that abandoning words for feelings is a necessary prerequisite of the revelation of self. That this process is recorded in, precisely, words is, of course, the heart of the paradox. It must also be said that this is an essentially Romantic paradox, but Miller and Millett express the resultant fertile ambiguity in a rich brew. Both *Flying* and *Tropic of Cancer* exploit the contradictions of the mobile consciousness as creative material.

The movement of the consciousness, expressed in Millett's metaphor of flying and Miller's image of the flow of a river, is a central subject. Millett's realisation that "my existence is astonishing, dramatic" (p. 248) is a crucial identification of the source from which autobiographical fictions are made. It is clearly also Miller's source: "The facts and events which form the chain of one's life are but starting points along the path of self-discovery. I have endeavoured to plot the inner pattern. . . ."[13] What is felt to be dramatic is not any sequence of events but the fluid, active, contradictory tensions embodied in the mobile consciousness. Millett's assertion in *Flying* that "This book is myself" (p. 486) reveals a profound sympathy with the method of construction that characterises Miller's *Tropic of Cancer*.

There are, then, fundamental correspondences between *Flying* and *Tropic of Cancer*. The subject matter in both traces the discovery of an essential self in a state of liberation from social restraint and convention. They share a similar assumption that the consciousness itself is dramatic subject matter. That assumption is expressed, in, for example, Millett's rhetorical question "Who will ever want to read this book, this collection of clutter in my mind?" The question is, of course, obliquely answered by the existence of the book itself, the doubt resolved by the act of completion and publication. The same resolution is implicit in *Tropic of Cancer*. The book encompasses the imperfections of "clutter," is created out of the apparently non-selective, promiscuous movement of consciousness precisely because, in Miller's terms, it expresses "the triumph of the individual over art" (p. 19). It thereby escapes, in Millett's terms, the tyranny of words.

Miller abandons the assumptions of literature as structured and selective experience and moves into the messy, cluttered areas of emotional complexity. The self is presented in debate with self, the consciousness in dramatic, often contradictory, movement. Miller's idea of self-collaboration as a mode of narrative is the source from which the work is made:

> Up to the present, my idea in collaborating with myself has been to get off the gold standard of literature. My idea briefly has been to present a resurrection of the emotions, to depict the conduct of a human being in the stratosphere of ideas, that is, in the grip of delirium.
>
> (*Tropic of Cancer*, p. 244)

In Miller's work there is an attempt to embrace, represent and celebrate the fragmentary nature of experience. In a letter to Michael Fraenkel he sees this fragmentation as "divine": "And as for the "divine jumble," I adore it. I see nothing to be gained by straightening it out."[14] Millett's "clutter" and Miller's "delirium" or "divine jumble" are expressions of the fertile fields from which the narratives emerge. A central metaphor in these fields is that of exploration, which is an introspective rather than geographical process. In *Tropic of Capricorn*, for example, Miller argues that "there is only one great adventure and that is inwards towards self, and for that, time nor space nor even deeds matter" (p. 11). The motif of flying that ends in Millett's vision of "chaos and serenity together" (*Flying*, p. 162) is, like Miller's metaphor of movement and flow, an expression of the essential nature of journeying. Movement is finally not into geographical space but into the contradictory complexity of self.

The journey recorded in *Flying* is from a position of political and ideological obligation to the realisation that "Finally all I had was who I am" (p. 487). There is throughout a tension between the public and the private self: "Going home for two more speeches. The last ones. Always the last ones. Then free: never the public person again. Out of it, the vulgar insanity" (p. 5).

Tropic of Cancer begins precisely from that point that Millett aspires to, "out of it," while *Tropic of Capricorn* describes the process of moving to that point. The narrator of *Tropic of Cancer* is a parody of that most American of archetypes, the self-made man. He is essentially an "unmade man" who has cast off all sense of a public self; has become an embodiment of a consciousness without status or power, an appetite without obligation or responsibility: "It is now the fall of my second year in Paris. I was sent here for a reason I have not yet been able to fathom. I have no money, no resources, no hopes. I am the happiest man alive" (p. 9). The narrator is passive, living in an environment that is, in a sense, a fictive idealisation of a world outside of life with its conventions, restraints and obligations. He is stripped of those accoutrements by which we define the social, public and political self. Thus the narrative voice can simultaneously assert "we are dead" (p. 9) and "Physically I am alive. Morally I am free. The world which I have departed is a menagerie" (p. 104). The "deadness" of the narrator is a device by which Miller achieves dual objectives. It creates a consciousness freed from public existence, from "life" in that sense. It also permits the establishment of an environment that moves between the real and the surreal. The simultaneous sense of the live and dead narrator offers a strategy in which Paris is both the real world of the American expatriate, and a landscape of dream and nightmare—a place of liberation and obsession that transcends the possibilities associated with the material world.

Miller's literary persona is, thus, a reversed Horatio Alger or a deconstructed Jay Gatsby. He embodies a profound alienation from the American ethos of material aspiration and upward social mobility. He manifests the political perspective that underlies Nathanael West's Lemuel Pitkin. West's figure in *A Cool Million* is literally "dismantled," whereas Miller's figure is, in a more subtle sense, unmade and consequently, deeply, un-American.

The figure allows Miller to express a complete realisation of the process described in Millett's *Flying*. The world as a "menagerie," and the attempt to escape the pressures of that world, is a common theme. This is apparent in *Tropic of Capricorn*, where Miller describes the imperatives of a working life that isolate the individual from the essential self. The world of work is a reductive pressure—a fundamentally destructive obligation. Millett, in contrast, suffers at the centre of a set of imperatives that emerge out of her political role within the feminist movement. In both *Flying* and *Tropic of Capricorn* additional imperatives afflict the narrators in the form of a family obligation. What unites both is the sense that they suffer pressures to adopt roles that are alien to an essential self. Thus the public stance is in direct conflict with private identity. The literary enterprise is both an expression of that conflict and an act of liberation in which the private self is asserted at the expense of the public persona. The public self, be it politically or domestically "responsible," is progressively "dismantled" in a process that finally reveals an essential self: naked, un-American and liberated.

At the heart of this process is the use that Miller and Millett make of sex and sexuality in their work. Sex is the mechanism through which the private or essential self is realised. It is a mode of action that expresses liberation from public roles, obligations and oppressive responsibilities. The naked self is literally and figuratively paramount in sexual action. The journey toward realisation of that self is a sexual one.

Inevitably, then, sexual action is closely related to philosophical exploration in the narratives. Miller sustains a complex and contradictory view of sexual action in *Tropic of Cancer*. The narrator moves between a view of sex as an act of sensual liberation, a metaphor for extreme social irresponsibility, and a version of sex as obsessional imprisonment. In *Sexus*,[15] for example, an orgy is the focus for a joyous rejection of all restraint: "There was such a feeling of freedom and intimacy that any gesture, any act, became permissible" (p. 350). Simultaneously, however, the figure of June, in various guises, haunts Miller's fiction—as she haunted his life. The figure of June as Mara or Mona is expressed in a sequence of imperatives and disjunctions that form and transform experience into what comes close at times to surrealistic nightmare. Anaïs Nin, still the most perceptive critic of Miller's work, recognised the impact of June's enigmatic character: "June's character seems to have no definable form, no boundaries, no core. This frightens Henry. He does not know all she is."[16]

The transaction between Miller's life and art is well documented in, for example, Jay Martin's *Always Merry and Bright: The Life of Henry Miller*. In this context, however, the significance of June is that Miller translated the figure into part of the contradictory perspective on sexuality that is expressed in the fiction. As Nin saw, Miller transformed the real person into a fictional device:

> What was June? What was June's value? Henry loves her with passion, he wants to know June, the perpetually disguised woman. June, the powerful, fictionalized character. In his love for her he has endured so many torments that the lover took refuge in the writer.[17]

In that refuge, the relationship is used to express the obsessional nature of sex as reflected in a relationship that, in *Nexus*, Miller called "an inferno of emotion."[18] The contradiction is clear: sexual action is both an expression of liberation and freedom, and simultaneously the reverse, a prison of obsession. The contradiction is not between sex and love: both dimensions are integrated around the figure of Mara. In the orgy of *Sexus* involving Mara, Lola Jackson and Ulric, a sense of freedom from constraint and convention is sustained. The orgy liberates the participants from the concerns of their public selves as shown, for example, in the figure of Lola:

> Lola Jackson was a queer girl. She had only one defect—the knowledge that she was not pure white. That made her rather difficult to handle, at least in the preliminary stages. A little too intent upon impressing us with her culture and breeding. After a couple of drinks she unlimbered enough to show us how supple her body was. Her dress was too long for some of the stunts she was eager to demonstrate. We suggested that she take it off, which she did revealing a stunning figure which showed to advantage in a pair of sheer silk hose, a brassiere and pale-blue panties. Mara decided to follow suit. Presently we urged them to dispense with the brassieres. There was a huge divan on which the four of us huddled in a promiscuous embrace. (p. 85)

The act of removing clothes corresponds to a casting-off of "culture and breeding." The public self is abandoned along with the underwear.

Sex is also used in Miller's work as a means of rejecting conventional moral standards. Sexual action is a rebellious gesture against a moral order that seeks to repress it. An orgy is a celebration of sensuality that, in Miller's version of a hostile America in *Sexus*, takes on the appearance, in the eyes of that society, of an "outlaw" act. The narrator fantasies the interjection of that hostile moral order:

> It was too good to be true. I expected the door to be flung open any moment and an accusing voice scream: "Get out of there, you brazen creatures." But there was only the silence of the night, the blackness, the heavy sensual odours of earth and sex. (p. 354)

The "outlaw" nature of sexuality is, in a sense, a dramatic expression of what is essentially a Romantic philosophy expressed, for example, in an assertion that Miller makes to Michael Fraenkel in the "Hamlet" correspondence: "You've got to ally yourself with Nature, with instinct, with desire."[19] That this state of alliance is an "outlaw" act is part of the narrator's consciousness expressed in one version of sexual action. This version enacts what Miller called "a real fight with the world"[20] and its rejected values.

This stance corresponds to Kate Millett's view that conventional morality and conventional sexual attitudes are oppressive. Both monogamy and heterosexuality are seen by Millett as the tools of a hostile moral order. They are those pressures from which the individual must seek liberation if the self is to be freed and realised.

The contradictions inherent in Miller's representation of sex are also expressed in Millett's work. Sex is seen as an ambiguous synthesis of liberation and obsession. Millett's *Sita* is, for example, a record of love transformed and distorted into shapes that approach nightmare:

> All love becomes vulnerability, the doorway to cruelty, the stairway to contempt. The very passion and adoration is now our undoing, the means of our evil. I in despising myself for loving, she in despising the one she had loved. Love turning back on itself, becoming its opposite. (p. 22)

In one of its manifestations, love is for both Miller and Millett a dark anguish that broods over their work, threatening to become a nightmare inversion of itself. For Miller this anguish is largely focused in June, for Millett in *Sita*. An extreme revelation of this obsessional element in sex and love is expressed in Millett's *The Basement*, where she creates a fictional version of the real-life torture and murder of a young girl. The nightmarish abuse of the central figure is presented as deriving, in part, from perverse sexual obsession.

That version of sexuality coexists with a view that is entirely consistent with Miller's. In *Flying*, sexual action is, in one manifestation, a means of achieving the real self freed from oppressive obligations and imperatives. Sex leads to both liberation and insight into the nature of essential experience:

> And tonight blots out all the voices of my life, their squalid words hitting like stones: sin, perversity, infidelity, scandal. Now I outcry them, certain, not only through joys of sense which in themselves become an ethic, but through a new perception that virtue, ultimately, is only another human being. Rejoicing in our bodies' woman's beauty, I can refute them, knowing that when I die I will have lived in these moments: when it comes to it, you have the world in your time, or you don't. Mine now is looking down on the gold of her head between my thighs while the white sky brings its first light through the ivy's green in the windows. (p. 40)

In that sexual action, the violent intrusion of moral convention ("like stones") is transcended. The "joys of sense" generate an ethic and lead, in a moment of lyrical epiphany, to a perception that reveals an essential self. The "outlaw" nature of sex in Millett is enforced by the recorded attitudes of society towards lesbianism. Both Miller and Millett employ sex as a means of rejecting moral values and social conventions that are presented as hostile. They share a profound anti-Puritanism.

For both writers sex is also, as I have argued, a means of exploring paradox and contradiction. Neither seeks to resolve these, precisely because they share a view of art which is not dependent on structural cohesion or resolution. The field of literature is not the well-made, "well-wrought urn," but the vast area of the active consciousness engaged in dramatic debate with self. Consequently, the narrative voice of *Flying* is consistent with that of *Tropic of Cancer* insofar as it is inclusive, promiscuous, ostensibly unedited. Millett's narrative voice is also radically different from the political/critical voice of *Sexual Politics*. Ideological rationality and political purpose give way to the greater energy of the creative voice in its paradoxical and contradictory exploration of the paradoxical and contradictory self. Anaïs Nin's description of her own and Miller's creative method applies equally to Millett's method of notebook narration in *Flying*:

> Henry's recollections of the past, in contrast to Proust, are done while in movement. He may remember his first wife while making love to a whore, or he may remember his very first love while walking the streets, travelling to see a friend; and life does not stop while he remembers. Analysis in movement. No static vivisection. Henry's daily and continuous flow of life, his sexual activity, his talks with everyone, his café life, his conversations with people in the streets, which I once considered an interruption to writing, I now believe to be a quality which distinguishes him from other writers. . . .
>
> It is what I do with the journal, carrying it everywhere, writing on café tables while waiting for a friend, on the train, on the bus, in waiting rooms at the station, while my hair is washed, at the Sorbonne when the lectures get tedious, on journeys, trips, almost while people are talking.[21]

Millett's description of her narrative method in *Flying* is an exact reproduction of this technique: "It's myself. It's a record as I go along doing my thing" (p. 220). The book is comprised, as are Nin's journals, of a sequence of notebooks which record "analysis in movement." Miller's description of his method of narration, in a letter to Anaïs Nin, clearly signals a similar technique:

> If anybody had written a preface to it [*Tropic of Cancer*], they might have explained that the book was written on the wing, as it were, between my 25 addresses. It gives that sensation of constant change of address, environment etc. Like a bad dream. And for that it is good.[22]

This connection between movement and narrative voice leads directly to a willingness to integrate contradiction into the fabric of the text, and it makes juxtaposition the key to both styles. What George Orwell called Miller's "flowing, swelling prose"[23] is a product of that procedure and that description is equally apt when applied to Millett's autobiographical voice. It is precisely a promiscuous voice that, in abandoning tight structure, creates a field of response through which the self moves without restraint of logic or convention.

The subject matter is the "naked" self and the self is, of course, most naked, metaphorically and literally, in the sexual act. For both writers, sex is given a dual function in the writing: it is used to assert a rejection of the moral absolutes of a conventional society, and it expresses an escape from the tyranny of time. A landscape is created which offers an area of action beyond, and outside of, material experience. Sex and love offer momentary transcendence of a real and oppressive world. This moment is recorded in *Flying*: "All time ceases, or is present together aloft in the sky like the two incongruous lights sinking and rising but arrested now as we are while we laugh or gaze or smoke, repeating our endless litany of love" (p. 583).

For Miller, in the opening of *Tropic of Cancer*, time similarly dissolves in the focus on Tania:

> It is the twenty-somethingth of October. I no longer keep track of the date. Would you say—my dream of the 14th November last? There are intervals, but they are between dreams, and there is no consciousness of them left. The world around me is dissolving, leaving here and there spots of time. The world is a cancer eating itself away. . . . I am thinking that when the great silence descends upon all and everywhere music will at last triumph. When into the womb of time everything is withdrawn chaos will be restored and chaos is the score upon which reality is written. You Tania are my chaos. It is why I sing. (p. 10)

The passage presents the focus of the desire as the "chaos" that defeats, and exists outside of, time and the material world.

The narratives are able to move freely between sexual action and metaphysical introspection precisely because sexual action reveals a self that transcends the material world. Sex is seen to liberate the self from the gravity of social or political obligation, and the narrative voice thus floats freely into areas of philosophical speculation. Miller's concept of "conversion" illustrates a direct transaction between the profane and the profound, between sex and introspection. The boundary between the two is eroded:

> As to whether the sexual and the religious are conflicting and opposed, I would answer thus: every element or aspect of life, however necessitated, however questionable (to us), is susceptible to conversion, and indeed must be converted to other levels in accordance with our growth and understanding.[24]

There is, consequently, no contradiction, in terms of the nature of the narrative, between a language of sexual description and a language of poetic or metaphysical intensity. Both narratives juxtapose these ostensibly contradictory idioms precisely because there is no felt contradiction between the sexual and the philosophical self. Miller's is the more dramatic juxtaposition:

> I am fucking you Tania so that you'll stay fucked. And if you are afraid of being fucked publicly I will fuck you privately. I will tear off a few hairs from

your cunt and paste them on Boris' chin. I will bite into your clitoris and spit out two franc pieces. . . .

Indigo sky swept clear of fleecy clouds, gaunt trees infinitely extended, their black boughs gesticulating like a sleep walk. Sombre, spectral trees, their trunks pale as cigar ash.

(*Tropic of Cancer*, pp. 13–14)

Within the persona of the narrator, there is a movement from a crude, violent sexual surrealism to a landscape invested, through simile, with a sense of the moribund—a comatose world. The explicit violence directed toward Tania is transformed by the surrealist device, "two franc pieces," into a dream sequence. Miller exploits surrealist potential both to "convert" violence into poetry and to express the contradictions of the consciousness, and the integration of those contradictions within the single self. Miller presents the consciousness as a set of reconciled tensions valuable in the dramatic intensity created. The stylistic mode of representing this field of tension is the juxtaposition of the poetic and the profane.

In less dramatic, more naturalistic form, Millett adopts the same kind of movement. Arriving, for example, in New York, the narrator in *Flying* moves from philosophical speculation to explicitly sexual thought:

Improbable that the fantasy I was living before England could support itself over time. A figment. Fictive. Most of all I inquire of myself in the earsplitting pressure of landing, feeling very New Yorker, most of all, am I gonna get laid? (pp. 15–16)

As in Miller, the shift in idiom has comic intention but it also serves to enforce the sense of a literature built on the "chaos" of self. The organising principle is not selectivity or order but inclusiveness. Millett's vision does not substantially differ from Miller's view of what constitutes the subject matter of literary art: "I said men, women and children. . . . They were all there, all equally important. I might have added—books, mountains, rivers, lakes, cities, forests, creatures of the air and creatures of the deep."[25]

There is another correspondence between *Tropic of Cancer* and *Flying* that relates directly to the theme of liberation. Both books express impulses that are common in American expatriate literature. They forge an image of Europe that exists as an alternative to American convention—a location in which the self can be freed from restraint. They also simultaneously sustain a sense of Europe as a landscape of cultural reference. America is the place of compulsion where the self is imprisoned. Europe is both freedom from that restraint and a place where the narrator engages with cultural complexity. Thus Millett's journey to Europe is a movement, literally and figuratively, from dark to light and an engagement with the past: "All night the plane flies against time toward the east, America's blackness becoming light, the day moving back and now the dawn. The old world is ahead like the sunrise. Ruminate on tradition, Italy and England" (*Flying*, p. 271). From London, New York is a "foreign madness" (p. 282). The same expatriate impulses pervade *Tropic of Cancer*. New York is "cold, glittering, malign" (p. 74). America is described as "a slaughterhouse" (p. 39). In *Tropic of Capricorn*, Miller's Paris is, in contrast, an area of possibility where the narrator asserts, "Everything happens here" (p. 27). It is also a place "saturated with the past" (p. 317).

For both Miller and Millett, there is an unreality about Europe: the place of dream that is familiar in American perceptions of Europe. There is, for example, no substantial difference between Miller's version of Europe as "golden peace" and Hawthorne's "poetic or fairy precinct, where actualities would not be so terribly insisted upon as they are, and needs be, in America."[26] The imperatives of social reality are suspended in the essentially conventional versions of the Old World created by Miller and Millett.

There is, however, a peripheral issue in this discussion. The basis of the relationship between Miller and Millett is that both writers assert the centrality of sex. For both, there is the notion of a real self which divests itself of gratuitous social, economic or political dimensions, and is revealed and celebrated in sexual action. In *Flying* Millett asserts, "Nothing I could accomplish in life is such a cause for pride, a gratitude straining the heart to watch her come, great lovely head back in ecstasy" (p. 434). What Miller calls his "night thoughts" lead toward the same conclusion, proposing the central importance of sex. Sex validates human activity: "Ideas have to be wedded to action; if there is no sex, no vitality in them, there is no action" (*Tropic of Cancer*, p. 43). With these shared assumptions, Miller and Millett present sex as the pathway to enlightenment; the interactions between sex and introspection is not simply a literary strategy but the cornerstone of a shared cosmic view. Sex is, for both writers, what Miller called the "omphalos" (*Tropic of Cancer*, p. 244), the central point of a system from which all else flows.

There is, then, a sense in which *Flying* contradicts the assertions of *Sexual Politics*. It goes beyond the ideological stance of that book and focuses on an inner self that seeks freedom from ideology and its imperatives. There is a further sense in which Millett's understanding of Miller is fuller and more perceptive in *Flying* than in *Sexual Politics*. In *Flying* she explores those areas of experience that transcend the ideologies of feminist criticism. She explores the same emotional landscape as Miller with the same tools. There is, as I have argued, a profound correspondence between the Millett of *Flying* and the Miller of *Tropic of Cancer*.

The Millett of *Sexual Politics*, the critical voice, approached Miller with a narrow perspective failing to recognise the comic persona of Miller's narrator. Anaïs Nin recognised that "what Millett did was to take his humorous, comic stance seriously."[27] Millett also failed, in Durrell's opinion, to identify Miller's real target: "His obscenity is not brutality . . . what he's trying to do down is the dreadful sentimentality which disguises brutality."[28]

The critical voice had other failures: the failure to recognise Miller's irony; the failure to recognise that *Tropic of Cancer* is, at least in part, a surrealistic foray into an underworld that has the texture of dream. Most significantly, perhaps, Millett failed to consider the distance between narrator and author, the degree to which Miller's work is not simply autobiography. This is signalled through the device of the "deadness" of the narrator but it is also a distinction perceived by Miller himself, and not identified by Millett the critic:

> I have endeavoured to plot the inner pattern, follow the potential being who was constantly deflected from his course, who circled around himself, was becalmed for long stretches, sank to the bottom, or vainly essayed to reach the lonely, desolate summits. I have tried to capture the quintessential moments wherein whatever happened produced profound alterations. The man telling the story is no longer the one who experienced the events recorded.[29]

However, the Millett of *Flying*, the creative voice, revealed a profound, if oblique, sympathy for Miller's position, and a deep insight into those characteristics of Miller's work that are beyond sexual politics.

On the ideological surface, Miller and Millett are strangers. Beyond ideology, in the innermost chambers of the contradictory heart, they both draw upon a rich vein of creativity which transcends issues of sexual politics and pornography. They share a capacity both to include experience and to transform it, to achieve, in Miller's words, an act of conversion out of which literary art is made: "What seems nasty, painful, evil can become a source of beauty, joy and strength, if faced with an open mind."[30]

Notes

1. "An interview with Lawrence Durrell," interview with Frances Donnelly, 1 October 1985.

2. Walter Allen, *Tradition and Dream: The English and American Novel from the Twenties to our Time* (London: Phoenix House, 1964) p. 181.

3. Norman Mailer, *Genius and Lust: A Journey through the Major Writings of Henry Miller* (New York: Grove Press, 1976) p. 10.

4. Richard Hoggart, "Art and Sex: the Rhetoric of Henry Miller," in *Speaking to Each Other*, vol. II: *About Literature* (London: Chatto and Windus, 1970) p. 102.

5. Kenneth Rexroth, "The Reality of Henry Miller," in *Bird in the Bush: Obvious Essays* (New York: New Directions, 1959) p. 166.

6. Kate Millett, *Sexual Politics* (London: Virago, 1977) p. 313.

7. Ibid.

8. Ibid., p. 279.

9. Ibid., p. 295.

10. Kate Millett, *Flying* (St Albans, Herts: Paladin, 1974); *Sita* (London: Virago, 1977). Page references in the text.

11. Henry Miller, *Tropic of Cancer* (London: Panther, 1968). Page references in the text.

12. Henry Miller, *Tropic of Capricorn* (London: Panther, 1969). Page references in the text.

13. Henry Miller, *The World of Sex and Max and the White Phagocytes* (London: Calder and Boyars, 1970) p. 101.

14. Henry Miller, "Letter to Michael Fraenkel, June 19, 1936," in *The Michael Fraenkel—Henry Miller Correspondence Called Hamlet* (London: Carrefour, 1962) p. 171.

15. Henry Miller, *Sexus* (London: Panther, 1970). Page references in the text.

16. Anaïs Nin, *The Journals of Anaïs Nin*, vol. II (London: Quartet Books, 1973) p. 35.

17. Ibid., p. 48.

18. Henry Miller, *Nexus* (London: Granada, 1981) p. 68.

19. "Letter to Michael Fraenkel, June 19, 1936" in *Fraenkel—Miller Correspondence*, p. 174.

20. Ibid., p. 175.

21. *Journals*, vol. I, p. 163.

22. Henry Miller, "Letter to Anaïs Nin, May 3, 1934," in *Letters to Anaïs Nin*, ed. Gunther Stuhlmann (London: Peter Owen, 1965) p. 158.

23. George Orwell, "Inside the Whale," in *Collected Essays* (London: Secker and Warburg, 1961) p. 123.

24. Miller, *The World of Sex*, p. 58.

25. Ibid., p. 66.

26. Nathaniel Hawthorne, *The Marble Faun* (London: Everyman, 1910) p. xv.

27. Anaïs Nin, "The Unveiling of Woman," in *A Woman Speaks* (London: Star Books, 1982) p. 100.

28. "An Interview with Lawrence Durrell," 1 October 1985.

29. Miller, *The World of Sex*, p. 101.

30. Ibid., p. 100.

Concrete Prose and the Cement Mind

John Ciardi

Law, I have been moved to argue in the past, is man's guilty conscience codified. More often than not, I have since concluded, law is that guilty conscience mystified. I know of no point at which the law represents itself as so self-evidently inferior to the conscience in which it dabbles as it is in those cases in which the legal mind feels itself summoned to haul literature into court.

I have from Grove Press copies of an "information" filed in the Brooklyn Court of Special Sessions of the Criminal Court of New York against Henry Miller, his publishers, and the distributors of "Tropic of Cancer" in the paperback edition. The document is dated October 15, 1962, and signed by Edward S. Silver, District Attorney, and heaven help the district. Here is the D.A.'s one-sentence prose form for the first charge (exclamation points mine):

The defendants, on or about and between January 1, 1961 and June 30, 1962, in the County of Kings, unlawfully sold, loaned, gave away, distributed, showed and transmutted (!), and offered to sell, lend, give away, distribute, show and transmute (!), and had in their possession with intent to sell, lend, distribute, give away, show and transmute (!) and advertised, and offered for loan, gift, sale and distribution, a certain obscene, lewd, lascivious, filthy, indecent, sadistic, masochistic and disgusting book, and written and printed matter entitled "HENRY MILLER, TROPIC OF CANCER" and bearing on its cover the legends "A BLACK CAT BOOK 95¢," "THIS IS THE COMPLETE UNEXPURGATED GROVE PRESS EDITION ORIGINALLY PUBLISHED at $7.50" which book and printed matter was copyrighted in 1961 by Grove Press, Inc., and is captioned "FIRST BLACK CAT EDITION 1961—THIRD PRINTING—MANUFACTURED IN THE UNITED STATES OF AMERICA," and which book and printed matter depicts and represents acts and scenes wherein the sexual organs of both male persons and female persons are portrayed and described in manners connoting sex degeneracy and sex perversion, and which acts, scenes and description were of such pornographic character as to tend to incite lecherous thoughts and desires; and the defendants designed, copied, drew, printed, uttered and published, and

Reprinted from *Saturday Review* 46 (9 February 1963): 17. Reprinted by permission of Omni Publications International Ltd.

manufactured and prepared said book and printed matter, and wrote, printed, published and uttered, and caused to be written, printed, published and uttered, an advertisement and notice giving information, directly and indirectly, stating and purporting so to do, where, how, and whom (!!), and by what means and what purports to be (!!!), the said obscene, lewd, lascivious, filthy, disgusting and indecent book and printed matter can be purchased, obtained and had.

I am tempted to submit that any man who can write, transcribe, and publish and utter with intent to transmute, or who causes to be written, transcribed, and/or published and uttered with intent to cause to be transmutted (great word, derived no doubt, from *trans* plus *smut* signifying "cross-smutted") any such hodgepodge of purported language is self-evidently in contempt of prose and should properly be declared incompetent in any action touching upon the human expression of human ideas. I invite any reader to play the game of deciding for himself how many of the D.A.'s piled-on verbiages contain a vestigial act of mind and how many made their own way from the dusty dictionary to the charge so filed, with no mind in attendance. I for one should especially like to know how a book can be sadistic and masochistic. And I should certainly welcome a grammatical note, among other things, "giving information . . . where, how, and whom, and by what means and what purports to be," etc.

But if in his "information" thus far, said D.A. has merely been pretentious, officious, illiterate, and pompous in the manner more or less expected of his office, he clearly leaves the world and even the fictive irrealities of D.A.'dom behind in a second citation in which he charges that Grove Press conspired with Miller to write the book in 1961—which is to say, twenty-seven years after the book was originally published in Paris, and more than a year after the hard-cover edition was published in the United States:

It was the plan of the said conspiracy that the said book and printed matter was to be prepared and authored by the defendant Henry Miller and was to depict and represent acts and scenes wherein the sexual organs of both male persons and female persons were to be portrayed and described in manners connoting sex degeneracy and sex perversion and were to be of such a pornographic character as would tend to incite lecherous thoughts and desires.

And in a final section of the information, captioned "Overt Acts," the D.A. further releases or causes to be released the following mental belch:

1. In pursuance of said conspiracy, and to effect the purposes and objects thereof, the defendant Henry Miller, on or about and between January 1, 1961 and June 30, 1962, in the County of Kings, prepared and authored the said book and printed matter entitled "HENRY MILLER, TROPIC OF

CANCER" and therein depicted and described acts and scenes where-in the sexual organs . . . etc.

So it would seem that between January of 1961 and June of 1962, Barney Rosset of Grove Press, and Henry Miller of Paris and California (he *was* born in Brooklyn) sat down in Kings County and conspired to author a book that had been written for twenty-seven years. Worse yet, as I get the picture, Barney Rosset sat there in Kings County nudging aforesaid Henry Miller while aforesaid was busily composing aforesaid, and did intermittently urge him to depict and describe yet another sexual organ or two.

Gentlemen of the law, we mere mortals have ever been constrained to sit still while you members of the Loophole Club exchanged your gibberish in the name of public order and private right. We must yet insist that when professional gibberish loses even its normally minor contact with reality and passes into that sort of disregard of plain fact usually associated with lunatic fantasy, the least any concerned citizen can do is to make public his censure of the legal officers involved in such a fantasy. What I mean, gentlemen, is that we used to have a gent on our block called Joe Pipedreams, so called because he seemed to specialize in such fantasies, and because we believed his special abilities to be the result of smoking opium. I do not know what the D.A. has been smoking, gentlemen, but let me urge the proper agencies to look into it. It will probably turn out to be no more than the fumes from some political back room. In any case, it would be well to have them analyzed. Something in the environment of the D.A.'s office certainly conduces to fantasy. And certainly, gentlemen, if the D.A.'s charges are the law at work, I for one must insist upon standing in contempt of it.

ORPHIC MILLER

◆

Henry Miller As Visionary

WALLACE FOWLIE

I believe the quality that first attracted me to Henry Miller's writings was his violence. Not the violence of the things said, but the violence of the way in which they were said. The violence of feeling has become in his work the violence of style which has welded together all of his disparate passions and dispersed experiences into the one experience of language. He has said in *The Wisdom of the Heart* that he doesn't believe in words, but in language, "which is something beyond words." Writing is a complete celebration for him in which shattered parts of experience are put together, in which elements are fused. These elements are not, however, fused into a system of thought and experience which can be learned or understood. They can only be "realized," more and more intuitively. Miller reveals in his art the gift of immediacy. His hungers of the present are never over. They never become past hungers to be recalled. From his vision of life, which is one self-perpetuating experience, comes his writing, integrated with the flowing steadiness of life, pulsating with the sameness of each day, incapable of being codified and explicated in accordance with the rules of "periods," of "genres," of "themes."

Henry Miller is a leading example of a special kind of writer who is essentially seer and prophet, whose immediate ancestor was Rimbaud and whose leading exponent was D. H. Lawrence. It is not insignificant that he considers the poet whose perceptions and visions blotted out his language— Arthur Rimbaud—one of the greatest writers. What characterizes this kind of writer is his vulnerability to experiences. He exposes himself to them all in a propitiatory frenzy. In a more histrionic sense, this artist is the scapegoat who feels physically the weight of the world's sins and who performs in his life the role of the clown. He relives all the incarnations of the hero which he calls, in his more modest language, his masks. Miller was also fascinated by the names Rimbaud used for himself in *Une saison en enfer: saltimbanque, mendiant, artiste, bandit, prêtre* (acrobat, beggar, artist, bandit, priest).

The reasons for this reduplicated role of the artist are difficult to state because they are so deeply imbedded in the spiritual problems of our age which, although they explain us, do not always explain themselves to us.

Reprinted from the Introduction to *Letters of Henry Miller and Wallace Fowlie*, Wallace Fowlie, ed. (New York: Grove Press, 1975), 9–18. Reprinted by permission of Grove Press, Inc., copyright © 1975.

Beginning with *The Tropic of Cancer* in 1934, and continuing in all of his writings through the most recent pamphlet, *On Turning Eighty*, of 1972, Henry Miller has been writing his autobiography, and at the same time the history of our age. In his frank acceptance of the world, he learned to perceive in it the forces of evil as well as the forces of good, and hence to prepare himself for the particular role of prophet which he has played so consistently and so brilliantly.

The very title of Mr. Miller's book, *The Wisdom of the Heart*, is a key to the artist's function, and in it, on page 45, there is a sentence that might well be a text to explain all of his books: "We are in the grip of demonic forces created by our own fear and ignorance." The little man who is terrified, and who is in reality greater than that which terrifies him, is the choreographic objectification of the artist. He is the homunculus who is physically crushed by the world but who spiritually dominates the world in his quest for the absolute. The heroes whom Henry Miller talks about the most often are all the same type of passionate clown: Rimbaud and Lawrence, Chaplin and Raimu, Christ and Saint Francis, Miller himself as hero in *The Tropic of Cancer*. When he writes about the French, it is always about the little man, the insignificant man, but who is the microcosmic representation of the age: the *garçon de café*, the store proprietor, the whore, the pimp.

On the homunculus falls more lucidly than on the proud and successful the shadow of doom announced by Spengler and Lawrence. Henry Miller continued the prophetic role of those two writers but preached less. Oswald Spengler, the prophet of cyclical history, D. H. Lawrence, the psychologist of love and sex, and Henry Miller, the visionary who perceives his wisdom in the microcosm of the heart, are all contained in the boy-prophet Arthur Rimbaud.

The prophet or the visionary is the man who daily lives the metaphysical problems of his age. How to live is the theme of all prophets. Peace is always the goal; and around the word "peace" cluster the plans and the dreams, the intuitions and the burning designs of those men who see into the heart of the living and into the future. The peace of the world is, for Henry Miller, associated with Paris, because there it is more possible for man, so divided in his natural heritages, to become one as artist.

In their creative activity, even if not always in their lives as men, some of the most notable among contemporary artists have attained a unity thanks to the spiritual role of Paris. It is impossible to measure the peace of Paris in the work of Frenchmen like Proust, Breton, Rouault; of the Irish James Joyce; of the Russian Chagall and Tchelitchev; of the Spanish Picasso; of the American Gertrude Stein, Hemingway, and Henry Miller. From some wellspring of ancient liberty, Paris has safeguarded a fertile power in the unity of her native and assimilated artists who, not only in the accomplishment of their work but in their understanding of man, defy the usual contemporary waywardness and bifurcations.

Throughout the history of American literature, there has been an uninterrupted preoccupation with the theme of evil, treated from a special viewpoint of horror and awesomeness and fixation. Poe, Melville, Djuna Barnes, and Julien Green in his French novels, are united in their conception of evil as being a sense of dark foreboding and the plotting of malign spirits. I believe that the work of Henry Miller (and by "work" I mean his presence, his spirit, and the profoundest meaning of his books) has interrupted the traditional American treatment of evil. The obvious reason for Miller's books not being published in America during the 40's and 50's is the obscenity of their language in some of the passages. But this violence was needed to redirect the American consciousness of evil. The obscenity in the two *Tropics* is a form of medication and catharsis, an extroversion needed after all the books of puritanical foreboding. Both Miller's dissoluteness in language and his fixation on the physical possession of woman were means of liberating himself from the Hamlet-soul which has dominated the American literary heroes during the long period between the revolution of 1789 and World War II. Miller's were *the* pioneer books in the freedom of language and attitudes toward sex in American books and films since the 1960's.

"And always I am hungry," Henry Miller writes in *The Wisdom of the Heart*. Alimentary and sexual hunger are one kind, and spiritual hunger is another. Both are centrally analyzed in Miller's books. The long line of heroes extending from Hamlet to Charlie Chaplin who have been awkward in the presence of woman and unable to express themselves in love have developed in woman a false role of domination which D. H. Lawrence was among the first to castigate. Lawrence was devoted to love, and Miller is devoted to life, but both have expressed fear of woman's role in the modern world and her usurping of man's position. Hence their treatment of woman, in order to undermine her role of mother for her husband and of frigid goddess for her lover. Lawrence treats woman as wife who is essentially mistress, and Miller often treats woman as prostitute. Their use of woman, rather than restoring her to her natural role, has become just one other perversion, comparable to man's excessive love for his mother, as in Proust, and his excessive hate for his mother, as in Rimbaud.

Henry Miller knows that there is no solution to the problem of man's sexual hunger. He writes in his book, *The World of Sex*, "I am essentially a religious person, and always have been." In the Paris television interview he gave to Georges Belmont in 1969, he said: "I am fundamentally a religious man without a religion. I believe in the existence of a supreme intelligence. Call it God if you wish." Flashes everywhere in his writing testify to a sensitivity that worships. Every action and every word, no matter how seemingly inconsequential, has a meaning for him and a part in the wholeness of things. The visionary is always akin to the religious, because to see the plenitude of the cosmos is to love it and to accept it. To read Henry Miller has always been for me to discover a kind of peace in the world. He is the one contemporary writer who has driven out from his nature all traces of hamletism, and yet he writes constantly about Hamlet. About Hamlet as death-sower.

All the aspects of Miller's art and his nature are unified. He is one person, one visionary. But his vision is multiple and changing and even contradictory. That is as it should be. Love is something else and Miller has defined it admirably in *The World of Sex*: "Love is the drama of completion, of unification." The purpose of life attracts him more than the complexities of any single existence. In his vision, details and debts are forgotten, and he sees only the dark results of corruption and the blazing projects of rejuvenation.

Despite his fame today, despite the notable success of his books throughout the world, Henry Miller at the age of eighty-three still tends to think of himself as a failure, *un raté*, as he said to Georges Belmont in the television interview. He identifies with the poor, the wretched, the unknown of the world. He has often spoken of his attraction to the story of D. H. Lawrence, concerning Jesus after the resurrection when he returns to earth and appears as an ordinary man, nondescript, almost an idiot. But that is when Jesus enjoyed life and found it exhilarating. If Miller himself is reincarnated and returns to the earth in another form, he hopes he will be a nobody, the most humble of men, unknown, and without an occupation.

In another age, he would have been a gnostic or a monk, and leading the kind of life in which all the contradictions of his nature would be explained and harmonized. Those friends who have perhaps understood him the best: Lawrence Durrell, Anaïs Nin, Brassai, Perlès, William Carlos Williams, in their praise have always spoken of the good influence he has been in the world, of his simplicity and honesty, of his ability to find himself the same man in his roles of clown and angel, the same man wherever he is living: Brooklyn, Dijon, Big Sur, Paris, Pacific Palisades. He has known suffering and upheavals in his personal life, anguish that brought him close to suicide, but more than most men, he is able to be at peace with himself in the midst of his conflicts. It is less important for Miller to be a writer than to be a man at peace with himself. By most people, he is thought of as the man who wrote the two *Tropics*, and they seldom consider the other lives he has led since that already distant time. His memory, faithful to itself, has become his work. It has continued to unfold and reveal itself in its ever expanding universe.

Henry Miller has always been surprised at his reputation of a writer about sex, and through the years has grown weary of the same question always asked him: "If you consider yourself a religious man, why do you write about sex as you do?" The answer is simple and Miller has repeated it on many occasions. Western civilization, Christianity in many of the forms it has taken, has created a conflict between the body and the spirit, which

Henry Miller has never felt. The façades of some of the great temples of India are covered with sculptured bodies of men and women in the most erotic postures that can be imagined. For Miller they are the work of religious spirits for whom sexuality, the worship of the human body, is the way leading to God. He has always looked upon his sexual life as normal and natural. He has written directly about sexual adventures which other men conceal under the words which they use. A close reading of Miller's books will show that actually he is timid in the presence of women. It is they who seduced him.

He admires woman for being more of the earth than he can be. He has often claimed that passion for woman remains personal, whereas man, more religious than woman, is passionate for abstract ideas and for God. Men are in error, he says, when they deliberately fail to cultivate the feminine element of their nature. The world as we know it is run by men, and badly run. Through the ages, man has impressed upon woman that she belongs to one man alone. This seems to Miller the source of much of the turmoil in the world, and nostalgically he thinks of prehistoric times when anthropologists tell us about matriarchies, about woman-dominated civilizations.

We may never learn what daemon inhabits Henry Miller, what spirit has made him into the honest writer that he is. But we do know beyond any doubt that he has remained totally faithful to his daemon. He is incorruptible. He cannot be bought by fame or money. He is more honest than most intellectuals. He has the integrity of a primitive living in a decadent world. He is not an exile from that world, but he is its critic. I would compare him, not so much to Rabelais as many critics have, but to Saint Francis. *Black Spring* is our contemporary "Hymn to the Sun."

It is tempting to compare Miller with Lawrence or Joyce or even Beckett. But there is no point to doing that—he does not possess the architectonic skill of a novelist. He is a world literary figure who has given us the best confessional writing since Jean-Jacques Rousseau. He has given us the best account of a writer's day-dreaming and reveries that are different from those of the layman.

Older than Steinbeck, Dos Passos, Hemingway, and Fitzgerald, he was not a member of the "lost generation" hesitating between exile in Montparnasse and commitment to the grapes of wrath. He has always been the pure singer of individual freedom who was a-political because he believed that to give up a capitalistic regime for a socialist regime was simply to change masters. His personal creed may be attached in part to the European utopia of the noble savage, and in part to the American tradition of the return to nature we read in Thoreau and Whitman. His sense of anarchy is partly that of Thoreau and partly that of the Beat Generation.

Miller is not a writer of pornography. He uses obscenity as a means of expressing natural forces in him that rise up against the constraints of civilization. His liberation begins with the liberation of his sexual drives. Obscenity is his battle cry against the air-conditioned nightmare. If one wanted to read about sex as a thesis, one would read Lawrence and not Miller. If one wanted to read about sex as sensuality, one would read Colette and not Miller. Sex is for Miller the symbol of the violent quest for experience that took him from an ordinary office job in America to the Paris of whores and bistros. He is the archetypal bohemian who to his newest readers today sounds like a sage rather than a tramp or a *clochard*. A young reader who was an adolescent in the decade of the 60's, on reading *Black Spring*, would equate the twenty-page passage "The Angel Is My Watermark" with the best pages of *Leaves of Grass* and *Howl*. He would be held, not so much by the episodes and the anecdotes in the books as by the intermittent explanations Miller is always giving us of what the artist is, as the man who has antennae and knows how to hook up to the currents that are in the cosmos.

The real thinkers of any age, the answerers to the really serious questions of humanity, have always lived as temporary exiles. They gain admittance to the company of the immortals by living just outside the rank of the mortals. During their lifetime they appear to most men as loafers, subversive, cranks, useless, and even dangerous to the establishment. Socrates was one of them, and Baudelaire, Thoreau, Henry Miller. They answer the questions of the few people who come to see them at the edge of Walden Pond, or at the top of Big Sur. They write, they paint, they hack away at the old forms of art and at the old forms of morals.

"Each man," Miller tells us in *Black Spring*, "is his own civilized desert, the island of self on which he is shipwrecked." Each artistic work is a flight off from this island of self, and he alludes to the classic flights of Melville, Rimbaud, Gauguin, Henry James, D. H. Lawrence. "The Angel Is My Watermark" is in one respect a treatise on the surrealist method of composition. In it Miller describes himself painting a watercolor. He feels like a watercolor and then he does one. He begins by drawing a horse. (Miller has vaguely in mind the Etruscan horses he had seen in the Louvre.) At one moment the horse resembles a hammock and then when he adds stripes, it becomes a zebra. He adds a tree, a mountain, an angel, cemetery gates. These are the forms that occur almost unpredictably on his paper. He submits it to the various processes of smudging, of soaking it in the sink, of holding it upside down and letting the colors coagulate. Finally it is done: a master-piece that has come about by accident. But then Miller says that the Twenty-third Psalm was another accident. He looks at the watercolor and sees it to be the result of mistakes, erasures, hesitations, but also "the result of certi-tude." Every work of art has to be credited, in some mysterious way, to every artist. So Miller credits Dante, Spinoza, and Hieronymous Bosch for his little watercolor.

Henry Miller as Orphic Poet and Seer

BERTRAND MATHIEU

1. "The Image's Truth"

"Here are hopes. But what will you see and hear of them, if you have not experienced glance and glow and dawn of day in your own souls? I can only suggest—I cannot do more! To move the stones, to make animals men—would you have me do that? Alas, if you are yet stones and animals, you must seek your Orpheus!"

Friedrich Nietzsche in *The Joyful Wisdom*

It may seem startling to suggest, in this opening chapter, that Henry Miller's characteristic major works were consciously structured with a view to updating and re-telling the myth of Orpheus in a systematic and consecutive fashion—the way James Joyce's *Ulysses* re-tells the myth of Odysseus or Eugene O'Neill's *Mourning Becomes Electra* the myth of Agamemnon and Clytemnestra. An artist as pugnaciously slapdash, as "anarchic," as Henry Miller prides himself on being could scarcely have aspired to anything of the kind.

Nevertheless, the image of Orpheus is clearly the mythopoeic backbone and *support* of Miller's entire output as a writer. The lineaments of "famous Orpheus" and of Orphic ways of seeing and experiencing things—almost invariably implicit, but very persuasive and uncannily consistent with the outlines of the ancient myth—are recurrent presences in all of Miller's well-known works, particularly in his masterpiece, *The Colossus of Maroussi*. In fact, I intend to argue in the course of a close analytical study of Miller's book on Greece that this extraordinary book belongs among the important examples of twentieth-century mythic writing in the genuineness of its mythic content and the beauty of its execution.

What *is* the Orphic myth? What role has it played in modern literature? Walter A. Strauss goes so far as to identify Orpheus with *poetry itself* in times of disaster like our own:

Orpheus is not only poetry; he has become, in modern times, the agony of poetry—a sort of ambassador without portfolio of poetry. He is the figure,

Reprinted from *Orpheus in Brooklyn: Orphism, Rimbaud, and Henry Miller* (The Hague, Paris: Mouton, 1976), 11–21, 22–33, 201–13. Printed by permission of author; copyright © Bertrand Mathieu. Footnote numbering has been altered.

the myth, entrusted with the burden of poetry and myth. His metamorphosis is the change in poetic climate itself, placed against an ever-darkening sky in which poetry recedes more and more toward secret and unexplored spaces, spaces that are obscure and must be illuminated by constellations of the mind ever threatened by disaster and extinction.[1]

Strauss' book on the Orphic theme in modern literature, *Descent and Return*, deals chiefly with Novalis, Mallarmé, Nerval, and Rilke. But such a study could equally have made room for figures like Rimbaud, Hart Crane, and Henry Miller—writers who taught themselves how to revindicate the role of poet in the face of modern horrors by tactically combining the stance of Prometheus and Orpheus, the defiant fire-stealer and the resourceful singer. In fact, Gwendolyn Bays' illuminating book, *The Orphic Vision*—to which I plan to return in later chapters—takes Rimbaud as the supreme exemplar of the Orphic writer in modern times. Since Miller, like Hart Crane, has again and again acknowledged the influence of Rimbaud on his development, the line of descent from their common progenitor, Orpheus, is made even more explicit.

Before giving a synopsis of the life and achievement of Orpheus, it may be useful to define what I mean by "myth" and "mythic writing." Although Henry Miller writes prose narratives, I intend to place him unhesitatingly among the poets and mythomanes. My reasons for doing so will be obvious by the completion of my study, but Miller—whose first serious writings were prose poems which he sold from door to door the way Whitman had done a century earlier—has repeatedly referred to himself as a poet[2] and is manifestly a writer of profound mythopoeic endowments. What he has achieved in *The Colossus of Maroussi*, as well as in the earlier *Tropic of Cancer* and *Tropic of Capricorn*, amounts to the creation of what Hugh Kenner would call a "homeomorph"[3] of the Orpheus myth. By recognizing the personal traits and outlook of the hero of a myth in his own personality, a writer acquires the power to instruct us in the urgencies and triumphs of that myth simply by telling us his own story.

Our word "myth" is derived from a Greek word which merely means "story," but "mythic writing" as I plan to use the term in this book has overtones and vibrancies that go well beyond mere storytelling. It is closer to what Mircea Eliade, the great Roumanian mytho-analyst, has in mind when he writes: "Myths reveal the structure of reality, and the multiple modalities of being in the world. That is why they are the exemplary models for human behaviour; they disclose the *true* stories, concern themselves with the *realities* (Eliade's italics)."[4] Eliade's use of words like "reveal" and "disclose" indicates that the mythic outlook is, in the most precise sense, a way of *seeing* reality and of transcribing, clearly, the results of what one has seen. The modern psyche, like its ancient counterpart, teems with half-remembered myths and hierophantic symbols. The triumph of mechanistic technology has not altered the fact that radiant residues of mythological matter survive for those who have the ability to *see* them.

Henry Miller, like Arthur Rimbaud, is committed to the doctrine that the true poet is a "seer." Neither writer would have found it difficult to agree with the words of Emerson: "What we are, that only can we see . . . Build therefore your own world. As fast as you conform your life to the pure idea in your own mind, that will unfold its great proportions. A correspondent revolution in things will attend the influx of the spirit."[5] The mythic writer has had to recognize the dynamics of a particular myth (as well as its significance for other people) *within himself* first of all. This is the secret of his "power." Wallace Stevens brilliantly describes the genus in this fashion:

> A mythology reflects its region. Here
> In Connecticut, we never lived in a time
> When mythology was possible—but if we had—
> That raises the question of the image's truth.
> The image must be of the nature of its creator.
> It is the nature of its creator increased,
> Heightened. It is he, anew, in a freshened youth.[6]

If "the image's truth" has been validated within the experience and art of the mythologist, Stevens suggests, it will prove to be identical with him but "anew, in a freshened youth." Mircea Eliade is completely in accord with the poet in this respect: Man is "contemporary with the cosmogony . . . because ritual projects him into the mythical epoch of the beginning. A bacchant, through his orgiastic rites, imitates the suffering Dionysos; an Orphic, through his initiation ceremonial, repeats the original gestures of Orpheus."[7] Renewal is as integral a feature of myth as is *repetition*, and this is the source of some of the greatest excitements and the greatest vexations in the study of the mythic temperament in action. There is nothing simple about the way a writer like Henry Miller (or Arthur Rimbaud or Rainer Maria Rilke) consciously, sometimes half-consciously, adopts the attributes of an Orpheus and projects the accents of his own inimitable humanness through the mask of the god.

The observations of the French scholar Eva Kushner on this subject seem to me highly pertinent. Professor Kushner considers myths highly complex realities which have the power to move people mysteriously, often independently of the skills of the author who employs them. Myths, she believes, are never merely stories. Primitive man genuinely *lived* the myths on which his mental universe was based. But modern man, with his hard-won knowledge, distrusts his own imagination and prefers to "stick to the facts." Every now and then, however, a contemporary writer allows himself to be seduced by a myth to the point of discovering in it the form *par excellence* of his own spiritual life or of an aspect of it. Whether this indicates a lack

of realism on his part depends entirely on how one defines the term "reality."
According to Professor Kushner, any writer who assigns a prominent role to
the myth of Orpheus in his work has merely opted for the view that reality
is not to be found in material objects alone but rather in the subtler connections that exist between man and his universe, sometimes perceptible, sometimes intelligible, and sometimes wholly elusive to human understanding.
But there is no simple, one-to-one connection between the latter view and
the intricate modalities of the Orphic myth. The truth, as Professor Kushner
puts it,

est beaucoup plus subtile, et comme le myth lui-même, elle échappe aux
abstractions toujours trop approximatives. Le rapport entre le poète et le mythe
ne se conforme à aucune loi générale car il est aussi personnel que l'âme de
chacun; la critique ne peut que s'en approcher avec respect, sachant que
l'analyse la plus scrupuleuse ne saurait en révéler le secret . . . Le contenue
de la mythologie est en mouvement perpétuel et soumis à de perpétuelles
transformations, même s'il lui arrive parfois d'être fixé dans le moule de
quelque tradition sacrée. Le mythe se donne à lui-même sa propre forme; il se
passe d'interprétations et d'explications. Comme la musique, il s'exprime
totalement lui-même. Ainsi, le mode d'expression mythologique est irremplaça-
ble, si bien qu'aucun autre moyen d'expression ne saurait en rendre la pléni-
tude. "Comme la musique a un sens intelligible qui, comme toute entité
intelligible génératrice de satisfactions, procure un contentement, ainsi en est-
il du mythologème. Ce sens, il est difficile de l'exprimer en langage de la
science, pour la raison même qu'il ne peut pleinement s'exprimer sur le mode
mythologique." Kerenyi conclut en disant que la seule manière de comprendre
le mythe, c'est de l'écouter simplement: d' "avoir de l'oreille" pour son sens
profond, de vibrer à l'unisson avec lui comme avec une oeuvre musicale.[8] [is
far more subtle and, like the original myth, it eludes mere abstractions which
are always too approximative. The relationship between the poet and the myth
does not conform to any general law since it is as personal as the soul of any
given individual. Criticism must approach it respectfully, conscious of the
fact that the most scrupulous analysis could scarcely reveal its secret. . . .
The content of mythology is in perpetual motion and subject to perpetual
transformations, even if it often happens to be embedded in the mold of some
sacred tradition. A myth gives itself its own specific form; it dispenses with
interpretations and explications. Like music, it totally expresses *itself*. Indeed
the mythological mode of expression is *sui generis*, such that no other means
of expression could give a sense of its plenitude. "Just as music has intelligible
meaning which (like all intelligible entities that can generate satisfactions)
provides contentment, so is it also with a mythologem. It is difficult to express
this meaning in the language of science, for the simple reason that science
cannot fully convey the mythological style." Karl Kerényi concludes by saying
that the only way to comprehend a myth is to listen to it, quite simply: to
"have an ear" for its deeper sense, to vibrate in unison with it as with a piece
of music. (My translation)]

Miller's own thinking on the subject of myth is much the same as that of Mircea Eliade and Eva Kushner. Toward the close of *The Colossus of Maroussi*, after commenting on the intoxication of the Greeks with their own myth, he writes:

> We forget, in our enchantment with the myth, that it is born of reality and is fundamentally no different from any other form of creation, except that it has to do with the very quick of life. We too are creating myths, though we are perhaps not aware of it. But in our myths there is no place for the gods. We are building an abstract, dehumanized world out of the ashes of an illusory materialism. We are proving to ourselves that the universe is empty, a task which is justified by our own empty logic. We are determined to conquer and conquer we shall, but the conquest is death.[9]

He concludes by apotheosizing the book's "colossal" hero and its principal avatar of Orpheus, George Katsimbalis—one of the many spellbinding myth-omanes in *Colossus* whom Miller, with the self-reflecting eyes of the Orphic, is so quick to identify and celebrate:

> There are men who are so rich, so full, who give themselves so completely that each time you take leave of them you feel that it is absolutely of no consequence whether the parting is for a day or forever. They come to you brimming over and they fill you to overflowing. They ask nothing of you except that you participate in their superabundant joy of living. They never inquire which side of the fence you are on because the world they inhabit has no fences. They make themselves invulnerable by habitually exposing themselves to every danger. They grow more heroic in the measure that they reveal their weaknesses. Certainly in those endless and seemingly fabulous stories which Katsimbalis was in the habit of recounting there must have been a good element of fancy and distortion, yet even if truth was occasionally sacrificed to reality the man behind the story only succeeded thereby in revealing more faithfully and thoroughly his human image . . . It was also taken for granted by everybody, it seemed to me, that Katsimbalis not only had a right to improvise as he went along but that he was expected to do so. He was regarded as a virtuoso, a virtuoso who played only his own compositions and had therefore the right to alter them as he pleased.[10]

One of the most eminent British historians of the Orphic movement in Ancient Greece, W.K.C. Guthrie, would have found nothing untoward about such a procedure. The Orphics in ancient times, according to Guthrie, also knew a thing or two about improvisation:

> The Orphic writers had taken what suited them from popular mythology. They had added something to its matter and much to its significance. It was a crystallization around a new centre, and the centre was the story of the

dismemberment of Dionysos, the revenge of Zeus on the Titans and the birth of mankind from their ashes.[11]

In order to provide a clear framework of reference for the case I want to make for Henry Miller as a writer of unquestionably Orphic orientation, I think it will be useful to provide here a detailed synopsis of the principal events of the career of the paradigmatic Orpheus. I will content myself largely with paraphasing the excellent accounts given by Robert Graves in *The Greek Myths* and the *New Larousse Encyclopaedia of Mythology*, although much more detailed accounts can be found in W.K.C. Guthrie's *Orpheus and Greek Religion* and Ivan M. Linforth's *The Arts of Orpheus*.

According to the original myth, Orpheus was the most famous poet and musician who ever lived. He was born in Thrace, in northeastern Greece, and was very early identified with the cult of Dionysos. Apollo had presented him with a lyre and the Muses had taught him how to play it, so that he not only enchanted wild beasts but made the trees and rocks move from their places to follow the sound of his marvelous music. At Zone, in Thrace, a number of ancient mountain oaks are said to be standing to this day in the pattern of one of Orpheus' dances. Orpheus not only possessed remarkable musical powers, but was also endowed (like a Siberian shaman) with the prophetic gifts of the seer.

After a visit to Egypt, Orpheus the voyager joined the Argonauts and sailed with them to Colchis. During the journey, the magical powers of his music helped the Argonauts overcome many of their difficulties. He even managed to charm the Sirens with his extraordinary singing voice so that the Argo and its crew escaped destruction. When he returned from his journey, Orpheus married Eurydice and settled in Thrace. One day, near Tempe, Eurydice met a young man named Aristaeus, who tried to seduce her against her will. She stepped on a snake while trying to escape and died of its bite. Orpheus, overcome with grief, decided to descend into Hades to try to bring her back among the living. He not only charmed the ferryman Charon, the watch-dog Cerberus, and the three Judges of the Dead with his beautiful plaintive music, but temporarily suspended the tortures of the damned. His music was so irresistible that he managed to soothe the savage heart of Hades and win permission to restore Eurydice to the upper world. Hades made only one condition: that Orpheus could not look behind him until Eurydice had crossed over the edge of the underworld into the light of the sun. Eurydice is said to have followed up through the dark passageway, guided by the sounds of his lyre, but just as they reached the outer limits of Hades, Orpheus turned around to see if Eurydice was still behind him. He thereby lost her forever and had to return to the upper world all alone. Some say that Orpheus thereafter avoided the company of women and introduced homosexuality into Greece.

Later, when Dionysos invaded Thrace, the myth tells us Orpheus neglected to honor the god. Instead, he taught the sacred mysteries and preached the evil of murder to the men of Thrace. Every morning he would rise early to greet the sun on the summit of Mount Pangaeum, preaching that Helios (whom he called Apollo) was the greatest of the gods. Angered by this, Dionysos sent his Maenads after him in Macedonia. First waiting until their husbands had entered Apollo's temple, where Orpheus served as a priest, the Maenads seized the weapons stacked outside, burst in, murdered their husbands, and tore Orpheus apart limb from limb. They threw his head into the Hebros River, but we are told it floated, still singing, down to the sea and was carried to the island of Lesbos. Tearfully, the Muses collected his limbs and buried them at Leibethra, at the foot of Mount Olympus, where the nightingales are now said to sing more sweetly than anywhere else in the world.

Some authorities, according to Robert Graves, hold that Orpheus had condemned the Maenad's promiscuity while he went about preaching homosexual love. This caused Aphrodite to be as angered as Dionysos had been. Her fellow-Olympians, however, could not agree that Orpheus' murder had been justified and Dionysos spared the Maenads' lives by turning them into oak trees, which remained forever rooted to the ground. The Thracian men who had survived the massacre decided, with a colorful flair for the cruelties of justice, to tattoo their wives as a warning against the murder of singers and priests!

As for Orpheus' head, after being attacked by a jealous Lemnian serpent (which Apollo immediately changed into a stone) it was laid to rest in a cave at Antissa, sacred to Dionysos. There it prophesied day and night until Apollo, finding that his oracle at Delphi was becoming deserted, came and stood over the head and said: "Cease from interfering in my affairs. I have stood enough from you and your singing!" Immediately after this, the head of Orpheus became silent. His lyre had also drifted to Lesbos and had been laid up in the temple of Apollo. At the intercession of Apollo and the Muses, the Lyre was placed in the heavens where it has been shining ever since in the form of a constellation called The Lyre, a symbol of the indestructibility of song.[12]

But at this point in the chapter we must ask ourselves how well acquainted Henry Miller was, exactly, with the specifics of the myth of Orpheus and Eurydice. Is it pure coincidence that all of the salient features of this myth form a loose choreographic plan for some of his most artful and most typical work? How *much* of the Orphic mythologem did the "unschooled" Henry Miller really know? A great deal. In fact, the evidence I have uncovered points to a rather detailed and obsessive interest in mythic materials such as those embodied in the myth of Orpheus. In *The Books in My Life*, published over ten years after *Colossus*, Miller indicates how far back into his childhood this interest extends:

When I stood amid the ruins of Knossos and of Mycenae did my thoughts turn to school books, to my penal instructors and the enchanting tales they told us? No. I thought of the stories I had read as a child; I saw the illustrations of those books I had thought buried in oblivion; I thought of our discussions in the street and the amazing speculations we had indulged in. I recalled my own private speculation about all these exciting, mysterious themes connected with past and future. Looking out over the plain of Argos from Mycenae, I lived over again—and how vividly!—the tale of the Argonauts [whose adventuring, it will be remembered, Orpheus had safeguarded with his music]. Gazing upon the Cyclopean walls of Tiryns I recalled the tiny illustration of the wall in one of my wonder books—it corresponded exactly with the reality confronting me. Never, in school, had a history professor even attempted to make living for us these glorious epochs of the past which every child enters into naturally as soon as he is able to read. With what childlike faith does the hardy explorer pursue his grim task! We learn nothing from the pedagogues. The true educators are the adventurers and wanderers, the men who plunge into the living plasm of history, legend, myth.[13]

In a special appendix to this book, Miller lists the one hundred books which influenced him most. The list conspicuously includes not only "Greek Myths and Legends," but at least a dozen other books that could have served him as sources of Orphic materials.[14]

The itch to emulate Orpheus is amply attested in essays Miller wrote before *Colossus*,[15] but there can be no doubt that it even antedates the publication of his first book. In a work schedule "drafted and used by H. M. during the Clichy period of 1932–1933," we find Miller reminding himself to "clarify the symbolism still more [in *Tropic of Cancer*]—mother's womb, hero-wanderer, labyrinth-throngs . . ."[16] An agenda prepared at that time lists Jane Harrison's *The Orphic Myths* and Dante as essential reading.[17] And in preparation for a book on D. H. Lawrence which Miller was beginning to write, he asks Anaïs Nin (in a letter dated October, 1933) to provide him with, among other things, the "Orphic myth (*Birth of Tragedy* gives it better than anything)."[18]

But Miller's letters to Anaïs Nin contain even more conclusive proof of his conscious discipleship to the myth of Orpheus and to his determination to put his own Orphic sensibility to formal use in his books. This passage, from a letter of February, 1934, strikingly illustrates both an Emersonian/Orphic tendency to see reality in terms of *himself* and a vivid consciousness of his own Orphic nature:

With the arrival of your note I've thrown everything on the floor. What I once thought was the material of a book lies about me, not in fragments, but in shreds. It would take a wizard to put it together—*and I am that wizard*! I've discovered in myself what I've been shouting about in the theory of annihilation, via Nietzsche, Jung, Father Orpheus, Mother Incest, etc. etc.

I've smashed the fucking thing into a million pieces in order that I may ingest it piecemeal and throw it out again in a macrocosmic poem. I am learning method, structure, order—teaching it to myself, the highest kind of order, of form and structure, the poem in itself, as it were. I use this word "poem" in a new sense, please notice. I borrow it from my friend Walter Lowenfels— my friend! Note! Yes, I feel proud of it—as if it were an achievement. It was a creation, if you like. Last night the great conjunction, the breaking down of all asymptotical relations by the creation of new orbits. Is it Lowenfels I see truly now, or myself? Same thing. I see that in him which was blind in me, or vice versa. I went down with him last night into some kind of chthonian underworld of the mind where the supreme point of identification is reached. I come home and order my book: Part 1.—Genetics of Idea; Part 2.—Poem and Exegesis. Important to note is "Poem." New meaning—*for me*. Here I have been complaining all along that I know no one in Paris with whom I can communicate, no man of sufficient stature. And by the most roundabout route I have come to exactly the man I wanted to meet. Did I create him, or did he create me? He is my counterpart, the other half of me which has been wandering through the underworld in search of Eurydice (Miller's italics).[19]

The reference to "Father Orpheus" is too pointed to require additional comment. The imagery of Miller's letter is saturated with Orphic notions and he is evidently intent on translating his Orphic "theory of annihilation" into more ambitious literary terms, in writings to come, as a result of his catalytic friendship with Lowenfels, which to all appearances has merely caused his own thinking to clarify itself. And I think a careful examination of the mythic elements in Henry Miller's key works will bear out my contention that Miller's literary strategies are those of a faithful follower and avatar of "Father Orpheus." The landscapes they describe—whether inner or outer, real or imaginary, in Brooklyn or in Greece—are quite simply what Wallace Stevens would term "supreme fictions" in the Orphic mode. They are a self-styled and self-taught Orphic writer's attempt to validate, within the limits of his own personal experience, "the image's truth" of a much larger paradigm.

2. Orpheus as Musician: The Spellbinder Motif

"I don't say that God is one grand laugh: I say that you've got to laugh hard before you can get anywhere near God. My whole aim in life is to get near to God, that is, to get nearer to myself. That's why it doesn't matter to me what road I take. But music is very important. Music is a tonic for the pineal gland. Music isn't Bach or Beethoven; music is the can opener of the soul. It makes you terribly quiet inside, makes you aware that there's a roof to your being."

Henry Miller in *Tropic of Capricorn*

It's as a singer and music-maker that Orpheus was famous in ancient times, and it's as a singer and music-maker that Henry Miller projects his author's *persona* upon the awareness of his readers at the very start of his career. *Tropic of Cancer*, his first published book, virtually opens with a gesture of self-identification with the singer Orpheus who must descend into Hades in search of Eurydice:

> To sing you must first open your mouth. You must have a pair of lungs, and a little knowledge of music. It is not necessary to have an accordion, or a guitar. The essential thing is to *want* to sing. This then is a song. I am singing . . . When into the womb of time everything is again withdrawn chaos will be restored and chaos is the score upon which reality is written. You, Tania, are my chaos. It is why I sing. It is not even I, it is the world dying, shedding the skin of time. I am still alive, kicking in your womb, a reality to write upon.[20]

It's entirely in keeping with what we know about Orpheus and his character for a writer like Henry Miller to connect the etiology of his own gift *with woman* and with the sense of desolation and hope evoked by woman. The Orphic theme of re-birth is immediately audible in these strains.

Not only did Miller at one time seriously aspire to become a concert pianist, but his books are saturated with musical terminology. He has referred to some of the characteristically Millerian literary devices which he uses as "cadenzas" and "codas" and he bears witness, in some of his earliest letters, to the crucial role music has played in his life:

> Now I really hear! I can relate these themes and motifs and big canvases and little to all things. It isn't music alone—it's all life, all history. And it has a great lulling and provocative effect, *both*. It drives you deep inward and permeates the tone of your feeling, your thought. Music purifies, no doubt of that. Especially, the highly organic, the great formal compositions . . . When I get to the subject of music I feel I am on the brink of something profound. Are you *sure* you get all that on music which Nietzsche gives (Miller's italics)?[21]

The Orphics, according to all the authorities, were not only greatly devoted to the arts of music but to the purification of the spirit.

Among his major books, *The Colossus of Maroussi* may easily be regarded as the *locus classicus* of Miller's attempt to re-enact the bewitching performances of Orpheus. It contains some of Miller's most dazzling monologues, but it is also a veritable gallery of portraits of great spellbinding "singers" in the Orphic tradition. From the opening paragraphs to Lawrence Durrell's glowing anecdote on the midnight cocks of Attica in the concluding coda, Miller treats his readers to a procession of human types who share his unique gift for casting a spell with words.

Here, to begin at the beginning, is the opening paragraph of *The Colossus of Maroussi*:

I would never have gone to Greece had it not been for a girl named Betty Ryan who lived in the same house with me in Paris. One evening, over a glass of white wine, she began to talk to her experiences in roaming about the world. I always listened to her with great attention, not only because her experiences were strange but because when she talked about her wanderings she seemed to paint them: everything she described remained in my head like finished canvases by a master. It was a peculiar conversation that evening: we began by talking about China and the Chinese language which she had begun to study. Soon we were in North Africa, in the desert, among peoples I had never heard of before. And then suddenly she was all alone, walking beside a river, and the light was intense and I was following her as best I could in the blinding sun but she got lost and I found myself wandering about in a strange land listening to a language I had never heard before. She is not exactly a story teller, this girl, but she is an artist of some sort because nobody has ever given me the ambiance of a place so thoroughly as she did Greece. Long afterwards I discovered that it was near Olympia that she had gone astray and I with her, but at the time it was just Greece to me, a world of light such as I had never dreamed of and never hoped to see.[22]

Betty Ryan, whose name faintly resembles that of Beatrice, Dante's irresistible guide to a Paradise that can only be reached after descending into the bowels of the Inferno, may be regarded as the prototype of a number of other beguiling Eurydices in the book: Lawrence Durrell's wife Nancy, the resplendent Jeanne Seferiades, the young Greek girl with the reddish-gold hair whose "slow, sustained smile" prompts Miller to liken her to "the dancers of Java and of Bali . . . the culminating expression of the spiritual achievement of the human race,"[23] and that "strange monster with six toes" who, according to Miller, "had the smile of the insatiable one to whom a thousand burning kisses are only the incentive to renewed assaults. In some strange and inexplicable fashion she has remained in my memory as that symbol of unbounded love which I sensed in a lesser degree in all Greek women."[24] All these women intimate the possibility of the paradisiac to Miller, but it is Beatrice/Betty Ryan's blandishments which actually persuade Miller to abandon Paris and make the "descent" south to Greece by way of the Dordogne region of France with its "black, mysterious river at Dômme."[25]

Although *The Colossus of Maroussi* is merely an implicit re-enactment of the Orphic drama in which the names of Orpheus and Eurydice are not mentioned once, it's interesting that at the very outset Miller identifies the "black, mysterious river at Dômme" with the poet Rainer Maria Rilke. The author of *Sonnets to Orpheus* seems a paradigmatic enough figure to Miller to deserve the place of initiatory presence at the outset of Miller's own *katábasis*. That presence presides, implicitly, over much of the book. The journey to Greece is taken under the patronage, so to speak, of Rilke. When Miller describes his first airplane trip in Part Two of *Colossus*, his attitude to the experience is a reminder that Rilke had devoted a good deal of his life to warning his own generation against the mechanization of their lives, and, as his biographer E. M. Butler puts it, to

imploring them . . . to turn their thoughts away from the beauty and complexity of aeroplanes, to the spaces they are traversing, that they [might] *become* those far-distant bourns. Determined though he was to glorify all existing things and to worship metamorphosis, Rilke could not affirm with any conviction the changes accomplished by the march of history and the industrial revolution. Our modern methods of haste and luxury, our mechanized lives have separated us from the gods of old; our sacred fires now burn in boilers; our strength has entered automatic hammers, and we are swooning like exhausted swimmers.[26]

Here is the way Miller expresses the same thought a few decades later:

I had never been in a plane before and I probably will never go up again. I felt foolish sitting in the sky with hands folded; the man beside me was reading a newspaper, apparently oblivious of the clouds that brushed the windowpanes. We were probably making a hundred miles an hour, but since we passed nothing but clouds I had the impression of not moving. In short, it was unrelievedly dull and pointless. I was sorry that I had not booked passage on the good ship Acropolis which was to touch at Crete shortly. Man is made to walk the earth and sail the seas; the conquest of the air is reserved for a later stage in his evolution, when he will have sprouted real wings and assumed the form of the angel which he is in essence.[27]

But Rilke is not the only Orphic poet whose music enchants Miller in the *Colossus*. Aside from being dazzled by the light-filled Greek landscapes, Miller is fascinated by the cunning art of contemporary Greek "singers" who, like their "Father Orpheus" before them, can enchant wild beasts and make the rocks and trees move from their places. *Colossus* pays tribute to the poet Seferis with his wonderful talk of poetry and American jazz; to Dr. Theodore Stephanides with his inexhaustible knowledge of "plants, flowers, trees, rocks, minerals, . . . diseases, planets, comets . . . and his hallucinating descriptions of his life in the trenches . . . during the World War";[28] to Captain Antoniou, the sea-voyager poet, with his feverish obsession with the American writer Sherwood Anderson, whose loneliness Antoniou shares with the sons of Orpheus in general; to Stavros Tsoussis, the bureaucrat-as-Orpheus, beside whose adroit machinations and dynamic doubletalk Miller believes a minor spellbinder like Adolf Hitler would seem a "caricature" and Mussolini "an old-fashioned Ben Greet player."[29]

The most important manifestation of the Orphic genius dealt with by Miller in *Colossus*, however, is George Katsimbalis. This well-known Greek magazine editor and bibliographer, who lived in the Athenian suburb of Maroussi at the time of Miller's journey in 1939, is the "colossus" of the title. Like everything he talks about with such verve, Katsimbalis as Miller describes him is considerably larger than life. From the first encounter with Katsimbalis, Miller is mesmerized by the man's extraordinary gifts as a raconteur. The quality of Katsimbalis' talk, despite his ailing health and "a great element of the tragic in him,"[30] could, according to Miller, "galvanize the dead."[31] One is reminded immediately that Orpheus not only charmed the ferryman Charon, the watch-dog Cerberus, and the three Judges of the Dead with his plaintive music, but temporarily suspended the tortures of the damned.[32]

Miller becomes eloquent himself, in the Orphic manner, when he attempts a portrait of Katsimbalis' self-infatuated technique. For, as he explains, Katsimbalis "talked about himself because he himself was the most interesting person he knew." Miller adds: "I liked that quality very much— I have a little of it myself."[33] Only an extended quotation could do justice to this *self*-entranced Orpheus *describing Orpheus*. And since paraphrases always invite some measure of distortion, I quote Miller's own words in their entirety:

It wasn't just talk he handed out, but *language*—food and beast language. He always talked against a landscape, like the protagonist of a lost world. The Attic landscape was best of all for his purpose: it contains the necessary ingredients for the dramatic monologue. One has only to see the open air theatres buried in the hillsides to understand the importance of this setting. Even if his talk carried him to Paris, for example, to a place like the Faubourg Montmartre, he spiced and flavored it with his Attic ingredients, with thyme, sage, tufa, asphodel, honey, red clay, blue roofs, acanthus trimmings, violet light, hot rocks, dry winds, *rezina*, arthritis, and the electrical crackle that plays over the low hills like a swift serpent with a broken spine. He was a strange contradiction, even in his talk. With his snake-like tongue which struck like lightning, with fingers moving nervously, as though wandering over an imaginary spinet, with pounding, brutal gestures which somehow never smashed anything but simply raised a din, with all the boom of surf and the roar and sizzle and razzle-dazzle, if you suddenly observed him closely you got the impression that he was sitting there immobile, that only the round falcon's eye was alert, that he was a bird which had been hypnotized, or had hypnotized itself, and that his claws were fastened to the wrist of an invisible giant, a giant like the earth. All this flurry and din, all these kaleidoscopic prestidigitations of his, were only a sort of wizardry which he employed to conceal the fact that he was a prisoner—that was the impression he gave me when I studied him, when I could break the spell for a moment and observe him attentively. But to break the spell required a power and a magic almost equal to his own; it made one feel foolish and impotent, as one always does when one succeeds in destroying the power of illusion. Magic is never destroyed—the most we can do is to cut ourselves off, amputate the mysterious antennae which serve to connect us with forces beyond our power of understanding. Many a time, as Katsimbalis talked, I caught that look on the face of a listener which told me that the invisible wires had been connected, that something was being communicated which was over and above language, over and above personality, something magical which we recognize in dream and which makes the face of the sleeper relax and expand with a bloom such as we rarely see in waking life. Often when meditating on this quality of his I thought of his frequent allusions to the incomparable honey which is stored by the bees on the slopes of his beloved Hymettos. Over and over he would try to explain the reasons why this honey from Mount Hymettos was unique. Nobody can explain it satisfactorily. Nobody can explain anything which is unique. One can describe, worship and adore. And that is all I can do with Katsimbalis' talk.[34]

One needn't feel as helpless as Miller acknowledges himself to be in the face of such accomplished musical performances, however. W.K.C. Guthrie tells us that the proto-Orpheus was first and foremost the musician "with magic in his notes," and surely there is a great deal in the virtuoso monologues of George Katsimbalis *and* Henry Miller that can be called "magic," that can legitimately make its hearers sense the "powerlessness" all magic is capable of producing. But it is a magic which, like that of any authentically skilled performance, will sustain a certain amount of analysis. As Richard Poirier has put it:

Performance is an exercise of power, a very curious one. Curious because it is at first so furiously self-consultive, so even narcissistic, and later so eager for publicity, love, and historical dimension. Out of an accumulation of secretive acts emerges at last a form that presumes to compete with reality itself for control of the minds exposed to it. Performance in writing, in painting, or in dance is made up of thousands of tiny movements, each made with a calculation that is also its innocence.[35]

Miller's most sustained solo performance in the *Colossus* is a seven-page monologue which owes its rhythmic style to Negro jazz improvisations and its violent imagery and mood to the example of Rimbaud. It is provoked by the prissy French wife of a Greek whose souvenir shop Miller visits in Crete and, on the face of it, it has the appearance of pure logorrhoea—a sassy and rather long-winded verbal jag. But there is extraordinary artistic control[36] in this outwardly fluid passage; its "thousands of tiny movements" have been carefully chosen and its spell is skillfully created. The monologue is a paean to the freedom-giving openness of music (as opposed to the stiff French-woman's love of "gardens with high walls") and the numerous variations on Miller's theme are improvised with a fitting "music": Miller orchestrates an imagery of angels, golden torques, blue skies, wild flowers, holidays, and open roads with fetching boogie-woogie rhythms. He even resorts to the "innocent calculation" of alliteration. In the following passage, for instance, the f's seem to suggest the fatuous Frenchwoman's windy passivity while the explosive b's (especially at the close) strongly suggest a tone of blunt rejection of what the woman stands for:

> *Madame*, there are always two paths to take: one back towards the com/ort and security of death, the other /orward to nowhere. You would like to /all back amongst your quaint tombstones and /amiliar cemetery walls. /all back then, /all back deep and /athomless into the ocean of annihilation. /all back into that bloody torpor which permits idiots to be crowned as kings. /all back and writhe in torment with the evolutionary worms. I am going on, on /ast the last /lack and white squares. The game is /layed out, the /igures have melted away, the lines are /razzled, the /oard is mildewed. Everything has become /arbarious again . . . Boogie woogie came /ack with /lood on his knees.[37]

Earlier in *Colossus*, Miller the poet makes an even more elaborate use of alliteration in a three-page cadenza on the planet Saturn, his lugubrious astrological nemesis. His mock-description of Saturn would have appealed to the *Symboliste* poet Gérard de Nerval, who referred to this planet as "le froid Saturne [qui] aime le plomb" in *Les Illuminés* (p. 376). Miller's insistent string of hissing s's, counterpointed with abundant f's and v's, almost too richly suggests the evil influences Miller associates with this planet:

> Saturn is male/ic through /orce of inertia. Its ring, which is only paperweight in thickness, according to the savants, is the wedding ring which signifies death or mis/ortunes devoid of all signi/icance. Saturn, whatever it may be to the astronomer, is the sign of senseless /atality to the man in the street. He carries it in his heart because his whole li/e, devoid of signi/icance as it is, is wrapped up in this ultimate symbol which, i/ all else /ails to do him in, this he can count upon to /inish him o/f. Saturn is life in suspense, not dead so much as deathless, i.e., incapable of dying. Saturn is like dead bone in the ear—double mastoid for the soul.[38]

Here the sinister impression created by a mass of sibilants and affricates is obvious to the point of redundancy, but Miller can be much more subtle in his handling of alliteration. There is a fine instance of this in a passage preceding the coda of Part One of *Colossus* in which Miller creates a remarkable extended melody based on the capacity of the phoneme /m/ to suggest pure delight and pleasurable self-awareness. The passage is doubly effective because Miller intimates that a transformation takes place as he enters the tomb of Agamemmnon. The "*m*an I a*m*" is metamorphosed before one's eyes and ears, as if through Orphic magic, into the larger onomatic figure of "Aga*m*e*m*non" (upon whose two m's the entire sequence of m's climactically converges). Whether or not Miller is entirely conscious of striving for this effect, the passage has a remarkably uniform insistence:

> I am still the man I might have become, assuming every benefit of civilization to be showered upon me with regal indulgence. I am gathering all of this potential civilized muck into a hard, tiny knot of understanding. I am blown to the maximum, like a great bowl of molten glass hanging from the stem of a glassblower. Make me into a fantastic shape, use all your art, exhaust your lungpower—still I shall only be a thing fabricated, at the best a beautiful cultured soul. I know this, I despise it. I stand outside full-blown, the most beautiful, the most cultured, the most marvellously fabricated soul on earth. I am going to put my foot over the threshold—now. I do so. I hear nothing. I am not even there to hear myself shattering into a billion splintered smithereens. Only Agamemnon is there.[39]

There is, in addition to the effective tonal arrangement of m's in this passage, another interesting trick used by Miller. It concerns the telling use of the personal pronoun "I." Very conspicuously, Miller uses this pronoun fourteen times in rapid succession to direct attention to the over-blown personal ego that comes to the tomb of Agamemnon. But that is clearly done to be able to annihilate it the more effectively when Miller puts his foot over the threshold: "Only Agamemnon is here." When the "I" reappears a little later in the paragraph, it is in the form of a highly chastened "I": "a nomad, a spiritual nobody." This obliteration of the too-assonantal "I" is also part of Miller's music.

Admittedly, there is a margin of subjectivity to all interpretations of alliterative and assonantal patterns, but the *presence* of such patterns on these pages can scarcely be doubted. Miller, in his own fashion, is "singing." And as the poet Rilke has put it,

> . . . *this* is Orpheus. His metamorphosis
> in this one and in that. We should not make
>
> searches for other names. Once and for all,
> it's Orpheus when there's song. He comes and goes.[40]

Miller comes closest to explicitly proclaiming his affinity with Orpheus in the description he gives of his trip to Delphi. If it is borne in mind that the Muse (woman/Eurydice/June) had given birth to Orpheus' powers of song and that the waters of the Castellian Spring were said to stimulate one's capacity to remember (thereby putting one more closely in touch with the materials of self-expression), it is possible to recognize, embedded in the matrix of Miller's casual-sounding account of his visit to the Castellian Spring, a genuine awareness of his Orphic mission. In order to facilitate the recognition of similarities between the two, I've placed this passage and a quotation from the great mythographer of Illuminism, Edouard Shuré, in parallel columns. Note that, aside from the difference of context *in time*, it is almost as if the two writers were talking about the same thing:

I. (Shuré)

II. (Miller)

In the sanctuaries of Apollo which possessed the Orphic tradition, a mysterious festival was celebrated at the vernal equinox. This was the time when the narcissus bloomed again near the fountain of Castalia. The tripods and the lyres of the temple vibrated of their own accord, and the invisible god was said to return to the country of the Hyperboreans in a chariot drawn by swans. Then the great priestess, dressed as a Muse and crowned with laurel, her forehead bound with sacred bands, sang before the initiates *The Birth of Orpheus*, the son of Apollo and of a priestess of god. The Muse called upon the soul of Orpheus, immortal and thrice-crowned, in hell, on earth, and in heaven, a star upon his forehead, walking among the constellations and the gods.[41]

We had a drink at the Castellian Spring where I suddenly remembered my old friend Nick of the Orpheum Dance Palace on Broadway because he had come from a little village called Castellia in the valley beyond the mountains. In a way my friend Nick was largely responsible for my being here, I reflected, for it was through his terpsichorean instrumentations that I met my wife June [whom Miller depicts as a sort of Eurydice/Muse type in *Capricorn* and *The Rosy Crucifixion*] and if I hadn't met her I should probably never have become a writer, never have left America [the voyager motif], never have met Betty Ryan, Lawrence Durrell, and finally Stephanides, Katsimbalis and Ghikas [whom Miller virtually regards as oracles and gods].[42]

Even the number three, sacred both to the Apollonian cult of Orpheus ("tripod," "thrice-crowned") and to Dante (the Trinity, terza rima), has a special hold on Henry Miller's imagination. Not only is *Colossus* divided into three parts, but things tend to occur in groups of three's with unsurprising regularity in the book (I intend to return to this subject in my chapter on Miller as a *Symboliste*). Certain leitmotifs which occur in all three parts of the book serve Miller the artist as clever ordering devices to hold together a book which, outwardly, seems to delight in the fluidity of its "improvisations." One of these is the sound of the flute. According to one authority, the flute "corresponds to erotic or funereal anguish"[43] in the sound it makes—precisely in accord with the ethos of the Orphic myth and in keeping with the use Miller makes of the symbol in all three parts of the book. It can be heard in distinctly "Orphic" settings in Part One[44] and Part Two.[45] But it is in Part Three that the sound of the flute conjures up one of the grimmest episodes in the Orphic myth: the dismemberment of the singer (*sparagmós*). The "plight of the creative artist" in the face of neglect and outright hostility is a favorite theme throughout Miller's *oeuvre*. Miller knows from experience that the fate of Orpheus is no more felicitous in the modern world than it was in the ancient. Jealous gods and maenads are always eager to tear apart the bringer of song and light. There are numerous illustrations of this in *The Colossus of Maroussi*, including the battered and luckless Katsimbalis himself, but the following episode is given the heightened quality of genuinely mythic treatment by Miller:

> It is Christmas Eve [in Corinth], but there is nothing here to indicate that anyone is aware of it. Approaching a lonely house lit up by a smoky kerosene lamp we are suddenly arrested by the queer strains of a flute. We hasten our steps and stand in the middle of the wide street to take in the performance. The door of the house is open, revealing a room filled with men listening to an uncouth figure playing the flute. The man seems to be exalted by his own music, a music such as I have never heard before and probably never will again. It seems like sheer improvisation and, unless his lungs give out, there promises to be no end to it. It is the music of the hills, the wild notes of the solitary man armed with nothing but his instrument. It is the original music for which no notes have been written and for which none is necessary. It is fierce, sad, obsessive, yearning and defiant. [It is easy to see, here, the analogy with Miller's own "improvisations."] It is not for men's ears but for God's. It is a duet in which the other instrument is silent. In the midst of the performance a man approaches us on a bicycle, dismounts and doffing his hat inquires respectfully if we are strangers, if we had arrived perhaps just to-day. He is a telegraph messenger and he has a message in his hand for an American woman, he says. Durrell laughs and asks to see the message. It is a Christmas greeting to the Countess von Reventlow (Barbara Hutton). We read it—it is in English—and pass it back to him. He goes off, peering like a scout into the darkness, ready no doubt to intercept the next tall woman with golden hair whom he sees dressed like a man. The incident reminded me of my own days in the telegraph service, of a winter's night when I came upon a messenger walking the streets of New York in a daze with a fistful of undelivered messages. Noticing the blank stare in his eyes I led him back to the office he had come from, where I learned that he had been missing for two days and nights. He was blue with cold and chattering like a monkey. When I opened his coat to see if he had any messages in his inside pockets I discovered that under the coarse suit he was naked. In one of his pockets I found a program of musical compositions which he had evidently printed himself since almost the entire list of pieces indicated him as being the composer. The incident came to a close in the observation ward at Bellevue where he was pronounced insane.[46]

There is nothing improvisatory about such effects. Clearly, the departure of the messenger in Corinth ("peering like a scout into the darkness") prepares the reader for the New York messenger/composer's final *sparagmós*. The hard fate of the music-maker is admirably evoked in a single anecdote by means of which Henry Miller apotheosizes the forlorn singer through the medium of music.

Toward the close of *The Colossus of Maroussi*, Miller states prophetically that parting from his Orphic companions in Greece to return to American will leave him often at the mercy of frightening and uncomprehending forces.

As soon as he boards the American boat to New York, he feels he is "in another world. I was among the go-getters again, among the restless souls who, not knowing how to live their own lives, wish to change the world for everybody."[47] Maenads are lurking everywhere. An Orpheus with Henry Miller's sense of humour could probably even be prompted to interpret the slashing and merciless attacks on him in such recent works as Kate Millett's *Sexual Politics*[48] as "symbolic" acts of maenadic fury! All that remains now is for the final apotheosis of the Lyre in the heavens to take place.

3. THE POET AS SEER

"Often when I attend the ritual procession on Good Friday, it is difficult for me to decide whether the god that is being buried is Christ or Adonis. Is it the climate? Is it the race? I can't tell. I believe it's really the light. There must be something about the light that makes us what we are. In Greece one is more friendly, more at one with the universe. I find this difficult to express. An idea becomes an object with surprising ease. It seems to become all but physically incarnated in the web of the sun."
George Seferis in *On the Greek Style*

The medieval philosopher Robert Grosseteste maintained that "just as physical light is the basis of all material forms, so the light of divine illumination is the foundation of our knowledge of intelligible things."[49] Obviously, what we refer to as "vision" is a twofold human activity. There is normal ocular perception with the eye (first sight) and supranormal or psychic perception (usually called "second sight"). The latter—the phenomenon of *voyance*— is manifestly what Arthur Rimbaud hankered after in his remarkable *voyant* letters to George Izambard and Paul Demeny, and what he actually practiced in *Illuminations*. It is also, I believe, what Henry Miller sought to perfect in himself and in his writings, most successfully in his illuminist travel book on Greece, *The Colossus of Maroussi*. The success of this attempt is writ large on almost every page of that book.

The revolutionary illuminists whom Rimbaud read believed that only by apprehending the supernal light which is circumambient among us in the universe would humanity succeed in changing life—that difficult aspiration so dear to Rimbaud's heart. Auguste Viatte cites illuminist/millenarian sources that bring to mind the programs of Arthur Rimbaud and Henry Miller:

Tous nous annonce une régénération universelle qui, en faisant le bonheur de tous, fera nécessairement la félicité de chacun. L'homme connaîtra sa veritable origine et le *bonheur qui lui est préparé*. Le Ciel ne changera pas, mais la pureté de nos âmes nous le fera trouver ce qu'il est. Tous les emblèmes, toutes les figures qui nous environnent, disparaîtront pour faire place à la vérité. *Sa lumière brille déjà à nos yeux*, ne la rejetons pas. Nous sommes arrivés au moment où nous avons plus qu'un espoir de la connaître, on ne nous dit pas: vous verrez la lumière; on nous dit: voilà la lumière; c'est en être bien près (italics mine).[50]

[Everything proclaims to us a universal regeneration that will of necessity ensure the happiness of each of us by ensuring the happiness of all. Humankind will know its veritable origins and the *happiness that is awaiting it*. Heaven will not alter, but our purity of soul will enable us to find out what it really is. All the emblems, all the figures that surround us will vanish in order to make room for truth. *Its light already shines before our eyes*—let us not reject it. We have reached the moment where we have more than a mere hope of knowing it. We are not being told: you shall see the light. We are being told: behold the light. That's how near we have come. (My translation and italics).]

This transcendent light which all the great illuminists have endeavored to put themselves in touch with is a topic of recurrent theoretical interest to Henry Miller, even before his trip to Greece.

In a pre-*Colossus* essay on the diary of Anaïs Nin, Miller had expressed thoughts on this subject which place him squarely in the illuminist tradition:

The totality of vision brings about a new kind of sympathy, a free, non-compulsive sort. . . . The eye too seems to close, content to let the body *feel* the presence of the world about, rather than pierce it with a devastating vision. It is no longer a world of black and white, of good and evil, of harmony and dissonance; no, now the world has at last become an orchestra in which there are innumerable instruments capable of rendering every tone and color, an orchestra in which even the most shattering dissonances are resolved into meaningful expression. It is the ultimate poetic world of *As Is*. The inquisition is over, the trial and torture finished. . . . This is the eternally abiding world which those in search of it never find. For with most of us we stand before the world as before a mirror; we never see our true selves because we can never come before the mirror unawares. We see ourselves as actors, but the spectacle for which we are rehearsing is never put on. To see the true spectacle, to finally participate in it, one must die before the mirror in a *blinding light of realization*. We must lose not only the mask and the costume but the flesh and bone which conceals the secret self. This we can only do *by illumination*, by voluntarily going down into death. For when this moment is attained we who imagined that we were sitting in the belly of the whale and doomed to nothingness suddenly discover that the whale was a projection of our own insufficiency. The whale remains, but the whale becomes the whole wide world, with stars and seasons, with banquets and festivals, with everything that is wonderful to see and touch, and being that it is no longer a whale but something nameless because something that is inside as well as outside us. . . . One lives within the spirit of transformation and not in the act. The legend of the whale thus becomes the celebrated book of transformations *destined to cure the ills of the world*. Each man who climbs into the body of the whale and works therein his own resurrection is bringing about *the miraculous transfigura-*

tion of the world which, because it is human, is none the less limitless. The whole process is a marvelous piece of dramatic symbolism whereby he who sat facing his doom *suddenly awakes and lives*, and through the mere act of declaration—the act of declaring his livingness—causes the whole world to become alive and endlessly alter its visage (italics mine).[51]

In an earlier essay, Miller had written even more inspiringly of the accessibility of this "light" to all people and of the quality of the changes it empowered them to bring about in their lives:

Jupiter, according to astrologic lingo, is my benevolent planetary deity. What a remarkable face Jupiter bears! Never have I seen anything so radiant, so bursting with light, so fiery and so cold at the same time. Coming away from my friend's roof that night suddenly all the stars had moved in closer to me. And they have remained thus, some astronomical light leagues closer—and warmer, more radiant, more benevolent. When I look up at the stars now I am aware that they are all inhabited, every one of them, including the so-called dead planets such as our earth. The light which blazes forth from them is the eternal light, the fire of creation. . . . Since then I have crossed the Equator and made my peace with the Neptunian forces. The whole southern hemisphere lies exposed, waiting to be charted. Here entirely new configurations obtain. The past, *though invisible*, is not dead. The past trembles like a huge drop of water clinging to the rim of a cold goblet. I stand in the closest proximity to myself in the midst of an open field of light. I describe now only what is known to all men before me and after me standing in similar relationship to themselves.[52]

The strange passivity that attends the seer-experience seems to be common to both Rimbaud and Miller. In *Tropic of Capricorn*, Miller had written:

People often think of me as an adventurous fellow; nothing could be farther from the truth. My adventures are always adventitious, *always thrust on me, always endured rather than undertaken*. I am of the very essence of the proud, boastful Nordic people who have never had the least sense of adventure but who nevertheless have scoured the earth, turned it upside down, scattering relics and ruins everywhere (italics mine).[53]

Rimbaud's ardent visionary creativeness manifests itself, according to Wallace Fowlie, in a similar state of passivity, in "total immobilization." In such a state, the poet "does not go to experiences"; rather they "offer themselves to him." Fowlie calls this "the inner vision of the voyant unfolding," an unpredictable state of being during which "stones can look at us and . . . a rabbit can say a prayer to the rainbow." Each *illumination* embodies

this power of the poet, his way of awakening everything that is habitually passive, of bestowing life on everything that habitually sleeps in the real world [cf. Miller's "(T)he whale becomes the whole wide world, with stars and seasons, with banquets and festivals, with everything that is wonderful to see and touch . . ."]. At the beginning of each prose poem, the curtain rises on a scene that is still and dormant. Then suddenly, with the magic lighting, the tableau comes alive, the vision takes on movement, and the action moves fast until the usual collapse comes at the end and the curtain is pulled down hurriedly [cf. Miller's "(T)he world has at last become an orchestra in which there are innumerable instruments capable of rendering every tone and color, an orchestra in which even the most shattering dissonances are resolved into meaningful expression. It is the ultimate poetic world of *As Is*."].[54]

There is a letter by Henry Miller to Anaïs Nin which further confirms Miller's understanding of the *consequences* the soul risked in embracing the light: the "death" of the everyday personality which is the necessary prelude to the "birth" of the *voyant*. It is dated January 12, 1940, just two weeks after Miller had left Greece and some time prior to his beginning work on *The Colossus of Maroussi*:

The last thing to disappear is the light, the light over the hills, that light which I never saw before, which I could not possibly imagine if I had not seen it with my own eyes. The incredible light of Attica! If I retain no more than the memory of this it will do. That light represents for me the consummation of my own desires and experiences. *I saw in it the flame of my own life consumed by the flame of the world. Everything seemed to burn to ash, and this ash itself was distilled and dispersed through the airs.* I don't see what more any country, any landscape, could offer than this experience. Not only does one feel integrated, harmonious, at one with all life, but—*one is silenced.* That is perhaps the highest experience I know of. It is a death, but a death which puts life to shame (first italics mine, second Miller's).[55]

One cannot but recall Rimbaud's *voyant* letter to Paul Demeny, at this point:

Ineffable torture où il a besoin de toute sa foi, de toute la force surhumaine, où il devient entre tous le grand malade, le grand criminel, le grand maudit,— et le suprême Savant!—Car il arrive à l'inconnun! Puisqu'il a cultivé son âme, déjà riche, plus qu'aucun! Il arrive à l'inconnu, et quant, affolé, il finirait par perdre l'intelligence de ses visions, il les a vues! Qu'il crève dans son bondisse- ment par les choses inouîes et innommables: viendront d'autres horribles travailleurs; ils commenceront par les horizons où l'autre s'est affaisé![56]
[Ineffable torture where he needs all his faith, all his superhuman strength, where he becomes in the midst of everybody else the great sick man, the great criminal, the great outcast—and the supreme knower!—since he reaches the unknown! On account of having cultivated his soul, already rich, more than anyone else! He reaches the unknown, and when, frantic, he ends up by losing the comprehension of his visions, *he's seen them!* Even if he croaks while gamboling among these unheard of and unnameable things—other horrible

workers will come along. They'll take up at the horizons where the other sank down! (my translation)]

Illuminist visions may come to the seer and be lost by him with equal unpredictability and with great risk to his personal well-being (I've already quoted both Rimbaud and Miller on episodes that led them both to the brink of "madness"), but, as Rimbaud poignantly observes, *"il les a vues!"* And one of the reasons he has "seen them" (i.e., the visions) is that he has dared make himself an extraordinary human being bent on achieving extraordinary things. His is a Promethean will power and, as Rimbaud points out in the letter to Demeny, he is *"vraiment voleur de feu."* E. R. Jaensch has pertinent things to say about the abnormality of what he calls "eidetic types"—i.e., people who *"see* something, although no object is actually present" and whose peculiar psychic endowments permit them to experience inordinately vivid mental images. Jaensch maintains that for the great majority of adults, an "unbridgeable gulf" exists between sensations and images. But it has "always been known," argues Jaensch, that this is not true "for a few individuals." Some people

> have peculiar "intermediate experiences" between sensations and images. From the description that such people have given of these experiences . . . we must conclude that their "experiences" are due to eidetic images. These phenomena, it is true, are rare among average adults. Their existence would, however, not have been doubted so often, and they would have been found to be fairly frequent even in adults, if those scientifically interested in such things had not always made their observations on people whose environment and interests were similar to their own, and therefore directed to abstract pursuits. . . . [S]ubjects should not always be taken from philosophical classrooms or psychological institutes, but occasionally from an academy of fine arts, or a group of people with artistic leanings and pursuits, to mention a group that is as widely different from the first as possible.[57]

Dr. Jaensch believes that the cultural spirit grows out of the spiritual life of such "different" individuals. Later in his book he cites the German poet Goethe—whom Henry Miller apostrophizes as "one of the best Virgo types the world has ever known"[58]—as a paramount example, an eidetic type who "experienced, in a purer and clearer form, what all or most of us feel in a confused way in the same circumstances in life."[59] It's interesting to note, while making this cultural-anthropological excursus, that both J. B. Bury and Äse Hultkranz consider the Orphic tradition (to which both Goethe and Miller clearly belong) to have been a tradition of seers and visionaries.[60]

The sheer frequency with which the word "light" appears in *The Colossus of Maroussi* would be enough to alert its readers to its extraordinary position in its author's thinking. I wouldn't necessarily want to suggest that there is any conclusive heuristic significance to word-frequency counts in works of literary scholarship, but one cannot help but be impressed with the fact that the words "light," "eye" (or "eyes") and "sun" (or variants such as "sunlight," "solar," etc.) occur one hundred and eighty-four (184) times in *Colossus*. In addition, the word "illumination" occurs twenty-one (21) times. This is an extremely high frequency for a book that is only two hundred and forty-four pages long. The incidence of the illuminist triad of "light," "sun," and "eye" is particularly high (and quite conspicuous) in Part One, where these three key words occur ninety-two (92) times on a mere ninety-seven pages—an average of almost once per page![61]

But, ultimately, it is to the *quality* ascribed to the "light" throughout *Colossus* and not to the mere frequency with which Miller invokes it that we must turn our attention. In the opening paragraph of his book, Miller refers to Greece as "a world of *light* such as I had never dreamed of and never hoped to see."[62] One of his finest evocations of this "light" occurs in a description of a walk he takes along the Sacred Way at Eleusis "from Daphni to the sea." Miller would probably agree with his friend, the Nobel Prize poet George Seferis, that "the light cannot be explained; it can only be seen."[63] But the passage on the "light" of the Sacred Way, in its impressionistic fashion, establishes both a vital connection and a distinction between the light which is seen by the naked eye and that which is seen by the "soul":

> Everything here speaks now, as it did centuries ago, of illumination, of blinding, joyous illumination. Light acquires a transcendental quality: it is *not the light of the Mediterranean alone, it is something more*, something unfathomable, something holy. Here the light *penetrates directly to the soul*, opens the doors and windows of the heart, makes one naked, exposed, *isolated in a metaphysical bliss* which makes everything *clear without being known*. No analysis can go on in this light: here the neurotic is either instantly healed or goes mad. The rocks themselves are quite mad: they have been lying for centuries exposed to this divine illumination: they lie very still and quiet, nestling amid dancing colored shrubs in a blood-stained soil, but they are mad, I say, and to touch them is *to risk losing one's grip* on everything which once seemed firm, solid and unshakeable (my italics).[64]

Miller is anything but a "deserter of the infinite" (in Ramon Fernandez' memorable phrase), but it is in keeping with his predilections as an alchemist of the word that he should know how to relate the "outer" light perceived by the eye—a "light" of secondary importance in the tradition of voyance—with the "inner" light of the psyche. He compares his own "illuminating voyage" from Poros to Tripolis to "the ascension of Séraphita, as it was glimpsed by her devout followers. It was a voyage into the light. The earth became illuminated by her own inner light."[65] Then, contrasting his own experiences with those of non-seers whose "inner eye . . . has now become a sickly gland," he gives us a vivid poetic picture of his encounters with the "light" at Corinth, at Arachova, at Leonidion:

In each place I open a new vein of experience, a miner digging deeper into the earth approaching the heart of the star which is not yet extinguished. The light is no longer solar or lunar; it is the starry light of the planet to which man has given life. The earth is alive to its innermost depths; at the center it is a sun in the form of a man crucified. The sun bleeds on its cross in the hidden depths. The sun is man struggling to emerge towards another light. From light to light, from calvary to calvary. The earth song. . . .[66]

The eidetic configuration made by the sun "in the form of a man crucified" and the extension of this trope to man's struggle "towards another light" is not, it goes without saying, something that every tourist to these spots in Greece would necessarily "see." But like the visions of the seer/poet Rimbaud, to whom he owes so much, one can say of Miller's visions, in view of the self-evident power of picturation with which he is able to transmit them to others: "*Il les a vues!*" And I would refer to such visual complexes—which are striking examples of the functioning of the eidetic or voyant sensibility— as a poetic eidolon. There are many others in *Colossus*.

The feeling of being "grateful for having eyes" persists at Phaestos, where Miller experiences what I regard as one of the most profoundly affective illuminations in the book. It's a small indication of his voyant's consistency that the word "eyes" appears six times during this five-page account of spiritual enlightenment. As in Rimbaud and their common Orphic ancestors, Miller's "light" leads via the eyes to inner awakening. This, after all, is the crucial meaning of *illumination*. The "light" not only radiates a greater glory *without* but leads to "life more abundant" within:

The rain has stopped, the clouds have broken; the vault of blue spreads out like a fan, the blue decomposing into that ultimate violet light which makes everything Greek seem holy, natural and familiar. In Greece one has the desire to bathe in the sky. You want to rid yourself of your clothes, take a running leap and vault into the blue. You want to float in the air like an angel or lie in the grass rigid and enjoy the cataleptic trance. Stone and sky, they marry here. It is the perpetual dawn of man's awakening.[67]

This is where "the descendants of Zeus halted" on their way to eternity and saw "with the *eyes* of innocents" that the earth "is indeed what they had always *dreamed* it to be: a place of beauty and joy and peace. In his heart . . . man is united with the whole world."[68] And considering the intensity of Miller's capacity to assimilate and transmit the "light" which has so be-witched him, it comes as somewhat less of a shock to the reader, later in *Colossus*, when Miller repeats Aram Hourabedian's somewhat hyperbolic prediction that he (Miller) would make a visit to the Orient from which "[he] would never return, neither would [he] die, but vanish in the light."[69] There has been sufficient forewarning built into the structure of the book.

Miller's awareness of himself as a *voyant* in the Rimbaud tradition can scarcely be doubted. Not only does he identify with Rimbaud's flair for dazzling visual phrase-making,[70] but he apotheosizes that quality in Rimbaud which he insists, with a democratic largesse, on also attributing to the rest of mankind—at least *in posse*:

> Man was given a second sight that he might see through and beyond the world of phantasmagoria. The only effort demanded of him is that he open the eyes of his soul, that he gaze into the heart of reality and not flounder about in the realm of illusion and delusion.[71]

In the development of this gift, Miller regards Rimbaud as a sort of absolute—as one "poised on the peak, a sort of *jeune Roi Soleil.*"[72]

Miller had been conscious of his own peculiar endowments as a *voyant* even before undertaking the *Colossus* trip to Greece in 1939; the brilliant light of Greece merely provided him with the luminous images necessary to give that faculty its "objective correlative" and help crystalize its most convincing extended statement. Here is a lengthy analysis of the phenomenon of voyance given earlier by Miller in *The Cosmological Eye* in the course of commenting on the work of a kindred artist, Anaïs Nin:

> The vision is first and foremost, always. And this vision is like the voice of conscience itself. It is a double vision, as we well know. One sees forwards and backwards with equal clarity. But *one does not see what is directly under the nose*; one does not see *the world which is immediately about*. [One is reminded here of Miller's sardonic comments on Rimbaud's "impracticality" and extreme lack of what is called "common sense" in many places in *The Time of the Assassins*.] This blindness to the everyday, to the normal and abnormal circumstances of life, is the distinguishing feature of the restless visionary. The eyes, which are unusually endowed, *have to be trained to see with normal vision*. Superficially this sort of individual seems to be concerned only with what is going on about him; the daily communion with the diary [the reference is to Anaïs Nin's *Diary* here] seems at first blush to be nothing more than a transcription of this normal, trivial, everyday life. And yet nothing can be further from the truth. The fact is that this extraordinary cataloguing of events, impressions, objects, ideas, etc. is only a keyboard exercise, as it were, *to attain the faculty of seeing what is so glibly recorded*. Actually, of course, few people in this world see what is going on about them. Nobody really sees *until he understands*, until he can create a pattern into which the helter-skelter of passing events fits and makes a significance. And for this sort of vision a personal death is required. One has to be able to see first with the eyes of a Martian, or a Neptunian. One has to have this extraordinary vision, this clairvoyance, to be able to take in the multiplicity of things with ordinary eyes. *Nobody sees with his eyes alone; we see with our souls* (emphases added).[73]

Both in eidetic and in strictly structural terms, *The Colossus of Maroussi* is Henry Miller's finest example of "a pattern into which the helter-skelter of passing events fits and makes a significance," as my first three chapters have partly made clear. But there's more.

To begin with, Part One of *Colossus* opens and closes with overt references to the ways of seeing. In the very first paragraph, Betty Ryan's lucid descriptions of her travels about the world make Miller *see* these travels vividly "because when she talked about her wanderings she seemed to paint them: everything she described remained in my head like finished canvases by a master."[74] And at the close, as we have seen earlier, Miller arrives, after multiple visitations and illuminations among the people and places of Greece, at "pure vision" and the wonderfully bedazzling eidolon of the "two men and a woman" with which the chapter comes to an artful close. It's in Part One that Miller makes the trip to the healing center at Epidaurus where, appropriately, the dirt that lingers in his eyes from the grubby *Tropic* experiences in Paris and New York will be washed clean and his remaining rags of prejudice stripped from him: "Everything here speaks now, as it did centuries ago, of *illumination*. . . . Here the *light* penetrates directly to the soul, *opens the doors and windows of the heart*, makes one *naked*, exposed, isolated in a metaphysical bliss which makes everything *clear*. . . ." He rounds off Part One, though, with very pertinent reminders that too many people have yet to avail themselves of their birth-right: "In our world *the blind* lead *the blind* and the sick go to the sick to be cured. We are making constant progress, but it is a progress which leads to the operating table, to the poor house, to the insane asylum, to the trenches."[75] And later, speaking of the archeologists at Mycenae, he writes;

> Spades and shovels will uncover nothing of any import. The diggers are blind, feeling their way towards something they will never *see*. Everything that is unmasked crumbles at the touch. Worlds crumble too, in the same way. We can dig in eternally, like moles, but fear will be ever upon us, clawing us, raping us from the rear.[76]

Part Two virtually opens with the assertion that "seeing" is not the function of the eye alone. After looking at the stars through the telescope at the Athens observatory, Miller writes:

> I am not more convinced of the reality of a star *when I see it* through the telescope. It may be more brilliant, more wondrous, it may be a thousand times or a million times bigger than *when seen with the naked eye*, but it is not a whit more real. To say that this is *what a thing really looks like* just because one sees it larger and grander, seems to me quite fatuous. It is just as real to me *if I don't see it at all but merely imagine it to be there* (my emphases).[77]

He then immediately launches into what he calls an "emotional photograph" of the planet Saturn which, in its astute blending of melopoeic and phanopoeic effects, could qualify as an eidolon set to music. Yet another eidolon, shorter and much more severely controlled in order to give *visual* pleasure, occurs in Part Two in the marvelous montage that begins with the "woman with a vase on her shoulder descending a little bluff in bare feet."[78]

Finally, in Part Three (which I have called the *Paradiso* section of *Colossus*), Miller treats his readers to the most eye-opening illuminations of all: the extended eidolons describing Thebes—where "the air was winey; we seemed to be isolated in the midst of a great space which was dancing with a violet light; we were oriented towards another world"[79]—and Delphi— where "victory and defeat are meaningless in the light of the wheel which relentlessly revolves. We are moving into a new latitude of the soul, and a thousand years hence men will wonder at our blindness . . ."[80] But most important of all, in terms of sheer eidetic power, is Miller's climactic catalogue of images of Greece at the very close of Part Three. Here, in a grouping of crisply visualized and hard-edged visionary details that recall such Rimbaud *illuminations* as "Enfance" (especially sections III and IV), "Villes I," "Mystique," "Scènes," and the irrestible "Génie,"[81] Miller gives us what may well be the quintessential *voyant* moment in his entire *oeuvre*. Surely, one of the most seductive aspects of this passage can be attributed to the specific attention Miller gives to the imagery of *seeing* and of *luminescence*:

> I *see* the violet *light* in which . . . the huge boulders . . . gleam like mica; I *see* the miniature islands . . . ringed with *dazzling* white bands; . . . I *see* the *figures* of solitary men . . . and the fleece of their beasts all *golden* fuzz . . . ; etc., etc.[82]

In such an ably *finished* prose poem, we see with our own eyes the genesis of a paradise which is inhabitable by anyone because it has been adequately visualized by *someone*. The seer's gift is a gift outright of what already belongs to all of us. With images variously derived and variously ordered but rendered with a simultaneity of effect that shocks us into a recognition of our own limitless potential for suprasensible vision, Henry Miller has combined the act of seeing with the bodily eye with the act of seeing something which is not yet present to the eye. In the process, he has actualized within himself and through the well-wrought work of art which he offers us "the image's truth" of what we all desire. The seer is inseparable from what he sees. But more important, he is inseparable from those *for whom* he sees. We all truly see only as the seer sees.

Notes

1. Walter A. Strauss, *Descent and Return* (Cambridge: Harvard University Press, 1971), p. 17.

2. Cf. *Colossus* (New York: New Directions, 1941), pp. 61 and 112, and *The Books in My Life* (New York: New Directions, 1952), pp. 147 and 166.

3. Hugh Kenner, *The Pound Era* (Berkeley and Los Angeles: University of California Press, 1971), pp. 33–34.

4. Mircea Eliade, *Myths, Dreams and Mysteries* (New York: Harper & Row, 1967), p. 15.

5. Ralph Waldo Emerson, *Essays of Ralph Waldo Emerson* (New York: The Book League of America, 1941), p. 363.

6. Wallace Stevens, *Opus Posthumous* (New York: Knopf, 1957), p. 118.

7. Mircea Eliade, *The Myth of the Eternal Return* (Princeton: Princeton University Press, 1971), p. 22.

8. Eva Kushner. *Le mythe d'Orphée dans la littérature française contemporaine* (Paris: A. G. Nizet, 1961), pp. 12 and 13, and p. 15

9. *Colossus*, pp. 236–237.

10. *Ibid.*, pp. 238–240.

11. W.K.C. Guthrie, *Orpheus and Greek Religion* (New York: W.W. Norton & Co., 1966), p. 153.

12. Robert Graves. *The Greek Myths* (Baltimore: Penguin Books, 1948), pp. 111–113 and *passim*, and *New Larousse Encyclopaedia of Mythology* (London: Prometheus Press, 1968), pp. 193–198 and *passim*.

13. *Books*, pp. 85–86.

14. *Ibid.*, pp. 317–319.

15. Cf. esp., *The Wisdom of the Heart* (New York: New Directions, 1941), pp. 187–191 and *The Cosmological Eye* (New York: Directions, 1939), p. 325.

16. Bern Porter (ed.)., *Henry Miller Miscellanea* (Berkeley, California: Bern Porter, 1945), pp. 20–21.

17. *Ibid.*. p. 25.

18. Henry Miller, *Letters to Anaïs Nin* (New York: G. P. Putnam's Sons, 1965), p. 70.

19. *Ibid.*, pp. 127–128.

20. Henry Miller, *Tropic of Cancer* (Paris: The Obelisk Press, 1934), p. 12.

21. *Letters to Anaïs Nin*, pp. 94–95.

22. *Colossus*, pp. 3–4.

23. *Ibid.*, p. 109.

24. *Ibid.*, p. 112.

25. *Ibid.*, p. 4. Pandelís Prevelákis, a close friend and biographer of the Greek novelist Níkos Kazantzákis, notes the same resemblance between the names of Betty Ryan and Beatrice in a very short article on Henry Miller entitled "Prospéro le jeune" in the Belgian magazine *Synthèses*, February/March 1967, p. 32: "Son Paradis fut la Grèce qu'il connut grâce à la médiation d'une femme nommée Betty (qui rappelle Béatrice)." But Prevelákis pursues this lead no further.

26. E. M. Butler, *Rainer Maria Rilke* (New York: Macmillan, 1941), p. 352.

27. *Colossus.*, pp. 112–113.

28. *Ibid.*, p. 17.

29. *Ibid.*, p. 169.

30. *Ibid.*, p. 28.

31. *Ibid.*, p. 30.

32. Robert Graves, *Greek Myths*, p. 112.

33. *Colossus*, p. 28.

34. *Ibid.*, pp. 30–32.

35. Richard Poirier, *The Performing Self* (New York: Oxford University Press, 1971), p. 87.

36. *Colossus*, pp. 138–145.

37. *Ibid.*, pp. 142–143.

38. *Ibid.*, p. 105.

39. *Ibid.*, pp. 92–93.

40. Rainer Maria Rilke, *Selected Works*, trans. by J. B. Leishman (New York: New Directions, 1960), p. 255.

41. Edouard Shuré, *The Mysteries of Ancient Greece: Orpheus/Plato* (Blauvelt, New York: Rudolf Steiner Publications, 1971), p. 35.

42. *Colossus*, p. 195.

43. Juan Eduardo Cirlot, *A Dictionary of Symbols* (New York: Philosophical Library, 1962), p. 105.

44. *Colossus*, p. 19.

45. *Ibid.*, p. 126.

46. *Ibid.*, pp. 213–214.

47. *Ibid.*, p. 233.

48. Kate Millett, *Sexual Politics* (Boston: Atlantic, Little-Brown, 1971), cf. esp. pp. 302–313.

49. Julius R. Weinberg, *A Short History of Medieval Philosophy* (Princeton: Princeton University Press, 1964), p. 160.

50. *Sources*, p. 233.

51. *Cosmological Eye*, pp. 285–286.

52. *Ibid.*, pp. 355–356.

53. *Capricorn*, p. 11. It's instructive to compare this passage with the following in Rimbaud's *Une saison en enfer*: "J'ai de mes ancêtres gaulois l'oeil bleu blanc, la cervelle étroite, et la maladresse dans la lutte. . . . Les Gaulois étaient les écorcheurs de bêtes, les brûleurs d'herbes les plus inepts de leur temps. D'eux, j'ai: l'idolâtrie et l'amour du sacrilège . . . surtout mensonge et paresse. . . . Ma race ne se souleva jamais que pour piller: tels les loups à la bête qu'ils n'ont pas tuée." (Cf. Rimbaud, *Oeuvres*, p. 220).

54. *Rimbaud*, pp. 177–178.

55. *Letters to Anaïs Nin*, pp. 193–194.

56. *Oeuvres*, pp. 270–271. Miller comments very perceptively on this passage in Rimbaud's letter in his study of Rimbaud, *The Time of the Assassins*: "Of what use is the poet unless he attains to a new vision of life, unless he is willing to sacrifice his life in attesting the truth and the splendor of his vision? It is the fashion to speak of these demonic beings, these visionaries, as Romantics, to stress their subjectivity and to regard them as breaks, interruptions, stopgaps in the great stream of tradition, as though they were madmen whirling about the pivot of self. Nothing could be more untrue. It is precisely these innovators who form the links in the great chain of creative literature. One must indeed begin at the horizons where they expire—'hold the gain,' as Rimbaud puts it—and not sit down comfortably in the ruins and piece together a puzzle of shards." (Cf. Henry Miller, *Assassins*, p. 87).

57. E. R. Jaensch, *Eidetic Imagery* (New York: Harcourt, Brace & Co., 1930), p. 36.

58. *Colossus*, p. 106.

59. *Eidetic Imagery*, p. 36.

60. Cf. J. B. Bury, *A History of Greece*, p. 312, and Äse Hultkranz, *The North American Orpheus Tradition* (Stockholm: The Humanistic Foundation of Sweden, 1957), pp. 309–310.

61. "C'est la vision des *nombres!*" one can hear Rimbaud guffawing sarcastically from a well-earned grave. Cf. *Une saison en enfer, Oeuvres*, p. 221.

62. *Colossus*, p. 4.

63. George Seferis, *On the Greek Style* (Boston: Little Brown & Co., 1966), p. 105.

64. *Colossus*, p. 45.

65. *Ibid.*, pp. 56–57.

66. *Ibid.*, p. 57.

67. *Ibid.*, p. 159.

68. *Ibid.*, p. 162.

69. *Ibid.*, p. 203.

70. Cf. esp. *Assassins*, pp. 17–19.

71. *Ibid.*, p. 42. He makes clear his belief, later in *Assassins*, that unless all society learns to cultivate the seer-artist's vision, the very existence of the artist is threatened: "The poet's passion is the result of his vision, of his ability to see life in its essence and its wholeness. Once this vision is shattered or deranged, passion dribbles away. . . . Despite all its powers, society cannot sustain the artist if it is impervious to the *vision* of the artist." (See Henry Miller, *Assassins*, p. 131).

72. *Ibid.*, p. 149.

73. *Cosmological Eye*, pp. 281–282.

74. *Colossus*, p. 3. In fact, the crucial closing word of this first paragraph is "see." The Greek world Betty Ryan shows Miller is "a world of light such as I had never *dreamed* of and never hoped to *see.*"

75. *Colossus*, p. 77.

76. *Ibid.*, p. 94.

77. *Ibid.*, pp. 103–104.

78. *Ibid.*, p. 126. This is one of the most *exclusively* visual passages in the book, "pure vision."

79. *Ibid.*, p. 188.

80. *Ibid.*, p. 195.

81. Cf. *Oeuvres*, pp. 177–178, 189–190, 193, 199–200, and 205–206.

82. *Colossus*, pp. 240–241.

Henry Miller, Emerson, and the Divided Self

PAUL R. JACKSON

In Henry Miller's *Tropic of Cancer* an Emersonian epigraph announces the romanticized autobiography that would become the staple of Miller's art. "These novels," Emerson asserts, "will give way, by and by, to diaries or autobiographies—captivating books, if only a man knew how to choose among what he calls his experiences that which is really his experiences, and how to record truth truly."[1] Along with Whitman—"In Whitman the whole American scene comes to life, her past and her future, her birth and her death"—Emerson stands as a clear, if surprising, link to those traditions of American writing that produced the prophetic autobiographer that Miller became.[2] Moreover, the extent of his early interest in Emerson is indicated by the selection of an epigraph, not from one of the standard Emerson essays, but from the *Journals* themselves, suggesting a familiarity with the New England transcendentalist somewhat at odds with Miller's reputation as a shouting, American vulgarian. Indeed Miller's preoccupation with Emerson in *Tropic of Cancer* is attested by a second quotation from the *Journals*, this one a comic appropriation of an 1847 entry. " 'Life,' said Emerson, 'consists in what a man is thinking all day.' If that be so, then my life is nothing but a big intestine. I not only think about food all day, but I dream about it at night" (p. 69).[3]

While Whitman has remained a perennial constant in Miller's literary enthusiasms, Emerson recurs only as a supportive figure in the Americanism that marks the volumes of a writing career that spans at least three decades and that binds the literary expatriate to the artistic roots of his own country. Yet Miller returns to Emerson often enough to suggest an attachment more significant than one would at first suppose. As late as 1957 in *The Books in My Life*, Miller listed *Representative Men* as one of the hundred books that influenced him most.[4] Whitman, Emerson, and Thoreau are noted in a list of "specific influences" (p. 124), and Miller laments the passing of excited interest in writers like Maeterlinck and Emerson, with their "inspiring references to great figures of the past." "Their spiritual pabulum is suspect nowadays. Domage! The truth is, we really have no great authors to turn to

Reprinted from *American Literature* 43 (May 1971): 231–41. Copyright 1971 *American Literature*. Reprinted by permission of Duke University Press.

these days—if we are in search of eternal verities. We have surrendered to the flux" (p. 129). Emerson remains an old favorite, a literary source to be returned to with enthusiasm. "I mentioned Emerson. Never in my life have I met anyone who did not agree that Emerson is an inspiring writer. One may not accept his thought in toto, but one comes away from a reading of him purified, so to say, and exalted. He takes you to the heights, he gives you wings. He is daring, very daring. In our days he would be muzzled, I am certain" (p. 184).[5] "The great influences," Miller wrote to Lawrence Durrell in 1949, "were Nietzsche, Spengler, yes, Emerson, Herbert Spencer (!), Thoreau, Whitman—and Elie Faure."[6] And to Anaïs Nin he reported: "I wanted to [p]raise Waldo Emerson to the skies, just to prove to the world that once there had been a great American—but more than that, because I once had been greatly influenced by him, he was bound up with a whole side of me that I consider my better side."[7]

Miller's indebtedness to general Romantic and Transcendental modes of thought emerges in his prophetic announcements, often with the cadences of a speaking voice reminiscent of that of Emerson himself. In *Sexus*, the first volume of *The Rosy Crucifixion* trilogy, for example, Miller proclaims the correspondence of the human and the divine: "The great joy of the artist is to become aware of a higher order of things, to recognize by the compulsive and spontaneous manipulation of his own impulses the resemblance between human creation and what is called 'divine' creation."[8] The ultimate is everywhere visible: "It is not necessary to die in order to come at last face to face with reality. Reality is here and now, everywhere gleaming through every reflection that meets the eye" (p. 425). "We are all part of creation, all kings, all poets, all musicians; we have only to open up, only to discover what is already there" (p. 35). Emerson's emphasis on intuitive understanding with its resultant reliance on childhood experience, dream, and vision is constantly echoed. "As a child it was impossible to penetrate the secret of that joy which comes from a sense of superiority. That extra sense, which enables one to participate and at the same time to observe one's participation, appeared to me to be the normal endowment of every one" (p. 24). Turning his back on an expiring cultural past, Miller can proclaim in perfect Emersonian tones, "My face is always set toward the future" (p. 33). Finally, the ecstatic merging of the emancipated individual with divine process is dependent, with the insistence of a contemporary Emerson, on self-reliance: "The world would only begin to get something of value from me the moment I stopped being a serious member of society and became—*myself*! The State, the nation, the united nations of the world, were nothing but one great aggregation of individuals who repeated the mistakes of their forefathers" (p. 261).

But while Miller's interest in Emerson does seem to issue in such varied and wide parallelism, he has been especially intrigued by a complex of Emersonian ideas concerned with the artistic necessity of using autobiographical fact, the relation of fiction to life and the difficulty of understanding the mystery of selfhood basic to autobiographical fiction. In *The Books in My Life*, Miller again chooses a quotation from Emerson, this time from "The American Scholar," as one of the five epigraphs for the book. " 'When the artist has exhausted his materials, when the fancy no longer paints, when thoughts are no longer apprehended, and books are a weariness—he has always the resource *to live.*' " Such elevating of life over books clearly reinforces Miller's own impulse, announced on numerous occasions, to give up writing altogether. "The act of dreaming when wide awake," he says in *Sexus*, "will be in the power of every man one day. Long before that books will cease to exist, for when men are wide awake *and* dreaming their powers of communication (with one another and with the spirit that moves all men) will be so enhanced as to make writing seem like the harsh and raucous squawks of an idiot" (p. 28). The supreme imperative is to live; books may indeed constrict that essential.

Nevertheless, Miller has gone on writing and living the literary life, and he has been most preoccupied with the recording and understanding of autobiographical fact. That preoccupation has involved the necessity of knowing, in Emerson's words, "how to choose . . . that which is really his experiences." Indeed, Miller returned to *Cancer's* epigraph in *The Books in My Life* in a passage commenting on the difficulty of expressing personal truth, of revealing the various selves in inevitable and constant competition.

> The autobiographical novel, which Emerson predicted would grow in importance with time, has replaced the great confessions. It is not a mixture of truth and fiction, this genre of literature, but an expansion and deepening of truth. It is more authentic, more veridical, than the diary. It is not the flimsy truth of facts which the authors of these autobiographical novels offer but the truth of emotion, reflection and understanding, truth digested and assimilated. The being revealing himself does so on all levels simultaneously. (p. 169)

The emphasis in this passage falls clearly on the "deepening" of autobiographical fact as it includes the essential truth that comes from the simultaneous revelation of all the levels of selfhood. Rejecting by implication the vitality of traditional fictional modes as well as the validity of unembellished confessional writing, Miller here announces a literary form that, whatever its sources in Romantic thought, constitutes for him a new departure for the contemporary novel.[9] The imaginative projection of autobiographical fact, especially the emotional life basic to biographical externals, will be the stuff of fiction. Neither fictionalist nor confessor, Miller would use the assimilated facts of his own experience in a mode that would bring together life and art in intimate association.

Throughout his career, Miller has been drawn to autobiographical writers of all sorts, and letters, diaries and confessions rank high in those books to which he has enthusiastically responded. Louis-Ferdinand Céline's *Journey to the End of the Night* was an early favorite in the thirties, and the list of books that influenced him most in the appendix of *The Books in My Life* emphasizes the biographical genres. Autobiography is represented by those of Cellini and Herbert Spencer, the diary by the anonymous *Diary of a Lost One* and Nijinsky's. Abelard's *The Story of My Misfortunes*, Chesterton's *St. Francis of Assisi*, Gide's *Dostoievski*, and Plutarch's *Lives* all further indicate the fundamental direction of Miller's literary interest. More immediately, his enthusiasm for the diaries of Anaïs Nin has been constant and public since the publication of *Un etre étoilique* in 1937. While the effects of many of these books may be traced in Miller's writing, Emerson clearly provided a basic clue to the autobiographical romance Miller made his own peculiar province. In Emerson's *Journals* and essays, Miller found that the divided self of the visionary seer in his long journey of emancipation into life was his subject.

The completeness with which Miller has been willing to confront Emerson's simultaneous levels of selfhood is nowhere better underscored than in one direct borrowing from Emerson's *Journals* in *Sexus*. This long autobiographical romance records the trying years of the 1920's; it begins with the turmoil of Miller's first marriage to the Maude of the romances and his initial meeting with Mona, the fictionalized second wife, chronicles his escape from employment with the telegraph company, his early attempts to begin writing, and ends on the night of his second marriage. At the close a life stretches before him that is to be marked by the ambiguities of the trilogy's title. Through the process of personal crucifixion paradoxically will come the new life.

Sexus ends with two parallel fantasies, the first taking place in a burlesque theater on the night of Miller's marriage to Mona. Watching the show unfold and allowing his mind to play with elements of his own predicament, Miller begins to fantasize about the death of a young soapbox orator he names Osmanli.[10] A "dark, sleek chap, nattily attired," Osmanli is "disguised as a boulevardier, a flaneur, a Beau Brummel." With all the appearance of success, he sports a roll of money, is suave and nonchalant, well read, has a taste for good music and has found that his love for words allows him to sway men. But his real aim is "to spread poison, malice, slander"; he is a "man without country, without principle, without faith, without scruples." In the fantasy, Osmanli stands on the steps of the Hotel Astor about to address the crowd and to create the confusion which as "a servant of Beelzebub" and a "free-wheeling ego" he finds it easy to do.

Yet this diabolically successful orator is a man of illusion. Priding himself on his freedom, he has no close friends of any kind. Moreover, his ability to sustain himself without love is incomplete; the series of masks behind which he has retreated has left an empty man who is now driven toward suicide. His thoughts of self-destruction bubble up from a self he is unable to recognize, a "hidden being" he has spent a life denying. Propelled by this essential self, Osmanli finds himself driven on down a street and, after discarding his money and possessions and presumably reaching his basic self, he is accidentally killed by a police bullet. In standard literary fashion, he thinks back over his life at the moment of his death.

In the flashback, Osmanli is deserted by his wife, who tells him she had never loved him. The effect of her declaration is to make Osmanli feel that for the first time he is free. And to test that freedom in the desperado fashion Miller loves, he cuts off the dog's head, rapes the maid, and leaves to commit a "few murders." And so began the life of the free-wheeling Beelzebub. But now at the moment of his death, Osmanli realizes that he had never finally been free. "To begin with, he had never chopped the dog's head off, otherwise it would not now be barking with joy." He is in fact a man who has denied his own vision and who has submerged his own vital self, living out a lie of heroic strength. "His flight . . . had brought him face to face with the bright image of horror reflected in the shield of self-protection. . . . He had reached his own identity in death."

Osmanli, of course, is a projection of Miller himself, a fantasized image of the autobiographical hero as he enters on a rocky, second marriage. "When Osmanli fell face forward on the sidewalk he was merely enacting a scene out of my life in advance. Let us jump a few years—into the pot of horror." The second fantasy explains the first, as Miller now dramatizes himself without the disguise of Osmanli. Married to Mona, he is living in a cellar with his wife and one of her female friends. Although Miller tries to rage against such inappropriate arrangements, he is soon reduced to the status of a pet dog. Escape fails and the hero returns to a life of emasculation and loveless manipulation. As domestic dog he is taken by his mistress to a dog show where he wins first prize. His reward is a knuckle bone "encircled by a gold wedding ring." With the ring appropriately mounted on his penis, the dog-Miller is carried off whimpering while the maternal wife comforts him. " 'Woof woof! Woof woof!' I barked. 'Woof! Woof, woof, woof.' "

The two fantasies complement each other. The dog-life significantly presents the reality of an emasculated existence with the very woman who is to free Miller from the shackles of a debilitating first marriage. It thus explains both the suicidal urge and the real illusion that govern Osmanli's sense of freedom in the first fantasy. While Osmanli acts with firm, if illusory, heroism in cutting off the dog's head, it seems clear that Miller is suggesting his own identification with the dog; at Osmanli's death the dog is still there to bark. The whole carries Miller's recognition that freedom was not to be gained simply by leaving wives or marrying them. In fact the two fantasies dramatize the discrepancy between the young Miller's expectations of his role in life and the honest awareness that freedom was still to be achieved.

It seems likely that Osmanli is Miller's version of Emerson's Osman, the alter ego who appears throughout the *Journals* and in the essay on "Manners." The change in his name presumably suggests a "manly" version of the ideal man Emerson secretly defined over so many years, a more masculine projection than that of the author Miller found at once "daring" and the writer of "pabulum." A comparison of Osman and Osmanli makes clear the hopes Miller entertained for himself as a young man and substantiates the technique that is basic to his art—the simultaneous projection of himself as heroic paradigm and the honest admission of the personal failures that marked much of his early adulthood.

Osman, the *Journals* tell us, was not especially noteworthy in youth. Underwitted while his brothers were ambitious, it is only at age thirty-five that he becomes known for his wisdom (V, 431–433; VI, 20). Since he has been so undistinguished, there is no need to hide anything from him; every man honestly reveals himself to him without a mask (V, 432). In his relations with others, Osman remains interested in the "rude self" beneath the mask, and although a remarkable man in middle age, "he was never interrupted by success" (V, 481; VI, 20). He is not interested in fine people but only in "highway experience"—he is a "poor and simple man," and "poor man's poet" (V, 431, 481). He prides himself on his "good constitution," believes in the vital force and self-denial (V, 563–564). He is a man of bold and free speech; a man of broad humanity who draws all sufferers to him.[11] At times he seems in his simplicity, Emerson says, to be a dog (V, 432). Rejecting all mercantile values, he emphasizes the reality of what a man is and what he communicates (VII, 260). He is well liked and sympathizes with the "sad angels who on this planet of ours are striking work and crying, O for something worthy to do!" He argues that we are all near the sublime (VI, 50). "Seemed to me that I had the keeping of a secret too great to be confided to one man; that a divine man dwelt near me in a hollow tree" (VI, 137).

Certain elements of this portrait would surely appeal to Miller. In a book detailing its author's late arrival on the literary scene—Miller was in his early thirties during the period dramatized here—Osman's neglected youth and the obscurity of his early adulthood closely parallel Miller's account of his own early years. In important ways a "poor man's poet" himself, generally preferring the responses of average men to professional critics, Miller has also taken pride in his simple ability to listen, a trait, we are told, that causes people to reveal the honest reality beneath their masks. Miller's concern with his own health, his broad humanity, and his ability to remain the same in spite of fame are all characteristics attested in his books or by friends. A writer of "bold and free speech," he too has argued for the closeness of divinity, the unimportance of mercantile values, and the crucial significance of communication in defining a man. Like Osman, he has been interested in the "rude self" and in "highway experience." In short, there is much in Emerson's portrait of Osman that corresponds to Miller's estimate of himself, at least with the "better side" he confessed to Anaïs Nin Emerson invoked. If he was a dog, he was also, in aspiration at least, many of the things Emerson hoped for himself.

There are, however, at least two essential differences between Osman and Osmanli, and Miller's fantasy creature is not the simple alter ego that his Emersonian counterpart had been. While Emerson's Osman is a "poor and simple man," without any touch of the violent, Osmanli is a desperado of action—in fantasy he cuts off the dog's head, rapes the maid, and spends a life promoting anarchy. Moreover, he is disguised as a dandy, "a boulevardier, a flaneur, a Beau Brummel." Both changes suggest the real pressures to which Miller felt himself subject in the twenties and the intensity with which he had to respond. The autobiographical hero of Miller's romances is generally conceived as a comic but nonetheless serious man of forceful, especially sexual, action. While other men vacillate in their responses toward women, Miller can depict himself as assured and bold. The final scene of *Cancer*, for example, shows a frightened and timid Fillmore, one of that group of closely knit expatriate males, confessing to a confident Miller all his sad affair with the tyrannous Ginette. "Look here, Fillmore, what is it you'd *really* like to do?" asks the assured and knowledgeable hero (p. 309). And helping Fillmore retreat to America is an act parallel to the sexual heroics of the forceful Millerian hero responding to women throughout the books. "I'm a desperado of love," the very American Miller announces at the beginning of *Sexus*, "a scalper, a slayer. I'm insatiable; I eat hair, dirty wax, dry blood clots, anything and everything you call yours" (p. 14). And generally with just such comic gusto he shoulders his way through ranks of threatening women.

Yet such heroics are undercut by the dramatization of himself as henpecked husband and canine lover. Hesitant and reluctant, Miller emancipated himself slowly and with the utmost difficulty. "People often think of me as an adventurous fellow," he confesses in *Tropic of Capricorn*. "Nothing could be farther from the truth. My adventures were always endured rather than undertaken. I am of the very essence of that proud, boastful Nordic people who have never had the least sense of adventure."[12] Osmanli, the forceful emancipator, is in fact a perfect projection of the ideal actor Miller, at the time, felt himself incapable of being. Himself a dog bound to an ambiguous mate in Mona, he could neither decapitate a dog nor rape a maid.

Similarly, Osmanli's dandyism functions as a parallel projection. The son of middle-class Brooklyn parents, Miller spent enough years as down-and-outer to dream of the amenities of the rich. Speaking of an attractively heroic friend in *Cancer*, Miller could remark: "I liked the way Collins moved against this background of literature continuously; it was like a millionaire who never stepped out of his Rolls Royce" (p. 203). And at the end of the book the sight of a French poodle riding in a taxi propels Miller to emulation. Spending all his newly acquired money on a taxi ride through the Bois, he remarks: "Inside me things were running smoother than any Rolls Royce ever ran. It was just like velvet inside" (p. 317). "Be a stevedore in the daytime and a Beau Brummel in the nighttime," Miller advises in *Capricorn* (p. 295). The self-assurance of the rich in fact merges with the assertiveness of the desperado to form a composite of the forceful, calm hero often comically expressing Miller's own aspirations.

But Osmanli is not a simple character of wish fulfillment, any more than he is a one-dimensional alter ego. He dramatizes a strength that, no matter how attractive, Miller felt was fictitious in himself, and he is presented as a hollow man, a straw hero who has to come to terms with his own hidden self. Beneath his ostentatiousness, Osmanli is essentially the kind of empty, trapped human being Miller evidently felt himself to be in the twenties. Bound and visionless, Osmanli is merely the mockery of heroic strength. Like the watch and money that he discards as he runs down the street, his outer self is mere sham, and behind the glibness of the words he finds it so easy to manipulate is a personal vacuum that turns words into empty gesture. Until emancipation is complete, freedom remains a fiction, strength an illusion. For Miller the hollowness of his life as he looked forward to it is symbolized by a dying man learning at the last moment that dogs were still there to bark in spite of his own futile acts.

By borrowing Emerson's own creation, Miller followed the direction the earlier American had indicated. If novels were to give way to autobiography, the personal statement would have to express the complexity of what it is to be human at any given time. For Miller in the twenties, his humanity involved the combination of competing hopes of forceful action and acknowledged fears that actions without selfhood would result at best in comic emptiness. Emerson's Osman eventually flowers into a wise and famous man; Miller's Osmanli dies the product of a freak accident, a parallel to the domestic dog who can only win blue ribbons for a demanding mistress. For Miller, the autobiographical novel has been indeed the vehicle with which he has presented "the truth of emotions, reflection and understanding, truth digested and assimilated." Emerson's secret Osman suggested the possibilities for dramatizing the simultaneous levels of being Miller felt in his own divided self.

Notes

1.   The epigraph is from an 1841 entry, *Journals of Ralph Waldo Emerson*, ed. Edward Waldo Emerson and Waldo Emerson Forbes (Boston, 1909–1914), V, 516. All quotations from the *Journals* are from this edition.

2.   *Tropic of Cancer* (New York, 1961), pp. 239–240. All quotations are from this edition.

3.   See *Journals*, VII, 319.

4.   *The Books in My Life* (New York, no date), p. 318. All quotations are from this edition.

5. In writing about Thomas Merton, Miller has commented: "Like Emerson and Nietzsche, he is a real radical." *Writer and Critic: A Correspondence with Henry Miller*, ed. William A. Gordon (Baton Rouge, La., 1968), p. 48. Many of Miller's later comments on Emerson emphasize his criticism of American culture. So [he does] in the essay "Henry David Thoreau" in *Stand Still Like the Hummingbird* (New York, 1962), pp. 111–118, and in the preface to that book, p. viii.

6. *Lawrence Durrell and Henry Miller: A Private Correspondence*, ed. George Wickes (New York, 1963), p. 261. Miller is given to such lists of influences; Emerson appears in a similar passage in "An Open Letter to Surrealists Everywhere," and again in "Autobiographical Note," both in *The Cosmological Eye* (New York, 1939), pp. 188, 370.

7. *Henry Miller: Letters to Anaïs Nin*, ed. Gunther Stuhlmann (New York, 1965), p. 58.

8. *Sexus* (New York, 1965), p. 270. All quotations are from this edition.

9. In *Writer and Critic*, p. 65, Miller again distinguishes his autobiographical writing from other forms: "All the backward and forward jumps have pertinence, from standpoint of 'true' autobiographical narrative, which, incidentally, bears no relation to Diaries or Confessions or Biographies."

10. The Osmanli episode in *Sexus* appears on pages 606–614. It is immediately followed by the second fantasy, pages 614–634.

11. See "Manners," in *The Complete Works of Ralph Waldo Emerson*, ed. Edward Waldo Emerson (Boston, 1903), III, 154.

12. *Tropic of Capricorn* (New York, 1961), p. 11.

AMERICAN MILLER

◆

Status

Norman Mailer

Literary criticism has left a space around Henry Miller. Fanfare in plenty has come his way, some grandiose, some opalescent—Miller would draw his share of critical rainbows—yet it is as if his reputation still lives in a void. Years later, Karl Shapiro would write to Durrell that they should "put together a bible of Miller's work" to be substituted for the Gideon Bible in every hotel room of America. Durrell, in his turn, would state, "American literature today begins and ends with the meaning of what Miller has done." Anaïs Nin began her preface to *Tropic of Cancer* by declaring: "Here is a book which, if such a thing were possible, might restore our appetite for the fundamental realities."

Yes, Miller has had his share of praise, and such literary maharajahs as Eliot and Pound and Edmund Wilson made their contribution. Pound contented himself with a remark from the fundament: "Here is a dirty book worth reading," and Eliot, who found Shelley satanic, nonetheless became a closet devotee of Miller's, and even sent a letter to the author (if no public pronunciamento). Wilson wrote one of the earliest laudatory (and starchy) reviews to be printed of *Tropic of Cancer*. George Orwell, in a fine essay, said, "it is the book of a man who is happy"—how close to the first virtue was happiness to Orwell! He added: "the only imaginative prose writer of the slightest value who has appeared among the English-speaking races for some years past."

That was in the Thirties. Miller has not lacked for adulation since. A small but accountable part of the literary world has regarded him as the greatest living American writer for the last four decades and indeed, as other American authors died, and Hemingway was there no longer, nor Faulkner and Fitzgerald, not Wolfe, not Steinbeck, nor Dos Passos, and Sinclair Lewis long gone, Dreiser dead and Farrell in partial obscurity, who else could one speak of as the great American author? Moreover, Miller provided his considerable qualifications. One had to go back to Melville to find a rhetoric which could prove as noble under full sail. Indeed one has to ask oneself if Miller could not out-write Melville if it came to describing a tempest at sea.

Reprinted from *Genius and Lust: A Journey Through the Major Writings of Henry Miller* (New York: Grove Press, 1976), 3–10. Copyright © by Norman Mailer. Used by permission of the author and his agents, Scott Meredith Literary Agency, Inc., 845 Third Avenue, New York, New York 10022, U.S.A.

Miller at his best wrote a prose grander than Faulkner's, and wilder—the good reader is revolved in a farrago of light with words heavy as velvet, brilliant as gems, eruptions of thought cover the page. You could be in the vortex of one of Turner's oceanic holocausts when the sun shines in the very center of the storm. No, there is nothing like Henry Miller when he gets rolling. Men with literary styles as full as Hawthorne's appear by comparison stripped of their rich language, stripped as an AP style book; one has to take the English language back to Marlowe and Shakespeare before encountering a wealth of imagery equal in intensity.

Yet it can hardly be said that the American Establishment walks around today thinking of Henry Miller as our literary genius, or one of the symbols of human wealth in America. Born in 1891, he will be eighty-five by December 26 of 1976, an artist of incomparably larger dimensions than Robert Frost, yet who can conceive of a President inviting him to read from his work on Inauguration Day, no, the irony is that a number of good and intelligent politicians might even have a slight hesitation over whether it is Arthur Miller or Henry being talked about. "Oh yes, Henry Miller," they might say at last, "the guy who writes the dirty books." There is such variety in America that everybody ends up being understood by a tag. Dirty books is the tag for old Henry.

Of course, there is the objection that one does not go for sound literary measure to a politician's judgments. Even in the literary world, however, Miller's reputation survives in a vacuum. It is not that he lacks influence. It is even not unfair to say that Henry Miller has influenced the style of half the good American poets and writers alive today: it is fair to ask if books as different as *Naked Lunch, Portnoy's Complaint, Fear of Flying* and *Why Are We in Vietnam?* would have been as well received (or as free in style) without the irrigation Henry Miller gave to American prose. Even a writer as removed in purpose from Miller as Saul Bellow shows a debt in *Augie March*. Miller has had his effect. Thirty years ago, young writers learned to write by reading him along with Hemingway and Faulkner, Wolfe and Fitzgerald. With the exception of Hemingway, he has had perhaps the largest stylistic influence of any twentieth-century American author. Yet still there is that critical space. Miller has only been written about in terms of adulation or dismissal. One does not pick up literary reviews with articles titled, "Ernest Hemingway and Henry Miller—Their Paris Years," or "The Social Worlds of F. Scott Fitzgerald and Henry Miller," no comments on "The Apocalyptic Vision of Henry Miller and Thomas Wolfe as Reflected in Their Rhetoric," no little studies about the similarities of place and time in Orwell's *Down and Out in Paris and London* juxtaposed to *Tropic of Cancer*, no, and certainly no biographies on Miller or the women in his life. If Scott had Zelda, and she was undeniably equal to a formal biography, so Miller had June Edith Smith and she may also be worthy of such treatment. No one seems in a rush to go near. Nor is there bound to be a work titled "Henry Miller and The Beat

Generation," or "Henry Miller and the Revolution of the Sixties." Young men do not feel they are dying inside because they cannot live the way Henry Miller once lived. Yet no American writer, not even Hemingway, necessarily came closer to the crazy bliss of being alone in a strange city with no money in your pocket, not much food in your stomach, and a hard on beginning to stir, a "personal" hard on (as one of Miller's characters nicely describes it).

The paradox therefore persists. It is a wonder. To anthologize Miller is to read just about all of him. To read that much of his work is to take in willy-nilly his dimension. He is a greater writer than one thought. If *Tropic of Cancer* is far and away his best work and nearly everyone who has read Miller has read it, that novel nonetheless offers a highly imperfect view of the rest of his future talent. Compared to Melville, Miller's secondary work is more impressive and considerably more varied. There is not one Henry Miller, but twenty, and fifteen of those authors are very good. Of course, when Miller is bad, he may be the worst great writer ever to be bad. His literary criticism can be pompous and embarrassingly empty of new perceptions. His work on Rimbaud, *The Time of the Assassins*, is disappointing. He may have nothing memorable to say about Lawrence or Balzac. His polemical essays read like sludge. At his worst, he sounds like a small-town newspaper editorial. He can even be corny.

At his literary best, however, as in "Jabberwhorl Cronstadt," he can do a parody—"vermiform and ubisquishous"—of *Finnegans Wake* which may as well set the standard for parodies of Joyce. In another year—it may as well be another life—he can write an undemanding account of trying to take care of his sick car in various garages in Albuquerque which has all the charm and publishability and perishability of the sort of piece *The New York Sunday Times Magazine* is always trying to find and never can. Or he will write a sustained memoir, *The Devil in Paradise*, about a complex and not unevil astrologer which is superior to Thomas Mann's "Mario the Magician" and nearly equal to "Death in Venice." He can create a gallery of characters in his trilogy *The Rosy Crucifixion* who match any equivalent group in the work of Thomas Wolfe, and the vividness of his creations need never give way to Balzac. He is a virtuoso. It is possible we have never had more of a literary acrobat.

In fact it would be tempting to say that he writes well about everything but his enthusiasms, which could explain why the ventures into literary criticism are not as good as one might expect. When Miller applauds, he is empty, he is loud. He is always putting his friends on his shoulders. For want of a new idea he is too quick to repeat the last one. Unable to develop a thought, be certain he bashes into the next. It is even tempting to say that he writes well about every situation in society but sex, except it is not true. One has to know where to look, but Miller has superb descriptions of sex. Even his standard writings about fornication, those accounts so famously empty of relationship, and stark, ergo, as pornography, can at least be read as pornography. He could have been a giant of pornography if he had chosen, right up there above John Cleland and Restif de la Bretonne; he could also have been the greatest writer *The New York Times Magazine* ever found; could have been a jewel of an avant-garde pen, the most poetic and surrealist protégé New Directions ever published; or a great travel writer; or a species of Beat Mencken—nobody hated America with better language than Henry Mencken unless it was Henry Miller; he could, with a little luck in his personal life, have written one of the great picaresque novels of the English language—reference is to *The Rosy Crucifixion*—somehow, he did not quite have that luck, something went wrong and large parts of his most ambitious work were written in years when he was miserably married and dragging his life uphill, far from the years of his exuberance in Paris after *Tropic of Cancer* was finally published. On the other hand, you could take any one of the paragraphs in his more surrealistic writing and recognize what an instinctive sense he had for film montage. In another career, he might have been an extraordinary movie director. He sees with more astonishment and savagery than most film artists.

> You step out along the Atlantic littoral in your cement suit and your gold-heeled socks and there's the roar of Chop Suey in your ears. The Great White Way is blazing with spark plugs. The comfort stations are open. You try to sit down without breaking the crease in your pants. You sit down on the pure asphalt and let the peacocks tickle your larynx. The gutters are running with champagne.
>
> *Black Spring*

The extent of his talent is that he has exhibited all these literary modes and styles in the thirty-odd years he kept writing after *Tropic of Cancer*, yet he had not even begun that book before he turned forty. Near to middle-aged and just about penniless, he was a middle-class failure who had used up his credit among friends. Leaving New York for Europe he was barely able to borrow ten dollars for pocket money on the boat. That is failure backed up in all the pipes. Yet living in Paris by his wits, living in Paris with the operative definition of what it means to live by your wits, he succeeded in putting together the manuscript of *Tropic of Cancer*, and it is one of the ten or twenty great novels of our century, a revolution in style and consciousness equal to *The Sun Also Rises*. You cannot pass through the first twenty pages without knowing that a literary wonder is taking place—nobody has ever written in just this way before, nobody may ever write by this style so well again. A time and a place have come to focus in a writer's voice. It is like encountering an archaeological relic. Given enough such novels, the history of our century could never be lost: there would be enough separate points of reference fixed forever in focus.

It is close therefore to incomprehensible that a man whose literary career has been with us over forty years, an author who wrote one novel which may yet be considered equal to the best of Hemingway, a better novel than anything by Fitzgerald, an author who at his richest gave us sustained passages as intense as anything in Faulkner, a writer who could probably produce more than Thomas Wolfe day by day, and beat him word for word, a wildwater of prose, a cataract, a volcano, a torrent, an earthquake—at this point Henry Miller would have fifty better words to string—a writer finally like a great athlete, a phenomenon of an avatar of literary energy who was somehow, with every large acceptance, and every respect, was somehow ignored and near to discarded, ignored indeed most—the paradox embeds itself in new paradox—in just those years when his ideas triumphed most, and the young of America, for the large part ignorant of Miller's monumental collection of writings, were nonetheless living up to the ears with his thoughts or spouting his condemnations. Turn on, tune in and drop out was old hat to Henry—he had been doing it all his life. Ecology came as no surprise; he and Lewis Mumford may have been the first to write about what was being done to the American landscape, and plastic was the stuff of nightmare with which they covered those air-conditioners he wrote about. Still, nobody was breaking down the doors to get to him. On any given night in any lecture hall of America, Buckminster Fuller—another genius— would draw an audience five to, would it be, ten times the size and Fuller cannot write a sentence which does not curdle the sap of English at its root.

We must assume there was finally something indigestible about Miller to Americans, something in his personality and/or his work which went beyond his ideas, for his condemnations are virtually comfortable to us today. No, it is as if there are authors whose complexities are in harmony with our own. Hemingway and Fitzgerald may each have been outrageous pieces of psychic work, yet their personalities haunt us. Faulkner inspires our reverence and Wolfe our tenderest thoughts for literary genius. They are good to the memories we keep of our reading of them—they live with all the security of favorite old films. But Miller does not. He is a force, a value, a literary sage, and yet in the most peculiar sense he does not become more compatible with time—he may be no better beloved today than twenty, thirty, or forty years ago—it is as if he is almost not an American author; yet nobody could be more American. So he evades our sense of classification. He does not become a personality, rather he maintains himself as an enigma. It is as if he is virtually disagreeable to confront—a literary ogre. There is something faulty in our comprehension of him. His work at its best is marvelously in focus, indeed that is the first virtue of his greatest work—he is one of the first to be forever telling it like it is, here and now, just like it is—yet his own personality is never clear. It is too complex and too vigorous, therefore too worrisome for us, too out of measure.

It is as if Henry Miller contains the unadvertised mystery of how much of a monster a great writer must be.

"History on the Side": Henry Miller's American Dream

ALAN TRACHTENBERG

Henry Miller left America in 1930, a man close to forty, hoping to find himself as a writer in Paris. There was nothing in America to hold him; from almost every point of view he was a failure, a restless drifter between ill-assorted jobs. Money, fame, position eluded him, and the values which supported the devotion to these ends came to seem hollow and inhuman. He tried to devote himself instead to writing, to become an artist as an alternative to the unhappy bourgeois life he had tasted. His first efforts, never published, were conventionally literary. But the journey to Paris worked a transformation, and by 1940, he was internationally known, well on his way toward the fame and wealth he now enjoys. Since his return to America Miller's prestige as a spokesman for the pursuit of personal freedom has grown enormously. The legal decisions which have made his books available represent a turning point in popular culture; they opened the door to a kind of frankness in regard to sexual matters unimaginable twenty years ago. To his readers Miller offers a "wisdom of the heart" which celebrates obedience to desire and loyalty to self. The often hilarious comedy of his early work has given way to a more earnest style of exhortation to love, to enjoy, to be. Miller's criticism of American values, especially the idea of deferring pleasure for the sake of future success, has a wide currency, from hippie culture, to the New Left, to the more sophisticated of the mass media. His idea of America, then, and his exact relation to the values he criticizes deserve closer attention and more precise judgment than they usually receive.

In his major work, the trilogy *Tropic of Cancer* (1934), *Black Spring* (1936), *Tropic of Capricorn* (1939), Miller had written of his contempt for modern America and of his attempts to purge its sickness from his system. In 1940, World War II forced him to leave Greece and return to the "home" of his earlier agonies. At first he imagined the visit would be short-lived: "unlike most prodigal sons, I was returning not with the intention of re-maining in the bosom of the family but of wandering forth again, perhaps

Reprinted from *American Dreams, American Nightmares*, Dave Madden, ed. (Carbondale: Southern Illinois University Press, 1970), 136–48. Copyright © Alan Trachtenberg. Reprinted by permission of the author.

never to return." Somewhat like Henry James almost forty years earlier, Miller felt a special need to explore the American terrain, "to effect"—as he wrote in the preface to the ensuing account of his explorations, *The Air-Conditioned Nightmare* (1945)—"a reconciliation with my native land." He wanted "a last look at my country . . . to embrace it, to feel that the old wounds were really healed." The book is a chronicle of a rambling automobile trek through the Midwest, the South and Southwest, and California. "My one thought," Miller explains, "is to get out of New York, to experience something genuinely American. . . . I want to get out into the open." In a way the jaunty excursion recapitulates the westward routes of pioneers in the last century. But civilization does not recede; it pursues Miller, and although he settled a few years later at Big Sur, the California of the book (in "Soirée in Hollywood") epitomizes the nightmare of the title. "Walking along one of the Neon-lit streets. A shop window with Nylon stockings. Nothing in the window but a glass leg filled with water and a sea horse rising and falling like a feather sailing through heavy air. Thus we see how Surrealism penetrates to every nook and corner of the world." Los Angeles frightens him as a sign of the future.

In its structure as a series of separate sketches of places and persons, and more interestingly, in the way the expatriate experience in Europe tempers observation and judgment, the book bears comparison with James's *The American Scene* (1907). For both writers America had been a troubling experience; both record premonitions of disaster, of "blight," in the money-getting and the frenzy of change; both search for such cultivated amenities as parks, respect for the past and old age, and are irritated to miss them in America; both discover in themselves a surprising attraction to and sympathy for the South, where Miller, for example, finds "a different rhythm, a different attitude." "You can sit on a bench in a tiny Confederate Park or fling yourself on the banks of a levee or stand on a bluff overlooking an Indian settlement, the air soft, still, fragrant, the world asleep seemingly, but the atmosphere is charged with magical names, epoch-making events, inventions, explorations, discoveries." As for the rest of America, except for the "boundless immensity," the sense of "the infinite *previous*" of the far West, as James put it, life is without grace, popular culture an "intellectual pablum," and "universal acquiescence" to profit-seeking and mechanization is the rule. "Nowhere," writes Miller, "have I encountered such a dull, monotonous fabric of life."

But these resemblances between the two books are superficial. In its mood of disengagement, of easy relations along the road, Miller's work is more in the spirit of Jack Kerouac's *On the Road* (1955) than of James's intense scrutiny of American society. James presents himself as a "restless analyst," whose responses, with their own special history and cultivation, play a major role in whatever he describes or relates. The drama of the book is held in the texture of each encounter, each struggle to attain a clear perspective. Miller is considerably less scrupulous about his responses. Often he is simply a passive reporter, a funnel for an indiscriminate flow of details. James worked up his material as a novelist; each detail is made to express larger patterns of feeling and idea. Details arouse associations which deepen the sense of personal history implicated in each encounter.

Miller's use of detail is more like that of a satirist than a novelist. "Everything is caricature here," he writes in a passage which demonstrates the flat, uninflected flow through which he achieves his characteristic effects:

> I take a plane to see my father on his death-bed and up there in the clouds, in a raging storm, I overhear two men behind me discussing how to put over a big deal, the big deal involving paper boxes, no less. The stewardess, who has been trained to behave like a mother, a nurse, a mistress, a cook, a drudge, never to look untidy, never to lose her Marcel wave, never to show a sign of fatigue or disappointment or chagrin or loneliness, the stewardess puts her lily-white hand on the brow of one of the paper-box salesmen and in the voice of a ministering angel, says, "Do you feel tired this evening? Have you a headache? Would you like a little aspirin?" We are up in the clouds and she is going through this performance like a trained seal. When the plane lurches suddenly she falls and reveals a tempting pair of thighs. The two salesmen are now talking about buttons, where to get them cheaply, how to sell them dearly. . . The girl falls down again—she's full of black and blue marks. But she comes up smiling, dispensing coffee and chewing gum, putting her lily-white hand on someone else's forehead, inquiring if he is a little low, a little tired perhaps. I ask her if she likes her job. For answer she says, "It's better than being a trained nurse."

Caricature is Miller's method in much of the book, and it is a method which accounts for the strength and energy of many passages. "Put the 58,956 crippled and killed this year back on the asphalt pavement and collect the insurance money. . . . Buy six Packards and an old Studebaker. . . . Dial 9675 and tune in on Bing Crosby or Dorothy Lamour. . . . Be sure to buy a slab of gum, it will sweeten the breath. Do anything, say anything that comes into your head, because it's all cuckoo and nobody will know the difference."

Like James, Dreiser, and Fitzgerald, Miller assails the American Dream of permanent wealth and happiness as the automatic reward of individual effort and excellence of character; he joins in the attack on the Dream as a hoax and a fraud. But where the others dramatize the process of belief and disenchantment, where they take account of losses and gains, analyze the social matrix of illusion and credit the desire for success as human facts worthy of compassion, Miller alternates between satire and direct assault. Less the novelist, he reveals himself as far more the moralist, which raises questions about the grounds of his moral fervor.

Since he settled in California in 1944, Miller's moral vision has become a major note in his writing. It is based on a vision of modern society as irredeemable, unchangeable, except through some form of apocalypse or shattering revelation. By "society" Miller means the way of life depicted in the caricature—the style of daily living, rather than the structure of social relations which gives that style a concrete historical setting. Any redemption must find its source outside social relations, that is, outside history. "To live beyond the pale, to work for the pleasure of working, to grow old gracefully while retaining one's faculties, one's enthusiasms, one's self-respect, one has to establish other values than those endorsed by the mob." The "mob" is Miller's indiscriminate label for American "society," the antithesis to which is the "artist." "It takes an artist to make this breach in the wall."

Miller devotes much of *The Air-Conditioned Nightmare* to portraits of artists, intensely private and often eccentric individuals who live apart from entangling relations and pursue their visions. Weeks Hall on his magnificent Southern plantation in Louisiana; Dr. Souchon, the surgeon painter; Albert Pike, the Arkansas dreamer; Dudley, the desperate, half-mad young writer of "Letter to Lafayette" (a portrait with premonitions of the Beats a decade later); Hilaire Hiler, the muralist; Edgard Varese, Alfred Stieglitz, John Marin—these are the main characters who people the book, and it is through them that Miller presents his hopes for redemption. His artists are a life-giving elite. "The world goes on because a few men in every generation believe in it utterly, accept it unquestioningly; they underwrite it with their lives. In the struggle which they have to make themselves understood they create music; taking the discordant elements of life, they weave a pattern of harmony and significance. If it weren't for this constant struggle on the part of a few creative types to expand the sense of reality in man the world *would* literally die out."

This redemptive function Miller assigns to his artists is a familiar idea with roots in nineteenth-century antibourgeois sentiment. Miller's artist is often the free bohemian, whose life on the fly is a deliberate slap at the order and routine of respectable life. But he is also something more. With all the eclecticism of Miller's thinking about art, and the important influence of European ideas, especially Surrealism, at bottom he is still attached to the idea of a particularly American function for his artist, or for personal liberation as such. To be sure, the idea does not often reach the surface of his writings, but there are enough clues to suggest that Miller hopes for a specifically *American* redemption—indeed, we discover, a return to traditional or mythic national values. How else are we to understand Miller's description of the present money-getting as a "bitter caricature" of the ideals of "our liberty-loving forefathers"? Or his mention of "a great social experiment . . . begun on this virgin continent"? "Here we are," he writes, "we the people of the United States: the greatest people on earth, so we think. We have land, water, sky and all that goes with it. We could become the great shining example of the world; we could radiate peace, joy, power, benevolence." These passages are all taken from *The Air-Conditioned Nightmare*. Later he writes in *Remember to Remember* (1947), "I would like to take this country of ours and recreate it—in the image of the hopes it once inspired"—a revealing comment and a revealing title.

The image of the "air-conditioned nightmare," in short, affirms implicitly a "dream" as a measure of judgment. In his earlier books America represented death and destruction of spirit. The American city suffocated him; he needed to escape. In *Black Spring*, the most successful of his books in evoking both the suffocation and the frenzy of release, he writes: "Swimming in the crowd, a digit with the rest. Tailored and re-tailored. The lights are twinkling—on and off, on and off. Sometimes it's a rubber tire, sometimes it's a piece of chewing gum. The tragedy of it is that nobody sees the look of desperation on my face. Thousands and thousands of us, and we're passing one another without a look of recognition." His feelings boil and verge on obscene violence: "Ought to grab a revolver and fire point-blank into the crowd." "*Smash it! Smash it!* That's all I can say." In large part his feelings arise from a sense of disillusion and defeat. "Once I thought there were marvelous things in store for me. Thought I could build a world in the air, a castle of pure white spit that would raise me above the tallest building, between the tangible and intangible, put me in a space like music where everything collapses and perishes but where I would be immune, great, godlike, holiest of the holies." Now that he has fallen and faced his reality (only a tailor's son), the dream of immunity seems an outrageous cheat. He feels lost and can find nothing in the American city to answer his needs for liberation. The solution is to destroy the old American world in himself, the world of fraud, materialism, gadgetry, the dream turned nightmare, and to die into a new, free being.

But does the new being Miller elicits from his desperate experiences really constitute a rejection of the American Dream? Or is it a translation of the values of the Dream from economic and social terms to psychological and aesthetic ones? To be "immune, great, godlike" remains the goal of his energetic assault upon the world, and in a sense he has freed himself to undertake that assault in a manner which has something in common with the fantasies of urban popular culture—fantasies of escape from conventions of family and work, of personal license in pursuit of pleasure, of "doing your own thing." If the heart of the American Dream is the image of the unfettered man "making" himself by accumulation of goods and credit, assuring a place for himself at the American banquet, Miller has detached the activity from any social end, and celebrated the act of accumulating experiences, especially sexual experiences, as an end in itself. Instead of a duty, life becomes an adventure—but still an adventure of self-aggrandizement and self-creation. By inverting the Horatio Alger style of the Dream, Miller discovers its essence, the desire to have what William James called a "moral holiday" as a permanent condition. "I have no money, no resources, no hopes. I am the happiest man alive."

The excitement in Miller's early work is its authentic emotion of release, its unhindered explorations of the suppressed fringes of middle-class fantasies, where respectability fades into criminality. It is a literature of pure disengagement and self-assertion, an act of aggression against all confining values. "For me the book is the man and my book is the man I am, the confused man, the negligent man, the reckless man, the lusty, obscene, boisterous, thoughtful, scrupulous, lying, diabolically truthful man that I am. I am thinking that in that age to come I shall not be overlooked. Then my history will become important and the scar which I leave upon the face of the world will have a significance. I can not forget that I am making history, a history on the side which, like a chancre, will eat away the other meaningless history. I regard myself not as a book, a record, a document, but as a history of our time—a history of *all* time." Exempt from convention, from personal ties, from history and politics, the self finds its realization in sheer flight. Its freedom is the escape from necessity.

The flight from history, from social ties and obligations, is the clearest mark of Miller's underlying commitment to an American Dream. The idea of a "history on the side" may have replaced the "castle of pure white spit," but the motive of immunity from time and society remains intact. Not wealth but voluntary poverty, not excellence of character but its exact reversal, become the means toward this immunity. Miller's career, as recounted in his books, can be taken as a quest for ultimate self-transcendence, for the perfect frontier where without any encumbrances the self can feed on the world without distraction.

Once we become aware of these familiar American aspirations in Miller, it is not surprising to discover other elements of the cultural pattern, especially the obsession with memory, the attempt to recapture an idealized past. While Miller rejects history as "meaningless," as a "cancer," his works are obsessed with the past. The personal past becomes a virtual alternative to world history. The pattern completes itself when we encounter passages which can only be described as "pastoral" in their yearning to recapture earlier moments of peace and harmony. To be sure, Miller's work will resist any reduction to a simple pattern. But in regard to his relationship to the American Dream, it is important to recognize what ideas and feelings he shares with his culture.

Miller is an urban pastoralist. "I was born in the street and raised in the street," he writes in "The Fourteenth Ward" (*Black Spring*). "The postmechanical open street where the most beautiful and hallucinating iron vegetation, etc." His memory is of iron gardens. "Where others remember of their youth a beautiful garden, a fond mother, a sojourn at the seashore, I remember, with a vividness as if it were etched in acid, the grim soot-covered walls and chimneys of the tin factory opposite us." The imagery suggests an infusion of pastoral feelings into a technological landscape. "No one seemed to notice that the streets were ugly or dirty. If the sewer mains were opened you held your nose. If you blew your nose you found snot in your handkerchief and not your nose. There was more of inward peace and contentment. . . . The foam was on the lager and people stopped to chat with one another."

The significant pastoral elements are found not only in the imagery of the Fourteenth Ward, but in the spirit with which Miller recaptures the "inward peace and contentment." To be born in the street, he writes, "means to wander all your life, to be free. It means accident and incident, drama, movement. It means above all dream." The Fourteenth Ward is in effect a dream, a dream of lost youth.

> In youth we were whole and the terror and pain of the world penetrated us through and through. There was no sharp separation between joy and sorrow: they were fused into one, as our waking life fuses with dream and sleep. We rose one being in the morning and at night we went down into an ocean, drowned out completely, clutching the stars and the fever of the day.
>
> . . . .
>
> And then comes a time when suddenly all seems to be reversed. We live in the mind, in ideas, in fragments. We no longer drink in the wild outer music of the streets—we *remember* only.

Now, after the "great change" of maturity, of loss of childhood, pastoral experience becomes the effort to recover the early moments in memory. "We walk the streets with a thousand legs and eyes, with furry antennae picking up the slightest clue and memory of the past. In the aimless to and fro we pause now and then, like long, sticky plants, and we swallow whole the live morsels of the past."

The natural imagery, the suggestion of yearnings for an organic relation with elements of the self, appear again in *Tropic of Capricorn*, where Miller describes the experiences which led to his escape from America. He roams the streets of New York with a sense of helplessness and strangeness. From Spengler he gains the conviction that the megalopolis is the last gasp of a dying civilization, and decides to purge himself, "to die as a city in order to become again a man." And the image which carries this wish is of a "natural park"—not forest or wilderness, but "park," an area made by design yet retaining its nourishing links with nature. "I shall be law and order as it exists in nature, as it is projected in dream. I shall be the wild park in the midst of the nightmare of perfection." Through such cultivated wildness Miller determines to awake from the American nightmare, the mad yearnings for money, possessions, status. Wildness will kill the nightmare, in order to release the dream.

By "wild park" Miller means in part the untamed, unformed impulses floating in his deep self. The "gob of spit in the face of Art," the "kick in the pants to God, Man, Destiny, Time, Love, Beauty . . . what you will," which introduce *Tropic of Cancer* are marks of this wildness, his rejection of conventional constraints upon expression. He will dishonor all pieties in order to honor the piety of free expression. In "Reflections on Writing" Miller connects his ideas of personal and aesthetic freedom. He is, he writes, "a man telling the story of his life," an inexhaustible process of surrender to the flow of existence. The writer needs to create an illusion of flux. Conscious technique, plotting, balancing of tone and weight, allowing patterns of words to judge and qualify each other, deliberating upon resonances—all this interferes with the pure act. Only by "the very accurate registering by my seismographic needle of the tumultuous, manifold, mysterious and incomprehensible experiences which I have lived through" is anything achieved. Of course this too is a convention, an artifice, chosen deliberately in order to render a sense of having freed oneself from all controls. "We are dealing," Miller writes, "with crystalline elements of the dispersed and shattered soul," and to convey the idea of dissolution faithfully, he will project his "self" as the *persona* of the "shattered and dispersed ego," manipulating "the flotsam and jetsam of the surrounding phenomenal world" through the *persona*.

The wild park, the park of the unconscious, which the writer both invokes as theme and employs as technique, is meant to dispel the nightmare of the city. Liberation is expressed in the act of writing, in its putative freedom from restraint. Flow takes the place of plot. The *persona* commands a range of styles—comic vernacular, high-flown prophecy and exhortation, surreal fantasy—but it does not possess any genuine plasticity. It is beyond change, beyond the ability to register experience as anything other than force, energy, impact. The effect is to make voyeurs of the readers, not participants. Self-absorption indulged on a scale of verbal magnificence is Miller's essential form of liberation. His "history on the side" is autobiography in which event and fantasy have identical status. To discriminate would be to falsify the flow, the tangled undergrowth of the "natural park" of the self.

The park image confirms Miller's attachment to Romanticism. But his version of the creed of the self is notably stripped of the social vision of Emerson, Thoreau, and Whitman. Miller's idea of freedom, of the natural and the wild, intensifies as his *persona* moves further away from society, from any relations in which history is an interference. Miller's Paris, for example, is portrayed as the perfect medium of his hero's release. It is the Paris of declassed expatriates, émigrés, failed artists. *Tropic of Cancer* conveys virtually no sense of Paris as a complex fact in the shared consciousness of people who live and work there. The book does not portray the way of life of Paris, but an idea of Paris where the raffish bohemian life seems the rule. In Miller's version, rootlessness *is* the way of life. The setting thus offers no social or historical resistance.

With all his apparent toughness and nonchalance, Miller's *persona*, unlike Céline's, has striking moments of softness. One such moment, in which the sentimental underpinning of Miller's romanticism becomes unmistakably clear, is the ending of *Tropic of Cancer*. Miller could hardly show himself as more American—one might even take a jaundiced view and say, as more of an American tourist—than in this conclusion, as he stands by the "green and glassy" Seine, thinks vaguely about New York, its crowded streets, the complications he left behind, and suddenly feels "a great peace" come over him. "Here," he writes, "where the river gently winds through the girdle of hills, lies a soil so saturated with the past that however far the mind roams one can never detach it from its human background." He feels "this river flowing through me,—its past, its ancient soil, the changing climate. The hills gently girdle it about: its course is fixed."

The tone of the passage, with its hints of portentous feeling, implies something of a discovery for the hero, a new understanding. But if we try to penetrate to the exact meaning of this feeling, if we ask what he means by "past," by "human background," we are left with a suspicion that the described moment is more a function of the inveterate Americanism of the hero than of the actual scene. His own history by now fragmented, oppressive, he is overcome with awe and reverence for the European "past"—not a specific past, but simply "the past."

In *The Colossus of Maroussi* (1941) the configuration becomes even clearer. Miller left France in 1939, choosing this critical moment in European history for a pilgrimage to the sources of Western civilization. "I felt completely detached from Europe," he wrote, which, as George Orwell pointed out, meant detachment from war, fascism, and resistance. The war was a fulfillment of sorts, the necessary and expected prelude to a new apocalypse. If the *Tropics* document the disease, *Colossus* projects a hearty sense of health and new life, suffused in the bright Aegean light. It is the least troubled, the most accepting and affirmative of Miller's books.

Once again the affirmation is decidedly American, a special mixture of verve and banality. What moves Miller more than anything else in Greece is the antiquity of the land. "Things long forgotten came back with frightening clarity." With "real" history raging about him in Europe, Miller discovers for himself a more meaningful history while exploring classical ruins.

I am a native of New York, the grandest and the emptiest city in the world; I am standing now at Mycenae, trying to understand what happened here over a period of centuries. I feel like a cockroach crawling about amidst dismantled splendors. It is hard to believe that somewhere back in the leaves and branches of the great genealogical tree of my life my progenitors knew this spot, asked the same questions, fell back senseless into the void, were swallowed up and left no trace of thought save these ruins, the scattered relics in museums, a sword, an axle, a helmet, a death mask of beaten gold, a bee-hive tomb, an heraldic lion carved in stone, an exquisite drinking vase. I stand at the summit of the walled citadel and in the early morning I feel the approach of the cold breath from the shaggy gray mountain towering above us. Below, from the great Argive plain the mist is rising. It might be Pueblo, Colorado, so dislocated is it from time and boundary. Down there, in that steaming plain where the automotrice crawls like a caterpillar, is it not possible there once stood wigwams? Can I be sure there never were any Indians there?

Later, lounging on the grass near Agamemnon's tomb, he watches some people in the distance measuring a plot of land, and has a flashing insight. "What is vital here is land, just land. I roll it over on my tongue—land, land, land. Why yes, *land*, that's it—I had almost forgotten it meant such a simple, eternal thing."

Land, wigwams, the Great Plains—it is as if Miller had to get to Europe to find the American frontier. Like Mark Twain's raftsman, the Greeks are "like men ought to be—that is to say, open, frank, natural, spontaneous, warmhearted. These were the types of men I had expected to meet in my own land when I was growing up to manhood. I never found them." It becomes clear that Greece helps him discover an American tradition—a tradition, it should be noted, which has its life mainly in literary convention—in the images of frontiersmen as heroes, of endless space in "nature" as the escape route from "society," of pastoral childhood. Wishing to make "history on the side," Miller slips into familiar American ways of evading history altogether.

In *Tropic of Cancer* he writes that he ceased to be an American when he realized that "everything American will disappear one day." This recognition, he felt, made it impossible for him to remain inside "the warm, comfortable bloodstream where, buffaloes all, we once grazed in peace." He at least is no buffalo—"not even a spiritual buffalo." He prefers "an older stream of consciousness, a race antecedent to the buffaloes, a race that will survive the buffalo." If the buffalo represents the destruction of the West, the failure of Americans to possess the land with the intimacy of Greeks and Indians, as well as the mindless herd instinct of modern Americans, then Miller's antecedent race sounds very much like the lost possibilities for purity and self-sufficiency and timelessness lamented with such monotony in American culture. As the historical possibility diminishes, the dream persists, becomes even more detached, becomes the American Dream. When Miller settled at Big Sur, one of the points farthest west on the continent, and later Los Angeles, to enjoy the fruits of a successful self-made career, he may have discovered that "reconciliation" with his native land was not such a difficult matter after all. In most essential matters he had never left home.

Henry Miller: The Success of Failure

John Williams

On July 4, 1845, Henry David Thoreau, who had been living in Boston, moved a few personal belongings into a hut on the edge of Walden Pond, a small lake near Concord, Massachusetts, the place of his birth. He was twenty-eight years of age. As he tells us in "Walden," he had tried a number of things before he made his escape into what he thought of as the wilderness. He had gone to Harvard and graduated; he had taught school for a brief time in his home town of Concord, and was by his own admission an unsuccessful teacher; he had thought of going into trade, and had worked briefly for his father, a small businessman who manufactured pencils; he had lectured before cultural groups in Concord, apparently without great success; he had written a few essays for the Dial; in exchange for room and board, he had performed odd jobs for Ralph Waldo Emerson; and he had been a tutor in the New York home of Emerson's brother William. Until his decision to abandon the "civilized pursuits" to which he was born, his was the ordinary life that any moderately intelligent young man, of no means but with some culture, education, and talent, might lead, given the conditions of his time and place. "The mass of men lead lives of quiet desperation. What is called resignation is confirmed desperation. From the desperate city you go into the desperate country, and have to console yourself with the bravery of minks and musk-rats. . . ."

Three generations later, in the year 1930, another Henry—Henry Miller, of New York City, the son of a lower-middle-class German-American family—sailed to Europe, where he had spent the year before as a tourist. He left behind him a first wife and a child, a second wife, and his other few worldly possessions. As we know from his many writings—the "Tropic of Cancer" and "Tropic of Capricorn," the five volumes that now constitute "The Rosy Crucifixion," and scattered essays and narratives in dozens of books—he had tried many things before finally making his escape from America. For two months he had attended the City College of New York, and failed to complete the semester; he had worked at a variety of clerical jobs, and in his father's tailor shop; he had been for three years a messenger

Reprinted from *Virginia Quarterly Review* 44 (Spring 1968): 225–45. Reprinted by permission of *The Virginia Quarterly Review*.

employment manager for Western Union; and for about ten years, intermittently, had tried unsuccessfully to become a commercial writer of articles, stories, and novels. He was, in other words, a member of a vast underground of lower-middle-class Americans who wander beneath the surface or on the periphery of our increasingly complex society, unseen by the very society that dominates their lives; men who exist marginally upon our culture, who for one reason or another have been unable to find a place in the social order that strives to give their lives substance or meaning.

He was, in short, a failure; and in "Tropic of Capricorn," the volume dealing with his pre-Paris years in New York, he announces that failure: "I couldn't waste time being a teacher, a lawyer, a physician, a politician or anything else that society had to offer. It was easier to accept menial jobs because it left my mind free. . . . The stabbing horror of life is not contained in calamities and disasters, because these things wake one up and one gets very familiar and intimate with them. . . . You know with a most disturbing certitude that what governs life is not money, not politics, not religion, not training, not race, not language, not customs, but something else, something you're trying to throttle all the time and which is really throttling you, because otherwise you wouldn't be terrified all of a sudden and wonder how you were going to escape. . . . One can starve to death—it is much better. Every man who voluntarily starves to death jams another cog in the automatic process. I would rather see a man take a gun and kill his neighbor, in order to get the food he needs, than keep up the automatic process by pretending that he has to earn a living."

One should recognize immediately that this is not the prose of prophecy or apocalypse, as it has often been taken; it is, in its peculiar tone of despair and in its very rhythm, the prose of the Depression. In a recent essay, "The American Left," Daniel Aaron quotes an anonymous letter published at the bottom of the Depression by one of the displaced; it might almost have been written by Miller himself.

"I wrote letters, I tramped hundreds of blocks to answer ads, I tried for jobs as teamster, clothing model, wringer man, floor-walker, garbage collector, truck driver. I wrote a Civil Service examination. I made ten dollars painting the ceiling of a barber shop. I managed an interview with my former superintendent, but he didn't remember me very well. I lived on a loaf of bread for ten days and then my money was all gone. . . . If it were necessary—if there were a famine, if I were a genius, an explorer, a martyr—I could endure cold and hunger, even degradation and insults, without a murmur. . . . But it is all so unnecessary, there is so little for me to look forward to, that I am beginning to think that it isn't so worthwhile to keep straight. The best I could look for, as a reward for going through another winter, or three, or five, like the last two, would be a job somewhere, sometime. And then could I feel secure? Another depression might catch me with no more resources than I had this time."

That Miller was not in this country during the worst of the great Depression does not matter; the "depressions" out of which both these passages spring are ones that are endemically American, always with us to one degree or another, in one way or another; they are more than political or economic; and the historical depression out of which the anonymous letter was written was only an intense symptom of a process that is implicit in our values and which has been with us nearly from the beginning of our country.

At the center of American life there is a polarity that I shall specify as the polarity of success and failure. This polarity has been generally recognized before, yet it is one whose precise identity cannot be seen except in a specific context of American history and culture.

The question of success and failure lies at the center of Thoreau's "Walden," and it lies at the center of much of Miller's work, especially his "autobiographical romances"—the "Tropic of Cancer" and "Tropic of Capricorn," "Black Spring," and "The Rosy Crucifixion." And the many statements of the two men upon the nature of success and failure are remarkably similar. Thoreau writes, "I would rather sit on a pumpkin and have it all to myself, than be crowded on a velvet cushion. I would rather ride on earth in an ox cart with a free circulation, than go to heaven in the fancy car of an excursion train and breathe a *malaria* all the way." In the opening section of "Tropic of Capricorn," Miller writes, "Everybody around me was a failure, or if not a failure, ridiculous. Especially the successful ones. . . . I think of all the streets in America combined as forming a huge cesspool, a cesspool of the spirit in which everything is sucked down and drained away. . . . The whole continent is a nightmare producing the greatest misery of the greatest number. I was one, a single entity in the midst of the greatest jamboree of wealth and happiness . . . but I never met a man who was truly wealthy or truly happy. At least I knew that I was unhappy, unwealthy, out of whack and out of step. That was my only solace, my only joy."

Some years ago, H. B. Parkes, in "The American Experience," wrote of the polarity between American political and theological theory: "In their political ideals, men give expression to what they wish to believe; but in their religion they show what they really are. A theology is, in fact, a kind of collective poem or work of art that records the secret emotional history of a community." It is that "secret emotional history" of the early American community that I should like to examine briefly.

In the strictly determined universe of the early New England Calvinist, mankind fell into one of two groups—the elect or the damned. This division was ultimately mysterious, but one who had a certain faith in God might feel reasonably sure of his own election; and it was a sign of that faith that he felt it a profound duty to impose his way of life upon his less fortunate fellows—by force if necessary. Life was a moral arena, and the battle was between Good and Evil; where one stood in that battle would not in theory influence the outcome, but it could give one a hint as to where he stood in the eyes of God—of the elect, or of the damned. Goodness, ultimately, was faith in God; action was merely a sign of that faith. And faith in God was faith in something beyond man and nature; for man, in nature, was corrupt, and his only salvation was to be saved from nature by the Grace of God. Thus, every impulse of nature tended to be evil, and any spontaneous emotion, such as love or even an excessive regard for another human being, was probably sinful. God was an ascetic ideal, and man found him in contemplation, not action.

But these settlers could, in their daily lives, be neither ascetic nor contemplative, even though Calvinist doctrine inexorably pushes man in upon himself. Their environment forced them to materialism, and their struggle against the wilderness was an external one, though it might have internal implications. Thus from the beginning the American Calvinist dangled between his sense of the doctrinal importance of his internal life and the practical necessities of his external life.

By the middle of the seventeenth century, however, the theology—that "secret emotional history"—had changed to accommodate necessity; and in the dim beginnings of American prosperity, the New England clergy began to preach that obedience to God was the way to worldly prosperity, though nominally such prosperity was valuable only insofar as it afforded an outward sign of inward grace. But one who saw prosperity as a *sign* of virtue did not have to step far to see prosperity as a *proof* of virtue. And as dogma weakened, it was almost inevitable that the prosperous man be profoundly convinced of his own virtue, and that he attribute that prosperous virtue to his own merits rather than to God's election.

Almost from the beginning, in America, the question of success and failure has been a religious question; and it remains so, to some extent, even in the twentieth century. Thus Miller's rejection of the standard American attitudes toward success is actually a rejection of a lingering Calvinist ethic that still works beneath the surface of our culture, though his rejection is not, as we shall see, as unequivocal as one might expect.

The popular view of Miller is that of the American who has rid himself of all that is most American; who has brought into American literature the invigorating strain of European modernism; who has rescued American literature from provincialism and brought the genuine avant-garde to our own traditional shores. In some respects Miller seems to share this attitude about his own work and to encourage it in others. Except for his repeated admirations of Whitman, Emerson, and Thoreau, his literary praise has always been for the figures of another culture: he has at one time or another admired and acknowledged indebtedness to such men as Dostoevsky, Van Gogh, Nostradamus, Dante, Nijinski, Elie Faure, Rimbaud, Nietzsche, H. Rider Haggard, D. H. Lawrence, the Oriental mystical writers, as well as to such modern avant-gardists as André Breton, Blaise Cendrars, Céline, Ionesco, Anaïs Nin, and a variety of lesser Dadaists and Surrealists. And nearly all of his writings make some gestures toward the European "modernism" of the twenties: the highly charged but never quite believable dreams, the long metaphoric flights that are simply extreme exaggerations of present reality, the passages of induced hallucination, the occasional excursions in automatic writing, and the literary affectations of madness.

But these are only gestures, and perhaps small debts, and one will not find the significance of Miller's work in them; for Miller is a writer who is essentially American, and American in a particular sense of that word.

If it appears perverse to suggest that in many ways Miller represents a nineteenth-and twentieth-century transformation of American Puritanism, it does so, I suspect, largely because of the celebrated question of his obscenity. One might wish to say that the issue of obscenity is in no way fundamental to Miller's work; and though one can almost say that, one cannot quite. For if Miller's use of obscenity is the most overt sign of his apparent rejection of the Puritan ethic, it is at the same time the covert revelation of the incompleteness of that rejection.

It should be clear to any serious student of American Puritanism that first the avoidance and then the symbolizing of sexual matters is one of the more obvious symptoms of the Puritan dilemma; and like many symptoms, it disguises more than it reveals. For obscenity and sexuality, in themselves, have little to do with the essential dilemma of American Puritanism; and when the more naïve among us wish to reject what we think of as the Puritan ethic, we turn immediately to the no doubt pleasant task of rejecting the Puritan sexual ethic—as if the taking of morphine might heal the wound.

In some ways Miller's obscenity is the most nearly innocent aspect of his art. The words he uses—the so-called Anglo-Saxon or four-letter words—we all know, else we would not be shocked by them. It is not a moral question, but a social one. If we are shocked by Miller's language, we are shocked not because our morality has been threatened but because our social standing has been; we are forced to confront and to admit the vital existence of one whose social standing appears lower than our own—one who would use such language, and so affront polite society. Thus snobbery subsumes morality, taboo overrides reason, and we are revealed to ourselves in all our cultural primitivism. We are made uncomfortable.

But though the language Miller uses is probably the basis for the widespread censorship of his books in this country, there are other pornographic techniques in Miller that are equally useful to his intention. Aside from the words, the sexuality and scatology found in Miller are of two sorts. First is that which is found with some frequency in the rather long, arty, and often irrelevant surrealistic fantasies that interrupt the narratives and expositions. By and large, such passages are so badly done that we have a hard time taking them seriously. Second, and more characteristic, are the sexual exploits that Miller attributes to himself in the autobiographical romances. And even these passages are strangely innocent; for they have that pathetic braggadocio and exaggeration of the lower-middle-class masculine world of the deprived adolescent (ugly, relentlessly shy, or merely poor) who finds himself outside the easy security of the promises of his society, and thus is committed to longing, talk, and the compensations of imagining.

When Miller is not indulging himself in quasi-surrealist nightmare sequences, or in the half-fantasies of symptomatic longing, his attitudes toward sex are almost embarrassingly moral, though not necessarily conventional. In the more straightforward narrative sections of the "Tropics," he reveals himself to be, if not altogether proper in sexual matters, at least not the monster that we might expect from the more literary passages; and when he speaks "seriously" of sex, in his rôle as latter-day sage, in his essays upon the subject, and especially in a work that remained until a few years ago unpublished in this country, "The World of Sex," his thinking is approximately as bold as that of a university-educated marriage counselor or sociologist—though the language in which he specifies this thinking is not likely to be found in either. Like Lawrence, he sees the rôle of sex as essentially religious, and he speaks sentimentally of its "mystery."

I do not wish to imply that Miller is a Puritan manqué, the archetypal American Calvinist in an outrageous disguise. I am, rather, suggesting that the dilemmas and polarities that have characterized American Puritanism are remarkably similar to the dilemmas and polarities that lie at the center of Henry Miller's most important and characteristic work.

As I have already noted, the Puritan doctrine of Election and Damnation has its secular counterpart in the American doctrine of success and failure. There are other counterparts, however, nearly as significant.

Fundamental to the Calvinist system was the notion that all men were by nature corrupt and wicked, and that only a few might be chosen by God for salvation. This was God's choice, not man's, and it was predestined and absolute. In theory, neither man's works nor his actions could influence this election. One might expect that such a system of belief would lead to spiritual inertia, fatalism, and acquiescence; the fact of history is that it did not. It led, rather, to a remarkable energy, an astonishing exercise of the will, and a forceful rejection of any sort of temporal acquiescence.

To understand this apparent contradiction, one must interpret the experience that it reflects; we return again to that "secret emotional history" of which the Calvinist theology is poem and text. The world and society tell man that only his works matter, and that he shall be judged by them; the Calvinist theology told him that he would obtain salvation not by works but by faith, and that faith was the free gift of God. Now, to the man who has any kind of insecurity about his own worth, nothing can be so devastating or paralyzing as to feel that that worth, in the eyes of his neighbors or of God, depends only upon the quality of his works. Thus, the Calvinist theology offered a profound alternative to the demands of a social world; and, as Parkes says in this connection, "Those persons who accepted this doctrine and applied it to themselves had an astonishing sense of liberation, as though a burden had suddenly fallen from their shoulders; they were immediately freed from doubt, insecurity, and anxiety. This instantaneous experience of conversion was, indeed, a kind of rebirth."

For the ten years preceding 1930, Henry Miller had engaged in the pursuits that he must have hoped would lead him to success, and he had failed. It was only when he rejected the approval of his neighbors and his country, and when he renounced the possible value of his works, that he came to feel himself free. In one of his essays of the Paris period, entitled "Peace! It's Wonderful!," Miller writes: "Night after night without money, without friends, without a language I had walked these streets in despair and anguish. . . . In any case, the important thing is that in [Paris] I touched bottom. Like it or not, I was obliged to create a new life for myself. . . . In this life I am God, and like God I am indifferent to my own fate. . . . Just as a piece of matter detaches itself from the sun to live as a wholly new creation so I have come to feel about my detachment from America. And like all the other suns of the universe I had to nourish myself from *within*. I speak in cosmological terms because it seems to me that is the only possible way to think if one is truly alive. I think this way also because it is just the opposite of the way I thought a few years back when I had what is called hopes. Hope is a bad thing. It means that you are not what you want to be."

This is the Calvinist formula in its nineteenth-century transformation, a transformation made possible by a weakening both of a specific sense of sin and by the inevitable deterioration of dogma. "God" or "Christ" becomes the "self," the "natural" or "social" world becomes "America," and "heaven" becomes the "universe." But the habit of mind is clear beyond the transformation, and it is Calvinist. Emerson, Whitman, and Thoreau had wrought the transformation, and Henry Miller inherited it.

The notion of rebirth is central to Miller's thought, and it usually is tied, directly or indirectly, to the escape from America to Paris, from hope to unhope, from success to failure. For Miller does not consider that his writing is in any sense of the word a "good work," whereby he hopes to earn the approval of his neighbors. In the first page of what is probably his best single book, "Tropic of Cancer," he announces his rejection of literature. "I have no money, no resources, no hopes. I am the happiest man alive. A year ago, six months ago, I thought that I was an artist. I no longer think about it. I *am*. Everything that was literature has fallen from me. There are no more books to be written, thank God.

"This then? This is not a book. This is libel, slander, defamation of character. This is not a book. . . . This is a prolonged insult, a gob of spit in the face of Art, a kick in the pants to God, Man, Destiny, Time, Love, Beauty . . . what you will."

It is, in other words, aimed precisely and destructively at all that we think of as Literature. In the biographical note at the end of "The Cosmological Eye," the first book of Henry Miller to be published in the United States, he declares: "I use destruction creatively . . . but aiming always towards a real, inner harmony, an inner peace—and silence. . . . Ninety-nine percent of what is written—and this goes for all our art products—should be destroyed. I want to be read by less and less people; I have no interest in the life of the masses, nor in the intentions of the existing governments of the world. I hope and believe that the whole civilized world will be wiped out in the next hundred years or so. I believe that man can exist, and in an infinitely better, larger way, without 'civilization.' "

Art, then, exists, not for its own sake, nor for ours, but for Miller's; and if the man who is Henry Miller has failed to the world, he may yet have succeeded to himself, who has become the object of his faith.

I am not the first to remark that, as pure theology, American Calvinism is a mess, a maze of contradictions, a chaos of impossibly opposed forces, a jungle of unresolved conflicts. In these respects, it resembles Miller's work, about which we could say many of the same things. I shall not attempt to resolve the illogicalities, to reconcile the opposing forces, or even to diminish the conflicts. The most I can hope to do is to offer some basis for understanding the conflicts, and perhaps thereby to suggest the significance and value that such an understanding may offer us.

One of the great conflicts in American Puritanism was between a mystical view of experience and a practical one. We find both impulses existing side by side in the early Puritan—one part of him is drawn toward the mystical being of God, and the other toward what is clearly a projection of God's strange will, the world itself. The Puritan conflict between idealism and realism is perhaps only another aspect of this earlier polarity, but it does have a peripheral identity in itself; in the Puritan ethic, that which exists in nature tends to be in conflict with that which exists in God's mind—hence our half-conscious aversion to sexuality, to bodily matters, to spontaneity, and to those shapes of flux and change that we must observe in natural processes. Yet the American Puritan found himself confronted with a natural world that he had to take with the utmost seriousness, if he was to survive; and in America, at least, the reconciliation of God and Nature has been an uneasy one.

And so has been the reconciliation of the conflict between aggressiveness and submission. Aggressiveness is supposed to be an almost exclusively American characteristic; and yet along with that aggressiveness, so often noted by foreign visitors, there is a deep strain of submissiveness that disguises itself in a number of ways. We may not willingly submit to fate, or even to simple fact; but we will almost without question submit to our neighbors' opinions of us. This, of course, is only a reflection of another pattern of aggression and submission; the Puritan had, by dogma, to submit to God's will; but, if he were to survive, he could not submit to the world—to nature, to the hostile environment that surrounded him; and, finally, in the historical evolution of Puritanism, he found himself in the curious position of becoming aggressive in the acquisition of worldly goods, the worldly goods being God's outward manifestation of inward Grace, and hence the sign of the aggressor's submission to God's will.

We need only to read in Cotton Mather's "Diaries" to find a recurring conflict between what might be called the apocalyptic vision and the practical vision, and between the impulse toward contemplative self-revelation and externalized activity. Certainly in a world view that is as rigidly deterministic as the American Calvinist's, the impulse toward the apocalyptic vision is inevitable; for if the course of the world is determined by God's will, and if that will is immutable, then one can predict events and make prophecies; for everything observable is a part of a meaning, and may be interpreted; a mouse gnawing through a Bible is a portent of whatever Mather can make of it, and the simple incompetence of a servant affords a prophetic view of things to come in the world at large.

But perhaps more important for our purposes is the Puritan conflict between self-examination, self-appraisal, and introspection, on the one hand, and practical, externalized activity and an examination of the world, on the other. Such a conflict sprang out of a psychological necessity imposed by the tenets of Puritanism itself; for if man's fate, his election or damnation, heaven or hell, was wholly at the mercy of God's whim, or his arbitrary will, and if the only evidence of that fate were those hints that God might place before the consciousness of man himself, then man inevitably would find one of his major occupations in constantly examining the state of his own soul, and at the same time examining those manifestations of the external world which impinged upon him and offered some hints as to his salvation or lack of it. Thus the external world, to the Puritan, was in one respect intimately linked to man's own internal being, and he tended to see the external world in terms of himself.

This view of the self and the world is everywhere observable in Henry Miller's work. It is not too much to say that virtually everything worthwhile and genuine in Miller is involved with Miller himself. George Orwell, an early admirer, praised Miller extravagantly for his social criticism, especially in the early "Tropics"; but what Orwell failed to understand, or at least to mention, was that Miller's social criticism was vital and worthwhile only when Miller himself was personally involved in the conditions of which he was writing. When he writes abstractly against social conditions in which he is not involved immediately and directly—as, for example, when he writes about war, which he is against—his remarks have all the depth and intensity of those we might find in a Sunday supplement article, or in a Time magazine essay. Unless his own person is immediately concerned, he is likely to be trite, unimaginative, verbose, or excruciatingly literary.

Everyone who has read the "Tropic" trilogy, and especially the "Tropic of Capricorn," has no doubt remarked the almost mechanical alternation of method—the rather long, naturalistic passages interspersed with equally long passages of self-revelation and self-exploration. Narrative and introspection, scene and revery; this is the structure, insofar as the books have a very definable structure. And part of the point I am trying to make about this structure is that the two modes are never really integrated; they remain in tense opposition, no doubt because the impulses remain in some opposition within Miller himself.

If one is still unsure of this matter, one has only to read Miller's so-called travel book on Greece, "The Colossus of Maroussi"; it is one of the most extraordinary travel books ever written, surpassing even Lawrence's study of "Etruscan Places" for its egoism and self-concern. Though passages of self-revelation and description are alternated, we soon become painfully aware that Miller is really concerned only with himself, and Greece is important insofar as that country and its landscape are capable of eliciting responses from him upon love, death, sex, the peasant, war, life, literature, time, poverty, America, or whatever else Miller might have within him, needing release.

And there are dozens of other confusions, or conflicts, or polarities in Miller's work that have been noted, and condemned or justified, by nearly everyone who has read him. The most vulgar, low, and colloquial language that we can imagine exists immediately alongside the most intellectual and literary language that we can also imagine; I take it that this is, among other things, a reflection of that conflict between idealism and realism that I mentioned earlier. Apocalyptic vision, nightmare, and phantasy exist immediately alongside passages of the utmost practicality and naturalism; this, I take it, is a reflection of that Puritan conflict between mysticism and practicality. And passages of the utmost sentimentality jostle passages of utter cynicism: Miller is almost endearingly American in his view that all prostitutes—at least all French prostitutes—have hearts of gold, and he is capable of rhapsodizing for pages upon their essential virtues; and at the same time he is capable of describing with relish his bilking them of their earnings and of viewing their degradation with pitiless and sometimes eager enjoyment.

Like the Puritan, he feels himself to be an alienated being, a man on the outside, looking for a way in. As the Puritan made a kind of occupation out of self-examination and an elaborate questioning of his relationship to God, so Miller's whole work is an occupation of self-examination and elaborate questioning of his relation to—what? Miller cannot say, and neither can we. But we can say this: whereas the Puritan, in his effort to allay that deepening sense of alienation, moved closer and closer to the world as it was, and felt less and less the theological impossibility of doing so, Miller has seemed to move farther and farther away from the world and its dictates and its demands—has moved deeper and deeper into himself, into his own impulses, his own wishes, and his own visions. He has moved aggressively upon the world, in what he has called an act of creative destruction, so that he might become more submissive to the dictates of himself.

It is customary in a paper such as this, which attempts a general survey of the work of a man, to arrive at a simple critical judgment of the value of that man's work. I must confess an inability to arrive at such a simple judgment, and I make the confession with a little chagrin, though I must admit that the chagrin is tinged with irony. For it is a judgment that should be easy, one way or the other. After all, several things are unequivocal and clear. Miller is, and has been for several years, one of the most extravagantly praised (and damned) of all modern writers: for Lawrence Durrell, "American literature today begins and ends with the meaning of what Miller has done"; for Karl Shapiro "Miller is the greatest living writer"; and for Kenneth Rexroth he is to be "ranked with Balzac, Goethe, and Baudelaire."

But beyond this praise it is clear that Miller as a writer is guilty of virtually every major fault that is possible for a writer to be guilty of. Stylistically, his work is a botch: he is incredibly prolix and repetitive, and many of his best effects are lost in jungles of approximate language; he is capable of an elephantine diction that sometimes makes Theodore Dreiser seem almost Flaubertian; the so-called "experimental" passages in his works often appear to be the kind of parodies, intentional or accidental, that the editors of a popular magazine might make upon some of the lesser Dadaists and Surrealists that in the twenties appeared in *transition* magazine; and he is capable of sentimentalities that would make a virginal New England school-teacher of a certain age blush with shame. He has almost no sense of structure, in either his longer or his shorter works: his work suffers from literary giantism, or disproportion, and one often has the dark suspicion that a passage is long or short, according to whether or not Miller might have been interrupted while writing it; and his solutions to structural problems are naïve to an extreme degree. Apparently conscious of the disorganization that dominates his work, he evokes the metaphor of a river, declaring that he "loves everything that flows," and attempts to justify his garrulous prose by that sentiment. He is incapable of constructing a dramatic scene, and he has no sense of character—except his own—and no ability to transmit the sense of another human being—except himself—to his reader. He is at his worst when he is most serious—that is, when he wishes his "ideas" to be taken seriously,—ideas which are, beneath the sometimes outrageous verbiage, so commonplace and old-fashioned as to be almost bewildering. And of the various costumes he wears—that of the innocent pornographer, the American abroad, the raucous prophet, the apocalyptic comedian, the outsider, the rebel, and the clown—none seems to fit him really closely. It is as if he had picked each of them up at some vast metaphysical rummage sale to wear as his mood suits him.

But after all this has been duly noted, and after we have read Miller, none of it seems really to matter; for cautious as we may be, we are left with the disturbing suspicion that we have been in the presence of an authentic genius, though a genius unlike any we have encountered in literature before. For in one respect, at least, we must take Miller at his word: he is not engaged in the act of writing literature. His work is, indeed, at bottom anti-literary, and anti-literary in a profound way that the Dadaists—those cultivated, highly educated, most humorous nihilists—could never have understood.

Miller's task has been, quite simply, to reveal himself, and to reveal himself as immediately and fully as his time and energy will allow him to do. Himself is the only subject he has ever had, and most of the time he has had the wit to know this, and not to pretend otherwise, at least to himself. He is not a novelist, and could never have been; for a good novelist must, perhaps, be offensively egotistic—that is to say, filled with pride and perhaps irrationally convinced of his own powers; but he cannot be egotistic—that is to say, so obsessed with the exclusive sense of his own identity that other identities have little reality, except insofar as they impinge upon him. And Miller is so consumed with a sense of his own identity that the question of his powers, or even the usual pride in his literary abilities, never really occurs to him. Nor, given his egoism, could he have been a philosopher, a social critic, an essayist—in short, he could not have been a writer, in the ordinary sense of that word.

Thus, seen in terms of its subject, the formlessness of his work begins to take on a new significance, so that the question of justification hardly arises. In a very real sense Miller is not engaged in writing books, or essays, or stories, or romances, or autobiographies, or whatever—he is engaged in writing, or revealing, himself, just as he is, or just as he thinks he is, at a given moment. And in Miller's view, to commit that self to a given literary form would be to betray it most profoundly; for finally he is not concerned that we see what he, Miller, *thinks* is true about himself; he wants us to see the thing itself.

And out of Miller's colossal, almost heroic egoism, the subject, Miller, is shown to us, not as a symbol of anything, not as a kind of everyman, but simply as itself. Miller never allows the integrity of his subject to be vitiated by lowering it to the level of myth or symbol; had he done so, it is likely that his work would have been without value to us.

It remains for me to suggest something of the nature of that character, that presence which constitutes the real subject of all that Miller has written; for it is in the nature of the subject that the significance of Miller lies.

I have said that at the center of Miller's work, and hence at the center of Miller himself, lies a set of polarities that curiously resemble the polarities found embedded in historical American Puritanism; but in saying that, I was not attempting to do anything very special, nor to imply any "mythic" quality to Miller's work. For the Puritan dilemma lies very near the center of the American experience, particularly at the center of what we might call uninformed American experience. And the polarities that we see in Miller are versions of the polarities that we encounter every day, in ourselves and in the life around us.

Miller's character is extraordinary in only one respect: and that is that it is so ordinary. This darling of the avant-garde, this prototype of the twentieth-century rebel, this almost legendary man, this candidate for the Nobel Prize—he is the most ordinary figure that we can readily imagine. Except for the fact that we have him on paper, we have seen him everywhere in America, if we have cared to look: the son of lower-middle-class immigrant parents, who for the first forty years of his life lived a lower-middle-class life, on the periphery of a middle-class society, with the usual ambivalent attitudes toward middle-class values and aspirations—a man indifferently educated, whose reading is scattered and eccentric and not really very wide— a man who had that most common of aspirations, to be a successful writer (what more middle-class ambition can there be?), and who, like most who have that aspiration, failed—and a man, finally, who, confronted with the failure that his life had become, found within himself a deep and compelling reservoir of indifference to all that he had been taught that mattered. We see such men around us every day—men who finally have been forced to the great freedom of genuinely not giving a damn; and we look at them with our ambivalence of contempt and envy.

But within the ordinariness that is the character of Henry Miller, what a vast humanity, finally, we find; and what a vast generosity of spirit. With the compulsive honesty that is possible only to the heroic egoist, Miller shows us this fleck of humanity in the chaotic arena of kindness and cruelty, sentimentality and cynicism, pretension and simplicity, tenderness and ob- scenity, suffering and ecstasy, hypocrisy and sincerity, falsity and truth, that is, humanity itself. And if finally we are shocked by Miller we are shocked because we see, in unflinching and crude and graphic terms, written upon the page, beyond our evasion, simply ourselves, our selves that we hide from others and too often from ourselves; we see what we have made of ourselves, out of our time and circumstance; our real shock comes from nothing other than a glimpse of our persistent, affirmative, essentially amoral, and un- homogenized humanity.

In what we may think of as a typically American way, with what we may even call Yankee ingenuity, Henry Miller has made a success of his failure. The ten years of his life in America before he went to Europe, ten years when his sense of worldly failure steadily increased into his saving despair, and the ten years he spent in Europe as an itinerant menial, beggar, and hack writer,—these years are the vital center of his work, and hence of his life. He made of these years of failure his great success, which is his work, which is himself. And he has shown us the degree to which a man can be free, even in the prison of his ideas and attitudes, his time and circumstance.

As has Thoreau, whose name I evoked at the beginning of this essay. But the parallels I have drawn between certain aspects of the thought of the two men obviously break down; and the dissimilarities in the later stages of both their careers are perhaps even more enlightening than the early resemblances. Miller left Europe and returned to the United States in the winter of 1940; Thoreau left Walden Pond and returned to Concord in the summer of 1847. For both men, the times away from their homes were the climactic periods of their literary lives, and their significant and vital work comes out of those times of exile.

But the end of Thoreau's life was dramatically unlike these late years of Miller's life. During his last two years, Thoreau was ill with tuberculosis, and he spent much of this time preparing a last group of essays for publication in The Atlantic Monthly. He did not live to see them appear there, but had he done so, he would have noted no untoward response to their publication. His first book—"A Week on the Concord and Merrimac"—was a failure from the beginning, and even "Walden" found but a very small body of readers during Thoreau's lifetime; most of his poems were not published, and those few that were went unnoticed; and his other essays were read as fugitive pieces in magazines. Thoreau died with the kind of worldly failure that he had, out of principle, courted for nearly all his life.

For the last several years, Henry Miller has been living in California. He is now a famous writer; he is moderately wealthy, sought after, widely admired and read; there is even a Henry Miller Society. Recently he was made a member of the American Institute of Arts and Letters, an eminently distinguished affair, our nearest equivalent to the Académie Française; I understand that he was pleased by his election. Miller has been living in a large modern house near Los Angeles; the house is most comfortably furnished, and like many southern California homes it has a large swimming pool on the spacious grounds. In his new prosperity, Miller has written almost nothing. But he is comfortable now, and I suppose at last he has earned his ironic success, which a few years ago he might have thought of as his damnation.

MILLER RECONSIDERED

◆

Letters from *Art and Outrage: A Correspondence About Henry Miller*

ALFRED PERLÈS, LAWRENCE DURRELL, and HENRY MILLER

FROM ALFRED PERLÈS TO LAWRENCE DURRELL

Dear Larry,

You ask me, and yourself, what he's like, but I'm afraid there's no ready answer. And if he himself told you what he was like his answer could not but be misleading. What's a kaleidoscope like if not unto itself? Always different but always the kaleidoscope: a million and one facets upon which, turn by turn, an accenting ray puts a varying emphasis. The attempt to coagulate all the possible image combinations into one rigid picture is as hopeless as trying to gauge the number and scope of all the books that can be written with the 26 letters of the alphabet. The number is infinite, and we'd be wasting our time looking for Henry in a haystack of Henrys. The *Happy Rock*, as you observed in your previous letter, reflects only an infinitesimal fraction of Henrys, all valid, none complete.

To get at his essence, a different approach seems necessary. Just interpreting the *intentions* of his work, does not strike me as efficacious for the purpose, either. For what exactly *are* his intentions? Has he any, in the first place? I'm inclined to doubt it. Intention diminishes the artist. Genius is unintentional. The sun does not *intend* to radiate heat, it radiates it. To my perhaps illogical thinking the term "intention" savours of propaganda, proselytism, promotion of ideas, etc., and somehow I prefer to think of Henry's work as intentionless. It's this intentionlessness, too, which accounts for his multiple "masks"!

As for his autobiographical form of self-expression, can you conceive a work of art—a poem, a symphony, or even a novel—that is not autobiographical? Any true work of art must needs be of an autobiographical nature, except perhaps in the case of a cathedral, which is anonymous. But none of Henry's masks can be said to be anonymous. *Alors?* His solipsism cannot be compared, by way of situating him in the mountain range of literature, with

The following three letters reprinted from Lawrence Durrell, Alfred Perlès, and Henry Miller, *Art and Outrage: A Correspondence About Henry Miller* (London: Putnam, 1959), 18–33. The first letter reprinted by permission of Anne T. Barret (Perlès).

that of other autobiographers, if for no other reason than his uniqueness. Apart from their respective uniqueness I can see no affinity between Henry, Rousseau, De Sade, Casanova etc. His sense of humour is only superficially germane to Rabelais's; for apart from the four centuries between them there's also a difference in the emphasis of their sense of humour: Henry's humour was born in the guts, Rabelais's in Holy Orders. And I refuse to consider Henry's evolution from the fleshly to the spiritual as a significant trait. Normally, such evolution would strike me as slightly suspect; nothing easier than to turn "spiritual" a fortnight before impotence sets in. Of course, this isn't Henry's case: the spiritual is always latent in the flesh and vice versa, even in the rowdiest passages of the *Tropics*. If a genius can at all be akin to any other genius, which I doubt, I should compare him to Till Eulenspiegel or the Hauptmann Von Köpernick rather than any of the solipsists you mention. In the exploits of the legendary captain, especially, there is something of the *acte-gratuit* nonchalance which, transposed to the literary level, is strongly reminiscent of Henry's narrative writings.

Why is it, I keep asking myself, that I am so wary of tackling him from a purely literary point of view? It isn't that I have nothing to say about him as a writer—far from it! But is it, should it be, our object to restrict these epistolary exchanges to literary criticism? There will always be critics, even a hundred years hence, ready and eager to dissect, analyse, interpret and misinterpret his work, but there won't always be you and I who knew the man before he turned into a legend. If we want to do him a service I feel we must look at his work through the man and pin him down without any possible literary loopholes. Unless we succeed in doing that the clue to his work would still be missing.

Let me put it another way; Henry's work, in its ensemble, strikes me as a huge crossword puzzle which can only be solved correctly if solved differently by each of his serious readers. Our job is to give them the clues, the 6 across, and 3 down etc. But they must fill in the words themselves; I dare say they prefer it this way. I, for one, get always irritated when some busybody leaning over my shoulders prompts me when I do the *Times* crosswords. Each of the clues we thus give would point to one of the "masks." No fear that we will unmask him completely but if we can manage to tear off, say fifty or seventy masks out of five or nine hundred, *ça sera toujours ça de gagné, non?*

To come to the point, I feel that Henry Miller is one of those peculiar geniuses who must be approached from the human rather than the literary end; it is the human being, in all his aspects, who reveals the artist, explains the genius. The failure of literary criticism, at least in England and America, to gauge the portent of his work, to apprehend the fundamental simplicity of his writings, is due to the fact that Henry cannot be shanghaied into any literary category. The critics, sensing that they're up against some intangible force, resent this and half unconsciously try to diminish his worth, attacking now his *simpliste* attitude, now his bogus philosophy, now his pornography. I am not trying to belittle the critics, who have no doubt been to the best schools and are certainly no morons. But it is easy for them to scoff at him: it's easy to scoff at a quack in all civilised sincerity and indignation, even when the quack achieves results in hopeless cases where the bona fide doctors give up in despair. Don't forget that it takes a hundred years, and often longer, for a saint to get canonised.

It is a fact that Henry invariably appeals to the pure at heart—to simple human beings albeit ignoramuses. That letter you sent me from Alexandros Venetikos, guardian of the Phaestos ruins, is significant in this respect: as significant as the hundreds of letters he received as personnel manager of the Western Union long before his first book was published (I believe we reprinted one of those letters in the *Booster*); as significant, too, as your urge to kiss the non-existing door knob at Villa Seurat. It is the love he inspires in the hearts of simple human beings which stands at the threshold of his genius. It is this love, too, which accounts for the fact that his genius does not always get through in his works. It is useless, therefore, to argue about him with those young men you mention, whose traditional and cultural pragmatism removes them from Henry's intrinsic vision. But the Alexandros Venetikoses will always sense his genius in their hearts and succumb to his colossal impact where the critics turn up their noses at him in refined disgust.

The clues. . . . Has it ever struck you how serious he always is in his commerce with children? I am not thinking now of his own children (though I had occasion to observe him in his intercourse with Tony and Val, which I found rather revelatory of the man); I am thinking of the trust he used to put in children long before he had any of his own. Walking the Paris streets with him I was often surprised when he would go to a child for directions rather than a grown-up or an *agent de police*, who might have directed him much better. Sometimes he would address a very small street urchin who couldn't possibly, one might think, have known what he wanted and was at first inclined to start screaming at his atrocious accent. Yet he always elicited an intelligent answer in the end; not even the most infantile practical joker would have sent him on a wild-goose chase for the street round the corner. I couldn't help marvelling at this. There was something about him, something of the endearing alienness of the spaceman, that conquered the malice of the most moronic infant. He brought the goodness out of the child, if you know what I mean: the same goodness he later brought out of Mademoiselle Claude (who was a whore), and Max (who was a spiv). And this, it seems to me, is a significant clue to Henry the human being *and* the artist. Why is it that he was always surrounded by morons and helpless neurotics if not to make them whole again, at least in his writings? Those he couldn't make whole, the Borises etc., had only themselves to blame: you can't cure a leper if the leper refuses to believe he's suffering from leprosy.

You seem amazed at Henry's self-confessed *pudeur* but the thing doesn't come as a surprise to me; I always knew it was there. I should imagine that every real artist has it. In the lesser artist it assumes the guise of tact or nicety. It isn't modesty, for no modest person could talk about his *pudeur* in the context Henry does. *Pudeur*, in the sense he probably means it, is not a sense of shame, an obscure remnant of the original sin, but a sort of priestly reluctance to reveal the contents of the tabernacle. For Henry, who doesn't adhere to any religious sect, who has torn up his spiritual passport as it were, is high-priest nevertheless. God, with him, suffers no intermediary; his footprints are all over Mount Sinai.

Fred.

FROM LAWRENCE DURRELL TO ALFRED PERLÈS

Dear Joe,

I agree with you about "intentions" in the sense of conscious and didactic purpose of a moral or philosophic kind. I meant something like *gestalt*—for of course our author is himself growing with his work, and his views about its own scope and meaning have broadened and deepened since the day when, with *Tropic of Cancer*, he cracked through the sound-barrier and found himself; he himself described *Tropic* as a gob of spit, a kick in the pants to Art, Truth etc. And there is no denying that it is a destructive book in a fecundating sense; but if it is tonic and inspiring it is because of the exultation that shines through it—the exultation of someone who revaluated the basic human values for himself, and emerged with a human morality of his very own, founded in his own bodily and spiritual experience.

I would not press any such general criticism on you (you know I hate criticism) were it not for the fact that we are discussing works which are not available to the reader, and it seems to me rather important to establish that Henry isn't another Sade or another Restif. Wherein does he differ? I think it important to stress that he is primarily a religious writer—which sounds of course a laughable paradox. And here I come to what I would call the basic intention behind his use of obscenity. He has effected an imaginative junction between the obscene and the holy—not exactly a new thing to the East but new and rather off-putting to the prurient West. The Ancient Greeks, for example . . . There was a shrine to Heracles in Rhodes which the devout could only approach uttering a whole litany of obscenities! In Rozanov I read that the central mystery of the Jewish faith centres about a word (did he call it "mikvah"? I have no books here) which is both the holiest and the most obscene of words at the same time. It is some of this terror and mystery that Henry conveys I think in his self-confessions and I suspect that later ages may read *Sexus*, parts of which are quite horripilating, with some of the patient awe that devotees visit those great Indian rock-cathedrals with their obscene-religious sculpture. Don't you think this is worth saying? At least someone who grasps the point will come to his work alertly and without prejudice and not feel he is just being insulted and spat upon. . . . I also think this factor explains Henry's own passion for the Eastern religious systems, for only these holy men would be able to read his spiritual adventure without prejudice, and would regard his books as a spiritual autobiography. A Japanese public seems no accident to me.

This is, to me, doubly important to state as in books like *Sexus* there is no specific statement of any such intention, and one has to read his essays out of the corner of the eye in order to sense the truth. Myself I had reservations about *Sexus* which turned upon this point; I felt that he had taken all the data about himself as equally important simply because it happened to him, and that a good deal of it added nothing to the pattern of this important book; it lay there unevaluated, as it were. But this is a criticism of craft. But the key to everything seems to me to be self-liberation and self-discovery—an important religious and artistic bias of mind. And surely this is what Keyserling meant by the telegram he sent him ("I salute a free spirit").

Nor could he have been anything but an Anglo-Saxon writer for only here and there in Europe does the printer's tabu have the same power as over ourselves and the Americans; the French, for example, are never shocked—but either interested or just plain disgusted. I think in *Sexus* a Frenchman would only deplore lack of volupté and tenderness. He doesn't look out for the "morally ennobling" but is rapidly disgusted by the coarseness of the Anglo-Saxon psyche. Moreover he sees most of our strains and stresses as fundamentally *laughable*—the result of living the wrong way. I have always found that the struggle of Lawrence isn't easily comprehended in Europe, because the Europeans are adults and are more amused than frightened of people in their pipi caca stage. But whether the French critics have evaluated Henry in these terms (I mean the religious) I don't really know; or whether they admire him as a tremendous creative writer. They are rather prone to admire a talent at the expense of a new temperament, a creative man *sui generis*.

This said, only a line or two about the masks. Certainly I did see several people peeping out of Henry. The most endearing were of course the childish ones—the clown, the American tourist, the gullible one (deliberately: did ever anyone enjoy so much being "taken in"? He never was, of course.) I also saw Mishkin, and once I caught a glimpse of the frightened man in the *Letters From The Underworld* . . . what was his name? But I think the best portrait of all—I mean the silhouette of his personality—is given by the character Sylvia on p. 54 of *Sexus*. I copy it out with a few light cuts (not for four-letter reasons, but because of length) . . .

". . . You will cause a lot of harm to others in defending yourself from your own fears and doubts. You are not even sure at this moment that you will go back to the woman you love. I have poisoned your mind. You would drop her like that if you were sure that you could do what you wanted without her aid. But you need her and you will call it love. . . . Because the woman can never give you what you want you make yourself out to be a martyr. A woman wants love and you are incapable of giving love. If you were a lower type of man you would be a monster; but you will convert your frustration into something useful. Yes, by all means go on writing. Art can transform the hideous into the beautiful. Better a monstrous book than a monstrous life. If you don't die in the attempt your work might transform you into a sociable, charitable human being. You are big enough not to be satisfied with mere fame, I can see that. Probably when you have lived enough you will discover that there is something beyond what you now call life. You may yet live to live for others. That depends on what use you make of your intelligence, for you are not as intelligent as you think you are. That is your weakness, overweening intellectual pride. . . . You have all the feminine virtues but you are ashamed to acknowledge them to yourself. You think because you are strong sexually that you are a virile man but you are more of a woman than a man. Your sexual virility is only the sign of a higher power which you haven't begun to use. Don't try to prove yourself a man by exploiting your sexual powers. Women are not fooled by that sort of strength and charm. Women, even when they are subjugated mentally, are always master of the situation. A woman may be enslaved sexually and yet dominate the man. You will have a harder time than other men because to dominate another doesn't interest you. You will always be trying to dominate yourself; the woman you love will only be an instrument for you to practise on. . . ."

I wonder if you will think all this nonsense?

Larry.

From Henry Miller to Lawrence Durrell

Dear Larry,

Your two letters to Fred, of which you so thoughtfully sent me carbons, excite me no end. Not because it's about *me*, but because of the nature of the project. What a task! Of course, you won't really get anywhere, you know. Take that for granted immediately—and you'll travel far and enjoy it.

There are many, many things come to my mind at the outset. Helpful hints and clues, for the most part. Though I trust you understand that I too

have difficulty putting my finger on "it," making the right, eternal statement. But I can offer some correctives and some new tacks, perhaps.

One of the first things that hits me between the eyes is this effort you
are making to discover the "intention." You speak of the difficulty of explaining or placing me with the younger generation. And with it you couple
this business of morality and iconoclasm. As the recipient of thousands of
letters, most of them from young people, I get such a different picture.
(Could it be that there is this difference in comprehension between the British
and the American youth?) At any rate, the young who write me do "get"
me to an amazing extent. Naturally, they "identify" with me, particularly
those who are trying to express themselves. But how interesting it is that
the same situations are at work eternally and eternally molding new artists.
One could almost sum it up, like Lawrence, and say our troubles are largely,
almost exclusively, societal. The social pattern remains the same, fundamentally, despite all the dazzling changes we have witnessed. It gets more
thwarting all the time—for the born individualist. And, as you know, I am
interested—like God—only in the individual.

One of the things which irks me most, with the critics, is the statement
you throw out—about being unlike myself.

This is simply impossible. I don't care who the artist is, if you study
him deeply, sincerely, detachedly, you will find that he and his work are
one. If it were otherwise the planets would be capable of leaving their orbits.
I think your trouble may lie here, that the part of me you don't know from
direct experience—I mean the me of youth, of long before we met—you
tend to idealize. The man you met in the Villa Seurat was a kind of monster,
in a way, in that he was in the process of transformation. He had become
partially civilized, so to speak. The tensions had eased up, he could be
himself, and his own, natural self was, at the risk of being immodest, what
you always sense and respect in me. (To myself I always think I was born
"ultra-civilized." Another way of saying it, a more invidious way, would of
course be to say that I was over-sensitive.) And I suppose it is always the
over-sensitive creatures who, if they are bent on surviving, grow the toughest
hides. This tough hide revealed itself in my case, more in what I passively
permitted to be done for me and to me than by what I did of my own
volition—vindictively, outrageously, and so on. The coward in me always
concealed himself in that thick armor of dull passivity. I only grew truly
sensitive again when I had attained a certain measure of liberation.

I don't want to embark on another autobiographical fragment! Stop me,
for God's sake. If I let myself go it is only because with the years I get new
visions of myself, new vistas, and their one value to me is that they are more
inclusive pictures of the parts that go to make the whole—the enigmatic
whole.

Here I disgress a moment to mention a noticeable difference in the
reactions of Europeans to my work. Seldom do they, for instance, speak of

these "discrepancies." Perhaps they have had too much contact with discordant authors all their lives. They seem to realize, without mentioning it, that all the contrarieties of make-up and attitude are the leaven necessary to the making of the bread. When they are shocked, to take another example, it is because of the language itself, what has been done to it and with it by the author, not by the moral or immoral implications of this language. There is a difference, do you see? And when I say shocked, I mean in a healthy, agreeable way. It is an aesthetic shock, if you like, but one which vibrates throughout their whole being.

And here, all the young, and often the old too, are unanimous in writing of the therapeutic value of my work. They were altered. They thank me, bless me, bless me for "just being," as they often say.

But to come back to "intentions." It is almost classic what I have to say on this score. I know it all by heart, and when you read again, if you read with this in mind, you too will see it very clearly.

(Oh, yes, but before I forget—one important thing! Remember always that, with the exception of "Cancer," I am writing counter-clockwise. My starting-point will be my end point—the arrival in Paris—or, in another way of speaking, the breakthrough. So what I am telling about is the story of a man you never met, never knew; he is mostly of a definite period, from the time he met June (Mona-Mara) until he leaves for Paris. Naturally, some of what he is at the time of writing comes to the fore. Inevitable. But the attempt is—I am talking only of the auto-novels, of course—to be and act the man I was during this seven-year period. From this segment of time I am able to look backward and forward. Very much as our own time is described—the Janus period, the turning-point, where both avenues become clear and recognizable—at least to those who see and think. Oof!)

I wanted so much, so much, to be a writer (maybe not to write so much as to *be* a writer). And I doubt that I ever would have become one had it not been for the tragedy with June. Even then, even when I knew I would and could, my intention was to do nothing more than tell the story of those years with her, what it had done to me, to my soul, if you like. Because it was the damage to the soul, I must tell you, that was the all. (And I doubt if I have made that at all clear in my writings!) And so, on the fateful day, in the Park Department of Queen's County, N.Y. I mapped out the whole autobiographical romance—in one sitting. And I have stuck to it amazingly well, considering the pressures this way and that. (The hardest part is coming—*Nexus*—where I must reveal myself for what I was—something less than zero, something worse than the lowest knave.)

With June I could not begin this magnum opus which, as you know, I thought would be just one enormous, endless tome—perhaps bigger than the Bible. My suffering was so great—and my ego too, no doubt—that I imagined it needed a canvas of that scope.

Note: *My* suffering I say. For *then* I was concerned with what had been done *to me*. As I wrote, of course, I began to perceive that what I had done to others was far more heinous. Whoever greatly suffers must be, I suppose, a sublime combination of sadist and masochist. Fred easily perceived the masochist that I was. But neither you nor he see so easily the sadist. Fred has touched on it in a subtly diabolical way—really too exalted to suit my case, I think. It was plainer, coarser than that. (But here you are up against the dilemma of not being privy to the facts of my life; it is my word as a man and a writer, against the apperceptions of readers and critics and psychologists. I admit that I have the power to warp what I honestly think may be the truth about my thoughts and actions. But I do believe I am nearer the mark than the outsider.)

So, as you hint, I coined this word Truth. The key to my whole work to be the utter truth. And, as you realize, I found it easier to give the truth about the ugly side of my nature than the good. The good in me I only know as it is reflected back to me in the eyes and voices of those I talk to.

Whether I *then* knew what later I have come to know absolutely is a question, namely—the words of Jesus, that the truth shall set ye free. If I had only set myself to tell the truth about myself, that would have been fine. But I also wanted to tell the truth about others, about the world. And that's the greatest snare of all: it sets you above the others if not precisely above the world. Time and again I try to cut myself down. You all know how I rant and rave. There's always some truth in these outbursts, to be sure, but how caricatural!

Yet I do feel that truth is linked to violence. Truth is the naked sword; it cuts clean through. And what is it we are fighting, who love truth so much? The lie of the world. A perpetual lie. But I'm going off again . . .

Let me tell you something more simple and yet revealing. I said I wanted nothing more of God than the power to write. Yes, this began in my late teens, I imagine. In my early twenties, confined to my father's shop, a slave to the most idiotic kind of routine imaginable, I broke out—inside. Inwardly I was a perpetual volcano. I will never forget the walks to and from my father's shop every day: the tremendous dialogues I had with my "characters," the scenes I portrayed, and so on. And never a line of any of this ever put to paper. Where would you begin if you were a smothered volcano?

And then, after the first attempt at a book—when with the Western Union and married to that woman B———, my first wife—I dream of making my entry into the lists—by the back door. To write something that will sell, that people will read, that will permit me to say—"There is my name signed to it, you see." Proof.

And then the break, thanks to June, the plunge. And I am free, spoon-fed, have leisure, paper, everything, but can't do it. Oh yes, I do write, but how painfully, and how poorly, how imitatively. And then when June left for France with her friend Jean Kronski, then I broke, then I mapped out my whole career. And even then, think of it, even after leaving for France, three years later, I still do not begin that great work. I write *Tropic of Cancer*, which was not in the schema—but of the moment. I suppose one could liken it to the volcano's eruption, to the breaking of the crust. (Only, let me say it as knows, it was such a feeble eruption compared to those imaginary street-walking ones I had every day, inwardly, walking to and from my father's shop!)

How well I know the tremendous décalage between what one wishes to do and what one does! Nowhere in my work have I come anywhere near to expressing what I meant to express. Now, if you can believe this, and I am sure you must because you must also suffer it, then imagine what sort of beast it is that a woman, any woman, has to live with who marries a writer. Imagine what happens to one who never says all, never does all, who smiles and nods his head in that civilized way and is all the while a raging bull. Well, what happens is that either the writer gains the upper hand eventually, or the man. One or the other must take the lead. My effort has been to give the lead to the man in me. (With what success others know best.) But there is no war involved, you must understand. It is rather a matter of leaning more this way than that, of shifting the emphasis, and so forth.

And I do not want to be a saint! Morality, in fact, drops out of the picture. Maybe the writer will drop out too. Or the man. Never the ego, rest assured. Nor do I give a damn about that.

I certainly do not hope to alter the world. Perhaps I can put it best by saying that I hope to alter my own vision of the world. I want to be more and more myself, ridiculous as that may sound.

Where the writing is concerned, I did nothing consciously. I followed my nose. I blew with every wind. I accepted every influence, good or bad. My intention, was there—as I said, merely to write. Or, *to be a writer*, more justly. Well, I've been it. Now I just want—to be. Remember, I beg you, that this infinitive is "transitive" in Chinese. And I am nothing if not Chinese.

Does this help? If not, walk on—and over me.

Henry.

Next day—April 2nd.
It's pouring and I feel like saying a bit more. . . .

Those fan letters I spoke of. If someone had the courage to publish these, volume after volume, what a broadside that would be. And how revealing! Here are the books which readers say have influenced them, enlarged their outlook on life, altered their being: The Colossus, Capricorn, Cancer, Wisdom of the Heart—primarily. But there are others in which *I* believe I have given most revelatory passages: the Books in my Life, Rimbaud, the Hamlet letters, even Aller-Retour New York. And in The Brooklyn

Bridge—where is that?—I am astounded each time I read it by what I have said "unknowingly."

There is another too, quite important: "The World of Sex." Noone has ever written me *against* this book—or the Colossus. Curious, what! When I speak of Books in my Life and the Rimbaud, I mean the passages about youth, as in the Rider Haggard chapter and the last chapter, called "The Theatre," where I dwell on the Xerxes society days.

Myself I like Plexus very much, not for the revelatory this time, but for the fantastic bits—about Stanley, about Mimi Aguglia and what follows, about John Brown, and Picodiribibi. Enough. . . .

What I can never write enough about are the "influences"—both men, haphazard meetings, books, places. Places have affected me as much or more than people, I think. (I find it the same with you here.) Think of my repeated journeys to Toulouse, or of the returns to the old neighbourhood (the 14th Ward), or to the places where as a boy I spent my summer vacations, or to the regions in America where I dreamed things my own way, only to find them so otherwise. Strange that I never think of the afterlife this way! Dear old Devachan, which Fred and Edgar and I spoke of so often. All I see there is a breathing spell, another "open" womb, so to speak, where all the senses and the intellect are intensified, clarified, unobstructed—and one learns just by looking, looking back at one's meagre, pitiable self in action.

But this business of youth—rebellion, longing for freedom—and the business of vision are two very cardinal points in my orientation. At sixty-six I am more rebellious than I was at 16. Now I *know* the whole structure must topple, must be razed. Now I am positive that youth is right,—or the child in its innocence. Nothing less will do, will satisfy. The only purpose of knowledge must be certitude, and this certitude must be established through purity, through innocence. Fred can tell you of the unknown man from Pekin who hangs above my doorway here. When I look at him I know he knows and is all that I expect a human being to be. (The photo of him is on the back of the Penguin edition of the Colossus. Study it. That is the person or being I would like to be, if I wanted to be someone else than I am.)

Coda: A Note on the Influence of *Tropic of Cancer*

WARNER BERTHOFF

While *Tropic of Cancer* remained under legal ban (as it did in English-speaking countries from 1934 to 1961), reading it was a kind of civic duty. Like *Lady Chatterley's Lover* and, earlier, *Ulysses*, the book was accepted, with its camouflaged wrappers and Paris imprint, as a symbol of the continuing struggle for both artistic and spiritual liberation; to be for it was to declare oneself on the side of freedom in the arts and natural honesty in human self-awareness. In its odd combination of outrage and unconcern at the catastrophes of modern history, *Tropic of Cancer* also came to be seen as symptomatic of a deepening crisis in the outlook for civilization as a whole. Orwell's notable essay only confirmed its standing in this respect.

The book has, then, a clear and not dishonorable place in the fluctuations of expressed moral and cultural attitude in our century, and conceivably of political attitude as well. How important is it, in addition, for the history of literature? To list its most vocal early partisans—beginning with Anaïs Nin and Lawrence Durrell—may be to suggest that its specifically literary influence has been peripheral and secondary. Even where the metaphor of cultural "cancer" has been kept in service, as fairly continuously by Norman Mailer over the past twenty years, the book as a whole—written in the exclamatory first person—may not seem much more than broadly corroborative of ways of going about the business of being a writer which would have persisted in any case, deriving as they do from long-standing American tradition. Mailer himself, though remaining loyal to this icon of his own apprentice years and willing to affix the word *genius* to an anthology of Miller's writings, acknowledges that Miller's reputation in literary circles has been isolated and idiosyncratic. Criticism has left a "space" around him; his reputation survives but "in a vacuum." Even at the point of asserting that Henry Miller may have "influenced the style of half the good American poets and writers alive today," Mailer effectively reduces this influence to a matter of atmosphere and inspiration. He remarks:

Reprinted from *A Literature Without Qualities: American Writing Since 1945* (Berkeley: University of California Press, 1979), 169–77. Reprinted by permission of the University of California Press, copyright © 1979 The Regents of the University of California.

It is fair to ask if books as different as *Naked Lunch, Portnoy's Complaint, Fear of Flying* and *Why Are We in Vietnam?* would have been as well received (or as free in style) without the irrigation Henry Miller gave to American prose. Even a writer as removed in purpose from Miller as Saul Bellow shows a debt in *Augie March*.

That is, Miller's writings, above all *Tropic of Cancer* ("far and away his best book"), encouraged others to take greater expressive risks, and worked generally to widen public tolerance and receptivity. But the title chosen as showing a "debt" turns out to be what is now commonly regarded as an important later author's least effective, most artificially constructed book.[1]

Writers absorbed (as both Mailer and Bellow have been) in registering the immediate moral and physical chaos of modern city life are writers of the sort we might expect to find at least abstractly sympathetic to Henry Miller. Expectably, too, for evidence of more substantial textual influence we can turn to Beat and neo-Bohemian writers of the 1950s and 1960s. Is *Tropic of Cancer* where Allen Ginsberg got the title for his breakaway poem?—"It may be that we are doomed, that there is no hope for us, *any of us*, but if that is so, then let us set up a last, agonizing, bloodcurdling howl, a screech of defiance, a war whoop! Away with lamentation!" (*Cancer*, 232). So, too, almost everything attributed to "Moloch," the devouring specter of Part II of "Howl"—"Robot apartments! . . . blind capitals! . . . granite cocks! monstrous bombs!"—has its place in *Cancer*'s rich outpouring of prophecy and invective, though rather surprisingly the epithet itself does not turn up in Miller's text.

In general, the line seems clear enough that runs from Miller's evocations of nightwalking in Paris and, in other books, New York and his native Brooklyn ("heart of American emptiness")[2] to Ginsberg's "negro streets at dawn" ("Howl") or Bob Dylan's "ancient empty streets too dead for dreaming" ("Mr. Tambourine Man"). Between Henry Miller, by the 1950s a fixture at Big Sur, and the California *jeunes sauvages* who went down the coast to claim him as patron, the correspondences, textual as well as biographical, are hard to miss. In part, perhaps, because Lawrence Ferlinghetti at City Lights too automatically arranged it, Jack Kerouac—as Ann Charters reports in her able biography—refused to make the ritual visit to Big Sur, notwithstanding an effusive preface Miller had written for Kerouac's *The Subterraneans*. But where besides Miller's "I just wanted to see and hear things" (*Cancer*, 260) was the formula established for Sal Paradise's "I didn't know what to say . . . all I wanted to do was sneak out into the night and disappear somewhere, and go and find out what everybody was doing all over the country"?[3] Similarly, what nearer precedent has the Aquarian-Age commandment to "go with the flow," motto in particular for Ken Kesey's transcontinental bus tour, than *Cancer*'s rhapsodic celebration of rivers, fluids, physical outpourings of every kind? The whole

Kesey fantasy of "Edge City" as the refuge of a perilously maintained existential freedom is anticipated in *Tropic of Cancer*'s insistence (as Karl Shapiro sums it up) that where everything in America conspires to make us "lead the lives of prisoners," "the only thing for nonenslaved man to do is to move out to the edge, lose contact with the machines of organization which are as ubiquitous . . . as in Russia."[4]

All this, however, may still be seen as belonging only incidentally to literary history. Where a conversational-journalistic vernacular has become more or less universal in prose, phrase-echoes inevitably abound; and echoes are not necessarily influences. Yet a book bearing with it the lurid reputation that even after twenty years of public legality still hangs about *Tropic of Cancer* is likely to leave more of an impression than it otherwise might; in such circumstances, as T. S. Eliot ruefully said of reading Edgar Allan Poe (that earlier "stumbling block for the judicial critic") in one's impressionable youth, "one cannot be sure that one's own writing has *not* been influenced."[5]

In any event, the proleptic echoes one begins to pick up in re-reading *Tropic of Cancer* do come from a broader performative field than the one so far indicated. If Miller's shudder at finding signs about syphilis and cancer posted in every Metro station (*Cancer*, 167) should remind us of Holden Caulfield's panic at discovering "Fuck you" scribbled on every wall, we are still on predictable ground. So are we, too, in catching an echo from *Tropic of Cancer* in the anthem, "Day by Day," of the rock musical *Godspell*—"The present is enough for me. Day by day," and again, "Day by Day. No yesterdays and no tomorrows" (*Cancer*, 46, 135)—but what about the title, *Day by Day*, Robert Lowell gave to what became the final volume of his long verse-almanac, a collection ending, in "Epilogue," pretty much where Miller had always been: "Sometimes everything I write / . . . seems a snapshot, / lurid, rapid, garish, grouped, / . . . Yet why not say what happened?" In an era defining itself as essentially under siege, programs of resistance and strategies of self-preservation converge. The lines by Adrienne Rich, "I am an instrument in the shape / of a woman trying to translate pulsations / into images," have their source in the circumstances of the poem itself, which is ostensibly about the woman astronomer Caroline Herschel. But the condition of mind they speak for, far from being peculiar to latter-day feminism, is Miller's explicit starting point: "I am a sentient being stabbed by the miracle of these waters that reflect a forgotten world"; "I am a writing machine" (*Cancer*, 6, 24).

Is this true also for one of the most admired and shocking poems of the whole post-1945 period, Sylvia Plath's "Daddy"? Do the lines, ". . . Dachau, Auschwitz, Belsen. / I begin to talk like a Jew. / I think I may well be a Jew," look directly back to the third page of *Tropic of Cancer*: "I too would become a Jew. Why not? I already speak like a Jew. And I am ugly as a Jew"? Or are they there perhaps by way of an intermediary text, Walker Percy's *The Moviegoer* (1961)?:

There is nothing new in my Jewish vibrations. During the years when I had friends my Aunt Edna, who is a theosophist, noticed that all my friends were Jews. She knew why moreover: I had been a Jew in a previous incarnation. Perhaps that is it. Anyway it is true that I am Jewish by instinct. We share the same exile.

There is more than one such echo of *Tropic of Cancer* in Percy's stylish novel. "For some time now," part two, section nine, begins, "the impression has been growing upon me that everyone is dead"—"We are all alone here and we are dead," is Miller's version, in the third and concluding sentence of *Cancer's* opening paragraph—and the last main section of *The Moviegoer* closes on an audibly Milleresque cadence: "Nothing remains but desire, and desire comes howling down Elysian Fields [the setting is New Orleans] like a mistral."[6]

For textbook literary history, though, the clinching case may prove to be Thomas Pynchon, who among other precocities was responsible for Henry Miller's first and only appearance in *The Kenyon Review*. When Pynchon's important early story, "Entropy," appeared in *Kenyon* in 1960, it sported an epigraph from page 1 of *Tropic of Cancer*:

> There will be more calamities, more death, more despair. Not the slightest indication of a change anywhere. . . . We must get in step, a lock step, toward the prison of death. There is no escape. The weather will not change.

The passage, we note, is interestingly abridged. Pynchon, already set on his own thematic course, omitted Miller's sentences attributing these desperate conditions to "the cancer of time" and to the fact that the heroes of contemporary life have all "killed *themselves* [my emphasis] or are killing themselves."[7]

A final instance will serve to suggest that *Tropic of Cancer's* capacity to influence began operating as soon as the book came into circulation, with consequences of unimpeachable literary seriousness. Eliot is known to have been one of *Cancer's* first supporters and admirers[8]—to Orwell this was further proof of the book's essentially twenties character—and though the central image-motifs in Eliot's poetry commonly have a multiplicity of textual sources, those who start digging for clues in writings which Eliot made a point of commending are rarely disappointed. Rivers and oceans, Miller chants in the apocalyptic climax of *Cancer* (231–233):

> . . . rivers that put you in touch with other men and women, with architecture, religion, plants, animals—rivers that have boats on them and in which men drown, drown not in myth and legend and books and dust of the past, but in time and space and history . . . oceans, yes! Let us have more oceans . . . oceans that destroy and preserve at the same time, oceans that we can sail on, take off to new discoveries, new horizons.

And "The Dry Salvages": "Unhonoured, unpropitiated / By worshippers of the machine . . . / The river is within us, the sea is all about us"; "Time the destroyer is time the preserver, / Like the river with its cargo of dead Negroes, cows and chicken coops, / . . . And the ragged rock in the restless waters"; "Not fare well, / But fare forward, voyagers,"[9] Of course, the confused discriminations Miller insists on in purest antinomian fashion—as between books and legends on the one hand and real people, real history, on the other—are a matter of indifference to Eliot's subtler, more knowledgeable vision. The convergence in this instance is merely in the poetry, which in both passages has the continental grandeur and freedom of American testaments generally.

All these possibilities of direct influence are of course merely speculative, at present. Moreover, most of the images and turns of phrase in question belong to a conspicuously traditional fund of idiomatic and metaphoric usage. With a writer as bookish as Miller, and bookish within fairly conventional limits, the whole matter may have to do, as much as anything, with the continuing availability of this fund for literary use. Nevertheless, the particular phrases and images I have cited come mostly from either the opening pages of *Tropic of Cancer* or its high rhetorical climaxes; and all are self-evidently central to the themes and major emphases of a book which for a quarter of a century after publication "everyone" made a point of reading—and then of reading again when it became legally available in 1961.

Notes

1. Norman Mailer, *Genius and Lust: A Journey Through the Major Writings of Henry Miller* (New York: Grove Press, 1976), pp. 2–4.
2. Quoted by Karl Shapiro, "The Greatest Living Author," p. xviii.
3. Jack Kerouac, *On the Road* (New York: Viking Press, 1957), p. 67.
4. Karl Shapiro, "The Greatest Living Author," p. xx. The bus tour of Kesey's Merry Pranksters is described in Tom Wolfe, *The Electric Kool-Aid Acid Test* (1968).
5. T. S. Eliot, "From Poe to Valéry" (1948), rpt. in *To Criticize the Critic* (New York: Farrar, Straus and Giroux, 1965), p. 27.
6. Walker Percy, *The Moviegoer*, pp. 88–89, 99, 228.
7. The "edge" metaphor, too, turns up in Pynchon, though now as a place of indeterminate terror; the "Zone" is "the new edge," we learn in *Gravity's Rainbow* (New York: Viking Press, 1973), pp. 722–723.
8. *Tropic of Cancer* received a favorable notice in *Criterion*, October 1935, as part of Montgomery Belgion's "French Chronicle," where it is called the most interesting new book of the Paris season: "The astounding thing is that the novel has qualities almost as great as its defects. There is no plot, but there is a pattern." There is also "a marked distinction in the writing," and, above all, a "dynamism" (p. 86). *Black Spring* was reviewed sympathetically in the April 1937 *Criterion* by A. Desmond Hawkins, who praised—"when Mr. Miller is not imitating other authors"—"the freshness of its idiom," describing this quality in thoroughly Eliotesque fashion: "This Paris-American idiom, loose and fragmentary as it may be, is the

one impersonal contribution to imaginative prose style in our time" (p. 503). In October 1937, Miller himself appeared as a *Criterion* author, with a review-article on Anaïs Nin and diary literature. A second and last contribution of Miller's was carried in the final number of *Criterion*, in January of 1939. It is a review of Erich Gutkind, *The Absolute Collective: A Philosophical Attempt to Overcome Our Broken State*, and it is printed just ahead of Eliot's own valedictory as editor.

9. T. S. Eliot, *Four Quartets* (New York: Harcourt, Brace, 1943), pp. 21, 24, 26.

The Body in the Prison-house of Language: Henry Miller, Pornography and Feminism

MARY KELLIE MUNSIL

Henry Miller's writing has proved deeply troubling to feminist critics, given the seemingly misogynist and sexually violent inclinations of the protagonist/author. Miller's career was punctuated by legal battles over the perceived "obscenity" of his startlingly frank autobiographical writings, and his difficulties in reaching print in the United States were linked primarily to the disturbing sexual content of his work. But the feminist response to Miller has proved little more sophisticated than that of his actual or would-be censors, addressed as it has been primarily, or exclusively, to this sexual content.

At least one major feminist writer (Susan Griffin) has branded Miller's writing pornography and lumped it with works more traditionally considered to be of that genre.[1] Another feminist approach, typified by Kate Millett's still important essay in *Sexual Politics* (1970), is to acknowledge Miller's work as serious literature—but a literature that is unfortunately marred by misogynistic views—and then to discuss only its misogynist aspects. Millett, for example, insists that Miller is "one of the major figures of American literature," applauds his skills as "an essayist, autobiographer and surrealist," and suggests that he is "misunderstood," but the primary focus of her essay is a scathing criticism of Miller's apparent contempt for women.[2]

For those feminists who, like Erica Jong, believe that Miller deserves a "place in the pantheon of poets,"[3] yet who are troubled by the sexism in his writing, neither of these approaches is sufficient to provide real insight into the power of Miller's work. It is becoming more and more necessary for feminists to read a text such as *Tropic of Cancer* in the light of the complex interplay of language and bodily experience.

SEXUAL AUTOBIOGRAPHY: FICTION, DESCRIPTION OR PRESCRIPTION?

Central to the debate over any work perceived as "pornographic" or "obscene" is the potential words or images have to incite action on the part of the reader

This essay was written specifically for this volume and is published here for the first time with the permission of the author.

or viewer. A number of critics, and not just feminist critics, believe that Miller's work has just such a potential, not only to promote dangerously perverse views but to inspire humanly destructive acts; that it serves, in short, as a manifesto. There is, in fact, much to suggest that *Tropic of Cancer* (1934) is a sort of manifesto. Miller's assertion that the book is intended as "a prolonged insult, a gob of spit in the face of Art, a kick in the pants to God, Man, Destiny, Time, Love, Beauty . . ."[4] bears a striking resemblance to assertions in the Russian futurists' 1912 manifesto *A Slap in the Face of Public Taste* and the French *Manifeste du surréalisme* of the 1920s. Thus, for feminists who view *Tropic of Cancer* as falling within the realm of autobiographical "pornography," Miller's descriptions of sexual violence can be read as prescriptions for such behavior.

Regardless of their political alignment, would-be censors usually claim to be interested in internalized responses to "obscene" or "offensive" materials only because of their potential to inspire antisocial or criminal actions, perhaps believing that this approach will help them to skirt the issue of free speech. For example, in the midst of the 1990 brouhaha over the homoerotic content of the NEA-sponsored exhibits of Robert Mapplethorpe's photography, Pat Robertson's Christian Coalition sent taunting letters to congressional supporters of the NEA, sardonically suggesting to them that "you may find that the working folks in your district want you to use their money to teach their sons how to sodomize one another" (*sic*).[5]

It soon becomes clear, however, that such self-appointed guardians of the public good find the existence of certain desires, thoughts, and fantasies unacceptable in themselves. Edward S. Silver, the district attorney who wrote Brooklyn's complaint against Henry Miller and Grove Press in 1962, after *Tropic of Cancer* was released in the United States, states in his brief that Miller's book

> depicts and represents acts and scenes wherein the sexual organs of both male persons and female persons are portrayed and described in manners connoting sex degeneracy and sex perversion, and which acts, scenes and description were of such pornographic character as to tend to incite lecherous *thoughts and desires*.[6]

Significantly, Silver does not point to the potential of the book to cause a reader to commit rape. For him the danger of the book lies in its creation of unacceptable mental and emotional states in the reader.

Most such critics, however, do suggest a causal relationship between "deviant" materials and deviant behavior. George F. Will, for instance, suggested in 1990 that the aggressive rap music of the group 2 Live Crew might have inspired the highly publicized gang rape of a Central Park jogger that year.[7] Feminists such as Susan Brownmiller likewise predicate their arguments against pornography on the behaviors (rape, sexual battery, child molestation) that may result from the consumption of such materials. And again like the right-wing moralists, antipornography feminists support an agenda that includes the suppression of certain internalized responses, or fantasies, that they deem offensive and threatening, in this case to women. Procensorship feminists such as Susan Griffin and Andrea Dworkin have gone so far as to suggest that the mere existence of pornography, regardless of its actual effects on the consumer (who is, significantly, presumed to be male), is a source of psychic pain for all women everywhere. Griffin claims that "a woman who enters a neighborhood where pornographic images of the female body are displayed . . . is immediately shamed. Once entering the arena of pornography, she herself becomes the pornographic image. It is *her* body that is displayed" (83).[8]

Perhaps it is because Henry Miller deliberately obscures the traditional distinction between author and character that the threat of Miller's more controversial sexual passages is "made real" in the minds of so many of his critics. His refusal to "divorce . . . [him]self as writer and [him]self as man," and his declaration that his "life itself became a work of art"[9] have led critics to wonder just how autobiographical his accounts of sex tinged with violence and misogyny might be, and to speculations as to his purposes in writing these passages.

In approaching Miller as a sexual autobiographer, the critics generally have fallen into three camps: (1) those who consider Miller's sexual descriptions to be comical, exaggerated, and/or fictional (ergo, not autobiography); (2) those who read such passages as hyperrealist indictments of social/sexual ills (ergo autobiography and/or social realism); and (3) those who read the material literally, often condemning Miller on that basis for promoting antisocial sexual behaviors or fantasies that his readers might enact.

The critics do not fall easily or neatly into these categories, however. Strangely, some who look upon Miller's work as dangerously subversive refuse to acknowledge it as autobiography. Susan Griffin, for example, characterizes a passage from a "novel" by Miller as a "list of pornographic *fantasies*" (90; italics mine). Even Francis Russell, a critic who is perfectly willing to dislike Miller and his "acolytes" on the basis of one reading of *Tropic of Cancer*, terming them "a crew of schizoid derelicts, fake artists, fake exiles, whores and whores" (*sic*), says that he finds Miller's sexual descriptions "unconvincing."[10] Miller, he implies, bad as he is, cannot be *that* depraved. Kate Millett best embodies this contradictory approach when she criticizes Miller for being too close to his literary persona, and then states that she doubts the veracity of the sexual exploits he recounts (Millett, 295).

Even some of Miller's supporters are apparently disturbed by the idea that his work is autobiographical. A number of them have asserted that the "sex maniac" narrator of *Tropic of Cancer* is not Henry Miller. Terry Southern, for example, writes that Miller's genius is in his ability to portray certain cultural realities, but he insists that Miller's form, "sometimes called 'the autobiographical novel' . . . is a misnomer; the word 'autobiographical' obtains merely because the narrator (that is, the created I) sounds so very real" (400). Southern even goes so far as to dispute Miller's own claims about his work: "Miller . . . when questioned about [his writing] . . . can say: 'Oh yes, that's all real, that really happened, that's me I'm writing about, etc.' which is, of course, nonsense."[11]

Not all Miller's supporters deny the links between his life and work. Some, agreeing with Southern that Miller's strength is in his depiction of sordid reality, suggest that he merely tells the truth of life as it really is, the implication being that whereas representing objective reality is permissible, influencing behavior is not. Stuart Sherman, defending the right to read *Tropic of Cancer*, which he characterizes as "a repulsive book," argues that "if the novel is sordid, it is because the life it reflects is sordid."[12] What Sherman considers to be the nauseating qualities of *Tropic of Cancer* are exactly what redeem it for him: no one, he suggests, would want to emulate the behavior depicted in the book.

Nor is this censorious fear of sexual autobiography a rare response directed only at Miller. Other writers whose works make little effort to conceal their autobiographical nature have faced hostile and contradictory *ad hominem* attacks, often from surprising quarters. Erica Jong's *Fear of Flying*, for example, was met with a kind of near-hysteria that clearly went beyond reactions to the shocking fact that a woman was writing openly about sex. That her narrator, Isadora White (Weiss) Wing, was all too obviously modeled on Erica Mann Jong, seems to have been largely responsible for the deluge of criticism from every corner, including some from feminists who branded Jong as a "male-identified" or "not feminist" woman, even as they denied that her work was autobiographical. Rosalind Coward, for example, writing about "quasi-autobiographical" women's novels, including *Fear of Flying*, suggests that such novels are not feminist, because their "preoccupation with sexuality, is not in and of itself progressive." She points out that "pornography, which frequently highlights the sexual experiences of women, is just one example of representations of sexuality which feminists have actually contested," thus suggesting that these novels are closely related to pornography and should be subject to the same scrutiny.[13] Coward concludes that writers like Jong are not feminists because they fail to answer to "a grouping unified by its *political interests*, not its common experiences." In other words, Jong and her ilk are not politically correct enough to qualify for membership in the feminist elite. Joanna Russ makes her objections to Jong's portrayal of sexuality more explicit. Novels like *Fear of Flying* "are tolerated [by patriarchal culture] because they are sexually (and economically) dishonest, women 'talking dirty' in a way that's acceptably cute."[14] Like

Miller, Jong is damned for her depictions of sex both because of their (possible) veracity and because they could not possibly be true.

Autobiographical works with controversial sexual content are thus perceived as especially scandalous not because American critics are merely Puritanical or unsophisticated, but because these works imply the unthinkable: that someone actually *did* those things, and that others might try them, too.[15] Indeed, Erica Jong, apparently disturbed by the potential of her early novels to inspire "a decade and a half of experimentation with random sexual freedom," later "recanted" in *Ms.*, claiming that she never promoted "free love," but rather documented it, concluding primly that "fantasy is meant to remain fantasy."[16]

Perhaps, too, these controversial works of autobiography are frightening to critics because they hit too close to home, exposing the reader's own "dirty little secrets" and mirroring what is submerged by language and culture. According to Mary Harron, the real threat of the English punk movement of the late 1970s, with its "load of teenagers . . . walking the streets in rubber trousers and manacles and dog collars," lay in its ability to embarrass the British by revealing that "bondage had been a dark secret in a culture that values repression and privacy."[17] So too, Miller's shock value lies in his exposure of the failures of communication (especially heterosexual communication), of the American dream, and of middle-class aspirations. John Ciardi agrees when he suggests that the legal response to the publication of *Tropic of Cancer* is typical of a society in which law "is man's guilty conscience codified" (Ciardi, 17).

Only a few critics—few of them feminists—have been willing to acknowledge that Miller's work represents a new form of autobiography and to accept this fact in the light of its potential for positive cultural subversion. Kenneth Rexroth's excellent 1955 review of Miller's work in the *Nation* is one of the few: he suggests that Miller offends because he refuses to lie about life. Discussing Miller's disturbing literary approach to sexual relationships, Rexroth writes that

> a real wedding of equals . . . may exist . . . but it certainly isn't very common. I don't see why Miller should be blamed if he has never found it. Hardly anybody ever does, and those who do usually lose it in some sordid fashion. This, of course, is the point . . . of all his encounters in parks and telephone booths and brothels. Better this than the lie. . . . And this is why these passages are not pornography, but comic.[18]

A feminist reading might be that these passages are not only comic, but subversively so, as they undermine male sexual supremacy precisely by insisting upon it so hysterically. That is, by accentuating his persona's sexual need, Miller, consciously or not, makes the persona seem laughable, even pitiable. This treatment is similar to the excesses of emotion and gesture typically found in melodrama, and as theorists of melodrama such as Peter Brooks have pointed out, the locations in a text that readers or viewers are most likely to find "excessive" are also those that tend to draw attention to themselves and, often, to subvert themselves.[19] Read in this light, the excesses of Miller's ongoing self-creation as virile male border on a self-parody that he may well *not* have intended. I will not go so far as to claim that Miller's approach to sexuality is nonsexist. I do suggest, however, that it may prove valuable to take Miller on his own terms and to explore how his excesses—sometimes located in passages more typically read by feminists as "sadistic"—allow the reader insight into the depths of male insecurity and despair.

PROBLEMS IN FEMINIST CRITICISM OF PORNOGRAPHY

If feminists have failed to address the subversive potential of sexually explicit writers like Henry Miller, it can be attributed more to the historical context in which the most recent wave of feminism arose than to any inherent blindness. Because the initial period of any civil rights movement is quite naturally marked by the identification of wrongs and demands for redress of those wrongs, it is not surprising that early criticism tends to focus on external forces of oppression and to vilify those figures who seem to embody these forces. Such has been Henry Miller's fate at the hands of some feminists. Underlying such feminist criticism is justified outrage over sexual violence committed against women and, more problematically, the perceived potential of pornography, especially violent pornography, to incite this violence. The limitations of this type of criticism of Miller require analysis, not as a means of salvaging Miller's reputation, but because readings of Miller and other writers of explicit sexual autobiography have potentially profound implications for gender criticism and theory.

Susan Griffin's influential *Pornography and Silence* (first published in 1981) discusses an enormous range of "pornographic" texts and images, including works by Miller, Sade, and Reage; skin magazines such as *Hustler*; stroke-books with titles like *Fatherly Love* and *Teenage Sadism*; and a variety of hard core porn films. Griffin does not differentiate between the various approaches taken by these texts to the subject of sexuality, much less evaluate their relative literary or cultural value. Indeed, she suggests that all contribute to the material oppression of women in the same way and to the same degree.[20] Griffin's methods and responses are typical of the antipornography feminists, the best-known of whom are Susan Brownmiller, author of *Against Our Will*, a book that suggests that pornography promotes rape; writer Andrea Dworkin and lawyer Catherine MacKinnon, proponents of an antipornography ordinance that defined pornography as "a form of discrimination on the basis of sex . . . the sexually explicit subordination of women, graphically depicted, whether in pictures or in words;"[21] and Robin Morgan, who popularized the slogan "pornography is the theory, rape is the practice."[22]

Antipornography feminists have all too often refused to make important distinctions, or oversimplified the complexities of gender and gender politics through their investment in a political view of women as constantly and immutably victimized by men. Dworkin, for example, agrees with Griffin that "pornography is not a genre of expression separate and different from the rest of life; it is a genre of expression fully in harmony with any culture in which it flourishes."[23] Yet, as Kate Ellis points out, this tendency to equate any "expression of sexism with others and say . . . they are part of a system that oppresses women . . . misses the unevenness of the system." After all, "if pornography were fully in harmony with [cultural institutions such as] the family, there would probably be much less interest in it" (Ellis, 43).

While Griffin's book is important in that it attempts to analyze, in psychoanalytic and cultural terms, the attractions for men of certain pornographic images, it falls far short of its goals. *Pornography and Silence* is undermined by Griffin's refusal to make important distinctions and her tendency to overgeneralize. Her insistence that women are always and everywhere victimized by the very existence of pornography runs counter to the experience of many women who are aroused and sexually empowered by such materials. Likewise, Griffin's reliance on essentialist assumptions about the nature of gender and gender relations, for instance that there is a "natural" female sexuality that excludes both violence and abuse of power, but includes what Ellen Willis calls the "goody-goody concept of eroticism," the idea that "lovemaking should be beautiful, romantic, soft, nice,"[24] are disturbing in their implications for those women and men who do not experience sexuality in Griffin's approved way.

A related issue is the not-very-convincing assertion of *Pornography and Silence* that all "pornography *is* sadism" (83), and therefore always unacceptable to feminism. Griffin quotes a charged sexual passage from *Sexus* to illustrate how "orgasm itself becomes a retaliation against a woman's words" (90):

"Shut up, you bitch," I said. "It hurts, doesn't it? You wanted it, didn't you?" I held her tightly, raised myself a little higher to get it in to the hilt, and pushed myself until I thought her womb would give way. Then I came— right into that snail-like mouth which was wide open.

Typically, Griffin takes the passage out of context (by neglecting to note that the female character, Elsie, has exhibited sexual enthusiasm in an earlier passage and is described as convulsing in orgasm in the next sentence) and fails to read the subtleties that might allow the passage to be read in terms other than sadism. Why do both Griffin and Millett (who also discusses and quotes this passage) interpret it as "brutality" (Millett, 306) rather than as a description of sexual intensity taken to an extreme, or, alternatively, as a rather pitiful demonstration of male desperation and inadequacy in the face of a woman's sexual demands? The answer is that both critics are operating according to a set of assumptions, including the belief that women are always victims; that women do not possess sexual or social power; and that sexual interactions that are passionate to the point of pain or temporary loss of reason are necessarily deviant.

Griffin—and she is not alone among feminist critics—believes that to eliminate the portrayal of deviant and "misogynistic" sexuality is to begin to annihilate misogynist thinking itself. In "Sadism and Catharsis: The Treatment is the Disease," she suggests that pornography and pornographic thinking are one and the same: both are expressions of the sickness inherent in sexist Western culture and only by eliminating the symptoms can the culture be "cured."[25] But Kate Ellis, finding the *issues* raised here by Griffin crucial for feminists, asks: "does sexuality begin as an unmediated 'it' that is later constructed by societal input, or is sexuality like language, only brought into being through the process of 'learning' it?" (45).

What is unfortunate, even dangerous, about Griffin's *approach* to these questions is her assumption of a normative sexuality (based on tenderness, monogamy, and other traditional values) that has been warped (especially in men) by social "sickness" and that must be regained by exercising self-denial, giving up our attachment to the "disease" (of pornography and/or sexist thinking and behavior) and returning to an idyllic, "natural," and "healthy" state. For those whose sexual desires, fantasies and activities do not correspond with Griffin's, these admonitions smack of the old Puritanism and, worse, of a new attempt at mind control. Even if feminists could agree on which portrayals are truly and dangerously misogynist and on what the "natural" state of human sexuality is, the potential for censorship to create undesirable limitations on intellectual and political expression far outweigh any possible benefits.

How, then, is a feminist to criticize a text like *Tropic of Cancer*, without censoring it and without giving it more credit than it deserves? One approach is to go beyond the superficial and "apparent" meanings of its language and ask of the text what it is "doing." Not surprisingly, given Miller's interest in surrealism and nontraditional narrative structures, his words are imbued with excess meaning, leaving the critic with significant gaps and inconsistencies which suggest that what *Tropic of Cancer* is, at least in part, "doing" is uncovering certain failures in the system of language that are important to gender studies.

NEW FEMINIST READINGS:
BODILY EXPERIENCE AND THE PRISON-HOUSE OF LANGUAGE

As we have seen, sexual autobiographies represent a highly threatening genre to would-be censors, because for all that such critics often attempt to maintain some separation of the text, the mind, and the body, for example by condemning the text for its possibly persuasive effects and yet refusing to read it as autobiography, they inevitably find themselves drawn into frightening and complicated connections between what is read (or written) and what is enacted. This is the problem Miller himself faced in writing *Tropic of Cancer*, a book in which he began to uncover the reciprocal relation between words, ideas, desires, and physical actions. In breaking down some of the mind/body dualism central to Western thought, Miller and other modernists anticipate structuralist theory; for if, as Miller's work implies, body and text each affect the other, then language must produce our experience as much as the other way around. That is, if we cannot name something, we have no means of identifying or experiencing it; it simply does not exist. In Heidegger's words, "language speaks us."

Miller himself suggests that words have a powerful potential to elicit certain responses from the reader's (or writer's) body. In *Tropic of Cancer*, when Van Norden recounts Carl's story of seducing the "rich cunt," he suggests that Carl's letter writing is "a form of masturbation" (119), but it is equally clear that Carl's storytelling has a strong physical effect on Van Norden as well. Again and again Van Norden affirms the erotic power of language: it "is the way [Carl] tells it" that excites him. He says to the narrator, "all night long I've been tossing about, playing with those images he left in my mind" (120).

If mind, body and text are interdependent, it is no wonder that Miller cannot imagine writing anything that does not answer to his own physical experience. In "Reflections on Writing" he calls himself "a man telling the story of his life, a process which appears more and more inexhaustible" (*Reader*, 242). The source of this inexhaustibility, I would suggest, is more than the fact of his continuing temporal existence that must be recorded. It must also be the constantly expanding network of life experience created by the interaction between Miller's writing and his physical experience of the world that makes "the story of his life" too big to encompass. It is likely that the "Miller" persona created by Miller to inhabit his books must have influenced Miller's self-creation and vice-versa. As the persona grew, so did the "real" Miller. Miller's understanding of this process may be behind his anguished insistence that "you can't put a fence around a human being" (*Cancer*, 59): like it or not, we all participate in a process of creating fictional selves, influenced by the fictions we read or write.

If our linguistic system caused us to experience the world in certain ways, would-be censors might have a solid argument for suppressing language with the potential to produce undesirable behavior; but this ignores the necessarily reciprocal and imperfect connection between language and action. Poststructuralists have suggested that the signs making up linguistic systems and the objects or ideas that these signs signify are linked only loosely and arbitrarily. For this reason, language cannot produce unmediated, uncompromised communication, but rather is doomed to produce failures, or slippages. Miller comments on this failure of linguistic connection again and again in *Tropic of Cancer*, as when, after an attempt at conversation with Moldorf fails, the narrator muses that "behind the word is chaos. Each word a stripe, a bar, but there are not and never will be enough bars to make the mesh" (11). If communication is a fabric formed by the interwoven "bars" of words (signs), Miller, like the deconstructionists, suggests that the fabric is necessarily unfinished and full of holes. Further, it may be possible to unravel this fabric, which offers a subversive hope, since uncovering the slippages and/or gaps in language may offer escape hatches from the "prison-house of language" (to borrow Jameson's phrase). It is when readers can find places in a text in which *language unravels itself*, demonstrates its own failures and excesses, that they can begin to subvert the seeming "wholeness" of Western (and, for a feminist, patriarchal) thought.

In *Tropic of Cancer* the failures of verbal communication are marked by hysterical physical excess: language is supplemented or replaced by attempts at physical connection. Miller's characters repeatedly try to express that which language cannot encompass by engaging in bodily acts including defecation, gluttonous eating, vomiting, farting, laughter, desperate sex, or violent outbursts. Sometimes these linguistic failures are expressed in purely transcultural terms: after Van Norden is unable to make a French hotel maid understand his English insults, he angrily resorts to taking a "photograph, his own photograph, and [wiping] his ass with it," and tells the narrator that he would like to "take a crap in the bureau drawer." Eventually he begins to destroy random objects in the room (122–23). Van Norden despairs of linguistic connection, but not only in being unable to talk with the maid, since he is also unable to write in his own language, though he calls himself a writer. Eventually, the only expression left to him is a tantrum.

More often, however, linguistic failures in *Tropic of Cancer* reveal themselves in attempts at communication between men and women. For Miller, there is little or no true communication across the lines of gender, and this gap must be bridged through the most primitive physical connection. Early in *Tropic of Cancer*, Miller's protagonist tries to "tell every cunt . . . [he is] *leaving in the morning!*" It is a cry of anguish, or exuberance, but the "blonde with agate-colored eyes" responds to his words only by taking his hand and "squeez[ing] it between her legs" (18). That Miller rarely records any conversations between men and women is often read by feminists to mean that he thinks of women only as bodies, or body parts; but it is equally possible that this significant omission represents his total despair at the impossibility of successful verbal communication, as when the narrator of *Tropic of Cancer* desperately cries out to Mona, " 'Just look at me . . . *don't talk!*' " even as he contemplates the imminent loss of her.

This is not to say that Miller and his persona do not make urgent attempts to connect with women, sometimes in ways that many women will consider offensive. The protagonist of *Tropic of Cancer* is almost beside himself at times in his desire to "get inside" women, in the most literal sexual sense, but also, I would suggest, in the metaphorical and communicative sense. And yet he fails, again and again, in a way that is less misogynistic than pathetic, because for all his attempts to understand "cunts" by describing, describing, describing, they remain "a hole without a key" (7).

Given Miller's repeated, desperate attempts to negotiate the chasm between male and female experience, not only through language but through gesture, and given the apparently inexorable failure of these attempts, are we to conclude that we are trapped within a misogynist "prison-house of language" that will never allow us to communicate across the gender gap? The answer for Miller—both the "real" Miller and his persona, tragically interlinked—was apparently in the affirmative, all too often. The resulting despair and fury in Miller's work create an unromantic view of gender relations, but as Rexroth has pointed out, it is an unhappily accurate view for many.

At issue are the dual problems of blame and responsibility. Feminists often lay the blame for failures of cross-gender communication on men (or, more obliquely, on male-created language), while refusing to ask women to take responsibility for their own participation in the processes of linguistic creation and self-creation. As women, we have, until recently, retreated behind the role of eternal victim of patriarchal culture and language, often refusing to acknowledge our own participation in these structures. Perhaps it is time now to seek out the significant gaps in the fabric of cross-gender communication and to take advantage of such openings to create ways out of the "prison-house of language."

Notes

1. Susan Griffin, *Pornography and Silence* (New York: Harper, 1981), 3. Griffin, commenting on "a reviewer's observation" that Miller's work concerns itself with " 'physical love for women,' " describes his interest in such love as "pornographic."

2. Kate Millett, *Sexual Politics* (New York: Touchstone, 1990), 294; hereafter cited in the text.

3. Erica Jong, "Goodbye to Henry-san," *Black Messiah* (Premier Issue 1980): 34.

4. Henry Miller, *Tropic of Cancer* (New York: Grove Press, 1980), 2; hereafter cited in the text.

5. Tom Mathews, "Fine Art or Foul?" *Newsweek*, 2 July 1990) 45–52.

6. Quoted by John Ciardi in "Concrete Prose and the Cement Mind," *Saturday Review*, 9 February 1963: 17 (my italics); hereafter cited in the text.

7. George F. Will, "America's Slide into the Sewer," *Newsweek*, 30 July 1990: 64.

8. Strangely, this passage demonstrates a conflation of body and text that has much in common with Miller's own explorations of the interplay between the two. In Griffin's reading, the physical body *becomes* the sign, and vice-versa.

9. Henry Miller, "Reflections on Writing," *The Henry Miller Reader*, ed. Lawrence Durrell (New York: New Directions, 1959), 243; hereafter cited in the text.

10. Francis Russell, "The Cult of Henry Miller," *National Review*, 12 August 1961: 92–94 (quotation on p. 92).

11. Terry Southern, "Miller: Only the Beginning," *Nation*, 18 November 1961: 399–401 (quotations on p. 400).

12. Stuart C. Sherman, "Defending the Freedom to Read: A case history of resistance to censorship and conformity," *Library Journal*, 1 February 1962: 479–83 (quotation on p. 480).

13. Rosalind Coward, "Are Women's Novels Feminist Novels?" in *The New Feminist Criticism: Essays on Women, Literature and Theory*, ed. Elaine Showalter (New York: Pantheon, 1985), 233.

14. Joanna Russ, *How to Suppress Women's Writing* (Austin: University of Texas Press, 1983), 29.

15. It is true that works that are entirely fictional, such as Bret Easton Ellis's *American Psycho*, have also aroused bitter controversy and attempts at censorship. What is absent from these attacks, however, is the kind of character assassination that has been directed at autobiographical writers like Miller and Jong.

16. Erica Jong, "Ziplash: A Sexual Libertine Recants," *Ms.*, May 1989: 49.

17. Mary Harron, "Brit Beat: Behind Closed Doors," *Village Voice*, 24 March 1987: 23.

18. Kenneth Rexroth, "The Neglected Henry Miller," *Nation*, 5 November 1955: 385–87 (quotation on p. 387).

19. Peter Brooks, *The Melodramatic Imagination: Balzac, Henry James, Melodrama, and the Mode of Excess* (New York: Columbia University Press, 1985).

20. Griffin makes one exception. Although she critiques passages with sadomasochistic content from Proust's *The Past Recaptured*, she insists that this is "a work which is not pornography" (85–86).

21. Kate Ellis, "I'm Black and Blue from the Rolling Stones and I'm not sure how I feel about it: Pornography and the feminist imagination," in *Caught Looking: Feminism, Pornography and Censorship*, ed. Kate Ellis et al. (New York: Caught Looking, Inc., 1986), 88; hereafter cited in the text.

22. Andrew Ross, *No Respect: Intellectuals and Popular Culture* (New York: Routledge, 1989), 187.

23. Andrea Dworkin, "Pornography and Grief," in *Take Back the Night: Women on Pornography*, ed. Laura Lederer (New York: Morrow, 1980), 289.

24. Ellen Willis, "Feminism, Moralism and Pornography," in *Caught Looking: Feminism, Pornography and Censorship*, ed. Kate Ellis et al. (New York: Caught Looking, Inc., 1986), 56.

25. Susan Griffin, "Sadism and Catharsis: The Treatment is the Disease," in *Made From This Earth: An Anthology of Writings*, ed. Susan Griffith (New York: Harper, 1982), 103–9.

Henry Miller, American Autobiographer

JAMES GOODWIN

Though a contemporary of the "lost generation" writers, Henry Miller did not establish an artistic life in Paris until nearly a decade after the expatriate phase in modern American literature had reached its height. More than forty years old at this point, Miller was acutely self-conscious that as yet he had no published or even finished work to speak of. In his twenties he had "authored" an imagined book, which someday he might actually write. During the subsequent years of halfhearted and frustrated efforts to write in earnest, Miller resigned himself to composing only personal letters to friends, which for a time he signed "The Failure".[1] Miller's first direct acquaintaince with a famous author is a comic paradigm of his artistic circumstance while living in New York. One regular customer of the tailor shop in which Miller reluctantly worked for his father was the British man of letters Frank Harris. A decade before the autobiography *My Life and Loves* (1922–1925) for which he is mainly remembered today, Harris was widely known as a critic, novelist, and the editor of important literary reviews. Miller introduced himself to Harris, then nearing sixty, while helping him into a pair of trousers.

In 1925 Miller resorted to the alternative of self-publication and direct sale to readers in emulation of Whitman. All but one of his sketches, however, was signed "June E. Mansfield," his wife's maiden name (though the surname was itself an assumed one.) Most of the sales were made in the New York saloons where June had cultivated a string of admirers. Miller had no Emerson to greet these pseudonymous efforts as the beginning of a great career. As long as he stayed in the United States Miller's writing remained, even in his own estimation, wholly derivative. For over six years his literary efforts, in feature journalism and fiction alike, were governed by the search for a marketable prose style. Because he habitually wrote in imitation of admired writers—whose ranks were numerous and offered models as diverse as Dreiser, Sherwood Anderson, Knut Hamsun, and Dostoyevsky—the search left him without an identifiable voice or persona.

By 1931 Miller's literary ambitions equivocated between a desire for acclaim as a popular novelist, as a romantic idol for Americans, and an

This essay was written specifically for this volume and is published here for the first time with the permission of the author.

acceptance of anonymity, following the principles of creative self-destruction advanced by bohemian friends. While the sensibility of American expatriates like Eliot, Pound, and Hemingway prized the formal purity and modern classicism of Flaubert and Cézanne, Miller gravitated toward Rabelais and Hieronymus Bosch, dadaism and surrealism. In Paris he finally realized that for his writing career to begin the "literary man" within himself "had to be killed off." *Tropic of Cancer*, published in 1934, would be the murder weapon.[2]

The breakthrough to discovery of his own, unique writing voice came through rediscovery of an originating impulse in our national literature—autobiography. With the placement of a statement by Emerson as inscription to *Tropic of Cancer*, Miller claims this tradition for his own: "These novels will give way, by and by, to diaries or autobiographies—captivating books, if only a man knew how to choose among what he calls his experiences that which is really his experience, and how to record truth truly." Emerson had made this prediction about the literary future of America in a journal entry for 1841.[3] And by the cultural canons that have prevailed through much of this century, autobiographies now comprise a large number of the classic works in our literature.

Elsewhere in his journal, Emerson identifies the potential significance in an individual's record of personal history:

> We are misled by an ambiguity in the use of the term Subjective. It is made to cover two things, a good & a bad. The great always introduce us to facts; small men introduce us always to themselves. The great, even whilst he relates a private fact personal to him, is really leading us away from him to an universal experience. . . . The more [the great] draw us to them, the farther from them or more independent of them we are, because they have led us to the knowledge of something deeper than both them & us. . . . The autobiography of the good is the autobiography of God. (December 1, 1839)

Setting aside for now consideration of the specifically masculine designation of "the good," the creative process Emerson proposes moves from experiential fact to ideal form and it is replicated in the reading process. The "good" is a universal Subject. The autobiography of the bad is instead solipsistic and self-seeking:

> But the weak & evil, led also to analyze, saw nothing in thought but luxury. Thought for the selfish,—became selfish. They invited us to contemplate Nature, & showed us an abominable self. . . . The little can see nothing in Nature but their own stake, & their most discursive regards are still economical. (December 1, 1839)

The American autobiographical tradition, and in important respects our national literature itself, derives from the figure most closely associated with just such an economic discourse of self, Benjamin Franklin, whose pamphlet *The Way to Wealth* (1758) was reprinted at least 145 times by 1800. Franklin worked on his *Life* (the term *autobiography* had not yet been coined) between 1771 and 1788 (and first published in part in 1791), the years during which the colonies waged a political and military struggle for independence, formed a confederation, framed the Constitution, and thus prepared for formation of a new nation in 1789. Franklin was a prominent participant in these events of course, but the *Life* breaks off in the year 1757, just when his career as a diplomat was beginning.

One expects that a statesman's memoirs will contain a full account of his political life, but Franklin's unfinished narrative covers only those formative events that preceded his career abroad as a representative of the rebellious colonies. Rather than national affairs, the *Life* is concerned with private and civic matters. Its chronicle of Franklin's rise from poverty and obscurity to affluence and prominence is an analogy to the revolutionary development of an independent country in the New World. Franklin's ethic of individual enterprise is a form of dissent against royal entitlements and landed wealth.

Through the *Life* Franklin lends his earlier life to the public domain. Writing about this period toward the end of a conspicuously successful career, Franklin acknowledges rhetorically the blessings of God but addresses posterity as a thoroughly self-made, self-ruled man. His name already engraved in national history, Franklin set out to shape profitable lessons from the personal history. Insofar as personal experience can lead to pragmatic results, it is universal and timeless. He reprints both the moral program and the accounting system for virtuous behavior to authenticate his youthful efforts to acquire the requisite qualities for success. The self-possessed Franklin conceives of life as a coherent succession of resolutions, decisions, and results.

The necessity for dissent and independence is redefined in Thoreau's autobiographical work *Walden* (1854). Having lived according to modest standards beside Walden Pond for over two years, Thoreau advocates voluntary poverty in the belief that affluence and reputation are incompatible with the highest human values. Rather unpragmatically, Thoreau instructs his readers in the nation's cities and towns to initiate their own primitive and frontier lives. *Walden* uses the segment of life on which it has focused to represent the whole and correlates one cycle of the seasons with the full course of human existence. To promote self-cultivation, Thoreau reckons the cost of his stay by the pond. The expense account included in "Economy" verifies how minimal the material requirements for an enriching life really are.

Franklin, on the other hand, maintained a bourgeois respect for matters of economy. He approaches life as a procedure whereby objective goals are formulated, then implemented, and his book provides all the data attendant to that procedure. The *Life*'s reckoning of accounts reflects his satisfaction in rising from inauspicious circumstances to wealth and fame. Thoreau is preoccupied with the less tangible processes of consciousness and his book is rich in reflections on the natural world, other lives, other eras, other literatures. *Walden* is a virtual history of the self; it renders experience through a sinewy, discursive style to convey the essentials of living.

The British writer Harriet Martineau, in her observations on the American people, makes one of the first uses of the word *consciousness* to denote a collective faculty and shared outlook. In *Society in America* (1837), Martineau terms consciousness "a self and mutual reference."[4] Such usage accords with concepts of the universal Subject developed in American Transcendentalism at the same time. A year after *Walden* was published, Whitman inaugurated his writing life with a constitutional declaration of union with readers of "Song of Myself":

> I celebrate myself,
> And what I assume you shall assume,
> For every atom belonging to me as good belongs to you.[5]

In his gregarious, unironic song, Whitman does not employ the paradoxical language of Thoreau, who invented a style that would differentiate and segregate himself from the American mainstream. Rather, Whitman pluralizes the egocentric perspective of conventional autobiography to incorporate the breadth of American democracy. In his epic survey of the homeland, the democratic utterance used most frequently is *you*. Prenominally, the *you* to whom the poetic *I* sings is both the individual reader and the book's prospective mass audience.

Whitman elevates egocentricism to Personalism, an identity of self that both individuates and binds individuals collectively. The poet of Personalism strives to free readers from their normative detachment by integrating them into the colloquy: "It is you talking just as much as myself, I act as the tongue of you (*Leaves*, 65)." His poetry is often a form of imaginative investment in the occupations and commonplaces that hold ordinary minds. In its creation of a literary future for both America and himself, the heroic age is realized with the constant, expansive, and multiform activity of daily social life. While Thoreau expresses consciousness through the topographic counterpart of Walden Pond, Whitman does so through the demographic keynote of "a word of the modern, the word En-Masse" (*Leaves*, 5).

In turning to the American tradition of autobiography from a context of European nihilism and avant-gardism, Henry Miller voices a new need for dissent and independence. *Tropic of Cancer* opens with an abusive denial: "This is not a book, in the ordinary sense of the word. No, this a prolonged insult, a gob of spit in the face of Art, a kick in the pants to God, Man, Destiny, Time, Love, Beauty . . . what you will. I am going to sing for you, a little off key perhaps, but I will sing. I will sing while you croak, I will dance over your dirty corpse."[6] Though not democratic, the voice here is demotic. Miller's discovery of a writing style came with acceptance of the street idiom he had used freely for years in conversation and personal letters.

Tropic of Cancer announces itself as the autobiography of a mundane and bad Subject. After citing Emerson's adage that "Life consists in what a man is thinking all day," its impoverished author explains that in that case "my life is nothing but a big intestine" (63). In a variation on the romantic aesthetic of negative capability, Henry Miller makes his appetitive obsessions the source of new heroic power. For a time Henry earns his daily bread as a newspaper proofreader. Reading the news of world depression with an eye only for typographical errors, he finds confirmation of the reductive hypothesis that "every man is potentially a zero" (135). Previously, while living in Brooklyn and struggling to write the great American novel, he had been deluded by the cultural maxim that "potentially every man is Presidential timber" (135). Such delusions were reinforced by the "luck and pluck" ethos of Horatio Alger, who had quickly recovered his American confidence after a brief period himself as a Paris bohemian.

In Europe, Henry has learned to live without worldly hopes and also without lasting despair. Through celebration of his own unrenowned individuality, he withdraws experience from consideration as a blueprint for success. No public acts or prior record of achievement legitimize his autobiography. Having considered the title "Cockeyed in Paris" and the authorial attribution "Anonymous" at different points, Miller wrote a book that he doubted he would see in print. With the costs of its publication in 1934 paid for by Anaïs Nin, *Tropic of Cancer* had no legitimate existence as an American book until its publication by Grove Press in 1961 and even then it faced censorship challenges in the United States over the next four years. At each stage in its publication history, Miller's principal claim to identity as a writer was the existence of the book itself.

Echoing Emerson, but subverting the Transcendentalists' higher laws, Henry claims that the autobiography written by a true individual would have an apocalytic impact: "If any man ever dared to translate all that is in his heart, to put down what is really his experience, what is truly his truth, I think then the world would go to smash, that it would be blown to smithereens and no god, no accident, no will could ever again assemble the pieces" (224–25). Anaïs Nin soon recognized the difference between Henry Miller the man and his textual creation. She wrote in her diary a few months after first meeting him, "I believe in Henry as a human being, although I am fully aware of the literary monster."[7]

Tropic of Cancer contains many departures from fact in its account of Henry Miller's life in his first four years abroad. As indicated through the usage of "Henry" and "Miller" in the discussion thus far, the book's authorial protagonist and narrator can be differentiated from its writer. Despite Henry's vow "not to change a line of what I write" (10), Miller undertook three complete revisions of the manuscript during the two years it awaited initial publication. This marginal dissociation between writer and persona does not disqualify the book as autobiography. Henry's self-referential consciousness gives Miller the means to convey authorial experience. *Tropic of Cancer* is more an autobiography of the writing activity than of the writer's life.

As a genre, autobiography combines discourse and history, the two axes of temporality and subjectivity in prose. In discourse, temporality is defined by the act of writing itself, which is the point of origin for the writer's identity. Discourse situates subjectivity within the moment of expression. In history, temporality is defined by past events arranged in a narrative order; in strict application, as in standard histories, it excludes signs of the writer's intervention with the material. History situates the subjectivity of its narrator outside the narrative itself. In reference to the prose classics of American autobiography already cited, the orientation of Franklin toward history and of Thoreau toward discourse is evident.

As *Cancer* opens, Henry is currently a resident in an uncomfortably sanitary apartment; he notifies readers: "I have moved the typewriter into the next room where I can see myself in the mirror as I write" (4). As early chapters unfold, Henry periodically informs us about changes in his physical condition and material circumstances and the progress of his writing. These chapters retain the rough-hewn quality of a work in progress. They are inscribed with disjunctive thoughts, discontinued sentences, and commentary like "I am merely putting down words" (7). There is little advance in the narrative or in terms of personal history because these chapters are given over to the ambulant, spontaneous purposes of discourse.

Henry's encounters with other unknowns like himself are, like the mirror before which he sits, reflective of his writing activities. Several of his expatriate friends fancy themselves as struggling painters or novelists whose genius languishes unacclaimed. The two would-be authors Carl and Van Norden have made unique accommodations to the demands of a writing life. Carl, a lowly journalist who insists that he can be a " 'writer without writing' " any published work, has enlisted Henry's literary aspirations in the epistolary courtship of a wealthy, but aged, Englishwoman (45). After describing to Henry the few caresses she has allowed in their first meeting, Carl admits his anxiety over the planned sequel and the prospect of greater intimacy. Terrified that this matron will then unman him, Carl concocts a fantasy in which his emasculation is a blessing. Carl imagines a future in which, paralyzed below the waist, he is married to her and has finally become an active writer: "Then I'd give them something to read, those pricks" (106). This bizarre scenario for a writing career, with its symptoms of a castration complex, is one variant in the diverse relationships between sexuality and textuality presented throughout *Cancer*.

Van Norden, a news columnist, protests that his sexual compulsions have interfered only temporarily with his calling as a serious writer. Another deterrent to the initiation of a career, however, is his monomaniacal insistence on being an "absolutely original, absolutely perfect" writer (120). Though his future book will be autobiographical, Van Norden's efforts to compose original material are constantly frustrated by the nagging suspicion that his thoughts echo passages from favorite authors. Thus unmanned as a writer, Van Norden dedicates his energies and talents to carnal matters.

Unlike these two authors manqué, for whom the pursuits of sex and writing are mutually exclusive, Henry achieves a state of mind in which these activities are dispassionately harmonious. In a statement that escalates Thoreau's polemics against the machinery of society, Henry proclaims: "Today I am proud to say that I am *inhuman*, that I belong not to men and governments, that I have nothing to do with creeds and principles. I have nothing to do with the creaking machinery of humanity" (229). His temperament does not prompt him to retire voluntarily from society, as Thoreau did in order to to cultivate his thoughts. On the contrary, this nonconformist is determined to "burrow into life again in order to put on flesh." Henry's credo is that of a grub writer: "I go forth to fatten myself" (90).

Henry gives an account of his scavenging excursions through the streets of Paris in search of sex and food. The only appetite that is truly insatiable, though, is curiosity about human behavior. In appeasing this appetite, Henry frequently becomes entangled in spite of his studied aloofness. At first he looks on clinically as Van Norden exhibits his staying power with an unenthusiastic prostitute. He is both amused by the performance and indifferent to the performers. As the two grind on mechanically, he decides finally to lend a helping hand and tickles Van Norden on the rump.

This sex spectacle is followed by Henry's explanation of the unexpected dispensation he now enjoys in his position as proofreader at the American news office where Carl and Van Norden are also employed. He praises the therapeutic effect of daily proofreading in bringing the world before his eyes while his only responsibility is to see that the spelling and punctuation are right. Henry attains a similar immunity when seated before his manuscript, upon which he teletypes this bulletin: "I am a writing machine. The last screw has been added. The thing flows. Between me and the machine there is no estrangement. I am the machine" (25). With a perverse sense of transcendence, he celebrates the strong flow of "bloated pages of ecstasy slimed with excrement" (229) and denounces a decayed civilization that is "slowly dribbling back to the sewer" (144–45). Henry differs from his uncreative friends in his willingness to plunge into writing and there make a spectacle of himself.

Henry insists that in these final, cancerous stages of Western decline only profane acts are creative: "A man who is intent on creation always dives beneath, to the open wound, to the festering obscene horror. He hitches his dynamo to the tenderest parts; if only blood and pus gush forth, it is something" (225). *Tropic of Cancer* finds the world in much the same condition that Henry Adams had found it thirty years earlier. The world's dissolution is reckoned by Miller in physiological terms, by Adams according to laws of mathematics and mechanics. It leaves the autobiographer of *The Education of Henry Adams* (privately printed in 1907, published in 1918) a nonentity, a cipher amid multiplicity and flux, hence his use of third-person forms of self-reference and historical forms of narration.[8] The autobiographer in *Tropic of Cancer* remains, in the tradition of the genre, a cynosure—but one often without a stable narrative context.

The Paris through which Henry wanders is described as alive with rot in imagery counterposed to the sterile urban wasteland evoked in T. S. Eliot's verse, which he mocks as "Intellectual trees, nourished by the paving stones" (35). He assumes responsibilities as a guide for readers to the city's working-class districts and pleasure quarters. He becomes an anatomist of the excretory-demiurgic functions: "To fathom the new reality it is first necessary to dismantle the drains, to lay open the gangrened ducts which compose the genito-urinary system that supplies the excreta of art" (149). Although Henry considers himself immune to the plagues of modern society in his remote position as a writer and proofreader, he welcomes the taints that his text inevitably bears.

Gertrude Stein's Paris, as portrayed in *The Autobiography of Alice B. Toklas* (1933), is the place where modern composition and modern genius, namely her own, take root. The advantage to her writing is that expatriate life leaves her "all alone with english and myself" and from that distance "the disembodied abstract quality of the american character . . . , mingling automobiles with Emerson," can be distinctly perceived.[9] By the 1930s, abstraction and experiments with structure had largely replaced the compassionate interest in mundane human experience that was evident two decades earlier in Stein's collection of fiction *Three Lives* (1909). While Stein, like Miller, adapted patterns from vernacular speech with its repetitions, discontinuities, and sound order, she develops them in a direction away from material, daily living and toward pure compositional elements. Though a mutual acquaintance urged her to meet Miller, Stein refused to admit into her salon this American renegade with his odor of the streets.

The most inventive passages in *Tropic of Cancer* are flights of discourse in which dream images and confessions mingle with ordinary speech, references to literary classics, and obscenity. These dynamic, half-formed extravaganzas display an amateur's passion for the writing process. Proclamations that this book of the self delivers a deathblow to art are farcically tempered by references to *The Last Book*, a "New Bible" Henry is co-authoring with his friend Boris and which is admittedly "colossal in its pretentiousness" (24). The portrait of another friend describes equally the principles that bring alive Miller's writing, moment to moment: "There is his mind. It is an amphitheater in which the actor gives a protean performance. Moldorf, multiform and unerring, goes through his roles—clown, juggler, contortionist, priest, lecher, mountebank. The amphitheater is too small. He puts dynamite to it" (7). *Cancer*'s best parts are living theater, variety acts with surreal flourishes and burlesque interludes. With the book Miller engages in a celebratory revision of the psychodrama of Strindberg's intimate theater and Artaud's theater of cruelty.

Miller is as intent upon representation of the act of expression itself as were Emerson, Thoreau, and Whitman before him. Reacting to the reading public's preference for sentimental fiction, Emerson in his journal called for an alternative literature: "Give me initiative, spermatic, prophesying, man-making words" (December 1841). Emerson's use of gender referents, as in the image "man-making" here, is not simply an idiomatic convention. Rather, it reflects a specifically masculine principle of self-reliance in ethics and art. Emerson's insistence that language be virile, that it requires man-making words as well as meter-making arguments to be viable, provoked fellow Transcendentalist Margaret Fuller to ridicule his principles as a form of impotent self-abuse. In 1844 Fuller caricatured Emerson as "a Jove, under the masculine obligations of all sufficingness, who rubbed his forehead in vain to induce the Minerva-bearing headache!"[10]

In "From Pent-up Aching Rivers" Whitman equates literary expression with sexual experience, "the act-poems of eyes, hands, hips and bosoms" (*Leaves*, 70). The demiurge and sexual urges correspond in "Spontaneous Me," where poetic conception rises from "This poem drooping shy and unseen that I always carry and that all men carry" (*Leaves*, 78) It is worth remembering that while Emerson privately praised Whitman as a brave and free voice, later reviewers judged *Leaves of Grass* to be a "mass of stupid filth."[11]

Condemnation of a book as vulgar and obscene became a basis for its interest to Miller. Humanity's lingua franca of bodily pleasures, as in Whitman, or bodily functions, as in Rabelais, offers the writer a rich resource: "every time a language is revitalized it is through the adoption and incorporation of the vulgar elements of that tongue. Everything is nourished from the roots."[12] It offers Miller a new vulgate for an American tradition that has linked writing about the self to experimentation with language. The obscene, as lived and spoken by common people in his time, belongs to a realm beyond the conventions of literary authorship. Its activities and language, as yet unspoken in the canons of high culture, contained the means of liberation for the writer in Miller seeking independence from his imitative habits. The vulgar and obscene retain a margin of humanity unreconstructed by the materialism and automatism of the machine age.

Another primary feature of Miller's language experiment in *Tropic of Cancer* is his use of the "gnomic aorist," as he termed it.[13] In linguistic terms, the aorist is a form of verb inflection that indicates the simple occurrence of an action without reference to its completeness, duration, or repetition. Though descriptive of the Greek language, the aorist in English is approximated by the simple past tense. For Miller's purposes, the inflectional form provides an undefined referentiality that allows his persona great mobility in relation to any chronological or narrative order of events. It affords full rein to the writer's vagrant thoughts, exhortations, incidental observations, and diffusive ideas. The apparent absence of plot, method, or plan in the early chapters is a means for the writer to free himself from history, both personal and literary.

Tropic of Cancer's opening attack against conventions is an assertion of a newly gained individuality, attained through dissent itself. Yet, near the book's midpoint Henry admits his vulnerability to a bookish sentimentalism where Mona is concerned. (Miller's second wife, June, is the basis for the Circe figure Mona, later renamed Mara in *The Rosy Crucifixion*.) The faintest memory of Mona can cause Henry to "dally with the dead stuff of romance" (163). Such indulgence comes at the expense of an otherwise joyous sense of life's comedy. A shift away from discourse and toward the conventions of storytelling becomes evident in *Cancer*'s later chapters. For instance, Henry recounts a chaotic night spent in Le Havre with fellow expatriates, but their debauch does not occasion an absurd epiphany, as had the earlier episode of a Hindu's visit to a Paris brothel, when the sight of two turds in a bidet reveals to Henry a liberating hopelessness in human behavior. The later escapade concludes with Henry and the night's comrades "getting sentimental, as Americans do" (187).

In the latter half of *Cancer*, the writer's spontaneous and protean performance often gives way to sustained narrative accounts of events such as Henry's journey down to Dijon and his brief term as an instructor of English at a lycée there. The complications in friends' intimate lives are also recounted and the book concludes with an elaborate tale of an expatriate's rescue from a calculating French girlfriend, with Henry acting as his duplicitous savior. Anaïs Nin observed in Miller a marked change of personality as he reworked the *Cancer* manuscript. In March 1933 she writes: "Henry talks about his Bohemian life with June, chaos, as a phase, not as his true nature. He likes order. He says all great artists like order. A profound order. So Henry is now trying to master chaos" (*Diary*, I, 189). A dependence on narrative and greater regularity in style within the book's concluding chapters are evidence of this concern for literary form.

Miller resumed his discursive practices in writing the pieces gathered together in *Black Spring* (1938), whose working title had been "Self-Portrait" when he began them in 1933. These compositions share with the early sections of *Tropic of Cancer* a spontaneous animation that is evocative of the writing performance. Miller invents a surreal jabberwocky in creating a bohemian's drunken prose poem for "Jabberwhorl Cronstadt." In "A Saturday Afternoon" he enthusiastically details the humble pleasures of reading while on the toilet and of stopping off at familiar pissoirs. "The Angel is My Watermark!" is a euphoric account of the metamorphic technique he employs to produce his "masterpiece," an amusingly absurd watercolor. Concluding with "Megalopolitan Maniac," Miller delivers a doxology of ruin for the modern city and a tribute to his own rebirth.

Twenty years later, in a letter to a companion from his Paris days, Miller grumbled that the work he had "botched the most of all was *Black Spring*" because he "was too happy then." He elaborates: "I might have written books and not the story of my life. . . . Fate had to remind me of my task." The fateful event was divorce from June after a decade of obsessive, tormented uncertainties. Her last visit in the winter of 1932–1933 compelled him to begin "the story of my suffering," the story of his struggle to become a writer while living with June in Brooklyn for seven years prior to settling in Paris.[14] *Tropic of Cancer* constitutes his final victory in that struggle, and it portrays his estrangement from June during her last trip to Paris. After two decades of effort to render the story of his suffering in narrative form, and suffering periods of prolonged self-doubt as a writer in the process, Miller looked back on *Tropic of Cancer* as simply "an attempt to blow off steam." Furthermore, he rates his first book as "a thing of the immediate present" and likens it to "the volcano's eruption, or the breaking of the crust. . . . It was such a feeble eruption."[15]

Miller determined that to achieve the effect proper to a story of suffering, he would have to develop a serious tone as an alternative to *Cancer*'s exultant and festive manner. By 1938 he proposes, under the influence of D. H. Lawrence, an aesthetic of art for life's sake. For the artist, "it is his almost impossible duty now to restore to his unheroic age a *tragic* note."[16] Thus *Tropic of Capricorn* (1939) is prefaced by an inscription Miller extracted from *Historia Calamitatum*, a spiritual autobiography written by the medieval clergyman Abelard. The inscription reads in part: "I [am] now minded to write of the sufferings which have sprung out of my misfortunes. . . . This I do so that, in comparing your sorrows with mine, you may discover that yours are in truth nought, or at the most but of small account, and so shall you come to bear them more easily."[17] While the quotation that introduces *Cancer* presents a statement of autobiographical method, this quotation indicates that Miller offers *Capricorn* as personal tragedy, as solace for mankind.

As *Tropic of Capricorn* unfolds, it is apparent that Miller has largely redirected his interests away from the contingent conditions of immediate experience. The extemporaneous, humorous configurations for the writing life present in *Cancer* are replaced by a recitation of the calamities of his aimless youth, of his position as a manager in the telegraph company, of a lifeless first marriage, of wasted efforts as a novelist, and of his fixation on the dancehall hostess Mara—a beautiful, damned, and lost soul. Though her presence in the story is confined to a matter of a few pages in the latter third of the book, *Capricorn* is dedicated "To Her," and Mara is the basis for its mythic and tragic claims. By the measure of the pathos of Abelard's love for

Heloïse, his moral agony and the castration he suffered, the misfortunes recounted in *Capricorn* are indeed minor. More often than not, however, Miller treats his misfortunes in all seriousness.

In a departure from the stereotype in the popular mind of the struggling writer sustained by a devotion to art, over the period represented in *Capricorn* Miller struggled to make a sustained commitment to the act of writing itself. He fully employs his gifts of redemptive comedy in depicting fruitless fantasies of authorship while seated before his "anchorage," a large pigeon-holed desk rescued from his father's tailor shop. Although he is at a loss to fix so much as one word or even a "pot-hook" on the blank sheet of paper before him, his imagination dictates an encyclopedia's worth of information, images, and ideas.

Discursive writing enlivens *Tropic of Capricorn* in the "cosmosexual" interlude "The Land of Fuck," which presents a burlesque on subjects ranging from "quiet thinking via the penis" to the "interstitial miscellany of Bloomingdale's" (184, 205). This Land is akin to Cockaigne, the world of leisure and plenty imagined in medieval carnivalesque. It is middle ground between Miller alone in bed with his night thoughts and the realm of men and women in intercourse. The music of the sexual sphere is like the "clanking of a great machine, the linotype bracelets passing through the wringer" (197). Miller's middle ground is the site of reverie, memory, fantasy, errant ideas, and essays in imagination. It is an altar, a womb, a birth canal for the words on paper he hopes will someday come. The situation conveys a new poetic conceit for ejaculation as expenditure. Not the waste of shame in an expense of spirit imagined in Shakespeare's "Sonnet 129," Miller's sexual pursuits in *Capricorn* are payment in advance, drawn from a reserve of promised but unrealized writing.

With war in Western Europe imminent in 1939, Henry Miller left France to visit his friend Lawrence Durrell in Greece and, after a few months, to return to the United States. The account of his experiences in Greece, *The Colossus of Maroussi* (1941), centers on the personality of translator and writer George Katsimbalis. A tireless storyteller as well, Katsimbalis embodies a spirit of protean immediacy: "I saw that he was made for the monologue," writes Miller. "I like the monologue. . . . It's like watching a man write a book expressly for you: he writes it, reads it aloud, acts it, revises it, savours it, enjoys it, enjoys your enjoyment of it, and then tears it up and throws it to the winds. It's a sublime performance."[18] Miller recognizes in Katsimbalis his own discoveries in the discursive mode, and the encounter confirms an intuition that "the best books [are] those whose plot I can never remember" (71).

The prose medium that most closely approximates monologue and in which Miller felt most himself is the personal letter. When stalled or without inspiration during the prolonged effort to find an individual style, Miller freed himself by writing to friends. These compositions would often become massive with accounts of dreams, reading, personal encounters, and the intentions for his other writing. While at work on *Tropic of Cancer*, Miller recognized the value of this material for the book and he sought to retrieve many of the letters. One draft for a conclusion is in the form of a letter to June in which Miller attempts to bring a resolution to both the book and their marriage. As he wrestled with the problems of narrating his "autobiographical romance" in the trilogy *The Rosy Crucifixion*—*Sexus* (1949), *Plexus* (1953), and *Nexus* (1960)—over the next three decades, Miller continued to engage in correspondence with "all and sundry (to my utter detriment, to be sure, but one of my 'weaknesses'—of character, perhaps)." Even if he regretted the time taken away from work on the trilogy, Miller acknowledged that "this vice has happily made me the kind of writer I am and not a literary figure" (*Durrell and Miller*, 340).

The joy of writing is the principal subject of discourse in Miller's life work. The struggle to begin writing is his principal subject of history and narrative. In 1927, with June off in Paris with her mysterious female companion Jean Kronski, Miller outlined in one sitting the general scheme for the project later titled *The Rosy Crucifixion*. The published story, after 1,400 pages, finally reaches this moment when, as Miller explains in *Nexus*:

> In a mood of utter despair, I sat down at the typewriter to outline the book
> I told myself I must write one day. My Domesday Book. It was like writing
> my own epitaph. I wrote rapidly, in telegraphic style, commencing with the
> evening I first met her. For some inexplicable reason I found myself recording
> chronologically, *and without effort*, the long chain of events which filled the
> interval between that fateful evening and the present.[19]

Were it true to the spirit of its inception, the trilogy would be a record of defeats and a chronicle of sorrows. Fortunately, it does not maintain these narrative intentions with great consistency and there are several wildly funny digressions and portraits in the books.

Although the trilogy romanticizes Miller the protagonist as our latter-day Man of Sorrows, the martyrdom is ultimately rosy in that it brings his ascension to the writing life. As its author, Miller has grown comparatively traditionalist in his concerns for creativity and art, and conservative in regard to literary form, even though his career as a writer is inaugurated with comic pronouncements in *Cancer* that "style, style in the grand manner, is done for" (5). Through *The Rosy Crucifixion* Miller explores his own utter "poverty and sterility" of spirit; his intention is to record a "life of 'senseless activity,' which the sages have ever condemned as death" (*Durrell and Miller*, 269). In reaction to the *Sexus* manuscript, which was due for publication in Paris within a matter of weeks, Lawrence Durrell bluntly advised Miller to with-

draw the book and completely revise it. Durrell found the book empty of
genuine passion and judged its prose to be "interlarded . . . with chunks of
puerile narrative" (*Durrell and Miller*, 266–67).

Miller was undeterred by this negative criticism, which came from an
admiring and trusted supporter, but commitment to the autobiographical
romance often deprived him of the joy of writing. Confiding to Durrell in
1959, Miller questioned the worth of the entire project. He feared that the
centerpiece of a life's work had become lifelessly alien and fraudulent:

> I'm going through some sort of crisis. Never felt more desolate. Yet underneath
> very hopeful. Two nights ago I got up in the middle of the night with the
> firm intent of destroying everything—but it was too big a job. So I'll hang
> on and finish *Nexus* (Vol. 2), then see. Writing seems so foolish, so unnecessary
> now. . . . The next step is to throw myself away. That's harder. One thing
> seems certain—that I've built on sand. Nothing I've done has any value or
> meaning for me any longer. I'm not an utter failure, but close to it. Time to
> take a new tack. Years of struggle, labor, patience, perseverance have yielded
> nothing solid. I'm just where I was at the beginning—which is nowhere. . . .
> What I feel like saying sometimes—when the whole bloody *Crucifixion* comes
> to an end—is "Ladies and Gentlemen, don't believe a word of it, it was all a
> hoax. Let me tell you in a few words the story of my tragedy; I can do it in
> twenty pages." (*Durrell and Miller*, 366, 376)

The original notes and outline composed in 1927 were longer by ten pages,
as a matter of fact.

Miller had contemplated that coda fully a decade before *Sexus* was
published when he announced in 1939 a future work to be entitled *Draco
and the Ecliptic* and to be composed in a prophetic vein, though he had not
finished one word of it other than the title. Once *Sexus* appeared, Miller
intended *Draco* to be a capstone to *The Rosy Crucifixion* when the trilogy
reached completion, and he expected: "Joy through work hereafter. No more
compulsion" (*Durrell and Miller*, 263). Ten years later, with only the first of
two proposed volumes of *Nexus* finished, Miller promises *Draco* again as a
cryptic account of the entire autobiographical romance, to be written in the
same inspired manner and for the same synoptic purpose as was the plan for
the romance itself, which he had recharted while at work on *Tropic of Cancer*.

Miller experienced prolonged anxiety over bringing *The Rosy Crucifixion*
to a conclusion. More than midway through the trilogy's composition in
1949, he regretted that completion meant "the autobiographical life will
then be done for," leaving him empty with only the alternative of creating
"sheer nonsense" (*Durrell and Miller*, 268, 263). Perhaps fearing them as
death notices to his writing life, Miller never finished *Nexus* or wrote *Draco
and the Ecliptic*. His dedication to rendering as narrative those formative seven
years, the final phase of his life before he began writing, causes him often to

disregard the credo announced in 1939 when he was flush with the break-through to a discursive identity in *Tropic of Cancer* and *Black Spring*:

> Even now I do not consider myself a writer, in the ordinary sense of the word. I am a man telling the story of his life, a process which appears more and more inexhaustible as I go on. Like the world-evolution, it is endless. . . . I learn less and realize more: I learn in some different, more subterranean way. I acquire more and more the gift of immediacy.[20]

A debt to Bergson is obvious in this sense of the ongoing creation of self by self. The sole context for life in this perspective is one contemporary with creation, not one prior to initiation into creativity. Happily, *The Colossus of Maroussi, Big Sur and the Oranges of Hieronymus Bosch* (1957), and *The Books in My Life* (1969) contain much writing created with a sense of actuality in the experiences recounted and in the recounting itself.

At age eighty Miller remarks how "tormented" he is by the thought that much of his life is left unexpressed in his writing. Rather than attempt to rectify his "sins of omission," however, Miller indicates that he is now content to enjoy "the luxury of *not* doing," of no longer recapturing the past for posterity. The "one strong, true desire" left in him is "to write absolute nonsense."[21] By persisting in this desire, already alive in him twenty years earlier, Miller violates the myth of his own autobiographical romance. Nonsense as the culmination of the writing life would subvert the teleological purpose of the narrative to *The Rosy Crucifixion*.

Instead of a second volume to *Nexus* or *Draco the Ecliptic*, in the 1970s Miller brought to a close the narration of his life in the Brooklyn and early Paris years with the illustrated memoir *My Life and Times* (1972) and the *Book of Friends* volumes (1976). The text of the memoir is edited from taped interviews with Bradley Smith. Miller reminisces in a tone of final retrospection and, on the eve of his ninth decade, he still boasts like a sturdy cocksman. Miller's role as a writer has been reduced to supplying captions for the numerous reproductions and photographs, with a few recent snapshots featuring him in the company of an irrelevantly naked woman. Chapters in the *Book of Friends* series return to painful events that are the foundation for *The Rosy Crucifixion* trilogy, but in a matter-of-fact, calmly anecdotal fashion.

In *My Life and Times* a fate of self-parody is glimpsed. The year of its publication, Norman Mailer remarked that in Miller's late works his origi-nally powerful autobiographical style and themes have diluted into subtle, unsuspected caricatures of themselves. In spite of this diminishment, Miller remains for Mailer exemplary in his individuality and heroic in his pursuits as a writer for starting relatively late in life and without any prospect of public success.[22] Miller's own private fears of futility, of arriving nowhere after twenty years of effort on the autobiographical romance, echo a textual pattern of truth not uncommon in American literary careers. Richard Poirier has described this pattern as an "entrapment that often turns American writers into imitators and finally into unconscious parodists of themselves."[23]

Henry Miller, however, did not remember himself, nor is he remembered by most of his readers, for lapses into self-imitation. The earliest recognition of Miller's artistic powers and the deepest appreciation for his books have come from fellow writers. Miller's comic and monologic gifts revived in modern prose, after the "lost generation" period, a performative and reflexive potential drawn from the American autobiographical tradition. Miller was also instrumental in delineating a modern sensibility rooted in sexual and self-exploration. His inventions in discursive style, and through them his invention of the writer Henry Miller, have stood as a powerful precedent for the Beat Generation, New Journalism, and other contemporary forms of personalist, confessional writing.

Notes

I wish to acknowledge support for my work on Henry Miller and American autobiography received through a UCLA Summer Faculty Fellowship and the University's Academic Senate Research funds.

1.   For such biographical information, I am indebted to Jay Martin, *Always Merry and Bright: The Life of Henry Miller* (Santa Barbara, Calif.: Capra Press, 1978).

2.   *Writers at Work, Second Series* (New York: Viking, 1963), 165–191 (quotation on p. 175).

3.   The Emerson quotation appears in *The Journals and Miscellaneous Notebooks of Ralph Waldo Emerson*, Vol. 7, *1838–1842*, ed. A. W. Plumstead and Harrison Hayford (Cambridge, Mass.: Belknap Press, 1969), 418–19; hereafter cited in the text by date of diary entry.

4.   This citation is given in the unabridged *Oxford English Dictionary*.

5.   Walt Whitman, *Leaves of Grass* in *Complete Poetry and Selected Prose*, ed. James E. Miller, Jr (Boston: Houghton, Mifflin, 1959), 25; hereafter cited in the text as *Leaves*.

6.   *Tropic of Cancer* (New York: Grove, 1961), 1–2; hereafter cited in the text.

7.   *The Diary of Anaïs Nin*, Vol. I, *1931–1934*, ed. Gunther Stuhlmann (New York: Harcourt, 1966), 134; hereafter cited in the text.

8.   These linguistic issues are discussed at length in my essay "The Education of Henry Adams: A Non-Person in History," *Biography* 6, no 2 (Spring 1983): 117–35.

9.   The quotations are taken from the complete text of the *Autobiography of Alice B. Toklas* included in *Selected Writings of Gertrude Stein*, ed. Carl Van Vechten (New York: Vintage, 1962), 66, 143.

10.   Fuller's remark is cited in Ann Douglas Wood, "Reconsiderations: Ralph Waldo Emerson," *New Republic*, 1–8 January, 1972, pp. 27–29.

11.   The review, from the New York weekly *Criterion*, is cited in Justin Kaplan, *Walt Whitman: A Life* (New York: Bantam, 1982), 203.

12.   Henry Miller, *The Books in My Life* (New York: New Directions, 1969), 262.

13.   *Lawrence Durrell and Henry Miller: A Private Correspondence*, ed. George Wickes (New York: Dutton, 1964), 221; hereafter cited in the text as *Durrell and Miller*.

14.   Lawrence Durrell, Alfred Perlès, and Henry Miller, *Art and Outrage* (New York: Dutton, 1961), 58.

15. The sources for these remarks are, respectively: *Henry Miller on Writing* (New York: New Directions, 1964), 191; *Writers at Work*, 175; and *Art and Outrage*, 31.

16. Henry Miller, *The Cosmological Eye* (New York: New Directions, 1939), 108–109.

17. *Tropic of Capricorn* (New York: Grove, 1961); hereafter cited in the text.

18. *The Colossus of Maroussi* (New York: New Directions, 1941), 28; hereafter cited in the text.

19. *Nexus* (New York: Grove, 1965), 165.

20. *The Wisdom of the Heart* (New York: New Directions, 1941), 19–21.

21. "On His Sins of Omission," *New York Times Book Review*, 2 January, 1972, pp. 10–11.

22. Norman Mailer, *The Prisoner of Sex* (New York: New American Library, 1971), 73–92.

23. Richard Poirier, "The Minority Within," *Partisan Review* 39, 1 (1972): 12–43 (quotation p. 43).

The Late Modernist

Jeffrey Bartlett

Henry Miller's place in twentieth-century American literature has been misunderstood often, since the beginning of his career as a writer. The notoriety given to *Tropic of Cancer*'s publication in France, its so-called obscenity, and the curtailed circulation of it and the two major books that followed, *Black Spring* and *Tropic of Capricorn*, in the United States and Great Britain were primarily responsible for this situation. Reviewers and a general audience were barred from reading the works (or without lurid expectations if they did). It is no wonder that for many years Miller was famous but unknown, set apart as an oddity from the mainstream of his contemporaries.

During the 1930s and 1940s, Miller was seen variously—as among the last derivative American expatriates of the 1920s; as an American picaro with literary pretensions; as a proletarian deficient in the appropriate leftist politics; as a bohemian anomaly both novel and outdated; and as a great genius come to revive a moribund literature. There is a tinge of truth in each of these caricatures, but two early essays show how critics tended to read his work in accordance with their own agendas.

One of the first notices *Tropic of Cancer* received in the United States (four years after publication) was from Edmund Wilson, then book reviewer for the *New Republic*. It exhibits Wilson's guarded interest in unconventional writing and is indicative of the way in which even charitable assessments dealt with the book. He calls it "the epitaph for the whole generation of American writers and artists that migrated to Paris after the war,"[1] a sentiment reflected also in the essay's title ("Twilight of the Expatriates"). He sees the book as an oddity left over from the 1920s, an essentially decadent work. It deals with a group of people—"expatriates"—for whom Wilson has little sympathy. Sharing the disdain loudly expressed by Hemingway and other "serious writers" in Paris of the twenties, he is tired of such literary poseurs, particularly since their time as a social phenomenon has passed.

Wilson's intentions are generous in reviewing a book that he believes

---

*This essay was written specifically for this volume and is published here for the first time with the permission of the author.

has gone unnoticed, and he admires it as "a good piece of writing" and a "remarkable book." But he treats it as if it were a novel like, say, *The Sun Also Rises*, though more picaresque and "low." He refers to the characters as "rogues" and the narrator as the "hero," a conventional designation completely foreign to the book. In calling *Tropic of Cancer* "the lowest book of any real merit that I ever remember to have read," Wilson reveals the platform of respectability from and to which he writes. He ends with a reading of the final section and concludes that Miller "gives us the genuine American bum come to lead the beautiful life in Paris . . . and lays him away forever" (708).

The trouble with this view is that it is so distant from the feeling in *Tropic of Cancer*. Perhaps Wilson and others think it is time the expatriates came home, but the book itself ends with a sense of freedom as Henry rejects the chance to return to America, instead embracing his life in Paris, regardless of its "sordidness." If we think of the book not as a novel and the narrator not as a fictional character to be portrayed and dispensed with, we may find that it is possible for an American to write well in and of Paris even in the thirties. As a species of autobiography, *Tropic of Cancer* may be the beginning of something, not the tag end of a tired trend. (Miller himself made these points, more or less, in a response sent to the *New Republic*, which Wilson reprints in his collection *The Shores of Light*.)

In a long essay published two years after Wilson's brief review, George Orwell agrees that "the subject matter of the book and, to a certain extent, its mental atmosphere belong to the twenties rather than to the thirties."[2] Yet he shows a better understanding of its autobiographical nature and finds *Tropic of Cancer* to be, like *Ulysses*, "a novel which opens up a new world not by revealing what is strange, but by revealing what is familiar" (11). This new world and the new man Miller represents are Orwell's focus in the rest of his piece, and they disturb him.

Actively involved in anti-Fascist politics, Orwell stresses the apocalyptic aspect of Miller's work because he sees such a drastic change fast approaching. He opposes the brutality of his times by writing in the English tradition of reasoned argument and goodwill and by going forth to fight this brutality (as he did in Spain). Underneath his reading of Miller is his evident anxiety that these measures may not be equal to the irrational, amoral chaos that is on the rise. As for Miller, "I should say that he believes in the impending ruin of Western Civilization much more firmly than the majority of 'revolutionary' writers; only he does not feel called upon to do anything about it" (42). Though Miller writes of "the lumpen-proletariat fringe" left in Paris after the glory days of the twenties, his attitude exhibits "a species of quietism" seemingly indefensible in the later thirties yet compelling nevertheless. Orwell ends by calling Miller "the only imaginative prose-writer of the slightest value who has appeared among the English-speaking races for some years past," but this evaluation carries no comfort. Rather, he thinks it "a demonstration of the *impossibility* of any major literature until the world has shaken itself into its new shape" (50).

Orwell cannot imagine that Miller's work itself might be an instance of a major new literature. Rather, he sees it as a symptomatic reaction to the negative forces afoot in the world. From his essay, one would picture *Tropic of Cancer* and *Black Spring* as enervated groans of apathy, not active celebrations of life no matter what the circumstances, which they are. The books show a new spirit but not one Orwell wishes to partake of. For him as for Wilson, Miller's work, whatever its good qualities, is outside the main currents of contemporary literature.

Despite criticism of its "commonness" and its social indifference, Miller's writing is in fact quite literary, dotted with references to modern art, imitations of modern writing, and departures from those models. This quality owes something to Miller's being largely self-educated, and it and his awareness of contemporary trends are affected by the advanced age and extreme circumstances at which he comes into his own as an artist.

While young American writers like Hemingway and Fitzgerald were achieving fame in the 1920s, Miller labored at obscure jobs, divorced his first wife and married his second, and struggled to write (unsuccessfully, from all reports). Eight years older than Hemingway, who published his first major book (the American edition of *In Our Time*) in 1925 at age twenty-six, Miller was forty-three when *Tropic of Cancer* appeared in 1934. His contacts with the avant-garde had been limited to an occasional art exhibition, books, and chats with his painter friend Emil Schnellock. For example, when the Armory Show in 1913 threw New York into an uproar and brought modernism to the American public, the Brooklyn boy was out of the city for one of the few times in his life up to then, working as a laborer in California and trying to get over a love affair.

Still, the modern spirit was in the air Miller breathed, even if he was unable to capture it in writing while in New York. He felt the anarchy of Dada and the unconscious forces and images of Surrealism, experienced life in cubistic fragments. Or so he recalls the past, especially in *Tropic of Capricorn*. Miller denigrates his earliest writing as "museum stuff, and most writing is still museum stuff and that's why it doesn't catch fire, doesn't inflame the world. . . . Even my dreams were not authentic, not bona fide Henry Miller dreams."[3] Only isolated bursts of inspired spontaneity gave him glimpses of his real self and the desire to continue. In such moments, although "I never read a French book and I never had a French idea," he says, "I was perhaps the unique Dadaist in America, and I didn't know it" (286).

The radically individual character of his early work distinguishes Miller from other writers more easily grouped together, as does his relative lateness in achieving publication. Nevertheless, he is a full member of the generation of modernists who flourished from the early years of the century until World

War II. The influence upon his work of major movements and figures in the arts can be documented clearly, though the results appear in forms clearly American and his own.

EXPRESSIONISM

By 1934, two of the defining characteristics of Miller's work were out of fashion. Individualism had given way to collectivism, and expressionism had given way to social realism. Inspiration for his efforts at expression comes from an earlier period and, as for many of his contemporaries, from the art form that drove the breakthrough: modern painting.

Perhaps the most drastic change that the twentieth century wrought upon the aesthetic of painting occurred in the artist's relation to his subject matter. Breaking away from the obligation to represent the world as it appears to the eye, the painter felt free to base his work on what Wassily Kandinsky called "an inner necessity." Painter and theorist, Kandinsky in 1910 wrote that "form is the external expression of inner meaning."[4] Henry Miller absorbs the idea of expressionism and approves its practice, as when he observes of a painter he knows, "Swift didn't give a fuck about Nature; he wanted to paint what was inside his head,"[5]

Kandinsky goes on to speak of two means for reaching his "ideal of composition": they are form and color (46). For the former, he chooses Picasso as exemplar, and for the latter, Matisse. Both names are invoked in *Tropic of Cancer*, but Miller, whose headlong rushes of imagery and leaps of attention displease formalist critics, is closer in temper and style to Matisse. He has been called worse than a "wild beast" and his iconoclasm and caricatures carry something of the playful spirit of the *fauves*. In almost the exact middle of the book, he visits a gallery showing Matisse's work, by which, he says, "I am drawn back again to the proper precincts of the human world. On the threshold of that big hall whose walls are ablaze, I pause a moment to recover from the shock which one experiences when the habitual gray of the world is rent asunder and the color of life splashes forth in song and poem" (146). This rhapsodic meditation lasts some four pages, during which Miller contrasts the vibrant color of Matisse with the decaying industrial landscape. Characteristically, Miller mixes the human senses and the arts of painting, poetry, and music into a polymorphous whirl of sensuality.

> In every poem by Matisse there is the history of a particle of flesh that refused the consummation of death. The whole run of flesh, from hair to nails, expresses the miracle of breathing, as if the inner eye, in its thirst for a greater reality, had converted the pores of the flesh into hungry seeing mouths. By whatever vision one passes there is the odor and the sound of

voyage. . . . He it is, if any man today possesses the gift, who knows where to dissolve the human figure, who has the courage to sacrifice an harmonious line in order to detect the rhythm and murmur of the blood, who takes the light that has been refracted inside him and lets it flood the keyboard of color. (*Cancer*, 147)

A whole section of the book spins to a stop with its visions of "the Paris that belongs to Matisse." Miller has participated in the work of Matisse and by writing has brought Matisse into his.

DADA

Miller's remark about being an unwitting dadaist suggests how congenial to his personality was the impulse behind this movement, which began as an artists' protest against World War I. Born in revolt, Dada is negation, but *modern* negation is creative. Breaking the old and recombining its pieces are fundamental tools in the modern method. The products of Cubism and Surrealism may seem more affirmative because they show the sensual affection of the artist for his materials, but Dada objects are dispensable, even "trashy," revalued by the compositional process but without the serious preciosity of Art. Dada is playful and its tone ironic, yet its purpose is violently earnest.

Dada is much less interesting as a movement—b. 1916, d. 1921— than as a Zeitgeist. It touched artists in all the other important "isms" of the time because it spoke to a common spirit of rebellion. According to Dickran Tashjian, "In contrast to Cubism, Futurism, and Surrealism, Dada was a deliberately incoherent phenomenon that went beyond such contemporaneous movements to appropriate the entire realm of creation as its concern."[6] Dadaists themselves realized after the war years that their impulse was ultimately personal and sustainable only individually, as Tristan Tzara emphasized in 1924:

Dada knows the correct measure that should be given to art: with subtle, perfidious methods, Dada introduces it into daily life. And vice versa. . . . The Beautiful and the True in art do not exist; what interests me is the intensity of a personality transposed directly, clearly into the work; the man and his vitality; the angle from which he regards the elements and in what manner he knows how to gather sensation, emotion, into a lacework of words and sentiments.[7]

The following well-known declaration from the first page of Miller's first book comes directly out of the anti-art impetus of Dada, echoing Tzara: "A year ago, six months ago, I thought I was an artist. I no longer think about it, *I am*. Everything that was literature has fallen from me." He insists that he is not writing "a book, in the ordinary sense of the word" and, ten pages later, elaborates: "There is only one thing which interests me vitally now, and that is the recording of all that which is omitted in books" (*Cancer*, 1, 11). He writes not to be understood but to express something of himself.

When Miller turns from his present life in Paris to the glum past in New York, the example of Dada still figures prominently, even literally. After a catalogue of European modernist events and artists he was "ignorant of," he copies into *Tropic of Capricorn* a passage from Tzara's first manifesto that includes the admonition, "Each page must explode," and continues, "If I had known then that these birds existed . . . I think I'd have gone off like a bomb." Miller's lateness in coming to the Dadaists fuels his enthusiasm for blasting the barriers of propriety. His summary of the spirit of their advance comments equally well on the commingled modes of destruction and affirmation in his own work: "To say Yes you have to be first a surrealist or a Dadaist, because you have understood what it means to say No. You can even say Yes and No at the same time, provided you do more than is expected of you" (*Capricorn*, 292–95).

Surrealism

Contrary to the nonrepresentational emphasis of Cubism, surrealist painting and writing exhibit strong narrative elements and, for the most part, are figurative, even symbolic. The startling modernity of these works is achieved through juxtapositions of recognizable images or objects not associated with one another by the logical mind. The Surrealists follow Freud in their attraction to the unconscious, which is a reservoir of images and scenes, and the dream, which is randomly sequential release of them. Fascination with the unexplored realm of "the great Mystery" that resides within humanity leads Breton to his first manifesto: "I believe in the future resolution of these two states, dream and reality, which are seemingly so contradictory, into a kind of absolute reality, a *surreality*, if one may so speak. . . . Let us not mince words: the marvelous is always beautiful, anything marvelous is beautiful, in fact only the marvelous is beautiful."[8] Like Kandinsky and Tzara, Breton appropriates the classical measure of art and redefines it to fit his new aesthetic. The primary aim of the dedicated Surrealist is the expression of psychic contents in a spontaneous flow unchecked by reason or ideas of "art."

The paradoxical revaluation of logical categories, partially influenced by Nietzsche, is a frequent component of surrealist thought and work. The essayist Walter Benjamin believes that the import of Surrealism lies in a "profane illumination" brought about "by virtue of a dialectical optic that perceives the everyday as impenetrable, the impenetrable as everyday."[9] This illumination is profane by birth, from the spirit of disgust and revolt central to Dada. Benjamin's phrase evokes the three Frenchmen who repeatedly are cited as the precursors of Surrealism: Lautréamont, Baudelaire, and Rimbaud. The first and last especially inspire Miller; their names appear ubiquitously in his writing of all styles, from the burlesque caricatures to the autobiographies to the essays. Illuminated figures themselves, their works light up the dark and cacophonic civilization in which they attempt to be heard. (Lautréamont's book, so unlike Walt Whitman's in temper, shares its desire to chant—and was published only thirteen years after the first *Leaves of Grass*.) Miller's sneering assertion at the beginning of *Tropic of Cancer* directly echoes the willfully accursed songs of Lautréamont and Rimbaud: "I will sing while you croak, I will dance over your dirty corpse. . . . The essential things is to *want* to sing. This then is a song. I am singing" (2).

He is the first major American author to apply the thought of these visionaries to his own work, to advance by way of them into the blasted world between the great wars. In an article celebrating the publication of *Maldoror* by New Directions, Miller marks the place of these founders of a literature: "The three great bandits were Baudelaire, Rimbaud and Lautréamont. And now they have become sanctified. Now we see that they were angels in disguise."[10] His fondness for the three is evident also in the rather bombastic turns of "poetic" language that dot his Paris books and which Edmund Wilson accurately characterizes as "old-fashioned and rhetorical in a vein of late romantic fantasy reminiscent of *Les Chants de Maldoror*" (706). Self-educated latecomer that he is, Miller sometimes has to swallow his influences whole and regurgitate them only partly digested.

Baudelaire possesses a refinement of style and self-image that is not unlike Breton's own; the difference between himself and Miller is analogous to that which Breton recognizes between Baudelaire and Rimbaud: "Baudelaire is Surrealist in morality. Rimbaud is Surrealist in the way he lived and elsewhere" (Breton, 27). Miller in action becomes a version of the writer Breton foresees in theory. His work abundantly demonstrates "the omnipotence of desire, which has remained, since the beginning, surrealism's sole act of faith" (Chipp, 416). And the flights of image and vision that occur most frequently and fully in the Paris books typify this observation on the unplumbed depths of association: "I certainly think that one must no longer underrate the hallucinatory power of some images or the imaginative gift some men possess independently of their ability to recollect" (Chipp, 421).

Beginning at the exact center of *Tropic of Capricorn* is "An Interlude" in "the Land of Fuck," a place in the author's mind that he visits while, among other things, making it with the Girl Upstairs. One particularly fantastic section begins with an explicit narration of their "impersonal personal" fucking, tinged equally with lust and humor, then drifts into a reverie that evokes the paintings of Dali or Tanguy, the early films of Buñuel, and animated cartoons. The transition from erotica to hallucination begins, "It was an enormous cunt, too, when I think back on it." We are carried along on a series of rapidly shifting images inside the imaginary womb, which, like the passage on Matisse referred to, petition all five senses. Sex for Miller is a source of and outlet for the imagination as well as a sensation, and writing is a way to celebrate its liberating energy. In this instance, he calls the process "thinking via the penis" and soon after elaborates: "It led absolutely nowhere and was hence enjoyable. The grand edifice which you might construct throughout the course of a long fuck could be toppled over in the twinkling of an eye. It was the fuck that counted and not the construction work." The Interlude continues on, because "when the penis gets to thinking there is no stop or let: it is a perpetual holiday, the bait fresh and the fish always nibbling at the line. Which reminds me of another cunt . . ." (182–86). The flow of this monologue indeed proves "the omnipotence of desire." Miller's drive to create is based not upon optimism or faith but on curiosity and the primal urge.

The tenets of Surrealism are adopted more deliberately in other writings from his Paris period. The tour de force "Into the Night Life" is a dream-flight through his past, full of Freudian images and seeming a bit like a textbook example of the surrealist method. "Scenario" is a lush, erotic film in writing, featuring two archetypally beautiful females around whom swirl and mutate a world of sensual visual images. "The Golden Age" is a meditation on cinema and the avant-garde based on Buñuel's film of the same name. All these were gathered in *The Cosmological Eye* (1939), Miller's first book published in the United States and intended to establish his reputation as a serious artist rather than a pornographer.

Also in that collection is "An Open Letter to Surrealists Everywhere," one of his finest essays. Miller casts a more critical eye on his French contemporaries than he does on their beloved predecessors, Rimbaud et al. Not surprisingly, the explicitly political side of Surrealism that Breton, Aragon, and others pushed from the early thirties on holds no value for Miller, nor does Surrealism as a "movement." The article, nearly fifty pages long, takes a strong polemical stance in which he rejects the idea that Surrealism, or any literary or artistic force, can or should serve mass sociopolitical ends.

The "Open Letter" undulates back and forth in response to its subject, revealing the certainty of vision that allows Miller to assimilate what he finds useful and to discard what is not. Of its creative surge he admits, "Scarcely anything has been as stimulating to me as the theories and the products of the Surrealists."[11] Surrealism has value in revolt against the "universal confusion" of its times, but adapting social ideas to the realm of the self makes it merely another demanding external force. Precisely in what it shares with such "progressivism" has Surrealism, for Miller, lost its way: "It seems to me that it is a very simple error which the Surrealists are guilty of; they are trying to establish an Absolute. They are trying with all the powers of consciousness to usher in the glory of the Unconscious" (181).

The primary importance of surrealist work, Miller agrees with the early

Breton, lies in finding "the possibilities of the marvellous which lie concealed in the commonplace. They have done it by juxtaposition" (193). However, even this is but a beginning; it does not establish a new creative vision. Miller's quarrel with Surrealism arises from a determination to take it seriously, not on principle but as a means for answering the urgent demands of the modern, the purpose of which is expression through new form, to produce "not even a representation of the Unconscious, but a necessity of the Unconscious" (173).

The theories of Freud, likewise, he sees not as administrable treatment but as "creative and anarchic," "a piece of art," or "purely aesthetic" (168–69). All art for Miller is expressive and individual; by creation he discovers that life in all its facets may appear marvelous. It enables him to write, in a fully affirmative way, "The artist's dream of the impossible, the miraculous, is simply the resultant of his inability to adapt himself to reality. He creates, therefore, a reality of his own—in the poem—a reality which is suitable to him, a reality in which he can live out his unconscious desires, wishes, dreams. The poem is the dream made flesh, in a two-fold sense: as work of art, and as life, which is a work of art."[12]

AN AMERICAN ORIGINAL

The last phrase quoted echoes Tzara and recalls Walter Benjamin's idea of the surrealist unity of the impenetrable and the everyday. These assumptions are fundamental to American forms of modernism because they restore integrity to actual experience while potentiating the spiritual. The open forms of Miller's "autobiographical documents," like his explicit statements, stress again and again that Mystery is inseparable from the flow of experience. The carnality of Miller's mind and writing holds him down to earth, and this rootedness supports his extravagant leaps into the intangible. "I do not have to look in my vest pocket to find my soul; it is there all the time, bumping against my ribs, swelling, inflated with song."[13] Frequently in *Tropic of Cancer* he speaks of his "health" and "optimism," admitting, "I'm a bit retarded, like most Americans" (45). Yet it is precisely his acceptance of factual conditions that makes for the wild imaginings a place in his life.

Though his literary models are largely European, especially French, his style, language, personality, and worldview are unmistakably American. His ideas are rather derivative but their articulation is strikingly new. Writing roughly a year and a half after Wilson, Paul Rosenfeld credits Miller with "giving surrealism new life" yet reminds us that he "is also conspicuously faithful to another tradition, recently neglected by newer American writers, and indisputably valuable. In general, it is the tradition of originality."[14] In a line of clear-eyed Americans who see through calcified propriety and pretense, which includes Ben Franklin, Walt Whitman, and Mark Twain among others, Miller owes nothing to orthodoxy, even when it exerts pressure by being topical.

Miller is a modernist in that he understands himself, however ambivalently, as of his times. The Zeitgeist of the modern helped him to break the constraints of writing "museum stuff" and to discover his personal voice. His tardy, hit-and-miss discovery of the artistic currents of the times (and, later, problems in publishing his work) insulated him from politeness and conventional literariness. For, despite the outbursts of Cubism, Dada, and Surrealism, and the vernacular directness of Hemingway and others, literature in English still needed the release his writings could give it—as the censorship of his and of Lawrence's late work testified.

By the later 1930s, some modernists had become respectable (such as Eliot), fashionable (Stein), and/or famous (Joyce), even if not massively popular like Hemingway. In that climate, however, Miller remained an outsider. Although he and Gertrude Stein were both Americans who lived in the same city and had written books considered unpublishable in large editions, the difference between their life-styles was extreme. The success of *The Autobiography of Alice B. Toklas* and a lecture tour of the United States in 1934 added public notoriety to Stein's position as leader of the official avant-garde. From her home she dispensed approbation and banishment in a royal manner not unlike Breton's during his reign as "the pope of Surrealism." A mutual friend, who asked if she would invite Miller to dine, says that she responded, "We're very particular who we pass meals to. . . . I have an instinctive feeling for when people are using me and when they really need a meal, and I cannot conceive of a situation where I would help Miller however desperate he might be."[15]

As a latecomer from the working class who presented indecorous subjects in explicit style, Miller sometimes proved as unwelcome to his established contemporaries as had Whitman to Emerson after the latter's enthusiastic initial response to *Leaves of Grass*. T. S. Eliot, by 1934 long freed from bank clerking and installed as an editor of the *Criterion*, had distanced himself so far from the American vernacular that Miller wrote, "Kahane was elated to know that the famous T. S. Eliot might print Pound's review [of *Tropic of Cancer*] in his magazine. I'm not." Less than a year later, Eliot rejected some of his epistolary collaboration with Michael Fraenkel, sending "a mildly sarcastic letter about it being more suitable for my 'admirers' and not calculated to 'widen my public.' "[16]

Eliot and Stein share a priori ideas about what good writing is and what it may include. Pound, despite his political and social prejudices, was more willing to consider new work on its own merits. He is credited with the pithy response to *Tropic of Cancer*: "Here is a dirty book worth reading." Pound wrote to Miller that he had notified two editors of his willingness to review the book, though no review ever appeared. In the same message, sent on two postcards, he praised it as "useful (I mean to the seereeyus critic) as means of allocating Joyce's kinks, and W. Lewis' ill humor." On the second card he continues,

> "Great deal more to the book than I thought when I wrote to you yester/ after reading about 40 pages. NEVERTHELESS, though you realize the force of money AS destiny, the one question you haven't asked yourself is:
> What IS money? who makes it/how does it get that way? . . ."[17]

In response to this attempt to interest him in Pound's hobbyhorse, economics, Miller wrote "Money and How It Gets That Way," printed as a pamphlet in 1936. Dedicated to Pound, it laughs at the issue in question (perhaps the only possible unjudgmental response) in doubletalk, burlesque, and parodies of scholarly knowledge. Yet Pound continued to speak positively of his work, though he didn't especially enjoy it: "Miller has considerable talent. Ultimately bores me, as did D. H. Lawrence. But that is private. . . . I am *not* the general reader; and Miller is too good for them. I mean more than they deserve; and I wish him luck."[18]

His writings of the 1930s emphasize Miller's status as outsider and unconverted "proletarian." He experiences the Great Depression firsthand, rather than protesting against it from the artist's privileged vantage. Though he pronounces himself "an artist," in doing so he drags the term off its pedestal. Once *Tropic of Cancer* became notorious, he attempted on a broader scale to enact what Henry does in the book: solicit support from well-wishers. In letters to magazines and in broadsides, he asked for money and goods (clothing, art supplies, and the like) that would help him continue to live while writing. In particular, *What Are You Going To Do About Alf* (1935; reprinted in 1938 and 1944) takes a stance that would make George Orwell, Gertrude Stein, and T. S. Eliot cringe, each for his or her own reasons. Miller does away with social commitment, polite manners, and the artist's nobility in a single paragraph, buttonholing the reader in a good-humored rant that is consistent with the ethic of his books:

> There are lots of people in this world who don't believe in charity any more. They want to overthrow the Government, set up a new economic order, establish higher ideals, etc., etc. *I don't believe in this crap. I believe in nothing except what is active, immediate and personal.* The reason for this is because I am practical and realistic. That sounds funny, I know, but it's a fact. For guys like Hitler, Roosevelt and Mussolini it's all right to talk about "the new order": they're in the gravy, and there's nothing to lose by it. But guys like us are at the bottom. We have to eat every day, and smoke, and what not. Five Year Plans don't interest us. Tomorrow doesn't interest us. It's today that counts—*and only today!* Do you follow me?[19]

Miller maintains a common-sense American slant on politics and artistic decorum. Possessing the anarchic spirit of modernism without leftist orthodoxy, he is aware of the history of Western civilization but indifferent to its demise because it has betrayed the human spirit. Conversely, living abroad enhances his ability to look at his native land. Europeans endure as models for the type of creative life he wants, despite reservations about some of their practices. Having returned briefly to New York in 1936, he writes to Fraenkel,

> Thinking of the letter I wanted to write you I was compelled to make a note of this phrase which kept repeating itself in my head all day: "How far we are from the world of André Breton." This was the clue by which I intended to recapture the complex bundle of emotions which this country inspires in me day after day. In reality all these emotions resolve themselves into one—my joy in realizing that I am free of this country. . . . I lived out my American problem; it is for the other 120,000,000 Americans to live out theirs. . . . By comparison with that other world of which André Breton is a native America is a far-flung empire of neurosis.[20]

Miller is most truly a modernist in the works he wrote before World War II. Leaving France in 1939 as the Nazis prepared to invade, he traveled first to Greece. The record of his journey, *The Colossus of Maroussi*, marks a turn from the explosive outrage of the early books toward more meditative work. In the forties, back in the United States, he wrote several important essays, including his antiwar piece, "Murder the Murderer," and the defense of his work, "Obscenity and the Law of Reflection." The successors to his early autobiographies, the three volumes of *The Rosy Crucifixion*, lack the fire and immediacy of his breakthrough books, often lapsing into windy recollection or near pornography. His finest book of the post-Paris years, *Big Sur and the Oranges of Hieronymous Bosch* (1957), takes as its tutelary spirit Thoreau rather than Whitman or the surrealists.

The modernist era itself ended with the coming of the war. Social disruption and the aging of the participants accounted for many deaths, the number increasing through the late thirties and the forties. Not the historically fastidious suicide of Harry Crosby (1929), coincident with the end of the Roaring Twenties, but the death of D. H. Lawrence in 1930 signaled the beginning of its decline. Hart Crane killed himself in 1932. The painter Charles Demuth died in 1935. In the next year began the slaughter of the finest Spanish poets of the time: Federico Garcia Lorca was murdered and Miguel de Unamuno died under house arrest. In 1937 Antonin Artaud, a living suicide, was incarcerated in a madhouse.

In 1939 the pace accelerated. W. B. Yeats and Ford Madox Ford died, as did Antonio Machado, having fled Spain while gravely ill, and Freud, having fled Vienna. Miller lost his publisher, Jack Kahane. In 1940 Walter Benjamin, sick and fearing he would not be admitted into France, committed suicide. Scott Fitzgerald and Nathanael West died in California, Paul Klee in Bern. James Joyce and Sherwood Anderson, as well as the French painter Robert Delaunay, died in 1941. In 1942 Miguel Hernandez expired after three years in a Franco prison. The community of painters suffered further losses: Marsden Hartley in 1943, Kandinsky, Piet Mondrian, and F. T. Marinetti in 1944. Theodore Dreiser, all but silent for ten years, passed on in 1945. Finally, 1946 saw the demise of Gertrude Stein, Alfred Stieglitz, and Paul Rosenfeld, as well as the artists Arthur Dove and Laszlo Moholy-Nagy.

The important writers who survived found themselves in a changed world, aged beyond the time of their high seasons, the 1920s and 1930s. A new generation came forward in America in the 1950s, many of them looking to the modernists for example and inspiration. By then, Henry Miller was established as an elder statesman of the avant-garde, and it hardly mattered that he had arrived late.

Notes

1.   Edmund Wilson, *The Shores of Light* (New York: Farrar, Straus, 1952), 706; hereafter cited in the text.

2.   George Orwell, *Inside the Whale and Other Essays* (London: Penguin, 1957), 9; hereafter cited in the text.

3.   Henry Miller, *Tropic of Capricorn* (New York: Grove Press, 1961), 284; hereafter cited in the text.

4.   Wassily Kandinsky, *Concerning the Spiritual in Art* (New York: George Wittenborn, 1947), 47; hereafter cited in the text.

5.   Henry Miller, *Tropic of Cancer* (New York: Grove Press, 1961), 200; hereafter cited in the text.

6.   Dickran Tashijian, *Skyscraper Primitives: Dada and the American Avant-Garde 1910–1925* (Middletown, Conn.: Wesleyan University Press, 1975), 13.

7.   *Theories of Modern Art*, ed. Herschel B. Chipp (Berkeley: University of California Press, 1968), 386–87; hereafter cited in the text as Chipp.

8.   André Breton, *Manifestoes of Surrealism* (Ann Arbor: University of Michigan Press, 1969), 14; hereafter cited in the text.

9.   Walter Benjamin, *Reflections*, ed. Peter Demetz, (New York: Harcourt, Brace, Jovanovich, 1978), 179 and 90.

10.   Henry Miller, *Stand Still Like the Hummingbird* (New York: New Directions, 1962), 169.

11.   Henry Miller, *The Cosmological Eye* (New York: New Directions, 1939), 188; hereafter cited in the text.

12.   Henry Miller, *The Wisdom of the Heart* (New York: New Directions, 1941), 4.

13.   Henry Miller, *Black Spring* (New York: Grove Press, 1963), 23.

14.   Paul Rosenfeld, "The Traditions and Henry Miller" in Henry Miller et al., *Of, By, and About Henry Miller* (Yonkers, N.Y.: Alicat Bookshop Press, 1947), 10–11.

15.   Bern Porter, *Observations from the Treadmill*, quoted in Norman Mailer, *Genius and Lust* (New York: Grove Press, 1976), 83.

16.   Henry Miller, *Letters to Anaïs Nin*, ed Gunther Stuhlmann (New York: G. P. Putnam's Sons, 1965), 144; Lawrence Durrell and Henry Miller, *A Private Correspondence*, ed.

George Wickes (New York: Dutton, 1963), 46. See also *Tropic of Cancer*, 35, in which Henry sees, "Intellectual trees, nourished by the paving stones. Like T. S. Eliot's verse."

17.   *Letters to Anaïs Nin*, 233. "Money and How It Gets That Way" is reprinted in *Stand Still Like the Hummingbird*, 119–56; see especially the Foreword. Miller copied Pound's message into his own correspondence.

18.   Ezra Pound, *Letters, 1907–1941*, ed. D. D. Paige (New York: New Directions, 1950), 301. For more admiring comments, see Ezra Pound, *Pound/Joyce*, ed. Forrest Read, (New York: New Directions, 1967), 256.

19.   Henry Miller, *What Are You Going To Do About Alf?* (Berkeley: Bern Porter, 1944), 9–10.

20.   Henry Miller and Michael Fraenkel, *Hamlet* (New York-Paris: Carrefour, 1939), 95–96.

The Anti-Aesthetic of Henry Miller

Welch D. Everman

All art, I firmly believe, will one day disappear.

—Henry Miller

This call for the disappearance of art is by no means unique in the writings of Henry Miller. Indeed, he insists again and again that art will and must exhaust itself—often he declares that it already has—and each time he announces the death of Western art, he does so joyfully, as if he were more than willing to do the job himself. The end of art—in particular, the end of literature—seems to be his most beloved project, a project announced in the opening pages of *Tropic of Cancer*.

> There are no more books to be written, thank God.
> This then? This is not a book. This is libel, slander, defamation of character. This is not a book, in the ordinary sense of the word. No, this is a prolonged insult, a gob of spit in the face of Art, a kick in the pants to God, Man, Destiny, Time, Love, Beauty . . . what you will.[1]

If *Tropic of Cancer* marks the beginning of that project, then here, at the very beginning of the beginning, we come upon an apparent contradiction. Miller's call for an end to literature comes from within literature itself, from within the text of a book—admittedly "not a book, in the ordinary sense of the word," but a book nevertheless—that would kill the book by way of the book. *Tropic of Cancer*, it would seem, begins by insisting upon its own impossibility, then proceeds to deny that impossibility by becoming, in fact, a book in its own right, yet another book. The book that would bring an end to all literature, including itself, seems rather to confirm literature in general and its own literariness in particular in and through its self-destructive project, like the suicidal scorpion in Julio Cortazar's *Hopscotch*: "The scorpion stabbing itself in the neck, tired of being a scorpion but having to have recourse to its own scorpionness in order to do away with itself as a scorpion."[2]

Miller, of course, would not be impressed by this argument—contradic-

This essay was written specifically for this volume and is published here for the first time with the permission of the author.

tions never seem to bother him—but, for our purposes, it is worth bearing in mind that if Miller's goal is the end of literature, and if literature itself is to be the means to that end, then his project is impossible, a failure even before it begins.

There is another apparent contradiction at work in Miller's call for an end to literature, to art: the contradiction between his refusal of art and his priviledging of the artist. "All art, I firmly believe, will one day disappear. But the artist will remain, and life itself will become not 'an art,' but art, i.e., will definitely and for all time usurp the field."[3]

For Miller, the purpose of art—of *all* art—is to destroy itself, and so the true artist is the one who works for that destruction and who does so, somehow, without sacrificing his or her own status as artist. "Unconsciously," Miller writes, "I think that every great artist is trying with might and main to destroy art."[4]

Again, the project of the artist would seem to be impossible. If the artist's job is to put an end to art, then the role of the artist must come to an end as well. On the other hand, if the artist insists upon remaining an artist—whose job it is to destroy art—then art itself must remain, if only to give the artist something to destroy.

How are we to make sense of all this? Do we have to? Perhaps the apparent impossibility of Miller's project isn't really a problem after all. Perhaps he is right in his refusal to take such contradictions seriously. What Miller seems to have in mind—and he makes this point with remarkable consistency throughout his writings—is an art that would break down the barriers between art and not-art, between art and life. The artist would be the one whose art would escape the limits of its own conventions and open out into the world, where art and life would be identical. Art would become itself by ceasing to be itself, as the artist would become the artist not by way of production but by way of loss.

Of course there is nothing new about Miller's desire to give art over to life and to do so by using art against itself. Among others, the romantics, the dadaists, and the early surrealists also called for an art that would transcend itself in favor of a reality grounded variously in ontotheology, in politics, in the Freudian unconscious, and so on. And of course Miller saw his own project as part of a history of art-against-art, of anti-art, if you will. He wrote about the great anti-artists, Blake and Rabelais, Céline, the dadaists, the surrealists, and one of his most important and striking books, *The Time of the Assassins*,[5] addresses that hero of anti-art, Arthur Rimbaud, who abandoned poetry in favor of life beyond the confines of art. Characteristically, the book is as much about the author as it is about Rimbaud, as if Miller were trying to find his place in what poet John Ashbery has called the "other tradition"[6] that grounds his own project.

For all this historical grounding, however, there is something about Miller's project that we might want to call, for lack of a better term, postmodern. Certainly Miller's works run counter to the modernist thinking that was prevalent during his most productive years, thinking grounded in traditional dichotomies (subject/object, high art/kitsch, presence/absence, self/other, art/life) that established art as a separate realm, answerable only to itself. "Modernism," according to Clement Greenberg, "reduces the work of art to matter-of-fact by analyzing it strictly in terms of its formal relations, and then regarding them as the final reality of the work."[7]

By this definition, modernist formalism would reject the very possibility of art's transcending itself. Modernist art is one thing, life another, and the project of the modern artist is to question his or her medium and its formal possibilities (Kuspit, 19). Certainly, as an artist, Miller has something very different in mind. He writes: "The artist's game is to move over into reality."[8]

If postmodern thought questions, blurs, or even collapses the distinction between art and life, as it questions, blurs, or collapses so much of our traditional thinking, then, for better or worse, Miller is a postmodernist. By saying this, I do not want to suggest that Miller was a forerunner of postmodernism, that he was merely "ahead of his time." The term *postmodern* is in many ways unfortunate, because it carries within it a sense of development, of progress—*after* modernism comes *post*modernism. And yet there is, of course, a historical dimension to postmodern thought; it is, I would say, Ashbery's "other tradition." In this sense, Blake, Rabelais, Céline, and Miller are as postmodern as, say, John Cage or Italo Calvino, regardless of the historical era in which they lived and worked. The term is probably worth keeping, if only because it suggests that our own era—the era *after* modernism—is a time in which the "other tradition" is becoming somewhat less other, but it is important to bear in mind that postmodernism designates not simply or even primarily a historical moment but a consciousness that opens to question the givens of our culture and that seems to be able to hold apparent contradictions in place without the need for resolution.

Certainly this designation suits Henry Miller, and certainly Miller has much in common with other artists working in a variety of media who use art against itself and who are usually discussed under the rubric of postmodernism—I'm thinking in this case of Marcel Duchamp, John Cage, and Robert Rauschenberg.

As early as 1915, Duchamp began selecting ordinary manufactured objects—snow shovels, bottle racks, urinals—and declaring them to be works of art. The Duchampian ready-made collapses any possible distinction between art and not-art, because it insists that any object can become a work of art and that anyone can "create" it; Duchamp claims that his ready-mades were selected without reference to aesthetic judgment. But if everything is art and if everyone is an artist, then the very notion of art breaks down, collapses under its own weight.

In 1952, pianist David Tudor offered the premier performance of John Cage's composition 4′33″, in which Tudor sat at the piano for four minutes and thirty-three seconds, doing nothing except closing and opening the keyboard cover to mark the beginning of each of the three movements. The ambient noise in the auditorium during the performance *was* the performance. If every sound is music, if everyone and anyone can be a concert musician or a composer (for surely it took no musical knowledge or ability to compose *4'33"*), then once again art ceases to be art. It gives up its priviledged status in favor of the commonplace, of life.

In 1961, Robert Rauschenberg presented "Black Market," one of his famous "combine paintings." The work consisted of a painted canvas and an array of small objects chosen more or less at random, and viewers were invited to take the objects that appealed to them and replace them with objects of their own choosing. Certainly, Rauschenberg had learned well from Duchamp and Cage. If "Black Market," *4'33"*, and the Duchampian readymades are works of art, they are works that transcend themselves as art—cancel themselves out—in favor of something else. And, though his strategies are quite different, the same might be said for the writings of Henry Miller.

Like Duchamp, Cage, and Rauschenberg, Miller is subversive as an artist, but the workings of a piece like *The Rosy Crucifixion* are less obvious and more complicated than overt pieces like *4'33"*. In his own way, Miller is every bit as outrageous as Cage, but he works from a somewhat different aesthetic. Or perhaps "aesthetic" isn't the right word. If an aesthetic establishes the conventions by which art is to be made and beauty realized, then Miller's end-of-art-by-way-of-art project would seem to call for an anti-aesthetic. This anti-aesthetic rejects the well-crafted novel of coherent characters and a logical cause-and-effect plot in favor of association, digression, and contradiction.

Certainly this is the way *The Rosy Crucifixion* works—or fails to work. The narrator is walking down a New York street, going nowhere in particular, and he notices a building and remembers something that happened there years before, or that happened in a building that looked much like this one. Or he remembers something that has nothing to do with where he is or what he is doing—he simply remembers. And often the memory has nothing to do with what comes before or after in the text. It is simply there. Again and again, the author interrupts the loose flow of the narrative to offer his views on life, love, or whatever, and often these views contradict ideas proposed elsewhere in the text. *The Rosy Crucifixion* does not develop; it simply unfolds in an exhaustive and exhausting flow of language that sometimes breaks down completely.

A shuttle moving back and forth, a bobbin ceaselessly bobbing. Now and then a dropped stitch. . . . Like the man who lifted her dress. He was standing on the stoop saying good-night. Silence. He blows his brains out. . . . Or the father flying his kites on the roof. He comes flying down out of the sky, like a violent angel of Chagall's. He walks between his race horses, holding one on either side, by the bridle. Silence. The Stradivarius is missing. . . . (*Sexus*, 329).

Ihab Hassan has written of *The Rosy Crucifixion*: "[I]t is interminable, perhaps the most tedious achievement of our time, perhaps the exemplary realization of anti-literature,"[9] and he is right, of course, though these comments, which would constitute a devastating attack on any other literary work, merely confirm Miller's project in *Sexus, Plexus*, and *Nexus*. The work *is* interminable, and purposely so, for it never could have been completed. *The Rosy Crucifixion* neither begins nor ends; it starts, continues for more than 1,500 pages, then stops. "No end, no conclusion, no completion. Perpetual becoming."[10] And it could be added to indefinitely, with another memory here, another digression there. The text is potentially infinite. "[T]his magum opus . . .," Miller writes, "I thought would be just one enormous, endless tome" (*Art and Outrage*, 30).

If Miller's project is the end of literature, his method in *The Rosy Crucifixion* seems to be to say everything, to exhaust the possibilities of language so that literature is no longer necessary, or even conceivable. *The Rosy Crucifixion*, if successful, would reduce literature to silence. Therefore, the work must be interminable, and Miller must contradict himself again and again, because if he is to exhaust the possibilities of what can be said, he must offer every idea, every thought, from every direction.

Anything and everything, every idea, every thought, every memory, every experience, and every dream can and must find its way into *The Rosy Crucifixion*. And so, just as for Duchamp every object is worthy of becoming a work of art, and just as for Cage every sound is worthy of becoming music, so for Miller every idea, thought, and so forth is worthy of becoming "literature." No passage in the text is more or less important than any other, and, on principle, nothing is to be excluded.

This is an impossible project, of course, a necessary failure, comparable only to the works of the Marquis de Sade, who also hoped to say everything and whose books are also tedious and seemingly interminable. But Sade's efforts to reduce literature to silence are based on a rigorously logical aesthetic of combination and permutation. By comparison, Miller's anti-aesthetic is seemingly without system, without method, without rigor, without logic.

And yet it is almost a truism to say that every anti-aesthetic—even Miller's—is an aesthetic in its own right, with its own method and its own goal. I have suggested that Miller's method is digression, association, and contradiction, and his goal is the dissolution of art in favor of life. Therefore, if Miller's anti-aesthetic *is* another kind of aesthetic, it is not an aesthetic of beauty and pleasure, for that would merely lead to more works of art. Miller wants not beauty but ecstasy, and his aesthetic is an aesthetic of the sublime.

Like Kant, Schopenhauer, and other thinkers before him, Jean-François Lyotard conceives of the experience of the sublime as a kind of threat. "[T]he sublime," he writes, "is kindled by the threat of nothing further happening."[11] In the literary realm, "nothing further happening" would be the end of literature, the eternally blank page, the silence that would remain after all the possibilities of writing had been exhausted. According to Ihab Hassan, this is what Henry Miller has in mind: "Obviously, Miller is an egregious instance of the prolific writer who aspires, beyond anti-literature even, to silence" (Hassan, 57).

But what might such an impossible silence mean? As every reader of Miller knows, his work is self-centered, sometimes to the point of egomania. And self, for Miller, takes shape in writing, sentence after sentence, page after page, book after book. To exhaust the possibilities of writing, to fall silent, to fall into that hypothetical silence on the far side of literature would be, for Miller, to lose the self, to transcend self in favor of—what? To experience this loss, this surrender of the self to the threat of nothingness ("Surrender, and the bliss which accompanies surrender")[12] is to experience the sublime. It is to be consumed by life, and by life, Miller means not everyday human life but life in a far grander sense. "Man does not look to the sun in vain; he demands light and warmth not for the corpse which he will one day discard but for his inner being. His greatest desire is to burn with ecstasy, to commerge his little flame with the central fire of the universe" (*Assassins*, 88).

This is the ecstatic aspect of Miller's work, the sublime experience of the loss of self which is the goal of writing and which the author clearly hopes to share with the reader—it is perhaps in this sense that Miller considers his writings to be "therapeutic" (*Art and Outrage*, 29).

This is also the religious aspect of Miller's project, and Miller is, in the words of Lawrence Durrell, "primarily a religious writer." Durrell adds that, given Miller's emphasis on the erotic, calling him a religious writer seems like "a laughable paradox" (*Art and Outrage*, 23), though of course it is not. Georges Bataille has argued that, because eroticism offers the possibility of a momentary loss of self, "all eroticism has a sacramental character."[13] The erotic experience, the religious experience, and the experience of the sublime all seem to be grounded in the same sense of loss—the loss of self and the promise of silence, of nothingness, of death. "Through loss man can regain the free movement of the universe, he can dance and swirl in the full rapture of those great swarms of stars. But he must, in the violent expenditure of self, perceive that he breathes in the power of death."[14]

The erotic experience, the religious experience, and the experience of the sublime—this is Miller's territory, his project, his goal. But the experience of the sublime would seem to be transitory at best. The self falls silent for an instant, dissolves for a moment, then returns to the mundane world, the world of selves and others, the world of literature in which the writer must keep writing in hopes of going beyond the literary and reaching that moment of ecstasy once again. No doubt this is why Miller so often refers to the experience of the sublime as the not-yet or the almost.

> A moment ago I had known what it was to pass beyond joy. A moment ago I had forgotten absolutely who I was: I had spread myself over the whole earth. Had it been more intense perhaps I would have passed over that thin line which separates the sane from the insane. I might have achieved depersonalization, drowned myself in the ocean of immensity. (*Sexus*, 311)

Failure seems to be built into an aesthetic of the sublime, and yet for Miller, the artist has nothing to gain by limiting his or her efforts to what can be done. Indeed, Miller seems to welcome failure, because, paradoxically, it is the recognition of impossibility that makes the impossible possible.

> I would like my words to flow along in the same way that the world flows along, a serpentine movement through incalculable dimensions, axes, latitudes, climates, conditions. I accept *a priori* my inability to realize such an ideal. It does not bother me in the least. In the ultimate sense, the world itself is pregnant with failure, is the perfect manifestation of imperfection, of the consciousness of failure. In the realization of this, failure is itself eliminated. (*WH*, 23)

Notes

1. Henry Miller, *Tropic of Cancer* (New York: Grove Press, 1961), 1–2.
2. Julio Cortazar, *Hopscotch*, trans. Gregory Rabassa (New York: Pantheon Books, 1966), 158.
3. Henry Miller, *The Wisdom of the Heart* (New York: New Directions, 1960), 24; hereafter cited in the text as *WH*.
4. Henry Miller, *The Cosmological Eye* (New York: New Directions, 1939), 167.
5. Henry Miller, *The Time of the Assassins* (New York: Pocket Books, 1975); hereafter cited in the text as *Assassins*.
6. "The Other Tradition" is the title of a John Ashbery poem in *Houseboat Days* (New York: Penguin Books, 1977), 2–3.
7. Donald B. Kuspit, *Clement Greenberg: Art Critic* (Madison: University of Wisconsin Press, 1979), 171–72; hereafter cited in the text.
8. Henry Miller, *Sexus* (New York: Grove Press, 1965), 273; hereafter cited in the text.
9. Ihab Hassan, *The Literature of Silence: Henry Miller and Samuel Beckett* (New York: Alfred A. Knopf, 1967), 85; hereafter cited in the text.
10. Lawrence Durrell, Alfred Perlès, and Henry Miller, *Art and Outrage: A Correspondence About Henry Miller* (New York: E. P. Dutton, 1961), 39; hereafter cited in the text.
11. Jean-François Lyotard, "The Sublime and the Avant Garde," in *The Lyotard Reader*, ed. Andrew Benjamin (Cambridge, Mass.: Basil Blackwell, 1989), 204.

12.   Henry Miller, *Plexus* (New York: Grove Press, 1965), 317.

13.   Georges Bataille, *Erotism: Death and Sensuality*, trans. Mary Dalwoöd (San Francisco: City Lights Books, 1986), 15–16.

14.   Georges Bataille, "Celestial Bodies," trans. Annette Michelson, *October* 36 (Spring 1986): 78.

Henry Miller: On the Centenary of His Birth

RICHARD KOSTELANETZ

Several critics, among them H. L. Mencken, Sir Herbert Read, and Lawrence Durrell, identify Miller as an excellent writer of English prose. Their evaluation is more true than false. Miller's prose resembles Mencken's in having the conversational directness of a man sharing confidences with his readers; we are pleased to listen to him, and continue listening, because keeping our attention is important to him. One measure of quality in his prose are many brilliant similes and memorable metaphors. "Everything is sordid, shoddy, thin as pasteboard. A Coney Island of the mind."[1] He characterizes his own aloof position in a decaying world as "like being in a lunatic asylum, with permission to masturbate for the rest of your life."[2] His short story "The Smile at the Foot of the Ladder" contains this touching metaphorical description of Auguste the Clown: "Within the radius of the spotlight lay the world in which he was born anew each evening. It comprised only those objects, creatures and beings which moved in the circle of enchantment."[3]

Miller is a master of explosive sentences that rise to the authority of prophecy:

> The saddest sight of all [in America] are the automobiles parked outside the mills and factories. The automobile stands out in my mind as the very symbol of falsity and illusion. There they are, thousands upon thousands of them, in such profusion that it would seem as if no man were too poor to own one. When the American worker steps out of his shining tin chariot he delivers himself body and soul to the most stultifying labor a man can perform.[4]

Some of Miller's descriptions are superlatively concise: "[Moldorf] has only one cane—a mediocre one. In his pocket are scraps of paper containing prescriptions for Weltschmerz."[5] He describes a seedy but pompous woman at a plush astrological party: "Her one desire was to get home as soon as possible, rip off her corset, and scratch herself like a mangy dog."[6] Remembering his visit to the stuffy promiscuous wife of a friend recently deceased, Miller writes, "When I rang the bell of the apartment I was trembling. I

An early version of this essay was prepared as an honors thesis at Brown University under the direction of Foster Damon.

almost expected her to come out stark naked, with perhaps a mourning band around her breasts" (*BS*, 208). Elsewhere his description of an airline stewardess is classic: "[She] had been trained to behave like a mother, a nurse, a mistress, a cook, a drudge, never to look untidy, never to lose her Marcel wave, never to show a sign of fatigue of disappointment, or chagrin or loneliness" (*SAW*, 21).

On the other hand, in his willful rejection of a literary voice, he often slips into the saddest clichés. He sounds like a slick popularizer when he concludes, "This, in a nutshell, is Bufano's philosophy."[7] Frequently he resorts to such clichés as this: "As far back as I can remember my ancestors were straining at the leash."[8] Equally distasteful is the weak sentimentality of "there she stands, the fair city of Paris, soft, gem-like, a holy citadel" (*BS*, 208). Although his language for sexual experience can be genuinely original ("I shoot hot bolts into you, Tania, I make your ovaries incandescent" [*Cancer*, 15]), more often he relies on the most familiar epithets. "One cunt out of a million, Llona," he writes in *Cancer*, while in *Sexus* Miller clumsily describes a letter he has sent as "smeared with cat shit, bird shit, dog shit, and one or two other varieties, including the well-known human variety."[9] Many of his sentences too obviously echo the prose of Louis-Ferdinand Céline: "In fact, almost all Montparnasse is Jewish, or half-Jewish, which is worse. . . . The Jews are snowing me under" (*Cancer*, 13). Finally, too many Miller metaphors are vague and clumsy: "Suffering is futile," he writes in *Capricorn*. "For me it is nothing more than an algebraic demonstration of spiritual inadaptability."[10] Especially in his later books, he tends to babble to an extent that cannot be quoted in an appreciation this short.

Compared with his contemporaries, Miller ranks among the finest American novelists of city life. Better than anyone else, Miller uses language to depict human qualities indigenous to the modern metropolis. He is skilled at capturing the distinctive characteristics of cities, particularly of New York, where he was born and raised, and of Paris, which he adopted as his home. Miller's New York is drab and depressing, the prototype of oppressive urban existence; yet he never ceases to remind us of his attachment to it. At the opening of *Black Spring*, which contains much of his finest writing, Miller proclaims, "I am a patriot—of the 14th Ward Brooklyn, where I was raised. But I was born in the street and raised in the street. To be born in the street means to wander all your life, to be free." Several lines later, he adds, "Nothing of what is called 'adventure' ever approaches the flavor of the street" (*BS*, 11). The streets of the ward were filthy with human trash and the soot from the nearby factories. No one was cleanly dressed, not even on Sunday. Most of the workingmen were visibly stained by their jobs. Although he recognizes the city's filth, Miller is willing to define himself as a product of it. "Practically all my life I have dwelt in big cities; I am unhappy, uneasy, unless I am in a big city. My feeling for nature is limited to water, mountain and desert." (CE, 346).

Miller not only has a keen sense for urban details but the ability to express his perception in energetic prose. As a Whitmanian, he identifies with the people of the Fourteenth Ward:

> In my dreams I come back to the 14th Ward as a paranoiac returns to his obsessions. When I think of those steel-gray battleships in the Navy Yard I see them lying there in some astrologic dimension in which I am the gunnersmith, the chemist, the dealer in high explosives, the undertaker, the coroner, the cuckold, the sadist, the lawyer and contender, the scholar, the restless one, the jolthead and the brazen-faced. (BS, 13)

In the following paragraph, Miller describes what makes the city so filthy with smoke and debris:

> I remember, with a vividness as if it were etched in acid, the grim, soot-covered walls and chimneys of the tin factory opposite us and the bright, circular pieces of tin that were strewn in the street, some bright and gleaming, others rusted, dull, copperish, leaving a stain on the fingers; I remember the iron-works where the red furnace blowed and men walked toward the glowing pit with huge shovels in their hands, while outside were the shallow wooden forms like coffins with rods through them on which you scraped your shins and broke your neck. I remember the black hands of the iron-moulders, the grit that had sunk so deep into the skin that nothing could remove it, not soap, nor elbow grease, nor money, nor love, nor death. Like a black mark on them? Walking into the furnace like devils with black hands—and later, with flowers over them, cool and rigid in their Sunday suits, not even the rain can wash away the grit. (BS, 13)

Miller relishes experiences that are singularly urban, such as sexual encounters in the subway: "Pressed up against a women so tight I can feel the hair on her twat. She's looking straight ahead, at the microscopic spot just under my right eye" (BS, 13).

Miller's Paris has a texture altogether different from his New York, and he credits Paris with curing him of the depression that forced him to leave America. "I was so desperately hungry not only for the physical and the sensual, for human warmth and understanding, but also for inspiration and illumination" (BS, 347). He concludes, in Remember to Remember, that "during the dark years in Paris these needs were answered" (309). Miller enjoys certain customs that he considers particularly Parisian: "After a day's work one can always find recreation. It costs almost nothing, the price of coffee merely. Just to sit and watch the passing throng. This is a form of recreation almost unknown in America" (Capricorn, 288). On the other hand, one of

Cancer's most famous metaphors is "Paris is like a whore. From a distance she seems ravishing, you can't wait until you have her in your arms. And five minutes later you feel empty, disgusted with yourself. You feel tricked" (205).

Miller describes features characteristic of other cities, in *The Colossus of Maroussi* capturing the distinctive quality of a night in Athens: "An electrical display which . . . is without parallel among the citizens of the world. The Greek is just as enamored of electric light as he is of sunlight. Athens sparkles like a chandelier." Elsewhere in the book, he writes that both Athens and New York are "electrically charged cities," full of excitement; but in praise of Athens, he adds that it "is permeated with a violet-blue reality which envelops you with a caress; New York has a trip-hammer vitality which drives you insane with restlessness" (181). Of European cities as well, Miller has a keen sense of what D. H. Lawrence called "the spirit of the place."[12]

Police commissioners, priggish businessmen, perfumed hens, and other guardians of our culture have said derisively of Henry Miller that he is a "filthy writer." This judgment is perfectly appropriate. Many Miller works are deeply concerned with scatology, the filth of human existence. He describes bodily smells, the lice that thrive in cheap hotels, the oppressive dirt of urban life, and our inability to escape from the unseemly. In his desire for a realistic literature, Miller has decided to include the scatological that has always existed in fact but rarely in fiction.

In making human filth a major topic of his work, Miller culminates a long, mostly hidden tradition. An early Church Father is remembered for having called the lice of his body his "pearls."[13] Artists and writers in the late Middle Ages attributed filth, particularly excremental filth, to man's relations with the devil. The painter Hieronymous Bosch, according to Miller, "in a panel depicting the world as Hell, enthrones Satan on a privy, from which the souls that have passed out of his anus drop into the black pit."[14] In his study *Young Man Luther*, Erik H. Erikson notes Luther's passion for speaking of the devil in anal terms. "Note this down," Luther tells the devil, "I have shit in the pants, and you can hang them around your neck and wipe your mouth with it." Luther defines anal excretions as a weapon of the devil: "A Christian should and could be gay, but then the devil shits on him." Luther uses anal references in his denunciation of Catholicism: "the only portion of the human anatomy which the Pope has had to leave uncontrolled is the hind one." About Luther's intimate concern with anal filth, Erikson has written, "Luther lived with the devil on terms of mutual obstinacy, an inability to let go of each other."[15]

Many years after Luther, Jonathan Swift wrote of the filthy base of love. "Should I the Queen of Love refuse, Because she rose from stinking ooze?" In another passage, Swift metaphorically speaks of the emotions of love as "tulips rais'd from Dung." Likewise, Swift's Yahoos in *Gulliver's Travels* represent the filth and smell of humanity: "The stink was somewhat between a Weasal and a Fox." Like Miller after him, Swift implicitly debunks the pretentiousness of those who regard humanity as the highest example of animal cleanliness.[16]

Ever since Charles Baudelaire initiated the modern revolt against gentility, filth has been a recurring preoccupation of French literature. In the poems collected as *Flowers of Evil*, Baudelaire both slyly suggests and overtly displays excremental imagery. The poem "Spleen" has such overtones:

> When the low heavy sky weighs like a lid
> Upon the spirit aching for the light
> And all the wide horizon's line is hid
> By a black day sadder than any night.[17]

In "Beacons," Baudelaire is yet blunter, speaking of human prayers as "exhaling from excrement" (*Howers*, 13). Arthur Rimbaud had similarly scatological concerns, exclaiming in an opening section of *A Season in Hell*, "My entrails are on fire." In the last, prose section of the poem, "Farewell," the poet turns to the filth and decay of his own body: "I see myself again, skin rotten with mud and pest, worms in my armpits and in my hair, and in my heart much bigger worms, lying among strangers without age, without feeling."[18]

In Alfred Jarry's *Ubu Roi*, first produced in 1896, as the curtain opens, the leading character steps forward and shouts directly at the audience "Merdre" (best translated as "shittr"). Père Ubu is obsessed with anal invectives: "Fart, shittr, it had to get him moving, but fart, shittr, I reckon I've shaken him all the same."[19] Mère Ubu's language is likewise filthy; for, as several critics have noted, the language and interests of *Ubu Roi* are more scatological than sexual. However, whereas Luther and Swift, say, are unself-consciously concerned with the scatological, Jarry intentionally wants to taunt his bourgeois audience by, in Roger Shattuck's phrase, "throwing dung in the public eye."[20] In the strictly French literary tradition, Jarry becomes a precursor of Louis-Ferdinand Céline, a French contemporary of Miller, with whom he is frequently compared.

Two major nineteenth-century American writers have incorporated a concern with human filth. Whitman in "Song of Myself" revels in the smell of his own armpits, deriving pleasure from the sweat of his body. "Divine am I inside and out, and I make holy whatever I touch or am touched from, The scent of these arm-pits aroma finer than prayer."[21]

Several years after Whitman's poems, in 1880, Mark Twain wrote his famous short fiction *1601*, which begins as an imaginary conversation in the court of Queen Elizabeth I. The narrator, Her Majesty's cupbearer, reports that "uin the heat of ye talk it befel yt one did breake wind." Each of the ladies present, including "The Duchess of Bilgewater," denies doing it. The stink was so great that Lord Bacon commented, "Not from my leane entrails hath this prodigy burst forth. . . . Haply shall ye find yt 'tis not from mediocrity this miracle hath issued." Sir Walter Raleigh admits he is the source and apologizes *not* for the act itself but for having "fathered such a weakling . . . in so august a presence. It was nothing—less than nothing, madam—." Later, the narrator confides that Raleigh "delivered he himself of such a godless and rock-shivering blast that all were fain to stop their ears." Because of *1601*'s notoriety, Twain was asked to address the Stomach Club in Paris. His topic was "Some Thoughts on the Science of Onanism."[22] (Although Miller writes in *Nexus*, "I was in such a state, that I felt like . . . jerking off,"[23] there is, to my recollection, no actual onanism in Miller's work.) Like Miller after him, Twain wanted to incorporate into literature human experiences that had been either forbidden or neglected.

Though many of the earlier scatological writers were modest and even ashamed in their treatment of filth, Miller is audaciously frank in his descriptions and absolutely guiltless about his concerns. Indeed, many of his funniest scenes are less erotic than scatological. In *Cancer*, Miller invites an Indian friend to come with him to a whorehouse. Seeing in the bathroom a bidet, the Indian mistakes it for a toilet and defecates into it, much to the hysterical horror of the house. In another scene, Miller is sleeping with a woman, admiring her long hair. "I look at her again, closely. Her hair is alive. I pull back the sheet—more of them. They are swarming all over the pillow." Miller and his girlfriend quickly dress and pack, sneaking out of the hotel, scratching themselves (*Cancer*, 29).

In *The Books in My Life*, Miller remembers an experience that nearly all of us urban children have had: "As a youngster in search of a safe place wherein to devour forbidden classics, I sometimes repaired to the toilet."[24] *Black Spring* contains Miller's ode to the toilet as a suitable place for reading:

> O the wonderful recesses in the toilet! To them I owe my knowledge of Boccaccio, of Rabelais, of Petronius, of *The Golden Ass*. All my good reading, you might say, was done in the toilet. There are passages in *Ulysses* which can be read only in the toilet—if one wants to extract the full flavor of their content. And this is not to denigrate the talent of the author. No harm, I say, can ever be done a great book by taking it with you to the toilet. Only the little books suffer thereby. Only the little books make ass-wipers. (*BS*, 57)

Furthermore, Miller does not shy away from telling his readers about his bowel movements, his occasional attacks of constipation, and his vomiting. Finally, as Kenneth Rexroth perceptively quipped of all Miller's works, "Over the most impassioned arguments and the bawdiest conversations lingers an odor of unwashed socks."[25]

In *Black Spring* is an acknowledgment of the pleasures of urination:

"And while the female squatting down to empty her bladder in a china bowl may not be a sight to relish, no man with any feeling can deny that the sight of the male standing behind a tin strip and looking out on the throng with that contented, easy vacant smile . . . is a good thing" (52). In a scene in *Cancer*, Miller compares literary creation to digestive and sexual excretion. One of his characters, "the great blind Milton of our times," proclaims to the world: "I too love everything that flows, rivers, sewers, lava, semen, blood, bile, words, sentences, . . . even the menstrual flow that carries away the seed unfecund. I love the urine that pours out scalding and the clap that runs endlessly" (249). Female menstruation occurs occasionally in Miller's books. In one example, in *Sexus*, Miller says of his friend who has just finished intercourse, "We all looked at Ulric: from the navel down to his knees he was a mass of blood. It was rather embarrassing for Lola."[26] For Miller, as for Twain (but unlike the Europeans acknowledged before), filth is first of all comic—until we realize that Miller is seriously asking us to acknowledge it as an intrinsic part of human existence.

If Miller is the finest American novelist of urban life as well as of scatology, he is comparatively weak in portraying sexual experience. Nearly all his female characters are shadowy nymphomaniacs with voluptuous bodies and limitless capacities for orgasm: "She kept right on coming, one orgasm after another, until I thought it would never stop" (*Sexus*, 72).[27] In his adult life, Miller, to my count, is never rejected in his sexual designs; he never encounters an inpenetrable or frigid woman. As noted before, he never resorts to masturbation. He doesn't suffer delicate negotiations with a woman who is either reluctant or erotically fussy. Though initially a loser in most of life's competitions, he portrays himself as consistently a winner with women. Sex in Miller is repetitive—the same techniques, the same easy conquests, and even the same phrases recur again and again, until the reader is barely able to distinguish one sexual encounter from another. Sex, even repetitive sex, is never depleting to Miller. Ironically, whereas he describes the scatological at a fairly high level of mimeticism, his portrayal of sex is definitely low mimetic.

By contrasting Miller with writers who handle sexual experience more sensitively we can measure how Miller fails. In his short story "The Time of Her Time," in *Advertisements for Myself* (1959), Norman Mailer depicts a sexual gymnast luring a college sophomore into his arenalike apartment, cajoling her into his bed and, after some bantering, finishing the act.[28] Mailer depicts both his characters as human beings reacting to each other and captures the specialness that such sex experience has for *both* participants. In the same way, Frank Harris in his five-volume *My Life and Loves* (1925) conveys to his readers not only the distinct personalities and bodies of the women he seduces but his care for them (for one thing, claiming never to publish a volume until after all the women portrayed in it have died), the problems of contraception (which Miller never considers), and the details of each act of intercourse.

In Alberto Moravia's novels we find something that is rare in Miller—sexually motivated complexity. That is, although Miller's characters experience sex freely, there is no sense that lack of sex can be frustrating and thus can lead to greater, if not perverted, thirsts. To Miller as an adolescent, lack of sex is like lack of money—tough luck. By contrast, for Moravia's Agostino of *Two Adolescents*, sexual inexperience is emotionally disturbing, a misfortune that both sets him apart from the other boys and separates him from further maturity.[29] In the short novel *Conjugal Love*, Moravia depicts a sensuous wife who is sexually snubbed by her writer-husband on the grounds that sex diminishes his desire for work.[30] Out of unsatisfied need she turns to the pudgy, greasy barber who comes to the writer's home every morning. The novel turns upon the reader's judgment as to whether the wife's infidelity is justified. Moravia's characters desire sex; this desire motivates their actions; frustrations do not eliminate desire. A feeling for these dynamics, coupled with his skillful characterizations and the absence of hackneyed symbolism, makes Moravia, in my opinion, a finer novelist of sexual experience whose Chekhovian success makes us only more aware of dimensions lacking in Miller.

Miller was a great admirer of D. H. Lawrence and devoted a number of his densest essays to him; but Lawrence too, despite his failings, is a better novelist of sex than is Miller. Where Miller describes intercourse in a paragraph or a page or two at best (unless, as in *Plexus*, he is engaged in an orgy), Lawrence devotes several pages to describing the delicate relationship between Mellors and Lady Chatterley. Lawrence evokes a symbolism for sex; and like Moravia, he sees how desire for sex is psychologically important to the characters. Lawrence's major failing is his attempt to make extramarital sex stand for individualistic rebellion; and as he moves between naturalistic and allegorical realms, Lawrence both overloads his fiction and confuses his purposes. Nonetheless, if only for his recognition of subtleties and complexities, Lawrence remains a better writer on sexual experience.

On the other hand, it is easy to distinguish Miller from the hard-core pornographer. Using the Kronhausens' distinction between pornography and erotic realism, Donald Phelps writes shrewdly, "Pornography isolates a single prism of experience—sex—from the context of sweat, fret, psychological tensions, and infinite finagling, with which—certainly in America—this experience is usually interwoven."[31] Sex in Miller, as noted before, is not so much isolated as symbolic.

There is one sense, however, in which Miller realizes a special novelistic insight into erotic experience—in his understanding of human beings as "polymorphously perverse." Like Sigmund Freud, Miller recognizes that people receive sexual pleasure not only from heterosexual intercourse but also from urinating, defecating, masturbating, and sucking, among other pleasures. Because he writes so truthfully and sensitively of these aspects of sexual experience, we can classify Miller as an excellent novelist of libidinal gratification.

Miller envisions the genuine artist as an apostle of a certain kind of self-liberation. Not only does sexual experience represent freedom but so do the acts of writing and reading about it. The fundamental theme of his books is less unfettered living than the unfettered response to unfettered living. His project as a writer is responding in print without any loss of vitality or freshness of response. In a key remark, he once said, "My books are not about sex but about self-liberation,"[32] and since, as noted before, seduction in his novels is minimally realistic, it is fair to say that sexual experience in Miller must be about something else: voyages to emancipation, in his case the narrator's (or his own) freedom. Miller's remark demonstrates that he thinks of liberation in terms broader than sexual promiscuity. Other components of his quest include a distaste for labor, for society's institutions, and for antihuman machines, coupled with a strong desire for mundane liberty and pleasurable play.

To understand Miller's conception of the artist we should turn to Freudian psychology, particularly as it has been interpreted by Norman O. Brown. Noting that Freud vacillated in defining a theory of artistic creation, with some of his essays expressing general schemes while others stated that the secret of art is beyond psychoanalytic understanding, Brown turns to one of Freud's early works, *Wit and the Unconscious*, for a psychoanalytic theory of art.[33] Recognizing the connections between wit and the pleasure-principle, Brown suggests that the purpose of art, as of wit, is "to undo repression" (Brown, 55–63). While dreams and neurosis give *expression* to the repressed unconscious, they are not capable of actually liberating it. In contrast, by actually liberating human instincts from their bondage, art joins wit in giving the psyche a positive libidinal pleasure denied to the neurotic dreamer (Brown, 64–65). "The function of art," Brown concludes, "is to help us find our way back to sources of pleasure that have been rendered inaccessible by the capitulation to the reality-principle . . . in other words, to regain the lost laughter of infancy" (60). "The function of childhood is play activity." Hence, Brown is led to associate art with libidinal activities: "Art as pleasure, art as play, art as the recovery of childhood, art as making conscious the unconscious, art as a mode of instinctual liberation, art as the fellowship of men struggling for instinctual liberation—these ideas plainly fit into the system of psychoanalysis" (65–66).

From this definition of art Brown can then identify the artist as the epitome of the pleasure-communicating human being. He characterizes the artist as one "who refuses initiation through education into the existing order, [and] remains faithful to his childhood being" (67). The child's foremost source of pleasure is his "polymorphously perverse" body, and in Brown's idea of sexuality and psychic health the polymorphously perverse child is the least neurotic human being (chaps. 3, 11, 12, 16). Therefore, the artist-as-child must be an "unneurotic" individual whose creations are devoured by a neurotic audience that turns to art for Eros's strength to oppose Thanatos, the death wish that is allied with repression.

It should be clear that Brown's concept of the artist aptly characterizes the first-person artist-narrator who writes about his endless struggle to realize a "natural," libidinal existence as a prerequisite to self-liberation. More prephallic than phallic, Miller's narrator generally prefers broad libidinal, polymorphously perverse pleasure to narrow genital pleasure. In a classic dichotomy, the artist emulates not Apollo but Dionysius (without indulging in drink). In his essays as well, Miller expresses many of Freud-cum-Brown's themes regarding the artist. In "An Open Letter to Surrealists Everywhere," Miller explains that "the artist does not tinker with the universe. . . . He knows that the transformation must proceed from within outward, not vice versa." A few lines later he describes this transformation in terms of making the conscious self aware of the unconscious self, which is to say by writing: "It is a process of expropriating the world, of becoming God. The striving toward this limit, the expansion of the self, in other words, is what truly brings about the condition of the marvelous" (*CE*, 193–94). Miller also speaks of the artist's greater penetration of the collective unconscious. In his essay "The Cosmological Eye," Miller writes of his prototypical example of the creative artist, Hans Reichel: "The cosmological eye is sunk deep within the body. Everything he looks at and seizes must be brought below the threshold of consciousness, brought deep into the entrails where there reigns an absolute night" (*CE*, 359). Penetration of the unconscious, combined with "expansion of the self," characterizes the act of artistic creation that also brings self-liberation.

Miller joins Norman O. Brown in believing that the true writer is able to aid his readers in their instinctual struggles. In his essay "Reflections on Writing," Miller writes of the redemptive value of writing. "The adventure is a metaphysical one: it is a way of approaching life indirectly, of acquiring a total rather than a partial view of the universe."[34] In this voyage the artist is able to penetrate essences and communicate these essences back to his readers. "By the force and power of the artist's vision the static, synthetic whole which is called the world is destroyed. The artist gives back to us a vital, singing universe, alive in all its parts" (*WH*, 3). On the same page Miller offers a more elaborate characterization of these essences: "This final reality which the artist comes to recognize in his maturity is that symbolic paradise of the womb, that 'China' which the psychologists place somewhere between the conscious and the unconscious, that pre-natal security and immortality and union with nature from which he must wrest his freedom." In the return to the womb, the artist finds liberty, play, security, contentment; in reaccepting his unconscious, the artist repudiates the reality-principle and thus the horrors of civilization. In communicating his experience, the artist has a redeeming power, becoming the avatar of liberated existence in a postanarchic world.

Though Miller the writer frequently equates literature with falseness, saying "what is not in the open street is false derived, that is to say, *literature*" (*BS*, 9), Miller himself was both a voracious reader of books and an occasional literary critic. In *My Friend Henry Miller*, Alfred Perlès reports that Miller often read a large portion of a book before eating breakfast.[35] In his introduction to *The Intimate Henry Miller*, Lawrence Clark Powell, the librarian at UCLA, describes how Miller came into the library and asked for a book by the Christian mystic Jacob Boehme. Powell took him to a shelf on an underground level. "He settled down on his haunches on the floor and began to leaf through it, read phrases, and talk more to himself than to me," Powell remembers. "I left Henry Miller reading on the cold floor, and when I returned two and a half hours later he was still here, like a Buddha, smiling and joyful."[36] Describing this as the start of a friendship "cemented in mutual bookishness," Powell adds that as a librarian he has personally taken a prodigious number of books, on a variety of topics, to Miller's home.

At times in his essays Miller drops the naive pose long enough to talk about his reading. In his "Autobiographical Note," he remembers that, though his father never read a book in his life, the son devoured "the dictionary and the encyclopedia." Until he was twenty-five he scarcely read a novel. Of the extensive reading of his thirties he identifies Dostoyevsky, Nietzsche, Élie Faure (the art historian), Spengler, Havelock Ellis, Emma Goldman, and Marcel Proust as the writers that influenced him most. Miller defines his place as in the mythic, as opposed to the naturalistic, tradition of American literature. "Of American writers the only real influences were Whitman and Emerson. I admit to Melville's genius, but I find him boring. I dislike Henry James intensely, and absolutely detest Edgar Allan Poe. As far as English literature, it leaves me cold, as do the English themselves; it is a sort of fish-world which is completely alien to me" (*CE*, 356ff.).

In 1952 Miller published *The Books in My Life*, a record of his reading. Although he asserts in the preface that "one should read less and less, not more and more," Miller goes on to praise Lawrence Clark Powell "for making books a vital part of our life" (*BML*, 11, 18). Miller's impressionistic criticism then convinces the reader of the pleasures to be gained from reading Jean Giono, Blaise Cendrars, H. Rider Haggard (a popular British novelist also favored by Carl Jung), Knut Hamsun, Hermann Hesse, and many other writers similarly more concerned with mythic undercurrents than with surface reality. In one chapter, Miller acknowledges a passion for the theater (though he has not written any notable plays): "Drama is the one category of literature into which I have delved more than any other" (*BML*, 287). At the end of the book, Miller offers a list of "the hundred books which influenced me most" (317ff.). Though Shakespeare, Cervantes, Dante, Hegel, St. Thomas Aquinas, Tolstoy, and T. S. Eliot are all conspicuously absent, the list includes a goodly number of such standard canonical writers as the Greek dramatists, Balzac, Cellini, Defoe, Dostoyevsky, Dreiser, Joyce, and Twain, in addition to a few less famous authors: Alain-Fournier, Céline, Paul Eltzbacher, Fenollosa, Dane Rudhyar, and Sikelianou—the last of whom is listed as the author of "Proanakrousma (in manuscript, translated)." All these references suggest that Miller, despite his pretense of intellectual naiveté, was an extremely literate man.[37] Indeed, what other major American prose writer has provided such an accurate list of his sources, including, for one test of honesty, a generous number of his contemporaries? Even Miller confirms the thesis that, as Malcolm Cowley put it, "all great writers have been great readers at some time of their lives."[38]

In addition to this book on books, Miller wrote several major pieces of literary criticism, most of which were included in his five books of collected essays. He also produced a book-length critical work, *The Time of the Assassins*, in which he identifies with the French poet Rimbaud, and for many years he worked on a lengthy study of D. H. Lawrence "only to end up in utter confusion."[39] Most of Miller's literary essays are impressionist in critical approach and flamboyant in tone. In "The Universe of Death," an essay on Marcel Proust and James Joyce, Miller makes several shrewd comments in the course of comparing the authors. "Where Proust held himself suspended over life in a cataleptic trance, weighing, dissecting, and eventually corroded by the very scepticism he had employed, Joyce had already plunged into the abyss" (*CE*, 111). Miller also traces their similarities: "They are naturalists who [unlike himself] present the world as they find it, and say nothing about the causes, nor derive from their findings any conclusions" (*CE*, 118). Neglecting Joyce's intentions, Miller offers his own impressionistic definition of Molly Bloom: "She is the quintessence of the great whore which is Woman, of Babylon, the vessel of abominations. Floating, unresisting, eternal, all-contained, she is like the sea itself. Like the sea she is receptive, fecund, vicarious, insatiable" (133).

In Miller's essay on the diary of Anaïs Nin, one of Miller's closest literary colleagues, he proclaims that the fifty-volume work is "a monumental confession which . . . will take its place beside the revelations of Saint Augustine, Petronius, Abelard, Rousseau, Proust, and others" (269). For twenty-two pages, he extols the values of this then-unpublished work, attributing to it the greatest universal themes and the most profound understandings. Nowhere in the essay does Miller quote from the text. When Miller the literary critic talks about the classics, his impressionistic comments are sensitive and pertinent; but when he tries to inflate the work of his friends, he becomes as hollow as a writer of blurbs.

* * *

Although most criticism of Miller has shirked basic evaluative tasks, it is possible to judge his work objectively and justly. He is a very good prose writer, though scarcely the finest or most original stylist in twentieth-century American letters. As a novelist of urban experience, he is superb, highly sensitive to the various aspects of city life and successful in communicating his reactions. In this respect, he surpasses all his American contemporaries. (Indeed, one can say that after he moved to coastal California, living away from cities, the quality of his writing declined perceptibly.) Miller is also a serious social critic protesting against the horrors of modern life, and his conception of history, as well as the artist's role in history, is both coherent and significant. Although his own position in relation to the decay of modern life is ambiguous and his philosophical discourse sometimes confused, he is deeply concerned with problems of meaning and the viable life. By no means is he, as some critics have tried to depict him, a shallow thinker. Although his treatment of sexual experience is more mythic than realistic or insightful, he is unique in acknowledging the filth in which most of us live. As a literary critic, he is sometimes analytical but usually impressionistic. His comments on other writers, albeit idiosyncratic, have critical value. In short, Miller ranks among the best writers of his generation. His work will be remembered not only as a symptom of his time, as George Orwell thought, but also for its literary merit.

In structure, Miller's novels are a series of vignettes. He is not a skillful fabricator of formally perfect novels. Hence, one returns to Miller not by reading an entire book again but by rereading one's favorite essays or passages: "Soirée in Hollywood," "Astrological Fricasee," "Max," "The Universe of Death," "Bufano," the opening sections of *Black Spring*, the chapter in *Tropic of Cancer* on the Dijon academy, the descriptions of the Cosmococcic Telegraph Company, and his memoirs of Knossos and Katsimbalis. These are portions of Miller's work to which even the most skeptical reader can profitably return.

Development as a writer is one criterion for measuring literary greatness in our time. We customarily praise James Joyce because each of his three novels transcends the preoccupations of its predecessor. Only in his first four books does Miller exhibit a sense of progress. To my mind, his second published book, *Black Spring*, surpasses *Cancer*, his first. Though the third, *Capricorn*, is worse than the first two, the fourth, *The Colossus of Maroussi*, contains some of Miller's best writing and his most interesting materials. The later volumes that constitute *The Rosy Crucifixion* trilogy are distinctly lesser. The humor is less effective, the sexual materials are methodically handled, the prose is not as exciting, and the characters are weaker. As he conceived of his autobiographical novels as parts of one great, seven-volume work, he did not experiment with alternative approaches to the problems of fiction. Although Miller's failure either to develop his talent or to experiment with literary possibilities diminish the value of his total achievement, such neglects do not devalue individual works.

The evidence presented here suggests that Miller has several literary virtues, some less obvious than others, along with numerous vices. While he is not one of the greatest American writers of his era, on the plane of, say, Faulkner and T. S. Eliot, he belongs to that group just below, authors of merit and distinction whom we call "major writers," in a generation that also includes F. Scott Fitzgerald, John Dos Passos, Ernest Hemingway, and Gertrude Stein. Even more important, perhaps, Miller, more than any of his contemporaries, offered images of liberation—both sociopolitical and literary—that would speak to the needs of succeeding generations. By freeing himself from the fear of exposing his deepest self in his writings, he transformed forever what writers could publicly say about their experience. The ultimate theme of his works and his life (to the extent that the two are one) is that freedom of speech is the essence of human liberation, and that this fundamental right is rooted in the body.

NOTES

1. Henry Miller, *Black Spring* (Paris: Obelisk, 1958), 173; hereafter cited in the text as *BS*.
2. Miller, *The Air-Conditioned Nightmare* (New York: Avon, 1961), 145; hereafter cited in the text as *ACN*.
3. Miller, *The Smile at the Foot of the Ladder* (San Francisco: Greenwood, 1955), 2; hereafter cited in the text as *SFL*.
4. Miller, *Sunday After the War* (New York: New Directions, 1958), 196; hereafter cited in the text as *SAW*.
5. Miller, *Tropic of Cancer* (Paris: Obelisk, n.d.), 18; hereafter cited in the text.
6. Miller, "Astrological Fricassee," *Nights of Love and Laughter* (New York: Signet, 1955), 90; hereafter cited in the text as *NLL*.
7. Miller, *Remember to Remember* (New York: New Directions, 1947), 378; hereafter cited in the text as *RR*.
8. Miller, *The Cosmological Eye* (New York: New Directions, 1944), 348; hereafter cited in the text as *CE*.
9. Miller, *Sexus* (Paris: Olympia, 1960), 23; hereafter cited in the text.
10. Miller, *Tropic of Capricorn* (Paris: Olympia, 1959), 338; hereafter cited in the text.
11. Miller, *The Colossus of Maroussi* (New York: New Directions, 1958), 208ff.
12. D. H. Lawrence, *Studies in Classic American Literature* (Garden City: Doubleday Anchor, 1954), ch. 1.
13. For this example and for guidance in much of the following discussion, I am indebted to Professor S. Foster Damon, in many ways my greatest teacher at Brown. For more on Damon's specialness, see my "S. Foster Damon," *Horns of Plenty* 3, no. 2 (Summer 1990): 45–47.
14. Quoted in Norman O. Brown, *Life Against Death* (New York: Modern Library, 1959), 207; hereafter cited in the text. For a print of the original painting, see "The Hell of the Musicians," pl. 12 in Wilhelm Franger, *The Millennium of Hieronymous Bosch* (Chicago: University of Chicago Press, 1951), opposite 84, as well as Franger's discussion, 84–85.

Miller praises Franger's volume in *Big Sur and the Oranges of Hieronymous Bosch* (New York: New Directions, 1957), x.

15. Erik H. Erikson, *Young Man Luther* (New York: W. W. Norton, 1958), 244ff. For more on Luther's anality, see G. Rattray Taylor, *Sex in History* (New York: Ballantine, 1959), 158–61.

16. Regarding Swift, see Norman O. Brown, "The Excremental Vision," *Life Against Death*, 179–201.

17. Charles Baudelaire, *Flowers of Evil*, trans. Marthiel and Jackson Matthews (New York: New Directions, 1958), 63; hereafter cited in the text.

18. Arthur Rimbaud, *A Season in Hell*, trans. Louise Varese (New York: New Directions, 1961), 27, 84.

19. Alfred Jarry, *Ubu Roi*, in *Four Modern French Comedies*, introduced by Wallace Fowlie (New York: Capricorn, 1960), 33.

20. Roger Shattuck, *The Banquet Years* (Garden City: Doubleday Anchor, 1961), 209.

21. Walt Whitman, "Song of Myself," in *The Laurel Whitman*, ed. Leslie A. Fiedler (New York: Dell, 1959), 53. In his introduction to this volume, Fiedler writes, "Surely one goal of any new selection from Whitman ought to be the redemption of that pristine poet, that 'dirtiest beast,' whom, in a world grown ever more genteel, we cannot afford to lose."

22. In the absence of the complete edition of *1601*, which was read under supervised circumstances, I have drawn these quotations from Phyllis and Eberhard Kronhausen, *Pornography and the Law* (New York: Ballantine, 1959), 43–55.

23. Miller, *Nexus* (Paris: Obelisk Press, 1960), 211.

24. Miller, *The Books in My Life* (New York: New Directions, 1952), 264; hereafter cited in the text as *BML*.

25. Kenneth Rexroth, introduction to *NLL*, 15.

26. For further insight into such displacements, consider Kenneth Burke's discussion of the "Demonic Trinity" in his *Grammar of Motives* (New York: Prentice-Hall, 1945), 300–303.

27. The following statement, by one of Miller's earliest advocates, does not, to my mind, exonerate Miller from my charge: "Mr. Miller proves countless times how much more [woman] is the object of sex and hunger. She is a kind of test both of the reality of man and of his function." Wallace Fowlie, "Shadow of Doom," *The Happy Rock* (Berkeley, Calif.: Bern Porter, 1945), 105.

28. Norman Mailer, *Advertisements for Myself* (New York: Putnam, 1959), 478–503.

29. Alberto Moravia, *Two Adolescents* (London: Secker & Warburg, 1952).

30. Alberto Moravia, *Conjugal Love* (New York: Signet, 1961).

31. Kronhausen, *Pornography and the Law*, 175–243; Donald Phelps, "A Second Look at Pornography," *Kulchur* 1, no. 3 (1961): 57–75.

32. *Henry Miller Newsletter* 2 (November 1960): 4.

33. For contradictions in Freud's theory of art, compare his "On the Relation of the Poet to Day-Dreaming," *Dream, Delusion and Other Essays* (Boston: Beacon, 1956) with his "Dostoevsky and Parricide," *Partisan Review* 14 (1945): 530–44.

34. Miller, *The Wisdom of the Heart* (New York: New Directions, 1958), 191; hereafter cited in the text as *WH*.

35. Alfred Perlès, *My Friend Henry Miller* (New York: John Day, 1956), 193.

36. Lawrence Clark Powell, *The Intimate Henry Miller* (New York: Signet, 1959); hereafter cited in the text as *IHM*.

37. In *IHM* (ix), Powell writes: "Along with Mark Twain, Jack London, and Upton Sinclair, Henry Miller is one of the widest read of all American writers."

38. Malcolm Cowley, introduction to *The Portable Hawthorne* (New York: Viking, 1948), 5.

39. *Henry Miller Reader* (New York: New Directions, 1959), 203.

MILLER IN RETROSPECT

◆

Reflections of a Cosmic Tourist: An Afternoon with Henry Miller

Jonathan Cott

> But you have so refined our sensitivity, so heightened our awareness, so deepened our love for men and women, for books, for nature, for a thousand and one things of life which only one of your own unending paragraphs could catalogue, that you awaken in us the desire to turn you inside out.
>
> —Henry Miller on Blaise Cendrars
> *The Books in My Life*

Henry Miller—"confused, negligent, reckless, lusty, obscene, boisterous, thoughtful, scrupulous, lying, diabolically truthful man that I am"; author of many famous and infamous books "filled with wisdom and nonsense, truth and falsehood, toenails, hair, teeth, blood and ovaries" (his words)—has been called everything from "a counterrevolutionary sexual politician" (Kate Millett) to "a true sexual revolutionary" (Norman Mailer); an author who neglects "form and *mesure*" (Frank Kermode) to "the only imaginative prose writer of the slightest value who has appeared among the English-speaking races for some years past" (George Orwell).

Now 83, and in spite of recent illnesses still painting and writing, Miller is still accepting what he once called our Air-Conditioned Nightmare with joyful incredulity, still continuing to find out and tell us who he is. This past year marks the 40th anniversary of the publication of the first Paris edition of *Tropic of Cancer*—Miller's first published book—and it is now indisputably clear that Miller's more than 40 subsequent volumes must be read simply as one enormous evolving work—a perpetual *Bildungsroman*—manifesting the always changing, yet ever the same, awareness and celebration of the recovery of the divinity of man, as well as of the way of truth which, Miller says, leads not to salvation but to enlightenment. "There is no salvation, really, only infinite realms of experience providing more and more tests, demanding more and more faith. . . . When each thing is lived through to the end, there is no death and no regrets, neither is there a false springtime; each moment lived pushes open a greater, wider horizon from which there is no escape save living."

Gentile Dybbuck (as he once called himself), patriot of the 14th Ward (Brooklyn), American anarchist, Parisian *voyou*, cosmic tourist in Greece, sage of Big Sur, Henry Miller is today an inhabitant of an improbable-looking Georgian colonial house in Pacific Palisades, Los Angeles—a house teeming with posters, paintings, sketches and photographs, all tokens and traces of Miller's ebullient, peripatetic life.

There are a number of his radiant "instinctive" watercolors hanging in the living room. ("If it doesn't look like a horse when I'm through, I can always turn it into a hammock," he once said of his "method" of painting in "The Angel Is My Watermark.") On one wall is a hand-inscribed poster listing the names of scores of places Miller has visited around the world—with marginal comments:

Bruges—the Dead City (for poets)

Imperial City, California (loss of identity)

Pisa (talking to tower all hours)

Cafe Boudou, Paris: Rue Fontaine

   (Algerian whore)

Grand Canyon (still the best)

Corfu—Violating Temple (English girl)

Biarritz (rain, rain, rain)

In the kitchen, posted on a cabinet, is his Consubstantial Health Menu, which announces favorite dishes: e.g., Bata Yaku! Sauerfleisch mit Kartoffel-klösze, Leeks, Zucchini ad perpetuum, Calves' Liver (yum yum) . . . and a strong warning: Please! No Health Food.

Across one end of his study is a floor-to-ceiling bookshelf containing hundreds of his own works translated into scores of languages, while two other walls are completely decorated with graffiti and drawings, all contributed by visitors, friends and by Henry himself: "Kill the Buddha!" "Let's Case the Joint!" "Love, Delight and Organ Are Feminine in the Plural!" "The Last Sleeper of the Middle Ages!" "Don't Look for Miracles. You Are the Miracle!"

Most fascinating of all is the author's famous bathroom—a veritable museum which presents the iconography of the World of Henry Miller: photos of actresses on the set of the filmed version of *Tropic of Cancer*, Buddhas from four countries, a portrait of Hermann Hesse ("Most writers don't look so hot," Miller says. "They're thin blooded, alone with their thoughts."), a Jungian mandala, Taoist emblems, a Bosch reproduction, the castle of Ludwig of Bavaria, Miller's fifth wife Hoki (from whom he's now separated and about whom he wrote: "First it was a broken toe, then it was a broken brow and finally a broken heart"), the head of Gurdjieff ("of all masters the most interesting") and, hidden away in the corner, a couple of hard-core photos "for people who expect something like that in here." (Tom Schiller's delightful film, *Henry Miller Asleep and Awake*—distributed by New Yorker Films—is shot in this very bathroom and presents the author taking the viewer around on a guided tour.)

"I really hate greeting you like this, in pajamas and in bed," Miller says as I enter his bedroom. Smiling and talking with a never discarded bristly, crepitated Brooklyn accent and a tone of voice blending honey and *rezina*, he continues: "I just got out of the hospital again, you see. They had to replace an artificial artery running from my neck down to the leg. It didn't work, it developed an abscess, and so they had to take out both the artery and the abscess. I'm really in bad shape, no?" Miller says, laughing. "And this is all attributable to those damned cigarettes. I was an athlete when I was young—don't you know? I was good at track and a bicycle rider. I didn't smoke until I was 25, and then it was incessant. And all my wives smoked, too. If I start again it means death. My circulation will stop, and they'll have to cut off my legs."

Again a smile and a gentle laugh. "Always Merry and Bright!"— Henry's lifelong motto.

"You'll have to speak to my left ear—the other one doesn't work. And I've lost vision in my left eye."

"Can you see me?" I ask.

"I certainly imagined you differently," Miller responds. "When I heard that someone named Jonathan was coming, I thought you'd be some tall, uptight Englishman with blond hair. But I'm glad I was wrong."

Henry, unlike his fellow expatriate novelist and namesake Henry (James)—it is impossible to think of two more wildly opposite types—is well known for his caustic Anglophobic attitudes. (Miller in a letter to Lawrence Durrell: "The most terrible, damning line in the whole of *The Black Book* is that remark of Chamberlain's: 'Look, do you think it would damage our relationship if I sucked you off?' That almost tells the whole story of England.") But strangely, it is the English Lawrence Durrell who, as a 23-year-old writer and diplomat living in Corfu, wrote the then 43-year-old Miller an ecstatic fan letter after reading *Tropic of Cancer*, calling it "the only really man-sized piece of work this century can boast of." They have been close friends and correspondents for almost 40 years, and in fact Durrell and his wife are expected this evening for dinner. (Durrell taught this past year at Cal Tech, one of the main reasons being to keep in close contact with his friend.)

Hanging on the wall alongside Henry's bed is a dramatic photo of a saintly looking Chinese man, whose face bears an uncanny resemblance to Miller's own.

"That's a photo of a Chinese sage I found in a magazine 30 years ago,"

Henry says, noticing my interest. "I framed it and kept it ever since. I regard him as an enlightened man, even though he wasn't known."

"You yourself once characterized the French writer Blaise Cendrars as 'the Chinese rock-bottom man of my imagination,' " I mention, pulling out my little black notebook to check the quote.

"I'm sure Durrell christened me that," Henry says. "Are you sure I said that about Cendrars?"

"Absolutely, it's in my book here."

Henry looks at me bemusedly. "That's really something," he exclaims. "I should have realized this before. But with that book you really look just like that guy Columbo on television. Peter Falk plays him, and he seems a little half-witted, you know, a little stupid . . . not conniving but *cunning*. Yes, I'd like to be like that. That's my idea of a man! . . . Go right ahead with . . . what is it you want to ask me? . . . Amazing, just like that guy Columbo."

"This isn't really a question," I say, rummaging through the book, "but speaking of the Chinese, I'd like to read you a little story by Chuang-Tze, the disciple of Lao-Tze. I wrote it down to read to you because to me it suggests something very deep and basic about all of your work."

"Just read it loudly and slowly, please," Henry says.

Chuang-Tze writes: "The sovereign of the Southern Sea is called Dissatisfaction (with things as they are); the sovereign of the Northern Sea, Revolution; the sovereign of the Center of the World, Chaos. Dissatisfaction and Revolution from time to time met together in the territory of Chaos, and Chaos treated them very hospitably. The two sovereigns planned how to repay Chaos's kindness. They said, 'Men all have seven holes to their bodies for seeing, hearing, eating and breathing. Our friend has none of these. Let us try to bore some holes in him.' Each day they bored one hole. On the seventh day Chaos died."

"That's a fantastic story," Henry says. "And it's interesting that you see that in my work."

"I was thinking of your idea of chaos as the fluid which enveloped you, which you breathed in through the gills. And of the fertile void, the chaos which you've called the 'seat of creation itself,' whose order is beyond human comprehension. And of the 'humanizing' and destruction of the natural order. And I was thinking, too, of your statement in *Black Spring*: 'My faltering and groping, my search for any and every means of expression, is a sort of divine stuttering. *I am dazzled by the glorious collapse of the world!*' "

"Yes, that's wonderful," Henry says. "I don't even remember some of these things you say I've written. Read some more from your notebook."

"I've been thinking about your obsession in your books with the idea of China, and that photo on the wall made me realize how much you look Chinese. 'I want to become nothing more than the China I already am,' you once wrote. 'I am nothing if not Chinese,' and you've identified *Chinese* with that 'supernormal life such that one is unnaturally gay, unnaturally healthy, unnaturally indifferent. . . . The artist scorns the ordinary alphabet and adopts the symbol, the ideograph. *He writes* Chinese.' And in many of your works you point over and over again to the fact that our verb 'to be,' intransitive in English, is transitive in Chinese."

"Yes, yes, that's become my credo. To be gay is the sign of health and intelligence. First of all humor: That's what the Chinese philosophers had, and what the Germans never had. Nietzsche had some, but it was morbid and bitter. But Kant, Schopenhauer . . . you can look in vain. Chuang-Tze is a genius, his marvelous humor comes out of all his pores. And without that you can't have humor. My favorite American writer, for instance, is the Jewish immigrant I.B. Singer. He makes me laugh and weep, he tears me apart, don't you know? Most American writers hardly touch me, they're always on the surface. He's a big man in my estimation.

"But speaking of the Chinese, I have intuitive flashes that I have Mongol and Jewish blood in me—two strange mixtures, no? As far as I know, I'm German all the way through, but I disown it. I believe that blood counts very strongly—what's in your veins. I've had that feeling. Because I'm a real German, and I don't like that. Not just because of the war . . . long before that: I was raised among them in a German-American neighborhood, and they're worse than the Germans in Germany. . . . Of course, there's Goethe, Schiller, Heine, Hölderlin, the composers. . . . Naturally they're wonderful.

"You know something? I was recently reading Hermann Hesse's last book, *My Belief*. And the very end of this book has to do with Oriental writers. He mentions how his perspective on life changed when he became acquainted with Lao-Tze, Chuang-Tze and the I Ching, of course. And I discovered these writers when I was about 18. I was crazy about the Chinese. I have trouble, however, with the novels like *All Men Are Brothers*—too many characters and there's no psychology—everything is on the surface."

"One of my favorite books of yours, Henry, is *Big Sur and the Oranges of Hieronymus Bosch*. Your meditations on and descriptions of your friends and life in Big Sur are so serene and lambent, like some of the great Chinese poems. I wish it had gone on and on."

"The poets who retired in old age to the country," Henry reflects. "Yes, that's right. I've tried to model myself on the Chinese sages. And they were happy, gay men. I've heard that the old men in China before the Revolution used to sit out on river boats and converse, drink tea, smoke and just enjoy talking about philosophy or literature. They always invited girls to come and drink with them. And then they'd go and fly a kite afterwards, a real kite. I think that's admirable. . . . We flew kites in Big Sur, but there we had big winds in canyons with birds being lifted by the updrafts. The kites got torn and smashed."

"I especially remember," I mention, "that passage in *Big Sur* where you describe the morning sun rising behind you and throwing an enlarged shadow of yourself into the iridescent fog below. You wrote about it this way: 'I lift my arms as in prayer, achieving a wingspan no god ever possessed, and there in the drifting fog a nimbus floats about my head, a radiant nimbus such as the Buddha himself might proudly wear. In the Himalayas, where the same phenomenon occurs, it is said that a devout follower of the Buddha will throw himself from a peak—*into the arms of Buddha.*' "

"Yes, I remember that," Henry says. "Your shadow is in the light and fog, overaggrandized; you're in monstrous size and you're tempted to throw yourself over."

"That reminds me of Anaïs Nin's comment." I mention, "that the figures in your books are always 'outsized . . . whether tyrant or victims, man or woman.' "

"That's true," Henry responds. "That's because I'm enthusiastic and I exaggerate, I adore and worship. I don't just *like*. I love. I go overboard. And if I hate, it's in the same way. I don't know any neutral, in-between ground."

Henry Miller's enthusiasms and exaggerations have led many persons to hold on to a distorted picture of the author as a writer only of six supposedly epigamic "sex" books (the *Tropics, Quiet Days in Clichy*, and *Sexus, Plexus* and *Nexus*) for a reading constituency consisting primarily of GIs in Place Pigalle, existentialist wastrels or academic "freaks" like Karl Shapiro (who called Miller the "greatest living author").

Of the above mentioned works, *Tropic of Capricorn* is certainly one of the most original works of 20th-century literature. And the fact that Henry Miller has been stereotyped so disparagingly is a peculiarity of American literary history, since his work is one that consistently evolves, perfectly exemplifying the ideas of rapturous change, metamorphosis, surrender and growth.

"The angels praising the Lord are never the same," the great Hasidic Rabbi Nachman once said. "The Lord changes them every day." One of Henry Miller's favorite statements is that of the philosopher Eric Gutkind: "To overcome the world is to make it transparent." And it is as if with the transparency of angels that Miller reveals an unparalleled literary ability to disappear into the objects and persons of his attention and thereby to allow them to appear in an unmediated radiance. Miller's heightened identification with everything he notices is made even more powerful by means of an astonishing descriptive presentational immediacy and an attendant sense of magnanimity.

Consider his meditation on his friend Hans Reichel's painting, *The Stillborn Twins*:

> It is an ensemble of miniature panels in which there is not only the embryonic flavor but the hieroglyphic as well. If he likes you, Reichel will show you in

one of the panels the little shirt which the mother of the stillborn twins was probably thinking of in her agony. He says it so simply and honestly that you feel like weeping. The little shirt embedded in a cold prenatal green is indeed the sort of shirt which only a woman in travail could summon up. You feel that with the freezing torture of birth, at the moment when the mind seems ready to snap, the mother's eye inwardly turning gropes frantically towards some tender, known object which will attach her, if only for a moment, to the world of human entities. In this quick, agonized clutch the mother sinks back, through worlds unknown to man, to planets long since disappeared, where perhaps there were no babies' shirts but where there was the warmth, the tenderness, the mossy envelope of a love beyond love, of a love for the disparate elements which metamorphose through the mother, through her pain, through her death, so that life may go on. Each panel, if you read it with the cosmological eye, is a throwback to an undecipherable script of life. The whole cosmos is moving back and forth through the sluice of time and the stillborn twins are embedded there in the cold prenatal green with the shirt that was never worn.

—"The Cosmological Eye"

Or read Miller's descriptions of the Paris photographs of the French photographer Brassai:

What strange cities—and situations stranger still! The mendicant sitting on the public bench thirsting for a glimmer of sun, the butcher standing in a pool of blood with knife upraised, the scows and barges dreaming in the shadows of the bridges, the pimp standing against a wall with cigarette in hand, the street cleaner with her broom of reddish twigs, her thick, gnarled fingers, her high stomach draped in black, a shroud over her womb, rinsing away the vomit of the night before so that when I pass over the cobblestones my feet will gleam with the light of morning stars. I see the old hats, the sombreros and fedoras, the velours and Panamas that I painted with a clutching fury; I see the corners of walls eroded by time and weather which I passed in the night and in passing felt the erosion going on in myself, corners of my own walls crumbling away, blown down, dispersed, reintegrated elsewhere in mysterious shape and essence. I see the old tin urinals where, standing in the dead silence of the night, I dreamed so violently that the past sprang up like a white horse and carried me out of the body.

—"The Eye of Paris"

Most persons seem to have forgotten (or have never known) not only passages like these but also: the great reveries on Brooklyn, the pissoirs in Paris and the madness of Tante Melia (all in *Black Spring*); the hymn to Saturnian effluvia and the talking-blues Dipsy Doodle passacaglia which tells the story of Louis the Armstrong and Epaminondas (*The Colossus of Maroussi*); his dreamlike discovery of the secret street in "Reunion in Brooklyn"; the letters to Alfred Perlès and Lawrence Durrell; the prose poems describing

Miller's obsession with painting (*To Paint Is to Love Again, The Waters Reglitterized*); the *Hamlet* correspondence with Michael Fraenkel (long out of print); and the essays on Balzac, D. H. Lawrence, Cendrars and H. Rider Haggard. All of these have been overlooked in the still raging debate concerning Miller's problematic attitude toward women.

The recent Mailer/Miller/Millett literary fracas presented Kate Millett in her book *Sexual Politics*, accusing Miller of depersonalizing women with his virulent and fear-ridden sexual attitudes, while Norman Mailer in *The Prisoner of Sex* defended him as a "sexual pioneer." There is little question, as Mailer points out, that Millett distorts Miller's escapades and determinedly overlooks the author's omnifarious, picaresque humor. But in terms of getting to the roots of Miller's sexual attitudes, neither Millett nor Mailer comes close to the perspicacious criticism of Miller's friend of more than 40 years, Anaïs Nin, nor to Miller's own comments on these matters in his correspondence with various friends.

In her diaries Anaïs Nin often mentions the paradox between what she sees as her friend's gentle and violent writing, his veering from sentimentality to callousness, tenderness to ridicule, gentleness to anger. And she suggests that because of what she saw as Miller's "utter subjection" to his wife June (Mona, Mara, Alraune in his novels), Miller used his books to take revenge upon her.

Miller himself has written: "Perhaps one reason why I have stressed so much the immoral, the wicked, the ugly, the cruel in my work is because I wanted others to know how valuable these are, how equally if not more important than the good things. . . . I was getting the poison out of my system. Curiously enough, this poison had a tonic effect for others. It was as if I had given them some kind of immunity."

Sometimes, in his letters, we find Miller protecting himself, describing himself as "a little boy going down into the street to play, having no fixed purpose, no particular direction, no especial friend to seek out, but just divinely content to be going down into the street to see whatever might come. As if I did not love them! Only I also loved others, too . . . not in the way they meant, but in a natural, wholesome, easy way. Like one loves garlic, honey, wild strawberries."

But he is unsparing of himself as well: "The coward in me always concealed himself in that thick armor of dull passivity. I only grew truly sensitive again when I had attained a certain measure of liberation. . . . To live out one's desires and, in so doing, subtly alter their nature is the aim of every individual who aspires to evolve."

The idea of self-liberation—what psychologists today like to call "self-actualization" or "individuation"—has always been Miller's great concern in all of his books, which progress from the *via purgativa* to the *via unitiva*. And even as his novels work counterclockwise (*Tropic of Cancer* tells of Miller's life in Thirties Paris, *Tropic of Capricorn* and *The Rosy Crucifixion* of his earlier life in New York City), Miller gives, as he tells us, in "each separate fragment, each work, the feeling of the whole as I go on, because I am digging deeper and deeper into life, digging deeper and deeper into past and future. . . . The writer lives between the upper and lower worlds: He takes the path in order eventually to become that path himself."

This path is often filled with the "strong odor of sex" which, to Miller, is "really the aroma of birth; it is disagreeable only to those who fail to recognize its significance." And it is a path which leads to his rebirth at the tomb of Agamemnon—described in *The Colossus of Maroussi* as "the great peace which comes of surrender"—and to his rebirth at the conclusion of *Tropic of Capricorn*: "I take you as a star and a trap, as a stone to tip the scales, as a judge that is blindfolded, as a hole to fall into, as a path to walk, as a cross and an arrow. Up to the present I traveled the opposite way of the sun; henceforth I travel two ways, as sun and as moon. Henceforth I take on two sexes, two hemispheres, two skies, two sets of everything. Henceforth I shall be double-jointed and double sexed. Everything that happens will happen twice. I shall be as a visitor to this earth, partaking of its blessings and carrying off its gifts. I shall neither serve nor be served. I shall seek the end in myself."

And this amazing passage suggests—if not that Henry is a prototype of Norman O. Brown—at least something quite different from what Millett and Mailer are arguing about.

Henry Miller is hardly an enthusiastic supporter of psychological criticism. "This seeking for meaning in everything!" he once exclaimed. "So Germanic! This urge to make everything profound. What nonsense! If only they could also make everything unimportant at the same time." But I decided to ask him about the woman question anyway.

"Henry," I say, "Anaïs Nin wrote in her diaries that in *Tropic of Cancer* you created a book in which you have a sex and a stomach. In *Tropic of Capricorn* and *Black Spring*, she says, you have eyes, ears and a mouth. And eventually, Anaïs Nin suggests, you will finally create a full man, at which point you'll be able to write about a woman for real."

"I don't remember her writing that," Henry responds. "That should have stuck in my head. That's quite wonderful. But it's interesting, isn't it? It's like that Chuang-Tze story you read me, about the drilling of the holes into Chaos, don't you know?" Henry smiles. "But if you saw Anaïs today I think she'd give you the feeling that I *am* a whole man today.

"Tom Schiller told me that there was a bomb scare in Copenhagen when they were going to show his film about me (*Henry Miller Asleep and Awake*). A woman's lib group called up the theater to stop the film from being shown—they showed it anyway—but I want so badly to write a letter to the women who are against me. The woman I could write it to would be Germaine Greer. I adore her—the others I don't know—and I'd like to say:

'My dear Germaine Greer, isn't it obvious from my work that I love women? Is the fact that I also fuck them without asking their names the great sin? I never took them as sex objects. . . . Well, maybe I did at times, but it wasn't done with evil thought or with the intention of putting the woman down. It just so happened that there were chance encounters—you meet and pass, and that's how it sometimes occurred. There never was any woman problem in my mind.' "

"You've been criticized, perhaps validly," I say, "for portraying women either as phantasmagoric angels disappearing into the clouds or as down-to-earth whores. Or do you think I'm distorting the picture?"

"I don't think that's true. I really don't," he replies. "To talk jokingly about it: They're all layable, even the angels. And the whores can be worshiped, too. Naturally. That's what Jesus did. The famous religious leaders always spoke well of whores."

"Again, Henry," I say, "Anaïs Nin has said that in *Tropic of Cancer* you seemed to be fighting off the idea of Woman because there was a woman inside of you whom you couldn't accept."

"It was my mother," Henry replies without hesitation, "whom I couldn't accept. I was always the enemy of my mother and she of me. We never got along—never. Not till her dying day. And even then we were still enemies. Even then she was berating me and treating me like a child. And I couldn't stand it. And I grabbed her and pushed her back on the pillow. And then I realized the brutality of it—I didn't hurt her—but the very thought of doing this to such a woman! And then I went out to the hall and sobbed and wept."

"I saw a photo of your mother recently," I mention, "and she looked like a strong, handsome woman."

"You really think so? Is that so?" Henry says with interest. "I always think of her as a cold woman. . . . But sometimes I think Anaïs analyzes everything too much. She believes so much that she's had such great help from psychoanalysts, and I'm always saying: Fuck the analyst, that's the last man to see, he's a faker. Now he isn't a faker, he's honest, and there are wonderful men. I read Jung and I know that Hermann Hesse said he was indebted to Jung and Freud. I can't read Freud today, but when I was 19 or 20 I fought a battle for him. Today I don't think it was worth wasting time on, but that's a prejudice again, and I don't deny that. I don't see why we haven't got a right to be prejudiced."

"But psychologically there are so many interesting things in your books, Henry," I say. "The conclusion to *Tropic of Capricorn*, for example, where you say that from then on you'd be both male and female—everything that happened would occur twice. Or the earlier, even more amazing 'Land of Fuck' interlude, which is a reverie about the purity and infancy of sexual desire, in which you seem to become the sexual process itself in an out-of-body journey."

"Yes," Henry agrees, "you're lifted out of the body of the narrative, you're floating somewhere and sex is something like x,y,z—you can't name it. You see, that was a windfall. Every so often you get a gift from above, it comes to you, you have nothing to do with it, you're being dictated to. I don't take credit for that interlude. . . . And the last part of *Capricorn* . . . yes, that was a wonderful passage. Sometimes I don't know what these things mean. They come out of the unconscious. It's interesting, these questions. No one picks these things out."

In order to lighten things up, I innocuously ask Henry about rock & roll—something I assume he likes.

"I detest rock & roll," he retorts passionately. "To me it's noise. I miss the beautiful melodies. But I suppose it's an omission. What rock & roll musicians do you like?"

"I like Bob Dylan for one," I say, "and I was thinking that some of your work must have influenced someone like Dylan. Like that passage in 'Into the Night Life' from *Black Spring*."

"Do you have it there in your book?" Henry asks. "How does it go?"

I read:

The melting snow melts deeper, the iron rusts, the leaves flower. On the corner, under the elevated, stands a man with a plug hat, in blue serge and linen spats, his white mustache chopped fine. The switch opens and out rolls all the tobacco juice, the golden lemons, the elephant tusks, the candelabras. Moishe Pippik, the lemon dealer, fowled with pigeons, breeding purple eggs in his vest pocket and purple ties and watermelons and spinach with short stems, stringy, marred with tar. The whistle of the acorns loudly stirring, flurry of floozies bandaged in Lysol, ammonia and camphor patches, little mica huts, peanut shells triangled and corrugated, all marching triumphantly with the morning breeze. The morning light comes in creases, the window panes are streaked, the covers are torn, the oilcloth is faded. Walks a man with hair on end, not running, not breathing, a man with a weathervane that turns the corners sharply and then bolts. A man who thinks not how or why but just to walk in lusterless night with all stars to port and loaded whiskers trimmed. Gowselling in the grummels he wakes the plaintiff night with pitfalls turning left to right, high noon on the wintry ocean, high noon all sides aboard and aloft to starboard. The weathervane again with deep oars coming through the portholes and all sounds muffled. Noiseless the night on all fours, like the hurricane. Noiseless with loaded caramels and nickel dice. Sister Monica playing the guitar with shirt open and laces down, broad flanges in either ear. Sister Monica streaked with lime, gum wash, her eyes mildewed, craped, crapped, crenelated.

"What a passage!" I exclaim. "That's certainly rock & roll to me."

"I'm glad you liked that," Henry says, "but I have no way of knowing whether Bob Dylan was influenced by me. You know, Bob Dylan came to my house ten years ago. Joan Baez and her sister brought him and some friends to see me. But Dylan was snooty and arrogant. He was a kid then, of course. And he didn't like me. He thought I was talking down to him, which I wasn't. I was trying to be sociable. But we just couldn't get together. But I know that he is a character, probably a genius, and I really should listen to his work. I'm full of prejudices like everybody else. My kids love him and the Beatles and all the rest."

At this point, Robert Snyder walks into the room. Snyder is the director of an excellent two-hour film entitled *The Henry Miller Odyssey* (distributed by Grove Press Films, which also handles Snyder's films on Buckminster Fuller and Anaïs Nin)—a film in which Miller is shown in his swimming pool reminiscing about his childhood, playing Ping-Pong, bicycling around Pacific Palisades, revisiting old friends in Paris and conversing with Durrell, Anaïs Nin and other friends.

Henry has been a film buff ever since his days in Paris, and his essays on *Ecstasy*, Buñuel's *L'Age d'Or* and the French actor Raimu are marvelous pieces of film criticism.

"Do you still see a lot of movies?" I ask.

"Well, as you can guess, I'm a little behind. Bob brought over a film to show here recently—a film that made me sob and weep: Fellini's *Nights of Cabiria*. I could see it again and cry again. And I just saw the original *Frankenstein* again. And of course, the original story ends at the North Pole where everything is ice, and that's the only proper ending for that monstrous story. It's really a work of art."

"There are films that you detest, Henry, aren't there?" Snyder asks.

"*Bonnie and Clyde*!" Henry exclaims. "Did I hate that! I was clapping to myself when they machine-gunned them to death at the end. Dynamite them! Blow them to smithereens! It was so vulgar, that film. I love obscenity but I hate vulgarity. I can't see how people can enjoy killing for fun. Also, there was a perverse streak there. There was a suggestion that the hero was impotent. I don't like that, I like healthy sex. I don't like impotence and perversion."

"What's perversion?" I ask.

"Well . . . what is it?" Henry laughs, confused. "You got me stumped for a moment. Perversion. Now you've got me stumped. Now I'm moralizing. Well, to get out of it nicely, I'd say it's what isn't healthy. I think you know what I mean, don't you?"

"Not exactly."

"Have you become so broad-minded—I'm not being sarcastic—that to you there's no such thing as perversion?"

"I have my preferences, but I wouldn't make a definite judgment."

"I once asked someone what he'd rather be: ignorant or stupid," Henry explains. "I'd rather be ignorant, but I've done stupid things every day of my life. I think we all do, don't you? Every day we're wrong about something. But I have no remorse, no regrets. That's what I call being healthy."

"Just to take you back for a minute, Henry," I say, "someone told me that you knew Gurdjieff when you were living in Paris. Is that true?"

"I wish I *had* met him," Henry replies, "because I think he's one of the greatest figures in modern times, and a very mysterious one, too. I don't think that anyone has ever come to grips with him yet. I was going to make a tour of France with one of my wives, and she didn't know how to ride a bike. So we went out to the park in Fontainebleau—and we drove around Gurdjieff's place, never knowing he was there. What a misfortune!"

"You often write about how it's possible to become aware and awake in the flash of a moment. This concern with being 'awake' was also important to Gurdjieff."

"I think there are two valid attitudes to this," Henry comments. "Because even in the Zen movement in Japan there are those who think you have to work at it, meditate, study hard, be ascetic. And then there's another group, whose attitude is exemplified by the story of the Master of Fuck. It was written by a famous American living in Japan, and it's about a young man whose parents sent him to become a Zen monk. He's a good student, disciplined, but after ten years he's not getting anywhere—he's not enlightened. After 15 years he feels he'll never make it and so he decides to live the worldly life, leaves the monastery and runs into a prostitute who looks wonderful. And in the middle of the fuck he attains satori. . . . I never thought of such a thing and naturally he didn't either, and that's why it happened. Do you know the quote from the Buddha: 'I never gained the least thing from unexcelled complete awakening, and for that very reason it is called that.' "

"Once you're awake, how do you keep awake?"

"I can't answer that question really. But: Do you believe in conversion and that it's sincere? Well, I do, I've seen it in people, and they don't have to struggle every day to hold on to it. It remains with you. I don't know if it ever really happened to me. But I think perhaps it did in Paris in 1934, when I moved into the Villa Seurat and was reading the books of Mme. Blavatsky. And one day after I had looked at a photograph of her face—she had the face of a pig, almost, but fascinating—I was hypnotized by her eyes and I had a complete vision of her as if she were in the room.

"Now I don't know if that had anything to do with what happened next, but I had a flash, I came to the realization that I was responsible for my whole life, whatever had happened. I used to blame my family, society, my wife . . . and that day I saw so clearly that I had nobody to blame but myself. I put everything on my own shoulders and I felt so relieved: Now I'm free, no one else is responsible. And that was a kind of awakening, in a way. I remember the story of how one day the Buddha was walking along and a man came up to him and said: 'Who are you, what are you?' and the

Buddha promptly answered: 'I am a man who is awake.' We're asleep, don't you know, we're sleepwalkers."

Henry is showing Robert Snyder some photographs. "Some fan of mine wanted to cheer me up," Henry says, "and so he sent me these postcard photos showing the house in Brooklyn where I lived from the age of one to nine. I spent the happiest times at that age, but these photos are horrible, they're like insanity. The whole street I grew up on has become like a jaw with the teeth falling out. Houses uprooted . . . it looks so horrible."

"What was your first memory of Brooklyn?" I ask.

"A dead cat frozen in the gutter. That was when I was four. I remember birds singing in the cage and I was in the highchair and I recited poems in German—I knew German before I knew English.

"I had three great periods in my life. Age one to nine was Paradise. Then 1930–1940 in Paris and Greece. And then my years at Big Sur."

"Why are you living here, Henry?"

"L.A. is a shithole. Someone selected the house for me and told me to move in. But it doesn't bother me because I have nothing to do with it. I'm in this house, this is my kingdom, my realm. It's a nice house, I have a Ping-Pong table, and when my leg was okay I used to play every day."

"Tell Jonathan about the new book you're working on," Bob Snyder interjects.

"It's called *The Book of Friends* and it's an homage I'm paying to close, intimate old friends. It begins when I was five years old—what happened 75 years ago is so fresh and vivid to me!—and it starts off with childhood friends. I always made friends easily—all my life, even now. And in this book I'm repeating myself often, overlapping, covering ground I've already written about, but from a different angle. It goes up to Joe Gray—an ex-pugilist, a stuntman and stand-in for Dean Martin. An uncultured guy but a great reader. After reading my books, he started to read everything else. He died two years ago, and he was a great friend. With each friend, you know, I was different."

"The last thing I wanted to ask you about, Henry," I say, leafing through my little book, "was the initiation ordeal imposed by the Brotherhood of Fools and Simpletons—an ordeal you've humorously written about in *Big Sur*."

"The Brotherhood of Fools and Simpletons?" Henry wonders. "I've completely forgotten what that was all about."

"Well, the Brotherhood asks three questions of the initiates. The first is: 'How would you order the world if you were given the powers of the creator?' The second: 'What is it you desire that you do not already possess?' And the third: 'Say something which will truly astonish us!' . . . How would you answer these questions?"

"Ah ha!" Henry exclaims. "That third question I borrowed from Cocteau and Diaghilev. They met in the dead of night and Diaghilev went up to Cocteau and said: '*Etonne-moi*! Astonish me!' The second question was a rhetorical question because there isn't any such thing. And the first question about ordering the world: I would be paralyzed. I wouldn't know how to lift a finger to change the world or make it over. I wouldn't know what to do."

Lawrence Durrell and his wife have arrived for dinner and are now chatting in the living room with Henry's daughter Val and his son Tony and Tony's wife. Henry appears in his bathrobe and speaks to Durrell with the generosity and gentleness that one might imagine a younger son would feel toward an adored older brother. And I am reminded of that beautiful letter Henry wrote to his younger friend in 1959:

> Ah, Larry, it isn't that life is so short, it's that it's everlasting. Often, talking with you under the tent—especially over a vieux marc—I wanted to say, "Stop talking . . . let's *talk*!" For 20 years I waited to see you again. For 20 years your voice rang in my ears. And your laughter. And there, at the Mazet, time running out (never the vieux marc), I had an almost frantic desire to pin you down, to have it out, to get to the bottom. (*What is the stars*? Remember?) And there we were on the poop deck, so to speak, the stars drenching us with light, and what are we saying? Truth is, you said so many marvelous things I never did know what we were talking about. I listened to the Master's Voice, just like that puppy on the old Victor gramophone. Whether you were expounding, describing, depicting, deflowering or delineating, it was all one to me. I heard you writing aloud. I said to myself—"He's arrived. He made it. He knows how to say it. Say it! Continue!" Oui, c'est toi, le cher maître. You have the vocabulary, the armature, the Vulcanic fire in your bowels. You've even found "the place and the formula." Give us a new world! Give us grace and fortitude!
>
> —A Private Correspondence:
> Lawrence Durrell and Henry Miller

As they sit down at the table, Henry says to Durrell: "This guy here mentioned three terrific questions asked by my Brotherhood of Fools and Simpletons. I'd really forgotten them."

"What were they, Henry?"

"What were they, Jonathan?"

I repeat them.

"I bet I know how you'd answer the first," Durrell says, "about how you'd order the world."

"What would you think?"

"Like a Gnostic," Durrell says, "you'd wipe it out."

"I said that I wouldn't know what I'd do, I'd be paralyzed," Henry replies. "But sometimes I do think the world is a cosmic error of a false god. I don't really believe things like that but I like the idea. Life is great and beautiful—there's nothing *but* life—but we have made of the world a horrible place. Man has never handled the gift of life properly. And it is a crazy world, everything about it is absurd and wrong, and it deserves to be wiped out. I don't think it's going to last forever. I think there is such a thing as the end of the world or the end of this species of man. It could very well be that another type of man will come into being.

"You know," Henry turns to me, "Larry recently gave me a book to read called *The Gnostics*. It's written by a young Jesuit, of all people. And you know something . . . you were asking me before about rock & roll and the happenings with young people in the Sixties. Well, when all that was happening, I wasn't aware that it was a revolution. Now they look back and they call it that. But the hippies are like toilet paper compared with the Gnostics. They *really* turned the world upside down. They did fantastic things. They were deliberately amoral, unmoral, immoral, contra the government and establishment. They did everything possible to increase the insanity."

A toast is proposed to insanity.

Even in his early days in Brooklyn, Henry Miller saw through the Social Lie as easily as through Saran Wrap, embodying the alienating Lie as the Cosmodemonic Telegraph Company in *Tropic of Capricorn*. While gainsaying Ezra Pound's dimwitted social-credit economics in a famous essay filled with sublime truisms ("Money and How It Gets That Way"), Miller rejected any and all "political" paths (for which he has been often criticized), preferring instead to lambaste every irruption of corporate mentality in any number of pasquinades—one of his most delightful being his attack on American bread:

Accept any loaf that is offered you without question even if it is not wrapped in cellophane, even if it contains no kelp. Throw it in the back of the car with the oil can and the grease rags; if possible, bury it under a sack of coal, *bituminous* coal. As you climb up the road to your home, drop it in the mud a few times and dig your heels into it. When you get to the house, and after you have prepared the other dishes, take a huge carving knife and rip the loaf from stem to stern. Then take one whole onion, peeled or unpeeled, one carrot, one stalk of celery, one huge piece of garlic, one sliced apple, a herring, a handful of anchovies, a sprig of parsley and an old toothbrush, and shove them in the disemboweled guts of the bread. Over these pour a thimbleful of kerosene, a dash of Lavoris, and just a wee bit of Clorox. . . .

—*Remember to Remember*

And in *The Colossus of Maroussi*, he writes: "At Eleusis one realizes, if never before, that there is no salvation in becoming adapted to a world which is crazy. At Eleusis one becomes adapted to the cosmos. Outwardly Eleusis may seem broken, disintegrated with the crumbled past; actually Eleusis is still intact and it is we who are broken, dispersed, crumbling to dust. Eleusis lives, lives eternally in the midst of a dying world."

Miller has always chosen reality over realism, action over activity, intuition over instinct, mystery over the mysterious, being over healing, surrender over attachment, conversion over wishing, lighthouses over life-boats, enlightenment over salvation and the world-as-womb over the world-as-tomb. Strangely, cosmologists have recently given credibility to the intuition that we probably all exist within a universe composed of space and time created by the original, erupting, fecundating "big bang"—all of us and all of our worlds trapped inside the gravitational radius of a universe from which no light can escape.

In the Forties George Orwell criticized Miller's idea of passive acceptance as it was revealed in the image of the man in the belly of the whale (the world-as-womb)—an image which Miller first presented in his impassioned introduction to and defense of Anaïs Nin's then unpublished diaries. Miller wrote:

> We who imagined that we were sitting in the belly of the whale and doomed to nothingness suddenly discover that the whale was a projection of our own insufficiency. The whale remains, but the whale becomes the whole wide world, with stars and seasons, with banquets and festivals, with everything that is wonderful to see and touch, and being that it is no longer a whale but something nameless because something that is inside as well as outside us. We may, if we like, devour the whale too—piecemeal, throughout eternity. No matter how much is ingested there will always remain more whale than man; because what man appropriates of the whale returns to the whale again in one form or another. The whale is constantly being transformed as man himself becomes transformed. . . . One lives within the spirit of transformation and not in the act. The legend of the whale thus becomes the celebrated book of transformations destined to cure the ills of the world.
>
> —"Un Etre Etoilique"

"The stars gather direction in the same way that the foetus moves toward birth," Miller has said. And his own books of transformations are remarkably in tune with the new cosmological perspectives of the universe. Rather than regressing to agoraphobic passivity, his books continually open themselves up to include and become a perpetually metamorphosing personality which itself becomes a "creation." "You have expanded the womb feeling until it includes the whole universe," Miller wrote Durrell after reading *The Black Book* for the first time—generously praising a fellow author, yet also accurately describing the direction of his own work.

Henry Miller has continued to foster his "cosmic accent" and his mantic gift but, like the Greek poet Seferiades whom he praises in *The Colossus of Maroussi*, his "native flexibility" has equally responded to "the cosmic laws of curvature and finitude. He had ceased going out in all directions: His lines were making the encircling movement of embrace."

As the world falls rapidly on its measured ellipse, Henry Miller is writing, painting and dreaming his life away in Pacific Palisades: "Some will say they do not wish to *dream* their lives away," he writes in *Big Sur*. "As if life itself were not a dream, a very real dream from which there is no awakening! We pass from one state of dream to another: from the dream of sleep to the dream of waking, from the dream of life to the dream of death. Whoever has enjoyed a good dream never complains of having wasted his time. On the contrary, he is delighted to have partaken of a reality which serves to heighten and enhance the reality of everyday."

TRIBUTES AND OTHER
RESPONSES TO MILLER

◆

To The Dean

William Carlos Williams

What should I say of Henry Miller:
a fantastic true-story of Dijon remembered,
black palaces, warted, on streets
of three levels, tilted, winding through
the full moon and out and
down again, worn-casts of men: Chambertin—
This for a head

The feet riding a ferry
waiting under the river side by side
and between. No body. The feet
dogging the head, the head bombing the feet
while food drops into and
through the severed gullet, makes clouds
and women gabbling and smoking, throwing
lighted butts on carpets in department stores,
sweating and going to it like men

Miller, Miller, Miller, Miller
I like those who like you and dislike
nothing that imitates you, I like
particularly that Black Book with its
red sporran by the Englishman that does you
so much honor. I think we should
all be praising you, you are a very good
influence.

Excerpted and reprinted from *The Happy Rock: A Book About Henry Miller*, Bern Porter, ed. (Berkeley, CA: Bern Porter, 1945), 97. Reprinted by permission of Bern Porter.

What Henry Miller Said and
Why It Is Important

BERN PORTER

Over the years from among all the words, the situations, the events, many will redescribe, many will remember this sequence, that scene, another episode; others will write, pay tribute, deride, criticize, imitate, be influenced, read, reread as others applaud, rewrite, fundicate, expand, elaborate, editorialize, comment, cross-file, index, catalogue and annotate. From the root comprising his initial billion words an overwhelming several billion more will multiply at the hands of countless others until in the resulting morass of verbiage the essential even simple, unsuspecting but all significant core will still remain undisturbed, even lost:

		air	
		bees	
		birds	
		city	
1.	*Sex is everywhere.*	country	
		earth	
		food	
		news	
A. It is in the		town	
		trees	
		streets	
		water	
		bed	
		songs	
		clothes	
		cars	
		factories;	
		clean	
		enjoyable	
		fun	
	boys		good
	husbands		healthy

Reprinted from *What Henry Miller Said and Why It Is Important* (Ashland, Maine: Bern Porter, 1961), 13–20. Reprinted by permission of the author.

                    males   2. *Sex is*   innocent
                    man   pleasurable
    B.   And in   females   pure
                    girls   natural
                    wives   normal
                    woman   wholesome.
    3. *And sex is not*   boring   shameful
                          damaging   sinful
                          dangerous   stupid
                          degrading   taboo
                          dirty   unclean
                          disgusting   undesirable
                          dull   unethical
                          evil   unnatural
                          filthy   wanton
                          hazardous   wicked
                          hostile   wrecking.
                          illegal
                          immoral
                          monotonous
                          revolting,
    Contrary to the law, the church, the state, the tradition,
                          argue
                          discuss
                          dream
                          give
                          have
              can   indulge
              does   partake
    one   must   perform   it.
              should   play
              will   read
                          receive
                          share
                          sing
                          speak
                          think
                          write
                          wish
                          desire
                          drive
                          power

More important the urge to fornicate (by whatever means) cannot be appeased, chastised, cheated, corrected, daunted, dazzled, deafened, debased, debilitated, disburdened, decontrolled, decreased, decrepited, deflected, deformed, defrauded, degraded, denied, devoured, diffused, diminished, dimned, disappeared, disappointed, disapproved, disarticulated, disassociated, disbanded, discarded, discerpted, disciplined, discontinued, discounted, discouraged, discreted, discredited, disengaged, disentitled, disgorged, disguised, dishabituated, disjected, disjoined, dislodged, dismembered, dismissed, disobeyed, disobliged, disordered, dispersed, displayed, dispirited, dissolved, dropped, eluded, emasculated, erased, expurgated, extenuated, extinguished, extirpated, extracted, fecundated, feigned, fixed, fooled, frustrated, guided, hood-winked, ignored, improved, killed, overawed, placated, repressed, restricted, reversed, shattered, sublimated, substituted, transferred, tricked, thwarted, untangled.

And all this the lawyer,
              the judge,
                   the sheriff,
                        the jailer,
                             the censor,
                                  the custom,
                                       the minister,
                                            the teacher,
                                                 the politician,
                                                      the doctor,
                                                           the commissioner,
                                                                the young,
                                                                     especially
                                                                          the young,
                                                                               must
                                                                                    know.

And know it not so much from the parent, from the cleric, from the teacher, from the medic as from an expert impartial OUTSIDER.

[Letter]

ISAAC BASHEVIS SINGER

June 27, 1979

I consider Henry Miller important for many reasons. First of all, he's a mighty good writer. In this epoch when many writers play around with words instead of observing life with all its mysteries and complications, Henry Miller is a man who gets inspiration first hand, or from the first well. It is not the words which are important to him, but what is behind them. His life and his writing cannot be separated in any way. The reader recognizes Henry Miller in every line of his works.

Henry Miller had also the courage and idealism to fight for literary freedom. He did it almost single-handedly. He was banned for years and excommunicated from the literary establishment. But he kept on fighting for what he considered just. And when victory came he allowed others to enjoy the spoils and in this respect he became a literary leader of the highest magnitude. The fear of censorship has left literature. Every writer can say what he wants and the way he wants nowadays.

As a person, Henry Miller is completely sincere, straightforward and as far from politics as a man can be. Although I don't write in his style, I cherish him as a writer and as a friend of everything which is genuine in the art of writing.

From a letter to Prof. Bertrand Mathieu. Reprinted by permission of Lescher & Lescher, Ltd. Copyright © by Isaac B. Singer.

[Letter]

JERZY KOSINSKI

December 21, 1990

Already in his *Tropic of Cancer* and *Tropic of Capricorn,* where sex stood for instinctual will to procreate—that is, to survive as one's own creation— Henry Miller had reached an unparalleled latitude of abandonment in his narrative expression. Driving sterilized morality morons beside themselves, and himself into exile, Miller nevertheless delved deeper into his narrative Self. A custodian of our innermost equator, he relentlessly watched over it with *The Cosmological Eye,* trying to come to terms with *The Colossus of Maroussi,* no less than with *The Air-Conditioned Nightmare* colliding full force with *Big Sur and the Oranges of Hieronymous Bosch,* or when confronting, as we all must, *The Rosy Crucifixion*: one's very own *Sexus, Plexus and Nexus.*

From a letter to Prof. Ronald Gottesman. Printed by permission of Jerzy Kosinski.

A Testimonial and Reflection

ROBERT CREELEY

Henry Miller's immense use to anyone of my generation was the rhetorical clarity of his writing. It was so clearly "personal" in the same sense that Whitman's was, the seeming fact of someone's simply talking. That he could gain that effect is an exceptional accomplishment in itself. His work constituted a large part of that useful "other" literature the university did not teach, not only because a part of it was significantly outlawed as "obscene," but because all of it did not conform with the ruling academic taste of the period either in its modes of composition or in its judgement of what to value. As if to underscore these differences, all of his active company were in like sense provocative: Durrell, Nin, Michael Fraenkel, Kenneth Patchen, the painters Abe Rattner and Beauford Delaney, to mention only those most familiar.

I loved Miller's heroes, his persuasive care for Rimbaud and Lawrence, for example. I felt his writing was grounded in practical, sensitive *humanness*, however vaguely that puts it. I thought his presumed "pornography" was again common-sense report, if it has to be still qualified. He fantasized with classic male chauvinist practicality but it was a relief, like it or not, in that period of bleak sexual confusion and innuendo. Unlike Lawrence, however, he wrote of sexual acts with humor and comfortable familiarity. For him they were obvious points of contact in the chaos of incessant human action.

The health of his work was always a pleasure, the insistent energy and appetite. He said of *The Colossus of Maroussi*, "What I like about it is that it's a joyous book, it expresses joy, it gives joy"—and that's true of his own work always, one way or another. He certainly wanted to be happy.

Years ago, in the mid-fifties, I remember listening with Jack Kerouac, who cared about Miller a lot, to a recording of him reading. The gravelly, utterly *city* voice was a great reassurance to us both in that time of discreet, literary accents. It was grass roots, basic American in all senses. Miller was such a useful bridge to writers as Hammett or James M. Cain, a range that Hemingway paradoxically left blocked out or that Faulkner was removed from in a curious way. When I was one time to teach a course on the Moderns, Robert Duncan suggested I begin with Stein and end with Miller.

Printed by permission of Robert Creeley.

It was a far more accurate location of that time. Henry Miller is still often taken out of the record, or simply made singular—like many of the writers of the thirties, in fact. Yet, as few others, he defines "writer" once and for all. He makes it possible for us to acknowledge that reality he knew we all long for, no matter what we may think we have to say.

Goodbye to Henry-san

Erica Jong

All of us—if we are honest—know that art is a fart in the face of God. Only the establishment artist—whose work exists principally to justify the injustices of the status quo—flatters himself that he is godlike. The renegade, the maverick, the rebel, the Henry Miller, the Petronius, the Rabelais, the Blake, the Neruda, the Whitman—knows that in part what makes his life's work valuable is its criminality. If somewhere along the line he is *not* banned, burned, deprived of his livelihood, cursed by the academics, denigrated by the self-appointed guardians of art, then he knows he is doing something wrong.

Henry Miller was such a criminal.

On his letter paper it said: "When shit becomes valuable, the poor will be born without assholes." On other sheets it gave the following quote from one of his friends—"Henry, sometimes I'm obliged to sleep in my car—but when I have to take a shit, I go to the Beverly Hills Hotel."

If Henry used the word *shit* a lot, it was because no other word so well conveyed what he thought of the world. But the word became clean in his mouth. He purified the excrement of life and made it roses. "I want a classic purity," he once said, "where dung is dung and angels are angels." He knew that angels could not be angels without dung, that a world of angels would be devoid of literature.

Those who criticized him, those who—to the end—denied him his place in the pantheon of poets—were in part, unknowingly, reacting to the fears his honesty roused in them. Like Swift, he lashed the world to bring it to its senses. Like Swift, he was a heartbroken lover of mankind, a naïf pretending to be a cynic. "Just a Brooklyn boy . . ." he often said of himself.

Sometimes, I used to think that the critics who hated Henry were really suffering from nookie-envy. He seemed to spend so much time fucking, and fucking so *guiltlessly*! How could the perpetually guilty be anything but envious? But even in his fucking, he was literary. Once, my husband asked him if he had *really* ever screwed a woman with a carrot—and he laughed uproariously and denied it—though he always maintained his books were autobiographies, not novels.

I disagree with him here. The Henry Miller of the novels is surely a comic *persona*, a picaro, a quester, a hero in search of the Holy Grail. "What is a hero?" Henry once wrote: "Primarily one who has conquered his fears." And in the *persona* of Henry Miller, the *real* Henry Miller created a fearless alter-ego, one who never quailed at a cunt, never wilted, never fainted, or failed. As the ancient hero was fearless in battle, the modern hero must be fearless in bed! Thus has our sphere of heroic action shrunk from a meadow to a mattress! Henry Miller knew that so-called "obscenity" in modern literature was the counterpart of the miraculous in ancient literature: "obscenity" was a device by which the poet awakened his reader and awakened himself. Obscenity was the means to enlightenment. "The real nature of the obscene," he wrote in *Obscenity & The Law of Reflection*,

> lies in the lust to convert. He (the master) knocked to awaken but it was *himself* he awakened, and once awake, he is no longer concerned with the world of sleep; he walks in the light and, like a mirror, reflects his illumination in every act. Once this vantage point is reached, how trifling and remote seem the accusations of moralists! How senseless to debate whether the work is of high literary merit or not!

Henry Miller admired the gurus and the sages even more than he admired the poets and the painters. Moreover, he knew that the essential characteristic of a sage is his gaiety. He would have agreed with Yeats' line: "Their ancient glittering eyes are gay." And so were Henry's eyes—even the blinded one—till the end.

I imagine him singing hosannahs on his deathbed and muttering to the maker of the cosmos. His death was clearly a much-sought release, at which all his friends and family rejoiced. I hear that he rejoiced, too. Trapped in an ailing body, he had failed from year to year. He deserved better than such frail flesh, and even in his death he has not left us.

I met him when he was already an old man—met him through literature, not life. Though he never read his contemporaries (except I. B. Singer), though he was said by his detractors to be a sexist and an anti-Semite, though he was blind in one eye and tired quickly, he was coaxed by a friend into reading *Fear of Flying*, and he responded with a torrent of applause, enthusiasm and unpaid agentry.

He was the most generous writer I have ever known (and I have known one or two who, in their generosity, flouted the general rule that writers hate all other writers, except the safely dead). He tirelessly wrote to German, French, Japanese, Dutch publishers on my behalf. Asked to do nothing, he did *everything*—from writing a preface to the French edition of my novel, to writing an essay on the Op-Ed page of the *New York Times* about it (an essay from which the word "horny" had to be deleted as unacceptable to a "family newspaper").

I was bowled over by his kindness. Day after day the letters arrived—written in black felt pen on yellow legal sheets or on his own stationery with its curious aphorisms at the bottom. My own replies were rather stiff at first. How to cope with the excitement of a living legend actually writing to me! It was daunting to say the least. But Henry's letters were so loose and spontaneous that you had to respond in kind. Having freed himself, it was his great gift to free everyone he touched. There was no question I would see him when I went to California.

I came at the most awful and wonderful time in my life. A bad marriage breaking up; a film promised of my first novel but turning to heartbreak before my eyes; sudden notoriety which alarmed me as much as it delighted me. Henry's house in Pacific Palisades became a refuge of peace in this maelstrom. At his dining room table, listening to him talk of Perlès and Cendrars, Picasso and Brassaï, John Cowper Powys and Marie Corelli, Gurdjieff and Knut Hamsun, Durrell and Anaïs Nin (and Isaac Singer whom he—and I—admired above all living writers), I felt safe and protected even in the city of the Lost Angels!

Henry was frail when I met him in 1974. Only rarely would he let me take him (and his friends) out to dinner—usually at the Imperial Gardens, a rather seedy Japanese restaurant on Sunset Strip, and his favorite eatery in Los Angeles. More usually, Twinka, his then-cook and companion, made us dinner at home and Henry held forth for the assembled throng. His house was full of young people—often including his kids, Valentine and Tony—and Henry would feed everyone—as, in his Paris days, everyone had fed him. In the last months (when I had already moved to Connecticut), it was rumored that some of his final caretakers exploited him. But that first autumn I knew him, he was still well enough to write in bed, to emerge for garrulous meals before he grew tired and had to be wheeled back into his room, and to appreciate his numerous nubile visitors though not—he maintained—to fuck them. He lived his last years (he once wrote in a letter to me) in the most delicious erotic fantasies. Now and then he copped a feel—though not of *my* breasts. I was not his physical type at all, I think—or maybe he thought of me as too bookish, for he always made a great point of how bookish I was. Henry loved women, but loved them more for the imaginary women he made of them than for themselves alone. He was a true romantic even to his rebellion against romanticism. Like both romantics and rebels, he did not always see people with perfect clarity. He loved or he hated. When his love failed, he often repudiated the object totally. When a friend died, he ceased to think about him. He claimed he never mourned. He lived in the present more completely than any person I have ever known. For this alone, he shone out from other men as an enlightened soul.

But he *hated* his reputation as a pornographer and he longed—despite himself—for literary respectability. He accepted the *Légion d'Honneur* with predictable derision but with unpredictable gratitude, and each year he lusted after the Nobel Prize. Each year, all his friends and disciples recommended him. Each year the dynamite factory passed him by.

When a publisher had the temerity to suggest that Henry and I collaborate on a book to be titled—humorlessly enough—*A Rap On Sex* (a sort of companion piece to Margaret Mead's and James Baldwin's *A Rap on Race*), Henry wrote back: "In the first place I am not an expert as you dub me—and secondly, though it may well be profitable, there's something in the idea that stinks . . ."

I thought the idea stank too, but I was not yet able to be so blunt in a letter to a publisher! *A Rap On Sex* indeed! This never-written book's title (with its unconscious pun) sounds more dated today than a title of a book by Marie Corelli (who happened to be—by the way—Queen Victoria's favorite author *and* Henry Miller's!).

His contradictions were many. Victorian and Bohemian, *schnorrer* and benefactor, sexual guru and tireless romantic. He made up women out of pen and ink (and often water color). Did he make up his autobiographies, too? In a way, he did. In a way, we *all* make up our autobiographies. He was more of a fabulist than he would have admitted—though the very word would have made him puke. He was "just a Brooklyn boy—dontcha know" and if he was the great force that liberated literature (I nearly wrote "liberature") in our age, he knew it in his gut, but did not know it at all in his brain. He desperately wanted public recognition of his genius and in the pursuit of that recognition, he gave far too many interviews, and entertained far too many conmen and *schnorrers*. Thus are even enlightened souls seduced by the lust for recognition! That we denied him such final pleasures is not only a measure of official literary meanness, but of his own greatness: he still—even to the end—had the power to shock the hypocrite, the faint of heart, the literary panty-waist.

I hope you get your Nobel Prize in Heaven, Henry, sent up on blasts of dynamite.

Henry Miller: A Reminiscence

ROBERT SNYDER

I am a filmmaker who happened to become Henry Miller's film biographer, or autobiographer. It's called *The Henry Miller Odyssey*. How did it all come about? Let me adduce as my starting point—given the fact that Miller's great hero was Walt Whitman—the concluding words of a D. H. Lawrence essay characterizing Whitman's poetry as "the exultant message of American Democracy, of souls on the Open Road, full of glad recognition, full of fierce readiness, full of joy of worship when one soul sees a greater soul—the only riches, the great souls."[1]

So, then, I set out to film this *great soul*—as before him I had filmed Pablo Casals, Willem de Kooning, and Buckminster Fuller in the mid-sixties. And I finally persuaded him to be filmed—against his initial refusal, and then only if I adhered to his most stringent ground rules. He did not want to know it was happening. He wanted no light meters pushed up to his face; no lights; no clap-sticks snapping at him (required to assure synchronization of the film to the soundtrack); no direction or manipulation; no retakes *Interdit, Verboten!* Now I had to persuade my young cameraman, Baylis Glascock, to meet the impossible challenge.

It was spring 1968. Baylis and Tom Schiller, a young apprentice, and I went over to his place with minimal, miniaturized equipment. Finding him in his (overheated) pool—doing his daily therapeutic stint for his arthritic hip of "walking the bar," hand-over-hand; tossing beach balls into floating styrofoam hemispheres; swimming a little, then floating—I ask him, "Henry, water being the element it is, and you in it, what's your earliest memory?" And he responds, the voice warm, seductive, yet gravelly, with the timbre of Humphrey Bogart and the New York/Brooklyn accent of Jimmy Gleason, "My first big memory, uhh, seeing a dead cat in the gutter . . . my first acquaintance with death, I really think so . . . being surprised that the cat was stiff, y'know, and already rotting away. And then there come a pile of them, like sitting by the window when I'm sick, convalescing, watching the snow fall against the windowpane—the ice formed on the window—and tracing patterns on it . . . sitting by the stove in the kitchen

This essay was written specifically for this volume and is published here for the first time with the permission of the author.

on a very tiny chair, and talking to my mother; mostly she was scolding me."

Flash-forward. One morning I go over—the evening before, he had said, "let's work tomorrow morning, and be sure to wake me, ten o'clock punkt!"—and find him sleeping, on his side, fetal position, smiling peacefully, angelically in the arms of Morpheus. Criminal to wake him; I only dare a whisper, "Henry, time to get up." He merely rolls slowly over to his other side. I step up the volume, "Henry, Henry," and get the same response. Dammit! he did insist that I wake him. I muster up my courage and yell, "HENRY, WAKE UP, YOU'LL BE LATE FOR SCHOOL!" He bolts upright, rubs his eyes, and, in the instant from the nightmare to daylight reality, is reassured. He heaves a sigh of relief; "Oh, Bob, it's you, thank God. For a moment, I thought it was my mother!"

We then revisited, in memory, his Brooklyn years, and, in fact, the Paris years; Greece; air-conditioned nightmare America: Los Angeles's Beverly Glen; Big Sur; and, "by a commodious vicus of re-circulation back to," his most unlikely two-story Georgian house in Pacific Palisades, for his seventy-seventh birthday celebration.

Two years and some fifteen hours of film later, he'd more or less answered the question I'd started with (was he "the worst writer who ever lived," or "the world's greatest living author"?) in what became the full-length *Henry Miller Odyssey*. In the course of this double odyssey, I became his amanuensis, chauffeur, social secretary, Ping-Pong opponent (he never gave an inch), listener, intimate, and confidant. Once entered upon his "ovarian trolley," I was overwhelmed by it/him, and have remained so ever since.

How to get a handle on this mercurial, quixotic chameleon, this omnivorous great whale, very like an omnidirectional crab? I am bogged down . . . and Henry, ole' Adam Cadmus, standing over my shoulder, whispers: "There you go again. Dotting your i's, crossing your t's; trying to impose structure on a voyage of discovery; damned intellectual." (He was always suspicious of my academic background, with a proper Columbia University Master's degree, yet.) "Spit it out, from the heart, from the subconscious; free-associate!"

Okay, Henry, you asked for it.

First impressions: He is a *gentle man*—smiling, gracious, almost a sweet man (is this the "high priest of obscenity?"). An *orderly man*: his desk carefully arranged, with pencils and pens in a drinking glass; writing paper neatly stacked next to the pile of letters he will answer today, in his own Spenserian penmanship; at hand, his almost encyclopedic address book. Laid out over his Ping-Pong table, when not in use, are his paints, washed brushes, cleaned paint box, alongside elegant blocks of French watercolor papers. "I attach no importance to what I do in *painting*, not at all," he volunteers. "I'm just having a good time, just playing. And I think that this is a very important part of life, that people learn how to *play*, and make life a game, rather than a struggle for goals, doncha know." When he sits down to an afternoon tea, or coffee, his *serviette* is rolled up in a wooden ring, "H.M." burned into it, and carefully placed at the right of the place he has carefully set. A *modest man*, in dress—indoors, he wears a blue denim work shirt, embroidered by a flower-child devotee; outdoors, for a ride on his velo, he is English checkered wool-capped and old corduroy bejacketed; on an evening out, he wears his three-piece herringbone tweed suit, natural shoulders (Brooks Brothers?), and, what with his bald, gray-ringed and bespectacled head, he could be mistaken for a bank manager of a small New England town. *Self-effacing* in manner—when I ask him to read on camera some passages from his work, perhaps his favorite person/portrait, Tante Melia (from *The Tailor Shop*) or "Peace in Epidaurus" (from his favorite book, *The Colossus of Maroussi*), he balks, insists I should get a proper actor, like, say, Gregory Peck. I protest that only Henry Miller could do honor to Henry Miller's prose.

He has total recall, whether of books (the countless pages he has written as well as the countless pages he has read), events, or places. He makes countless lists: things to do; places to go; books to read; movies and art shows to see; words to learn to use. We have a session at the Henry Miller Archives, Special Collections, UCLA Library, which houses a sheet of wall paper on which he had charted his "Capricorn plan": ideas, obsessions, descriptive bits, styles—"let me see that"—Dostoyevsky for Xerxes Society . . . Hamsun . . . Tagore . . . Spengler . . . Anatole France . . . Somerset Maugham . . . Dos Passos . . . Ingersoll and Tolstoy . . . Sinclair Lewis for rantings—"ranting, y'know"—Dreiser for desertion theme . . . Sherwood Anderson for yearnings and introspection—"y'get me? You see what a cunning bastard and, what shall I say, a cheat; still I'm saying what style can I use, not my own, you understand!"

I come upon him clowning in front of his bathroom mirror: "The day I graduated from high school," he tells me, we were all asked what we would like to be? I had no idea what I wanted to be, so I said, 'I think I'm going to be a clown, a symbol of man's suffering on earth, you might say, and of his conquest over it, too.' But I was saying a great truth, because at bottom I think there is a great deal of the clown in me. I'm kind of a schizoid type, who laughs and cries at the same time." And I see him entering the world, en route to the breakfast table, passing this huge red-lacquered wooden drum, and dancing around in front of it, chanting, "Nam miyo-ho, renge-kyo; Nam miyo-ho renge-kyo." He clowns at the piano, mimicking a great virtuoso, arms flailing, hands banging away, and rippling up and down the keyboard in a performance that is pure Dada, da-da/da-da/da-dah. "Music . . . you sound a note; that leads to the next note; one determines the next, do y'see. And when you get right down to it philosophically, as in Zen, the idea is to live from moment to moment; this move decides the next. Think only of what is right there, what is right under your nose to do. It's such a simple thing—that's why people can't do it."

He loved films, admired Fellini and adored his wife, the Chaplinesque Giulietta Massina. "Why can't we have a little film society at home?" I would rent some 16 mm prints for home viewing, and we'd invite over some friends (suggesting they might kick in). He especially liked *La Strada*, which was about a clown and a traveling circus. "But Henry," I'd tell him, "Fellini's *I Vitelloni* and *The Nights of Cabiria* are much better." I got hold of *Cabiria* for the following Saturday. He murmured, "Can I preview it, privately, on Friday?" Of course. After that first running, he simply sat there, "mmmm, mmmmmm, hmmmmm." On Saturday evening, the friends are gathered and I project the film. As the end titles roll, we hear sobbing from Henry's chair, growing in volume, and as the lights go up, there he is, head down in his hands, shoulders shaking. He looks up, smiles apologetically, and excuses himself with an embarrassed little laugh: "I thought you'd all be shedding tears."

Did he ever get angry with me, really mad? Yes, while he was recalling some of the steamiest passages depicting the Clichy days, I asked whether there wasn't a bit of Walter Mitty romanticizing in them. He got very mad, indeed. "Dammit, it's all true!" What is truth?

By way of concluding, I quote a memo that he dashed off, "from the top of my head," while we were filming:

> What are we here for if not to enjoy life eternal, solve what problems we can, give light, peace and joy to our fellow-man, and leave this dear fucked-up planet a little healthier than when we were born. Who knows what other planets we will be visiting and what new wonders there will unfold? We certainly live more than once. Do we ever die—that is the question. In any case, thank God we are alive and of the stars—unto all eternity. I suppose I should say, Amen.

Notes

1. D. H. Lawrence *Studies in Classic American Literature* New York: Penguin Books, 1977, 187.

The Naked Tongue

DIANE MILLER

Henry Miller, my father-in-law, was the first person to show me what it meant to write naked. He branded his name into everyone's psyche with his original naked tongue speaking truth through the fire and ice of his vision so that no one who read his words was left untouched or perhaps even unscathed. Henry strode across the page in all his brilliant audacity spilling his heart and his guts, his incisive mind cutting through anything that might even hint at dissembling. For Henry was not a dissembler. He was a truth teller. And he loved the naked page or a naked woman because they were there for him to fill up with his vision, for him to plunge into, his own nakedness raw and sharp-edged as he gave birth to something greater than himself. His words an avalanche of joy, mysticism, self-scrutiny, and soul-purging as he penetrated into the bloody core of life. His hands never came out clean. They always drew blood.

Some women have a difficult time dealing with the Henry Miller version of woman telling. Many of them feel raped by his naked tongue, and that his words have ravaged them into a humiliating submission. But it was only that Henry left the lies to those who must always be carefully dressed in public. Henry was not willing to compromise truth for a socially acceptable front or for a kind heart.

Every stone was turned over one by one to bare its mossy underside, the part that no one sees unless they care enough to look more deeply. And Henry cared enough to plumb the depths of truth. Henry cared enough about women to look at their mossy undersides and still to exalt them in the end. This was the place where truth and vision melded for him. A woman was ultimately a sacred vessel of desire, but first she was witnessed in her civilized depravity and then worshiped in her resurrected, primal beauty. She was brought to her knees by Henry in the most searing humility and then crowned and put upon the throne inside the temple of his spirit. For woman was the quintessential enigma whom he adored and to whom he presented his words as a sacrificial offering of his lifeblood. She was the sacrament and he the humble recipient of this woman flesh and spirit that transposed his words into the inside and outside of truth. She was the goddess

Reprinted by permission of the author.

of dichotomy, stretching out her golden wings, her tiny horns almost hidden in the folds of her hair. But Henry always got caught in her horns, where he descended into the chambers of hell and was then transported on her wings back into the sublime realm of divine passion, where they both lay naked within the womb of truth.

Henry showed me how to be naked, how to be the naked truth seeker poking and prodding into every dark corner, how to go where only the eyes of spirit can see and the ears of spirit can hear and then to come back and write the naked tongue into words that stand unyielding to the stones of judgment that are cast by those who are afraid to stand naked before their own truth.

Selected Bibliographies

◆

PRIMARY WORKS

The Air-Conditioned Nightmare. New York: New Directions, 1945.

Aller Retour New York. Paris: Obelisk, 1935.

The Angel is My Watermark. Fullerton, Calif.: Holve-Barrows, 1944; reprinted, New York: Harry N. Abrams, 1962.

Art and Outrage: A Correspondence About Henry Miller (with Lawrence Durrell and Alfred Perlès). London: Putnam, 1959; New York: Dutton, 1961.

Big Sur and the Oranges of Hieronymous Bosch. New York: New Directions, 1957.

Black Spring. Paris: Obelisk Press, 1936; New York: Grove, 1963.

Book of Friends: A Tribute to Friends of Long Ago. Santa Barbara, Calif.: Capra, 1976.

The Books in My Life. Norfolk, Conn.: New Directions, 1952.

Collector's Quest: The Correspondence of Henry Miller and J. Rives Childs, 1947–65. Edited by Richard Clement Wood. Charlottesville: University Press of Virginia, 1968.

The Colossus of Maroussi. Norfolk, Conn.: New Directions, 1941.

The Cosmological Eye. Norfolk, Conn.: New Directions, 1939.

Crazy Cock. New York: Grove Weidenfeld, 1991.

Dear, Dear Brenda: The Love Letters of Henry Miller to Brenda Venus (with Brenda Venus). New York: Morrow, 1986.

A Devil in Paradise. New York: New American Library, 1956.

The Durrell-Miller Letters, 1935–1980. Edited by Ian S. MacNiven. New York: New Directions, 1988.

First Impressions of Greece. Santa Barbara, Calif.: Capra, 1973.

From Your Capricorn Friend: Henry Miller and the Stroker, 1978–80. Edited by Irving Stettner. New York: New Directions, 1987.

Gliding into the Everglades. Lake Oswego, Oreg.: Lost Pleiade, 1977.

Hamlet (with Michael Fraenkel). 2 vols. Volume I, Santruce, Puerto Rico: Carrefour, 1939; Volume II, Mexico City: Carrefour, 1941.

A Henry Miller Miscellanea. Berkeley, Calif.: Bern Porter, 1945.

Henry Miller's Book of Friends: A Trilogy. Santa Barbara, Calif.: Capra, 1987. (Includes *Book of Friends, My Bike & Other Friends,* and *Joey.*)

Henry Miller on Writing. Edited by Thomas H. Moore. New York: New Directions, 1964.

Henry Miller: Years of Trial and Triumph, The Correspondence of Henry Miller and Elmer Gertz. Carbondale: Southern Illinois University Press, 1978.

Insomnia, or, The Devil at Large. Euclid, Ohio: Loujon, 1971.

Into the Night Life (with Bezalel Schatz). Berkeley, Calif.: Privately published by Henry Miller and Bezalel Schatz, 1947.

Joey: A Loving Portrait of Alfred Perlès Together with Some Bizarre Episodes Relating to the Opposite Sex. Santa Barbara, Calif.: Capra, 1979.

Just Wild about Harry: A Melo-Melo in Seven Scenes. New York: New Directions, 1963.

Letters to Anaïs Nin. Edited by Gunther Stuhlmann. New York: Putnam's, 1965.

Letters of Henry Miller and Wallace Fowlie, 1943–1972. New York: Grove, 1975.

Maurizius Forever. San Francisco: Colt, 1946.

Max and the White Phagocytes. Paris: Obelisk, 1938.

Money and How It Gets That Way. Paris: 1938; Berkeley, Calif.: Bern Porter, 1945.

Mother, China, and the World Beyond. Santa Barbara, Calif.: Capra, 1977.

Murder the Murderer. Berkeley, Calif.: Bern Porter, 1944.

My Bike and Other Friends. Santa Barbara, Calif.: Capra, 1978.

My Life and Times. Chicago: Playboy Press, 1972.

Nexus. Book 3 of *The Rosy Crucifixion.* Paris: Obelisk, 1960; New York: Grove, 1965.

Obscenity and the Law of Reflection. Yonkers, N. Y.: Alicat Book Shop, 1945.

Of, By, and About Henry Miller. Edited by Oscar Baradinsky. Yonkers, N. Y.: Alicat Book Shop, 1947.

On Turning Eighty. Santa Barbara, Calif.: Capra Press, 1972.

Patchen, Man of Anger and Light. New York: Max Padell, 1946.

The Plight of the Creative Artist in the United States of America. Berkeley, Calif.: Bern Porter, 1944.

The Paintings of Henry Miller. Edited by Noel Young. San Francisco: Chronicle, 1982.

Plexus. Book 2 of *The Rosy Crucifixion.* Paris: Obelisk Press, 1953; New York: Grove, 1965.

Quiet Days in Clichy. Paris: Obelisk Press, 1956; New York: Grove, 1965.

Reflections. Edited by Twinka Thiebaud. Santa Barbara, Calif.: Capra Press, 1981.

Reflections on the Death of Mishima. Santa Barbara, Calif.: Capra, 1972.

Remember to Remember. New York: New Directions, 1947.

Reunion in Barcelona. Northwood, England: Scorpion, 1959.

Scenario (A Film with Sound). Paris: Obelisk, 1937.

Semblance of a Devoted Past (with Emile Schnellock). Berkeley, Calif.: Bern Porter, 1944.

Sexus. Book 1 of *The Rosy Crucifixion.* Paris: 1949; New York: Grove, 1965.

The Smile at the Foot of the Ladder. New York: Duell Sloan and Pearce, 1948.

Stand Still Like the Hummingbird. New York: New Directions, 1962.

Sunday after the War. Norfolk, Conn.: New Directions, 1962.

The Time of the Assassins: A Study of Rimbaud. Norfolk, Conn.: New Directions, 1956.

To Paint Is to Love Again. Alhambra, Calif.: Cambria, 1960.

Tropic of Cancer. Paris: Obelisk Press, 1934; New York: Grove, 1961.

Tropic of Capricorn. Paris: Obelisk Press, 1939; New York: Grove, 1962.

Varda, the Master Builder. Berkeley, Calif.: Circle Editions, 1947.

What Are You Going to Do About Alf? Paris: Obelisk Press, 1935; Berkeley, Calif: Bern Porter, 1943.

The Wisdom of the Heart. Norfolk, Conn.: New Directions, 1941.

The World of Lawrence. Edited by Evelyn J. Hinz and John J. Teunissen. Santa Barbara, Calif.: Capra, 1980.

The World of Sex. Printed by J[ohn] H[enry] N[ash] for Friends of Henry Miller, 1940; rev. ed., Paris: Olympia, 1957; New York: Grove, 1965.

Writer and Critic: A Correspondence with Henry Miller (with William A. Gordon). Baton Rouge: Louisiana State University Press, 1968.

SECONDARY WORKS

Baradinsky, Oscar, Editor. *Of, By, and About Henry Miller: A Collection of Pieces by Henry Miller and Others.* Yonkers, N.Y.: Alicat Bookshop Press, 1947.

Berthoff, Warner. "Coda: A Note on the Influence of Henry Miller." Pages 169–77 in *A Literature Without Qualities: American Writing Since 1945.* Berkeley: University of California Press, 1979.

Ciardi, John. "Concrete Prose and the Cement Mind." *Saturday Review* 46 (9 February 1963): 17.

Cott, Jonathan. "Reflections of a Cosmic Tourist: An Afternoon With Henry Miller." *Rolling Stone* (27 February 1975): 41–46 and 57.

Durrell, Lawrence, and Henry Miller. *The Durrell-Miller Letters, 1935–1980.* Edited by Ian S. MacNiven. New York: New Directions, 1988.

Durrell, Lawrence, Alfred Perles, and Henry Miller. *Art and Outrage: A Correspondence About Henry Miller.* London: Putnam, 1959.

Fowlie, Wallace, editor. *Letters of Henry Miller and Wallace Fowlie.* New York: Grove Press, 1975.

Fraenkel, Michael. "The Genesis of the *Tropic of Cancer.*" Pages 38–56 in *The Happy Rock: A Book About Henry Miller*, edited by Bern Porter. Berkeley, Calif.: Bern Porter, 1945.

Jackson, Paul R. "Henry Miller, Emerson, and the Divided Self." *American Literature* 43 (May 1971): 231–41.

Jong, Erica. "Goodbye to Henry-san." Pages 34–36 in *Black Messiah* (Premier Issue). Ellensburg, Wash.: Vagabond Press, 1981.

Mailer, Norman. "Status" and "Narcissism." Pages 3–10 and 173–94 in *Genius and Lust: A Journey Through the Major Writings of Henry Miller.* New York: Grove Press, 1976.

Mathieu, Bertrand. "The Image's Truth," "Orpheus as Musician," and "The Poet as Voyant." Pages 11–21, 22–33, and 201–13 in *Orpheus in Brooklyn: Orphism, Rimbaud, and Henry Miller.* The Hague-Paris: Mouton, 1976.

Millett, Kate. *Sexual Politics.* Garden City, N. Y.: Doubleday, 1970.

Mitchell, Edward B., Editor. *Henry Miller: Three Decades of Criticism.* New York: New York University Press, 1971.

Nin, Anaïs. *The Diaries of Anaïs Nin, Vol. I, 1931–1934.* Edited by Gunther Stuhlmann. San Diego: Harcourt Brace Jovanovich, 1966.

Porter, Bern. *What Henry Miller Said and Why It Is Important.* Ashland, Maine: Bern Porter, 1961.

Porter, Bern. Editor. *The Happy Rock: A Book About Henry Miller.* Berkeley: Bern Porter, 1945.

Rexroth, Kenneth. "The Reality of Henry Miller." Pages 154–67 in *World Outside the Window.* New York: New Directions, 1947.

Saunders, Jack. Editor. *Black Messiah* (Premier Issue, 1981).

Schnellock, Emil. "Just a Brooklyn Boy." Pages 7–25 in *The Happy Rock: A Book About Henry Miller*, edited by Bern Porter. Berkeley, Calif.: Bern Porter, 1945.

Trachtenberg, Alan. " 'History on the Side': Henry Miller's American Dream." Pages 136–48 in *American Dreams, American Nightmares*, edited by David Madden. Carbondale: Southern Illinois University Press, 1970.

Wickes, George. Editor. *Henry Miller and the Critics.* Carbondale, Ill.: Southern Illinois University Press, 1963.

Wickes, George. "Henry Miller: Down and Out in Paris." Pages 239–76 in *Americans in Paris.* Garden City, N. Y.: Doubleday, 1969.

Williams, John. "Henry Miller: The Success of Failure." *Virginia Quarterly Review* 44 (Spring 1968): 225–45.

Williams, William Carlos. "To the Dean." In *The Happy Rock: A Book About Henry Miller.* Edited by Bern Porter. Berkeley: Bern Porter, 1945.

Wilson, Edmund. "Twilight of the Expatriates." Pages 705–10 in *Shores of Light.* New York: Farrar, Straus and Giroux, 1952.

Woolf, Michael. "Beyond Ideology: Kate Millett and the Case for Henry Miller." Pages 113–28 in *Perspectives on Pornography: Sexuality in Film and Literature*, edited by Gary Day and Clive Bloom. London: Macmillan, 1989.

Index

♦